# The Gourmet's Guide to
# Northwest Wines & Wineries

*"The Best Guide
To Northwest Wine Touring"*

by
### Chuck Hill

### with Stephen Gaddis
### & Kurt Krause

## Speed Graphics
### Seattle, Washington

## About the Author

Chuck Hill has been involved with the Northwest wine industry since 1976, following the rapid development of Washington, Oregon and Idaho wineries. In this ever-changing environment he has found a challenge in keeping the consumer informed about the best in Northwest wines and the most enjoyable of winery visits.

The exciting emergence of food and wine pairing as a popular culinary exercise has increased interest in Northwest wine and in this area, Chuck co-authored the cookbook *Food and Wine Northwest Style* in 1991.

As a past member of the Board of Directors of the Seattle Chapter, Enological Society of the Pacific Northwest, Chuck contributed to the Society's goal of exploring the realms of wine and food. His nine years as the editor of the Seattle Chapter's newsletter gave him additional insight into the diversity of appreciation for wines from the Northwest and beyond.

## Acknowledgments

Special appreciation is due to **Stephen Gaddis** for his enthusiasm of wine touring, his persistent reminders to stay on task, and his willingness to work on the less glamorous aspects of producing a book such as this. Much more, his open-minded philosophical nature lends a depth to research that adds a new dimension. As a travelling companion and excellent adventurer, Steve's interests complement my own. Whether rating restaurant experiences, looking for local activities or trying to find our way through the wilderness, we always seem to make it home enriched culturally and socially, if not monetarily.

And my thanks to **Kurt Krause** for his excellent assistance in pursuing the latest wines and the rare bottlings from Northwest wineries and selecting wines and wineries to be listed as the best from our region. Kurt's years as sommelier for Ray's Boathouse and other Seattle restaurants have given him insights into what makes a great wine better than a good wine and how wines and foods become greater than the sum of their parts.

Continued appreciation is due Marie Hardie at the Washington Wine Commission, the Yamhill County Winery Association, and the Oregon Winegrowers Association.

## Credits

Cover photograph by John Rizzo, courtesy of King Estate Winery.
Photographs used throughout the book were taken by Chuck Hill, Stephen Gaddis, Kurt Krause and Anne Nisbet, or were provided by the winery or individuals pictured.

## Copyright © 1998 by Speed Graphics

## Printed in the United States of America

ISBN 0-9617699-8-X

To Jeffrey William Hill
*My brother and advisor,*
*confidant and friend,*
*and uncle to Andrew.*

# On the front cover of this edition
# King Estate Winery

King Estate winery of Eugene, Oregon has been a tremendous success story during the 1990s. The owners developed their 550-acre estate by planting over 200 acres of vineyard, building a showplace 110,000 square foot winery, establishing a grapevine propagation operation and creating a culinary program that has resulted in two delightful cookbooks and exciting television cooking shows.

This view of vineyard and winery on a beautiful Northwest afternoon typifies the spectacular scenery that can be enjoyed by wine tourists as they travel throughout the region.

Our special thanks to King Estate for providing this photograph for use on the cover of The Gourmet's Guide to Northwest Wines & Wineries.

On the back cover is a photo of a beautiful stained glass window that is the showpiece of the BC Wines Information Center in Penticton, British Columbia. The photo was taken by the author, Chuck Hill, during a visit to the Okanagan Valley in May of 1998. The photo of ripening Pinot Noir grapes at Rex Hill Vineyards is also from the author's archive.

The tempting wine country meal on the back cover was photographed by John Rizzo at King Estate Winery in Eugene, Oregon. Used by permission of King Estate.

In addition to creating the superb photographs included in King Estates's Pinot Gris Cookbook and Pinot Noir Cookbook, photographer John Rizzo serves many Northwest and national clients through Rizzo Studio in Portland, Oregon. Anyone needing quality photography should contact Rizzo Studio at:

**Rizzo Studio**
725 NW Flanders St. #307
Portland, OR 97209
(503) 243-2605

# TABLE OF CONTENTS

## Northwest Legends of Food & Wine

## All About Northwest Wine

## Washington Wine Country

## Oregon Wine Country

# TABLE OF CONTENTS

## Idaho & Montana Wine Country

## British Columbia Wine Country

## Appendix & Index

# ★ ★ ★ Northwest Legends of Food & Wine ★ ★ ★

# Great Recipes for Wine from Our Northwest Friends

After ten years writing about wine touring and enjoying hundreds of meals paired with Northwest wines, we thought it might be time to honor some of the restaurants and individuals who have done a great job with Northwest food and wine. Without many of these restaurants, the Northwest wine industry would have had great difficulty getting off to such a fast and successful start. Without some of the individuals who have promoted high quality, fresh regional foods, there would have been quite a lack of national and international interest in the Northwest culinary scene. Together, the wineries, the food suppliers and the hospitality industry have really put the Northwest on the map.

We are featuring in this edition of The Gourmet's Guide to Northwest Wines & Wineries 30 restaurants and individuals who have made significant contributions to your enjoyment of wine.

## How were they selected?

Our criteria for selection had a basic requirement of at least five years in the business of working with Northwest wines and foods. Most of this year's participants have at least twice that and some even longer. They varied from restaurants who have consistently had a strong Northwest representation on their wine list, to food industry luminaries who have used their national prominence to bring our region's great wines into the limelight. Other participants represent wine producers who's insights into food and wine pairing have always been a part of their personality and program.

Certainly there are more than 30 individuals and firms who qualify as Northwest Legends of Food & Wine. Due to space limitations in this edition, we invited about 40 of these to participate. Some were unable to accommodate our deadlines and some asked for a "rain check" to participate next time.

We already have a list going for the next edition and we invite your suggestions as to restaurants, wineries and food producers who deserve recognition as those who have succeeded in making the Northwest food and wine experience better for everyone through their chosen direction.

## How do I find each recipe?

We had quite a struggle in determining whether to list the recipes as one section in a sort of mini-cookbook or to scatter them throughout this edition to represent their region. Further, do we place each participant in their hometown or in the region represented by the wine suggested for the dish?

Ultimately, we chose a bit of a hybrid approach. Many restaurants were placed in the section of the book where they are located (i.e. Rover's and Canlis are in the Seattle Area section). Some, however, cried out to be next to the winery they singled out as their favorite with their particular recipe (i.e. Flying Fish is listed with Torii Mor Winery in the Yamhill County, Oregon section).

Realizing that our choices would not be intuitive to everyone, we present on the following page an alphabetical listing of the participants complete with their recipe title, wine selection and the page number of the recipe in this book.

## Let us know your favorites!

Please do let us know your suggestions for those we should include in our next edition. Send your nominations to: Gourmet's Guide Selections, Speed Graphics, 17919 2nd Ave. NW, Shoreline, WA 98177. You may email responses to: speedgraph@aol.com and look for our upcoming web site at nwgourmet.com.

# ★ ★ ★ Northwest Legends of Food & Wine ★ ★ ★

# NORTHWEST WINE COUNTRY

The wineries of the Pacific Northwest are producing some of the finest wine in the United States. Whether you are counting gold medals won in prestigious competitions or consulting chefs from the nation's finest restaurants, you will find that Northwest wines are world-class enological efforts.

The wines of the Northwest have evolved with the number of wineries and the sophistication of the consumer. As winemakers have learned to make better wine with each vintage, wine lovers have learned to appreciate the difference. Vineyardists have expanded the number of varietals and have learned ways to grow better fruit. New vineyards and wineries are being developed by Northwesterners and by investors from California, the Midwest and abroad.

Wine touring in the Northwest affords the opportunity to experience not only the fruits of the vineyards but the fruits of orchard and field as well. Mountain peaks, towering evergreens, vast waterways and welcoming, livable cities are additional attractions. The wine scene in the Northwest has not conglomerated to the extent of the Napa Valley and you can still find wineries clustered in small numbers around the vineyard areas of Oregon and Washington.

You can tour major facilities in mid-season if you choose, or you can visit smaller wineries on weekdays to have a few private moments of conversation with the winemaker. You can enjoy the variety of winery sizes and personalities.

This book is designed to provide the wine tourist with enough information to travel, tour, eat and sleep without additional references. Experiences related here are genuine and recommendations are sincere. A state highway map is a useful addition to the touring knapsack, along with a chunk of cheese, some flavorful bread and, of course, a corkscrew!

The Pacific Northwest is defined geographically by several dominant features. The Columbia River and her tributaries provide water to agricultural areas in all three Northwestern states. The mountains of the coast range and the Cascade range in Oregon, Washington and British Columbia define rainfall amounts and season temperatures in the eastern and western sections of each state. Idaho has several mountain regions – foothills to the Rocky Mountains – which have determined the course of rivers and the locations of fertile ancient flood plains where agriculture now thrives. British Columbia's Okanagan Valley is a wonder of remarkable scenery and quality sites for superb vineyards.

The development of successful vineyards is a fairly recent development in the Pacific Northwest. Plantings of grapes in the Northwest date back into the 19th century with most of those vineyards having been destroyed or having fallen to fend for themselves. Any attempts at making table wines from local grapes had only moderate success, and prohibition destroyed whatever fledgling wine growing industry had developed prior to the 1930s.

Successful plantings of vitis vinifera (wine grapes) in the Northwest really began in the 1940s and 1950s (Washington State) with little demand for the finished product. Not until the national wine boom of the 1960s was there enough interest in table wine to create the demand necessary to help both vineyards and wineries make a go of it.

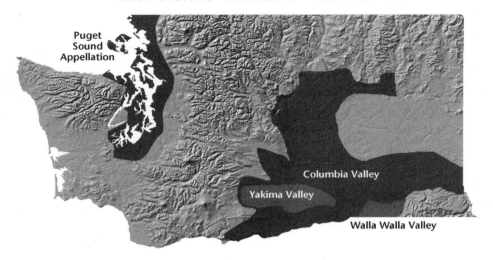

The wine growing regions of Washington State are defined by her dominant geographic features. The Cascade Mountains bisect the state into two halves – one wet and green, the other hot and dry in the summer and cold and dry in the winter. Irrigation has made viticulture possible in dry Eastern Washington, and careful selection of grape varieties and the warmest planting sites has established successful vineyards in Western Washington.

The Yakima River Valley of Eastern Washington is itself an appellation (approved viticultural area) and is included entirely within the larger Columbia Valley appellation. The Columbia River Valley (Columbia Valley) and the Walla Walla River Valley both include parts of Washington and Oregon within the recognized appellation boundaries. As the Columbia River meanders from the Canadian border to the Pacific Ocean it offers water for irrigation to farmers and vineyardists from Kettle Falls to Wenatchee to the Tri-Cities and through the Columbia Gorge.

While these appellations are east of the Cascade Mountains, the newer Puget Sound appellation is located in Western Washington on the islands and valleys of the Puget Sound basin. The challenge of finding climatically warm pockets to plant vineyards has occupied several dedicated growers who forged the Puget Sound Appellation and are owed the credit for its ongoing success. Their conviction that "wine is of the place where the grapes are grown" continues to be the mantra of Puget Sound area wine growing.

The most important grape-growing regions in Washington are far from the main population centers. Consequently, several of the state's largest wineries have placed their facilities near Seattle and bring the ripe grapes (or field-crushed juice) over the mountains to the winery. This is convenient to residents and tourists alike, who can enjoy a tour of the wine country without leaving the amenities of the big city.

# WINE COUNTRY GEOGRAPHY - OREGON

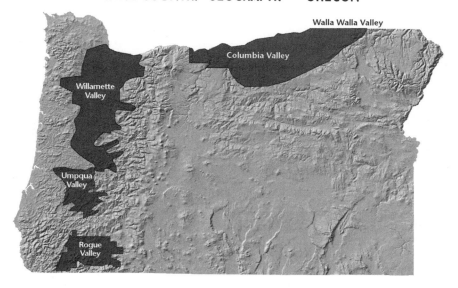

Oregon's Willamette Valley Appellation follows the Willamette River from the northern border of the state south to the area around Eugene. The appellation is cradled east and west by the Cascade Mountains and the Oregon coast range embracing a warm, fertile valley with rolling hills and ample rainfall. Smaller river valleys further south form the Umpqua Valley Appellation and the Rogue Valley Appellation. Roughly following the Interstate 5 corridor, Oregon's wine country is right at hand for tourist access from Portland, Salem, Eugene, Roseburg, Grant's Pass, Ashland, and many points in-between.

# WINE COUNTRY GEOGRAPHY - IDAHO, BRITISH COLUMBIA

Idaho agriculture follows the Snake River plain as it crosses the state from Caldwell/Nampa in the west, through Twin Falls, Pocatello and Idaho Falls. Wine growing activity is generally limited to the lower elevation areas in the west (Caldwell/Nampa/Wilder) where the marine influence of the Pacific Ocean reaches 300 miles inland to provide a long growing season and relatively mild winters. The beautiful scenery of southern Idaho along with recreation opportunities for skiers, fishers and other sportspeople provide an eager market for local winemakers year 'round.

Like Washington State, British Columbia has two wine regions, one west of the Cascade Mountains and one east. In the west, Vancouver Island and the Fraser River Valley each have similar problems to Puget Sound Appellations in Washington. Dedicated B. C. wine growers have found suitable microclimates to create good wines in both areas.

The Okanagan Valley was reborn in the late 1980s as cool-climate grape varieties were replaced with vinifera which have thrived in selected warm areas along Lakes Okanagan, Skaha and Osoyoos. Look for great things from this exciting region.

# ALL ABOUT WINE – WINEMAKING

As in other winegrowing regions, most Northwest wines are made from the grape species vitis vinifera – wine grapes. The grapes arrive at the winery from the vineyard in large bins or boxes and our story begins . . .

Grape clusters are dumped into the mechanical crusher/stemmer where rollers break the grape skins releasing juice and pulp for fermentation. Stems are removed by fast-rotating impellers that throw the berries off the stems and then deposit the stems into a collector where they are later hauled to the vineyards for use as compost.

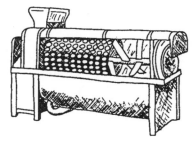

White grapes (and red grapes destined to be white wine, blanc de noir) are pressed after minimal skin contact. The Willmes bladder press gently extracts the juice by inflating a neoprene balloon inside the mass of skins and pulp. The pulp is pressed against a stainless steel wire cage and the juice trickles into a trough from where it is pumped into tanks.

Fermentation is carried out in stainless steel tanks, large wooden tanks, open-top plastic bins or oak barrels. White and blush wines are chilled in special refrigerated tanks for a cool fermentation.

Red wine fermentation is carried out on the skins and pulp during which color is extracted to give the wine its deep ruby hue. The fermenting wine is "punched down" or "pumped over" to maintain contact between wine and skins. Aging in tanks or barrels is followed by filtration or other clarification methods.

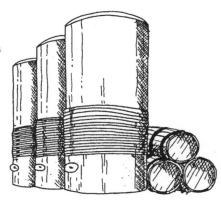

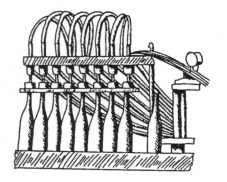

Modern, self-contained bottling lines are used at many wineries. The bottles are sterilized, then filled, corked and labeled. The capsule spun onto the top of the bottle is more decorative than functional and is nowadays most often made from aluminum alloy or plastic. Lead capsules have been banned from use.

# ALL ABOUT WINE – BARREL AGING

Most red wines and and many white wines spend time in oak barrels before being bottled and sent to you for enjoyment. Two things happen when wine is stored in a barrel: slow, controlled exposure to air through the pores of thewood; and flavoring of the wine with oaky character. Without the slow, controlled oxidation of wine that takes place in the barrel, some red wines might take an extraordinarily long time to smooth out and become drinkable. With the amount of flavor added to wine—especially with new oak—some would argue that the wines become undrinkable with longer and longer barrel age!

For white wines the term "barrel fermented" indicates that the wine's primary fermentation took place in an oak barrel (very often a new barrel) and the wine was allowed to rest on some or all of its fermentation solids that precipitated out (also called "lees"). This process adds a toasty, buttery character to the wine, especially if the wine undergoes a secondary *malolactic* fermentation. Barrel-fermented white wines generally spend 6 months to a year in barrel.

Red wines can stand up to a lot more oak than whites due to their full flavor and body. Because red wines need skin contact to gain color, the first fermentation takes place in large tanks. Once the wines are pressed off the skins, they are placed in barrel. New oak barrels quicklly impart a woody flavor to the wine and winemakers often rotate wines through newer and older (more neutral) barrels. Even with the full flavor and rich tannins, many red wines today are quite perceptibly oaky. This flavor is preferred by most consumers, or at least that's what many winemakers tell us.

Oak that is used to make 60-gallon wine barrels comes from both French and American sources. The flavor that is imparted to the wine varies both with the oak species and the region from which the oak was harvested. Blending wines aged in different oak types gives the winemaker the role of a chef seasoning his final blend.

Wine barrels are "coopered" in the style that originated in France. Trunk sections from oak trees are split - not sawn - to provide the barrel side pieces or "staves." These pieces are stacked and aged for several years to dry and season. When ready they are shaped to provide a tight fit in the assembled barrel.

Since staves do not naturally conform to the barrel shape, they are warped with steam and heat over a fire. A partially assembled barrel is placed over the flame to heat the wet wood and a wire is drawn tight to pull the staves into the final shape. The heads of the barrel are the last part to be assembled.

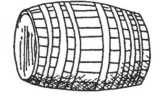

The barrel's inside is scraped to remove some of the smoky flavor of the fire. The remaining "toast" (smoky flavor) is classified by the barrel maker as light, medium or heavy, depending on how much wood was scraped away.

# ALL ABOUT WINE – THE COMPONENTS OF WINE

**Acidity** - the major acid present in grapes and wine is tartaric acid. The puckery sensation on the sides of the tongue tell you how much acid is present. Acidic wines are referred to as 'crisp' or 'tart,' low acid wines as 'flabby.'

**Alcohol** - Ethyl alcohol and carbon dioxide are the products of yeast fermenting sugar. Content can be from 9% to 15%.

**Aroma** - The smell of a wine related to the grape varietal used in its making.

**Balance** - When the acidity, alcohol, sugar and tannin of a wine are in correct proportion, the wine is said to have good balance. A refreshing sensation on the palate is a telltale sign.

**Body** - The sensation of viscosity on the palate. A 'watery' wine is thin in body. A thick or syrupy wine is heavy in body. Alcohol and residual sugar add body to a wine.

**Bouquet** - The smell of the wine relating to aging and to the handling of the wine. Oak aging adds a certain 'bouquet' and wines with considerable bottle age often exhibit complex, pleasant smells referred to as 'bottle bouquet.'

**Dry** - In wine tasting terms, the opposite of sweet. Generally a wine with less than 1% residual sugar.

**Fermentation** - The process whereby wine yeast converts grape sugar to alcohol and carbon dioxide.

**Finish** - After the wine is swallowed, the sensation left on your palate. The finish often reflects the flavor of the wine, but it also can be alcoholic, bitter or woody.

**Floral** - The natural aroma of many riesling wines that is reminiscent of fresh cut flowers.

**Fruit, Fruity** - A catch-all term describing a pleasant sensation of the flavor or aroma of a particular wine. Most useful when indicating the intensity of aroma or flavor, i.e. 'light fruit in the nose' or 'intensely fruity flavor.'

**Must** - Unfermented grape juice or a combination of juice and crushed grapes.

**Nose** - The term used for the overall olfactory sensation of a wine. It includes both the aroma AND bouquet.

**Oak** - The wood from which most wine-aging barrels are constructed. The term can also refer to the flavor or smell of oak as it is found in wine.

**Off-Dry** - A wine with residual sugar of 1% to 3% is off-dry.

**Oxidation** - The chemical reaction of the alcohol in wine with oxygen turning first into acetaldehyde (sherry odor) and then into vinegar.

**Sweet** - The opposite of dry. A wine with more than 3% residual sugar and/or low levels of balancing acidity.

**Tannin** - The substances present in all wines but most obvious in reds where they provide a textural astringency on the palate that cuts through fatty foods. This is part of the tradition of red wines accompanying red meats which contain high levels of animal fat.

## Wine Label Terminology

**Vintage Year** - by federal law, 95% of the grapes had to be harvested in the year specified.

**Winery Name** - The name of the bonded winery or a proprietary name used by the winery.

**Appellation /Viticultural Area** - Defines the origin of the grapes that went into the wine. All viticultural areas that appear on wine labels in the United States are approved by BATF (Bureau of Alcohol, Tobacco and Firearms). To use the name, 85% of the grapes must originate in that area.

**Grape Variety** - If a varietal name is used, at least 75% of the wine must be of the named variety. In Oregon, their state law requires that 90% of the wine must be from the named grape.

**Producer Information** - Tells the consumer if the wine was actually fermented at the named winery or just bottled there.

**Alcohol Content** - The percentage of alcohol in the wine as measured by volume. Must be accurate to ± 1.5%.

# ALL ABOUT WINE – WINE TASTING

Wine is a complex solution of water, ethyl alcohol, various organic (fruit) acids, a little sugar, and compounds that give wine its color, aroma and flavor. Let's take a quick tasting tour through a glass of wine then talk about how it's made.

*Take a look . . .*

**1. Appearance & Color** - The appearance of wine is very important to your enjoyment of it. Fortunately, modern winemaking technology has made bright, sediment-free wines the rule rather than the exception. Your wine should be free from floating particles and should have no visible cloudiness.

White wines often range in color from almost water-clear to golden yellow. Most Northwest white wines are somewhere in-between and are described as 'pale straw' in color. Red wines can be anywhere from dark ruby to pale garnet in hue. Lighter colored red wines often have lighter flavor and less **tannin**. Wines with prominent amber color (whites) or dark brown color (reds) may be oxidized and well-past their prime. Confirm your suspicions by using your nose.

*Take a sniff . . .*

**2. Aroma & Bouquet** - Swirl the wine in your glass and take a deep sniff to appreciate the smell of the grape type (**aroma** or '**fruit**') and the smell of the aging and treatment (i.e. oak, etc.) of the wine (**bouquet**). Together the two sensations can tell you much about the quality of the wine and its origin. Professional wine tasters often make many of their judgements based on a wine's smell rather than simply on the taste of the wine. If a wine looked oxidized, then you should try to detect a smell of sherry on the nose. Other flaws discovered by smelling the wine relate to sulfur compounds that can smell like sewage, rotten eggs, or sweaty socks. Several micro-biological spoilage problems may also be detected at this stage.

*Take a sip . . .*

**3. Flavor & Balance** - Take a small amount of wine in your mouth and swirl it around your tongue. The **flavor** of a good quality wine will often echo the aroma and bouquet. Additional factors influencing '**mouthfeel**' include **acidity**, **sweetness** and **alcohol** content of the wine. The **balance** between acidity (sour) taste and sugar (sweet) taste is very important to high-acid Northwest wines. Most rieslings, chenin blancs and other 'sipping' wines have **residual sugar** left in the wine to balance the acidity and thus provide a 'refreshing' feeling on the palate. Alcohol in the wine provides viscosity or '**body**' but if too high can leave a hot sensation on the palate after swallowing. Red wines provide a tactile, drying sensation in the mouth from the **tannins** extracted mostly from the grape skins. The **finish** is the combination of sensations and flavors you encounter after swallowing. Lingering fruitiness and toasty vanilla from **barrel fermentation** are often encountered. Evaluation of the taste of wine generally focuses on bitterness or an imbalance

## The authors' favorite wine producers for each varietal:

Whether you prefer red wines or white, there is a varietal produced in the Northwest just for you. From deep-colored, tannic Cabernet Sauvignons to delicate Rieslings and Chenin Blancs, the Northwest states produce a variety of styles to please the most discriminating wine lover. Recent years have seen the planting of varieties new to the region and new clones of varieties such as Chardonnay and Pinot Noir.

*Chinook Wines*
*Columbia "Red Willow Vineyard"*
*Preston Premium Wines*

## Cabernet Franc *(CAB air nay frahnc)* is one of the main blending grapes in red French Bordeaux and has become popular for the same purpose in the Northwest. Varietal bottlings of Cabernet Franc are offered by several wineries and feature berry, herb and vegetative notes in the aroma with berry flavors on the palate and a tannic finish.

*Andrew Will*
*Canoe Ridge Vineyard*
*Chateau Ste. Michelle (vineyard designated wines)*
*Chinook Wines*
*Columbia Winery (vineyard designated wines)*
*L'Ecole No. 41*
*La Garza Cellars*
*Leonetti Cellar*
*Portteus Winery*
*Preston Premium Wines*
*Quilceda Creek Vintners*
*Woodward Canyon*

## Cabernet Sauvignon *(CAB air nay SAW veen yawn)* is the major red wine grape of the Bordeaux region in France. In the Northwest, a few distinct growing sites have proven the best at providing the finest fruit for making complex, powerful wines. Cabernet grapes from the Red Mountain area, Portteus Vineyard near Zillah, Mercer Ranch, and others are highly sought after. Two distinct styles of Cabernet are crafted in the Northwest: a light, fresh, intensely-fruity version and a fruity-with-plenty-of-oak version. Winemakers claim consumers love the oaky style but wine critics often like a softer blend of fruit with oak. Some leading wineries are softening their oak approach – an encouraging sign. Pair your Cabernet with lamb, beef, veal, richly-sauced pastas, or even chocolate desserts.

*Bethel Heights "Reserve"*
*Canoe Ridge Vineyard*
*Cascade Ridge*
*Chateau Ste. Michelle (vineyard des. and reserve)*
*Chehalem "Ian's Reserve"*
*Domaine Drouhin Oregon*
*Hamacher*
*Ken Wright Cellars*
*McCrea Cellars*
*Woodward Canyon*

## Chardonnay *(shar doe nay)* is the queen of white grapes in the Burgundy region of France and it has found a home in winegrowing regions throughout the Northwest. A trend toward barrel-fermented wines finds rich, buttery, toasty, mouthfilling chardonnays that are quite remarkable and linger on the palate. A leaner style is also popular, clinging to the tenet that "food wines" don't need all that oak but should have crisp acidity and aromas and flavors of tropical fruit. The truth is that the very best are somewhere between the two styles. Oakier chardonnays don't do well with light dishes but a touch of smoke from the grill helps forge a flavorful pairing.

*Covey Run*
*Cuvee Lulu (Andrew Will)*
*Hogue Cellars*
*Kiona Ice Wine*
*L'Ecole No. 41*

## Chenin Blanc *(SHEN in blahnc)* is less well-known as a varietal wine these days but several wineries carry the torch with good results. Dry versions have proven to be good food wines – especially with oysters! The best off-dry styles continue to offer aromas of pear, apple and vanilla with a lightly-sweet palate making them good sippers for hot afternoons. Chenin Blanc ice wine and other late harvest styles have been consistent award winners and are also popular with dessert.

16

## Authors' Favorites

*Amity Vineyards*
*Brick House Vineyards*
*WillaKenzie Estate*

**Gamay** *(ga MAY)* is the red wine grape of Beaujolais but has become a confusing di-varietal in America. The upright clone of Pinot Noir was the official American *Gamay Beaujolais* but now the varietal *Gamay Noir a jus blanc* is taking its rightful place since it is the true grape of France's Beaujolais wines. Go figure. The former is most often crafted into a lightly sweet rosé or red wine while the latter produces a richer, complex red wine for several Oregon wineries.

*Amity Vineyards "Dry"*
*Canoe Ridge Vineyard*
*Covey Run "Celilo Vineyard"*
*Hoodsport Winery*
*Tyee Wine Cellars*

**Gewurztraminer** *(gaVERTS trah meener)* is a difficult grape to grow successfully and a difficult wine to make in a marketable style. The most varietally-true examples are still off-dry sipping wines. Dry style gewurztraminers have been attempted in recent years with some success. The natural finish of this varietal is slightly bitter (due to the ripeness of the grape required to achieve the spicy character) and a slightly sweet palate helps to overcome this problem. Dry styles should, therefore, be accompanied by food.

*Thurston Wolfe Grenache*

**Grenache** *(gray NAHSSH)* has found a couple of new champions in the Northwest industry and promises to have a future as a Rhone-style medium-bodied red wine instead of the rosés of the past. Blended with 10% to 30% merlot, it takes on a quality not unlike pinot noir but with a unique character all its own.

*Covey Run Vintners*
*Kiona Vineyards*
*Powers Winery*
*W. B. Bridgman*

**Lemberger** *(LEM burger)* is a red variety (originally from Northern Europe and badly in need of a name transplant) that is grown primarily in Washington State. It offers wines with berry fruit and a simple plummy-cherry palate. Lighter versions and more full-bodied styles compete for the title of barbecue red wine *extraordinaire*.

*Mount Baker Vineyards*
*Lopez Island Vineyards*
*Whidbey Island Vineyards*

**Madeleine Angevine** *(MAD a lin ANJ a vin)* is a varietal cross that is grown mostly in Western Washington's Puget Sound appellation. It produces a distinctively aromatic wine with a spicy-herbal character that finds a small but devoted group of fans. Off-dry and late harvest versions can be found at several Puget Sound area wineries.

*Panther Creek Wine Cellars*
*Ken Wright Cellars*

**Mélon** *(mel OWN)* has somewhat disputed origins but is generally agreed to be the grape that makes the flavorful white wines of Muscadet in France (the OTHER Melon is from Burgundy and is related and similar in style). Fresh and crisp, Melon is a superb wine to accompany seafood. The variety is sparsely planted in Oregon.

# ALL ABOUT WINE – NORTHWEST WINE GRAPES

## Authors' Favorites

*Andrew Will*
*Barnard Griffin*
*Canoe Ridge Vineyard*
*Caterina*
*Chateau Ste. Michelle*
*Chinook Wines*
*L'Ecole No. 41*
*Leonetti Cellar*
*Preston Premium Wines*
*Seven Hills Winery*
*Waterbrook*
*Woodward Canyon*

**Merlot** *(mare-LOW)* is second only to Cabernet Sauvignon as the most planted varietal in Bordeaux, France. It is often blended with Cabernet to soften that varietal's rough edges and add complexity. On its own it produces a rich and plummy wine that is gentle on the palate. Now the most popular red varietal with American consumers, wineries are scrambling to produce a variety of styles from ripe, rich oaky monsters to softer, more affordable everyday wines. Black cherry, berry and toasty oak aromas are today's merlot hallmarks. It is an excellent food wine for rich meats, garlicky sauces and, surprisingly, it may be a better match for chocolate than Cabernet! As wineries discover the best vineyard sites for merlot (Canoe Ridge for one), consumers can expect richer, more complex wines.

**Mourvedre** *(more VED ra) or (more VED)* comes to the Northwest from France and (most recently) California, where the cult of finding a new Rhone varietal to champion each year is running out of names on the list. A red wine of earthy character with a heavy palate, this will be (sigh) much talked about in years to come.

*Autumn Wind Vineyard*
*Bainbridge Island Winery*
*Chateau Benoit*
*Kramer Vineyards*
*Mount Baker Vineyards*

**Muller Thurgau** *(MOO ler TER gaoo)* is a German grape used mostly in that country to produce Liebfraumilch. In the Northwest, the best versions are off-dry, light and fragrant with herbal notes on the palate that make it an enjoyable pairing with lighter cheeses and meats.

*Bookwalter Winery*
*Horizon's Edge*
*Silvan Ridge*

**Muscat** *(MUSS cat)* is widely grown in Italy where it is the major component in Asti Spumante among other wines. An exceptionally fragrant wine, excellent Northwest versions can be found in both off-dry sipping wines and sweet late-harvest styles. Its name similarity to fortified *Muscatel* have hurt its marketability among beginning wine consumers.

*Cavatappi Winery*

**Nebbiolo** *(nebbi OH low)* was brought to Washington by Peter Dow who worked with Mike Sauer at Red Willow Vineyard in Yakima to nurture a small planting of this Italian varietal, the pride of Piedmont. Peter's winery, Cavatappi, produced the first Northwest Nebbiolo wine, but the jury is still out on the varietal's future in the Northwest.

*Cameroni "Giovanni"*
*Erath Vineyards*
*Ken Wright Cellars*
*WillaKenzie Estate*

**Pinot Blanc** *(PEE noh BLAHNC)* is a relative of Pinot Noir and is grown at many sites throughout Europe. Certain soils and vineyards are able to coax more character from the grape and experimental planting in Oregon has yielded promising results. The best wines produced from this varietal are bright and fragrant with hints of mineral and earth.

## Authors' favorites

*Columbia "Otis Vineyard"*
*Cooper Mountain Vineyard*
*Erath Vineyards*
*The Eyrie Vineyards*
*King Estate "Reserve"*
*Ponzi Vineyards*
*Tyee Wine Cellars*
*WillaKenzie Estate*

*Archery Summit*
*Autumn Wind Vineyard*
*Beaux Freres*
*Bethel Heights Vineyard*
*Brick House Vineyard*
*Broadley Winery*
*Chehalem*
*Cristom*
*Domaine Drouhin Oregon*
*Ken Wright Cellars*
*St. Innocent Winery*
*John Thomas*
*Torii Mor*
*Westrey*

*Argyle "Dry Reserve"*
*Chateau Ste. Michelle*
*"Reserve"*
*Columbia Crest Ice Wine*
*Hogue Cellars*
*Ponzi "Vino Gelato"*

*Andrew Will*
*Cavatappi Winery*

**Pinot Gris** *(PEE noh GREE)* another relative of Pinot Noir that has been highly touted as the perfect food wine for many Northwest seafoods. The best examples have a flinty-yet-fruity character with citrus notes and a crisp finish. Plantings in Oregon have increased dramatically resulting in increased production and a great variety of styles including barrel-fermented and barrel-aged versions that resemble Chardonnay. Several plantings in Washington have yielded flavorful wines that have enjoyed success with consumers.

**Pinot Noir** *(PEE noh NWAHR)*, the great red grape of Burgundy, has taken root in the Northwest with many Oregon producers sometimes beating the French at their own game. Many techniques influencing production levels and quality have evolved over the past two decades including intensive vineyard management, cold-maceration of the grapes to extract more color, and praying for better weather. The wines are offered in a variety of styles from rich and tannic to light and quaffable. The best versions marry toasty/smoky oak with earthy/berry qualities in the fruit to produce complex wines that offer an expansive palette of aromas and flavors to eager Pinot-philes. These cherry, berry, smoke and earth components combine with meaty characters to create what many believe to be the Northwest's most exciting food wine.

**Riesling** *(REEZ ling)* White Riesling and Johannisberg Riesling are the same grape. While Oregon's state wine law prohibits the use of the name Johannisberg Riesling, Washington and Idaho use the names interchangeably. A convention of usage has evolved where wines labeled 'White Riesling' are often sweeter versions and those labelled 'Johannisberg Riesling' are dry or off-dry. With thousands of acres in Washington alone, this prolific producer has contributed greatly to the success of that state's wine industry. Dry Rieslings offer aromas of apples and pears and a crisp palate begging for food accompaniment. Sweeter, late harvest versions lean toward peach and apricot aromas and flavors.

**Sangiovese** *(SAN geo VAYS ee)*, the red grape that makes up a good percentage of Italian Chianti has arrived in the Northwest. Small plantings in the Columbia Valley have produced tiny crops and several vintners have crafted a barrel or two of experimental wine.

## Authors' Favorites

*Arbor Crest*
*Carlo & Julian "Croft Vineyard"*
*Caterina*
*Cavatappi*
*Chateau Ste. Michelle "Horse Heaven Vnyd."*
*Chinook Wines*
*DiStefano*
*Hogue Cellars*
*Sineann "Smith-Cerne Vnyd."*
*Waterbrook*

**Sauvignon Blanc** *(SAW veen yawn BLAHNC)* The white grape relative of Cabernet Sauvignon, this is also the variety that, when aged in oak, becomes Fumé Blanc. Much improved versions of this variety are surfacing as more wineries blend in small amounts of semillon and use vineyard canopy management to soften the herbaceous character. Sauvignon Blanc is particularly important to Northwest restaurateurs since many of our local seafoods pair extremely well with this wine.

*Barnard Griffin*
*Chinook Wines*
*Columbia Winery*
*L'Ecole No. 41 "Fries Vnyd."*

**Semillon** *(SAY me on)* is a major white grape of Bordeaux and is grown successfully in Washington where it has come into its own as a popular food wine. The melon and apple aromas and flavors complement lighter meats and cheeses, as well as a wide variety of lighter seafoods.

*Columbia "Red Willow Vnyd."*
*Glen Fiona*
*McCrea Cellars*

**Syrah** *(sir AHH)* comes to the Northwest from France's Rhone Valley. Small plantings at Red Willow Vineyard and elsewhere have produced spicy, full-bodied red wines that promise good things for the future.

*McCrea Cellars*
*Waterbrook*

**Viognier** *(vee own YAY)* is a white varietal from France's Rhone Valley that has achieved popularity in California. Several small plantings are testing the variety's ability to thrive (perhaps just to cope!) in the Northwest's climate. A refreshing and flavorful white - not unlike Pinot Gris, this wine currently commands a higher price due to its rarity.

*Barnard Griffin*
*Hood River Vineyards*
*Portteus Vineyard*
*Thurston Wolfe*

**Zinfandel** *(ZIN fon dell)* is California's spicy red grape that has gained fame as a blanc de noir table wine of little character with a low price to match. Plantings near The Dalles in Oregon and at Portteus Vineyard in the Yakima Valley have shown that, given the proper microclimate, Zinfandel can grow in the Northwest and make a palatable, medium-bodied red wine of some character.

*Argyle*
*Mountain Dome Winery*
*St. Innocent*

**Sparkling Wines** are a romantic part of the wine industry. The excitement of celebrating with bubbly brut creates demand that entices winemakers to try their hand at this category. Sparkling wines are usually made from slightly underripe grapes of Pinot Noir, Chardonnay, Pinot Meunier or other varietals. Good sparkling wines are fairly common, great sparkling wines are rare.

# LOOKING AT THE BEST NORTHWEST WINES

Any "Best of" list is bound to be controversial. Are the wines available to buy? Is the producer consistent at producing the varietal? What about new wineries making their mark?

We have divided this "Best of" list into three categories. The first listing for each varietal is the best Northwest wine we've tasted recently regardless of whether the wine is available. This category may be frustrating to some but it tends to identify some truly superb bottlings and single out some excellent winemakers. The second category is the best up-and-coming wine. These wines are from new wineries or represent new varietals or production areas for existing wineries. The third category is a Northwest "standby." A wine that can be easily found, offers fair value for quality, and is close to the Northwest ideal for that varietal.

## Sparkling Wines
*Superb but Hard to Find*
**St. Innocent Brut**
*Up and Coming - Wines to Watch*
**Alexia Blanc de Noir**
*Faithful Standby*
**Argyle Brut**

## Riesling
*Superb but Hard to Find*
**Chateau Ste. Michelle Reserve**
*Up and Coming - Wines to Watch*
**Terra Blanca**
*Faithful Standby*
**Argyle "Dry"**

## Semillon
*Superb but Hard to Find*
**L'Ecole No 41 "Fries Vineyard"**
*Up and Coming - Wines to Watch*
**Hogue "Genesis"**
*Faithful Standby*
**Chinook Wines**

## Sauvignon Blanc
*Superb but Hard to Find*
**Carlo & Julian "Croft Vineyard"**
*Up and Coming - Wines to Watch*
**Ch. Ste. Michelle "Horse Heaven Vineyard"**
*Faithful Standby*
**Arbor Crest Wine Cellars**

## Pinot Gris
*Superb but Hard to Find*
**St. Innocent**
*Up and Coming - Wines to Watch*
**WillaKenzie Estate**
*Faithful Standby*
**The Eyrie Vineyards**

## Pinot Blanc
*Superb but Hard to Find*
**Blue Mountain "Reserve"**
*Up and Coming - Wines to Watch*
**Cameroni "Pinot Bianco Giovanni"**
*Faithful Standby*
**WillaKenzie Estate**

## Chardonnay
*Superb but Hard to Find*
**Chehalem - Ian's Reserve**
*Up and Coming - Wines to Watch*
**Brick House Vineyards**
*Faithful Standby*
**Woodward Canyon**

## Pinot Noir
*Superb but Hard to Find*
**Hamacher Wines**
*Up and Coming - Wines to Watch*
**Archery Summit**
*Faithful Standby*
**Domaine Drouhin**

## Merlot
*Superb but Hard to Find*
**Portteus "Reserve"**
*Up and Coming - Wines to Watch*
**Walla Walla Vintners**
*Faithful Standby*
**L'Ecole No 41**

## Cabernet Sauvignon
*Superb but Hard to Find*
**Leonetti Cellar**
*Up and Coming - Wines to Watch*
**Dunham Cellars**
*Faithful Standby*
**Quilceda Creek**

## Syrah
*Superb but Hard to Find*
**McCrea Cellars**
*Up and Coming - Wines to Watch*
**Glen Fiona**
*Faithful Standby*
**Columbia "Red Willow"**

## Late Harvest
*Superb but Hard to Find*
**Andrew Rich - LH Gewurztraminer**
*Up and Coming - Wines to Watch*
**Columbia Crest Ice Wine**
*Faithful Standby*
**Ponzi Vineyard "Vino Gelato"**

# ALL ABOUT WINE TOURING

Imbibing beverage alcohol and getting behind the wheel of a car is dangerous. Wine is beverage alcohol and wine touring is getting behind the wheel of a car. It doesn't take a rocket scientist to figure out that something's wrong with this picture. Bring along a friend who agrees not to drink wine on the tour and reward him with a bottle of wine to take home afterwards. This designated driver idea has saved hundreds of lives and hopefully will save many more. If you choose not to designate, then spit (this is a practical and time-tested custom for those who truly want to evaluate the wines).

## Navigational Remarks

Almost all the maps in this book are oriented so north is up, west is left, etc. Hold the book right side up and you should be just fine. Landmarks have been noted where necessary and some mileage distances are given when appropriate. Use your odometer, trip meter or trip computer to figure out distances. Out in the wine country you'll find that your travels often begin on a fancy, paved four-lane highway and end up on a dusty gravel road. That's the way it's always been and I don't think a change is coming any time soon. Dings on the paint job are no fun so drive carefully and be considerate of the guy behind you.

## Eating and Sleeping

Restaurant and lodging suggestions are provided for most touring regions. Sections featuring larger cities offer listings for for unique, high quality lodgings and many wine-friendly restaurants. Rural areas include listings for resorts, inns and restaurants that enhance the ambiance of the wine country of that particular region.

Motels and hotels listed vary from basic accommodations to the fanciest, big city palaces. Many wine country recommendations have a pool and other diversions for the younger set. Northwest Bed & Breakfasts have become much more than a "home stay." Rooms often have private baths with showers, and breakfasts take on proportions that eliminate the need for lunch. All that I have

recommended are clean, well-run and savvy to the needs of the wine tourist.

Eating establishments have been chosen – at least partly – with their attitude to the Northwest wine industry in mind. Many of the suggestions for dining have expansive selections of Northwest bottlings at fair prices, as well as Northwest wines by the glass.

## Northwest Microbrews

Microbreweries and brewpubs are listed after the wineries section in each regional chapter. Some regions have dozens of entries while others have none. Enjoy these great Northwest beers!

## Regional Activities

The Pacific Northwest is home to some of the world's best family activities. Most towns have interesting museums, parks and historic sites. Community pools, beaches and sport fields provide recreation, exercise and fresh air. Listings for the best of these areas are included.

## Winery Listings

The over-250 wineries listed in this book are arranged alphabetically within each touring region section. The regions have been determined by geographic common sense and by clustering of wineries open for touring. To provide you a sense of each winery's personality, most listings include:

**Statistics** such as address, phone number, fax (if available), size of facility, owner and winemaker

**Winery History** encapsulated into a few accurate sentences

**A Visit to the Winery** with hours, amenities, directions, etc.

**The Wines** describes the winemaking style and current releases.

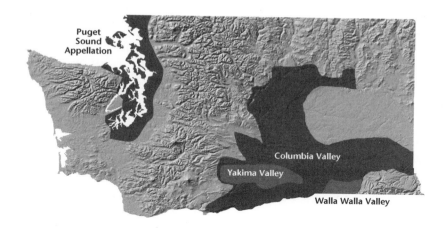

Puget Sound Appellation

Columbia Valley

Yakima Valley

Walla Walla Valley

# Washington Wine Touring

# NORTHWEST WINES & WINERIES
## Seattle Area Wine Touring

Within a one hour drive of downtown Seattle are some of Washington's best known and largest wineries as well as some small, family operations and several wineries in between. The Seattle area listings include all wineries within a one hour driving radius.

### Bainbridge Island

The temptation to hop a ferry and visit this independent community just across Puget Sound is irresistible. You can walk on if you plan to limit your visit to **Bainbridge Island Winery** and downtown Winslow. Add an appointment to visit **Rich Passage Winery** and you'll need your car.

### Vashon Island

Reached by a ferry from West Seattle, Vashon Island is home to two wineries and several unique agricultural businesses. An appointment on Friday or Saturday is needed to visit **Vashon Island Winery. Andrew Will Winery** is not open to the public.

### West Side of Lake Washington

On the Seattle side of the lake only one winery is open with regular hours for public touring. In the industrial area of south Seattle **E. B. Foote Winery** invites you to stop by on Saturdays or selected weekday evenings.

**Wilridge Winery** is open by appointment, and the winery has an annual open house. Look for owner/winemaker Paul Beveridge's red wines for sale at local wine shops.

### Eastside Wineries – Woodinville, Bellevue, and Points North and East

The Woodinville area is now home to four wineries open to the public with regular hours and other facilities open by appointment. The grand **Chateau Ste. Michelle** is better than ever with ample picnic facilities and **Columbia Winery's** broad veranda encourages visitors to cross the road and stay awhile.

**Facelli Winery** is just north on Hwy. 202 where you'll get a warm welcome from Lou and Sandy Facelli and their daughter Lisa. **Silver Lake Sparkling Cellars** is close to downtown Woodinville on the banks of Little Bear Creek. You can stop by for tasting or for one of their numerous winery events.

Other Woodinville-area wineries require an appointment for a visit or tasting. **DeLille Cellars**, located near Hollywood Corner, offers special dinners and events through their newsletter. Matt Loso's **Matthew Cellars** facility and the new **Di Stefano** winery are open for visits and tastings by appointment. Gordy Rawson has been making his **Alexia** sparkling wine in borrowed space in Woodinville, but you can call him at his home office in the U-District.

Before you leave Woodinville be sure to visit the **Red Hook Brewery** facility. Tours, tastings and a great pub!

**Cafe Juanita**, just a block north of Juanita Beach Park near Kirkland, is home to **Cavatappi Winery**. The winery is not open to the public but the restaurant serves some of the Seattle area's finest Italian cuisine. Cavatappi wines are on the list, of course.

North of Woodinville **Silver Lake Winery's** winemaking facility near Mill Creek and **Quilceda Creek Vintners** winery near Snohomish are each open by appointment for tasting and sales.

Traveling east on Interstate 90, **Hedges Cellars** has opened their spectacular visitor center east of downtown Issaquah. **Snoqualmie Winery** has closed their visitor facility.

### South of Seattle

In Kent, David Larsen's **Soos Creek Wine Cellars** plans an annual open house but is otherwise not open for visits.

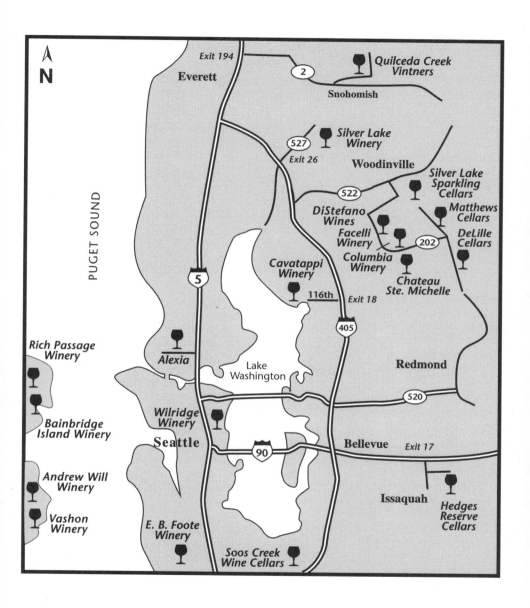

# Alexia Sparkling Wine

620 N.E. 55th Street
Seattle, WA 98105
(206) 985-2816
**Email:**
gordyrawson@msn.com

**Tasting Room Hours:** By appointment only, Saturdays or Sundays.

**Owner/Winemaker:** Gordon Rawson
**First Year:** 1997

Gordy Rawson has been tinkering with making sparkling wine at home for years and he now has crafted enough to share with local Seattle area wine lovers. Alexia Brut is a methode champenoise sparkler with tiny bubbles, a rich toasty nose and a crisp palate suited for pairing with appetizers or entrees.

Look for Alexia sparkling wine in better Seattle wine shops and restaurants.

# Andrew Will

12526 SW Bank Road
Vashon, WA 98070
(206) 463-3290
Winemaker:
  Chris Camarda
First Year: 1989

**Winery History**

Andrew Will winery is named after the nephew and son (respectively) of owners Chris and Annie Camarda. The winery outgrew its original location near downtown Seattle and is now located at the owners' home on Vashon Island. As winemaker, Chris brings experience gained in the culinary arts working at Il Bistro restaurant in the Pike Place Market for many years. His gentle sense of humor reveals that he "finally found some use for the chemistry classes I was forced to take in high school." The reputation of Andrew Will winery was established from the beginning with widely acclaimed bottlings of Cabernet and Merlot. The winery is not open to the public but the winemaker participates in several local wine fairs where interested parties can discuss the wines and winemaking philosophy.

*Continued on page 28.*

## Kathy Casey
## Kazzy & Associates

As a true Legend of Northwest Food and Wine, Kathy Casey is celebrated for paving the way for the emergence of Northwest cuisine on a national level. She was hailed as an "inventor of dishes that dazzle the eye and the palate" by Craig Claiborne in the New York Times. Casey received her first acclaim at age 23, as Executive Chef for Fullers restaurant in Seattle where she was named "one of the 25 hot new American chefs" by Food & Wine magazine.

Consultant to many Northwest restaurants and other food purveyors, Kathy leads her team at Kazzy & Associates in recipe and menu development, strategic planning and concept development.

"Where else but the Paciifc Northwest are you surrounded with such pleasurable bounty - the freshest fish and shellfish from the waters of Puget Sound, wild mushrooms from our forest floors, the crispest vegetables and an abundance of berries from our lush farmlands . . . and of course wonderful Northwst wines to perfect these gifts. Always use the best ingredients you can find and never be afraid to try different wines with different foods . . . you never know what kind of fun food and wine pairing you'll cook up!"

Kathy suggests that her Northwest seafood stew is a great dish to enjoy at the beach after a day of fishing, clamming and mussel gathering. Just make the Seafood Stew base ahead and pack in your ice chest. Take along a stew pot; add a good bottle of Northwest wine and a loaf of crusty bread to your picnic basket and you're all set for a beach feast.

# Northwest Seafood Stew

*Serves 4 to 6, Serve with:* Domaine Drouhin Oregon Pinot Noir

## Northwest Seafood Stew Base

| | | | |
|---|---|---|---|
| 1/4 | cup olive oil | 2 | cups clam juice |
| 1 | cup thinly sliced white onion | 3 | cups chopped ripe tomatoes or |
| 1/2 | cup thinly sliced red pepper | | diced canned plum tomatoes with juice |
| 1/2 | cup thinly sliced green pepper | 1 | tsp salt |
| 1 | tbs. minced garlic | | dash of Tabasco sauce |
| 1 | cup thinly sliced mushrooms | | freshly cracked black pepper |
| 1 | cup thinly sliced fennel bulb | 1/4 | tsp. crushed, whole dried rosemary |
| | (about 1 small bulb) | 1 | tsp. dried basil |
| 1-1/2 | tsp. finely grated orange zest | 1/4 | tsp whole dried thyme |
| 1/2 | cup dry white vermouth or dry white wine | | |

Pour the olive oil in a large stew pot or Dutch oven and place over moderate heat. When it is hot, add the onion, peppers, garlic, mushrooms, fennel and orange peel. Cook, stirring often, for about 4 - 5 minutes until the onion is translucent.

Add the vermouth, clam juice, tomatoes and seasonings. Turn the heat to high and bring mixture to a low boil, then reduce heat to low and simmer for 6 - 8 minutes. Remove from heat and adjust seasoning if necessary. If not using immediately, cool and refrigerate until needed.

## To finish the recipe:

| | | | |
|---|---|---|---|
| 1/4 | cup olive oil | 1/2 | lb. mixture of fresh boneless, skinless, |
| 3/4 | lb. little neck clams in the shell | | firm-fleshed fish, such as salmon, cod |
| 1/2 | lb. cleaned mussels, shells scrubbed, | | or halibut, cut in 1-1/2 inch pieces. |
| | debearded | 4 | small (1- to 2-inch) cooked red potatoes, |
| 1/2 | lb. large shrimp, peeled and deveined | | cut in half |
| | (about 8 shrimp) | 1/4 | cup Pernod liqueur (optional) |
| 1/4 | lb. large scallops, sliced in half | | fresh fennel fronds for garnish (optional) |

## To finish the stew:

Pour the olive oil in a stew pot or Dutch oven and place over moderately high heat. When oil is hot, add the clams, mussels, shrimp, scallops and fish. Sauté for 30 seconds, turning fish and scallop pieces as necessary. Add potatoes and Pernod. Cook 30 seconds more then add the seafood stew base.

Cover pot and cook until clams and mussels just open. Immediately remove from the heat and divide fish and shellfish among individual large bowls. Ladle in the broth and vegetables. Garnish with fennel fronds. Serve immediately with warm French bread for dipping.

**The Wines**

The vineyard-designated Cabernet Sauvignons and Merlots produced by Andrew Will are intense, oak-aged versions requiring further bottle age to realize their full potential. Chardonnay and Chenin Blanc under the Cuvée Lulu label also have a loyal following. Check with Seattle wine merchants to find out what new bottlings Chris Camarda is creating. His Sangiovese is a recent addition to the line.

# Bainbridge Island Winery

682 State Hwy. 305,
Bainbridge Island, WA
98110
(206) 842-9463

**Tasting Room Hours:**
Wednesday through Sunday, Noon to 5 PM

**Owners:** Gerard and JoAnn Bentrynn
**First Year:** 1982
**Winery Capacity:** 7,000 Gallons

**Winery History**

The first vines were planted at Bainbridge Island Winery in 1978 with the purpose of producing low alcohol, German-style wines from grape types suited to the climate of the Puget Sound region. A decade later, the winery declared independence from Eastern Washington grape growers by making wine only from grapes grown at their two Bainbridge Island vineyards.

**A visit to Bainbridge Island Winery**

The handsome winery building and immaculate vineyards stand ready to welcome visitors with tastings and tours. The wine museum in the tasting room reflects the life-long hobby of JoAnn Bentryn, collecting antique wine glasses, and most of the pieces are for sale. Out in the vineyard, a self-guided tour explains the grape-growing process to visitors. The owners encourage visitors to enjoy a picnic on the grounds or to call for information on special events held throughout the year.

**The Wines**

Gerard Bentryn grows several early-ripening varieties including Muller Thurgau

*Bainbridge Island Winery near Winslow, Washington.*

and Siegerrebe, though Chardonnay and Pinot Noir grown at the winery have proven very popular with visitors. Fruit wine lovers enjoy the winery's limited releases of raspberry wine and strawberry wine made from delicious fruit grown on Bainbridge Island.

# Cavatappi Winery

9702 NE 120th Place
Kirkland, WA 98034
(206) 823-6533

**Owner/Winemaker:**
Peter Dow
**First Year:** 1984
**Winery Capacity:** 2,000 Gallons

**Winery History**

Peter Dow's Cavatappi Winery is located in a cellar adjacent to his locally-famous Cafe Juanita restaurant. The Italian focus of the restaurant is echoed in the wines of Cavatappi as Washington's first Nebbiolo was crafted by Dow using traditional techniques including natural yeast fermentation. Grapes for Cavatappi's *Maddalena* (Nebbiolo) come from Red Willow vineyard near Yakima. The most enjoyable way to discover Peter Dow's wines is to have dinner at Cafe Juanita. Additional distribution is limited to a few Seattle-area retail outlets and to selected restaurants in San Francisco and New York. Winery visits are offered by appointment only.

*Continued on page 30.*

## Cafe Juanita
### Owner Peter Dow and Chef John Neumark

*Peter Dow and his Cafe Juanita have become culinary icons in the greater Seattle area. Patrons comment that Dow is at once charming and irreverent, yet dedicated to quality and success. Not a person to be turned away from his passions, he personally jumped the hurdles to get Nebbiolo planted at Red Willow Vineyard and personally fought the battles to get a winery license for the basement of Cafe Juanita.*
*Working together at the restaurant, Dow and his longtime chef John Neumark enjoy each other's sense of humor as both men aspire to create a superb dining experience for each restaurant guest.*

❖ **A RECIPE FROM CAFE JUANITA** ❖

## Coniglio con Ripieni
## "Rabbit Braised with Sweet Peppers"

*Wine Recommendation:* Cavatappi Maddalena

| | |
|---|---|
| 2 | 3 lb. rabbits, portioned (see below) |
| 4 | sweet peppers (mixed colors) cut into 1-inch squares |
| 1 | yellow onion, sliced thin |
| 1 | Tbs chopped Italian parsley |
| 1 | tsp. anchovy paste (Don't be a wuss! Just use it, You won't taste it, and it adds depth and dimension to the dish.) |
| 1 | Tbs. tomato paste |
| 2 | bay leaves |
| | olive oil |
| | salt and pepper to taste |
| | flour for dusting rabbit pieces |

With a cleaver, portion the two rabbits into 18-20 uniform pieces. You get two pieces from each hind leg; 2-3 from the saddle-loin area; one piece from each foreleg; and two pieces by splitting the rib area in half pole-to-pole.

In a large heavy-bottomed casserole-type pan (12-16 inches in diameter please) heat oil to generously cover the bottom of the pan until it ripples. Having dusted the rabbit pieces in flour ahead of time, shake off any excess flour and add the pieces to the pan taking care not to overcrowd. Gently brown the rabbit, turning as needed to create a nice golden crust. You will have to cook the rabbit in batches. After all the pieces are browned, wipe out any excess oil and browned flour bits.

Add enough oil to the pan to barely cover the bottom and when hot add the onion and cook very gently for 20-30 minutes stirring occasionally. When soft and lightly colored add the Italian parsley and anchovy. Stir and cook over very low heat for another 15-20 minutes. Add the pepper squares and cook over very low heat until softened; 20-25 minutes. Add the rabbit back to the pan along with two bay leaves, the tomato paste, and water to barely cover the solids. Bring to a languid simmer; add salt and pepper to taste and cook gently, stirring occasionally until the rabbit is meltingly tender but not falling off the bone. You may have to add a bit of water during the cooking process. The peppers will have disintegrated into the sauce, which should be somewhat thick, not unlike gravy. Check seasoning and serve. Polenta would be an appropriate accompaniment. It's amazing how simple this recipe is. It's a revelation to taste what a little time, patience and restraint can contribute to a dish. *From John N. by way of Tornavento Ristorante, Treiso, Italy.*

**The Wines**

The above-mentioned Maddalena is Peter Dow's pride and joy. The wine features the distinct varietal character of Nebbiolo presented in a medium to lighter style. Other wines of recent release include a rich and toasty Cabernet Sauvignon, Bayless Blanc (a Sauvignon Blanc named after the late Washington wine pioneer Alec Bayless) and Molly's Muscat after Dow's younger daughter.

# Chateau Ste. Michelle

P.O. Box 1976
Woodinville, WA 98072
(206) 488-1133, FAX (206) 488-4657
Email: info@ste-michelle.com
Web: www.ste-michelle.com

**Tasting Room Hours:** Daily, 10 AM to 4:30 PM

**Owner:** Stimson Lane Vineyards & Estates
**Winemaker:** Mike Januik
**First Year:** 1967
**Winery Capacity:** 1,000,000 Gallons +

**Winery History**

The Chateau Ste. Michelle winery dates back to the 1930s when Washington's bountiful harvest of fruits, berries and grapes were vinified to produce some of the Northwest's first wines. The grand Woodinville Chateau was constructed in 1976 as a showplace winery and tourist attraction within a half-hour's drive of metropolitan Seattle. The 87 acres of parklike grounds were originally designed and landscaped by the Olmstead brothers (designers of New York City's Central Park) in 1912 as part of Northwest lumber magnate Frederick Stimson's Hollywood Farms.

**A visit to Chateau Ste. Michelle**

The combination of superb architecture, lush landscaping and perfect picnicking make Chateau Ste. Michelle a stop not-to-be-missed on any Seattle-area wine tour. Exploring the grounds you'll find a large pond and picnic area adjacent to the demonstration vineyard. Tucked away under the trees next to the amphitheater are the original trout rearing ponds of Fred Stimson. These concrete tanks are often stocked with trout and are patrolled

*Chateau Ste. Michelle winery in Woodinville.*

by flotillas of hungry mallards. Winding paths through the gardens lead you to many enjoyable surprises of horticultural note.

In the winery, tours of the cellar describe the winemaking process and conclude with a tasting of Chateau Ste. Michelle wines. The gift shop offers a broad selection of wine, picnic fare and wine-related gifts.

**Special Events**

Special events at Chateau Ste. Michelle are too numerous to mention individually, but you can call the winery to request a monthly calendar of happenings. The outdoor amphitheater is now the setting for a variety of concerts, the ballet and plays throughout the summer. Culinary events have been added under the direction of Executive Chef John Sarich and a curriculum of wine appreciation classes are offered by Bob Betz, M.W.

**The Wines**

Winemaking at Chateau Ste. Michelle is in the capable hands of Mike Januik. A native Northwesterner, Januik gained experience making wine for several other wineries before joining Chateau Ste. Michelle. His insightful handling of the winery's many varietals and vineyard sources are testament to his innate ability as a winemaker. Among the best of his efforts are Chardonnay and Sauvignon Blanc, while Cabernet and Merlot are favorite reds. Artist series red wines are popular and the winery released its first Syrah in 1998.

Tuscan winemaker Piero Antinori joined with Chateau Ste. Michelle in 1998 creating the inaugural bottling of *Col Solare*, a red wine blended from Cabernet, Merlot and Syrah. This venture testifies to the Italian's admiration for hearty Columbia Valley wines.

### John Sarich
### Culinary Director
### Chateau Ste. Michelle

*Passionate about fresh, regional foods paired with world-class wines, John Sarich has been part of the Seattle area culinary scene for over 20 years. In his current role as culinary director for Chateau Ste. Michelle he has the opportunity to share his enthusiasm and knowledge with both local wine lovers and wine and food professionals around the world.*

*John joined Chateau Ste. Michelle winery as a tour guide in 1976 when the winery first opened its doors. He taught cooking classes in the Chateau's historic Manor House and later moved into sales.*

*In 1980, Sarich took a hiatus from the winery and founded the acclaimed Adriatica Restaurant above Lake Union. Lauded by Esquire magazine as one of the country's hot new chefs, he later opened Dalmacija Ristoran in Seattle's Pike Place Market.*

*John returned to Chateau Ste. Michelle in 1992 as Culinary Director and hosted the Emmy-nominated cooking show* Taste of the Northwest *for four years. His cookbooks* Food & Wine of the Pacific Northwest *and* John Sarich at Chateau Ste. Michelle *have inspired wine-loving cooks across the nation and around the world.*

## ❖ A RECIPE FROM JOHN SARICH ❖

# Braised Lamb Shanks

*Serve 4 - Serve with:* Chateau Ste. Michelle Merlot

| | |
|---|---|
| 4 | lamb shanks |
| 1/4 | cup flour, seasoned with 1 teaspoon salt and 1/2 tsp. black pepper, for dredging |
| 2 | Tbs. olive oil |
| 1 | large yellow onion, sliced thin |
| 3 | cloves garlic, minced |
| 1 | cup diced Roma tomatoes |
| 1 | Tbs. tomato paste |
| 1 | cup Chateau Ste. Michelle Merlot |
| 1 | Tbs. chopped fresh rosemary |
| 1 | bay leaf |
| 1 | Tbs. chopped fresh Italian parsley |
| 1/2 | Tbs. dry mustard |
| 1 | clove |
| | salt and freshly ground pepper to taste |

Preheat the oven to 350° F. Dredge lamb shanks in the seasoned flour. Shake off excess flour and set aside. Heat a heavy ovenproof skillet over medium-high heat. Add the olive oil and, when sizzling, add the lamb shanks. Cook, turning occasionally, until golden brown on all sides. Remove shanks and set aside. Add the onion and garlic. Cook, stirring often, until softened, about 5 minutes. Add the tomatoes, tomato paste, Chateau Ste. Michelle Merlot, rosemary, bay leaf, parsley, dry mustard, clove, salt and pepper. When the mixture comes to a simmer, add the lamb shanks.

Transfer the skillet to the preheated oven and bake for about 1 hour (basting occasionally with the sauce) or until the lamb is very tender. Top the lamb shanks with a generous amount of sauce before serving.

# Columbia Winery

14030 NE 145th,
Woodinville, WA 98072
(206) 488-2776
FAX (206) 488-3460
**Email:**
info@columbiawinery.com
**Web:** www.columbiawinery.com

*Columbia Winery in Woodinville, Washington*

**Tasting Room Hours:** Daily, 10 AM to 7 PM

**Owner:** Associated Vintners, Inc.
**Winemaker:** David Lake, M.W.
**First Year:** 1962
**Winery Capacity:** 250,000 Gallons

## Winery History

Columbia Winery is the descendent of Associated Vintners (AV), a group of amateur winemakers that bonded a winery in 1962. Led by Dr. Lloyd Woodburne, a professor at the University of Washington, this group is credited with producing the first premium varietal wines made in the state.

In the 1970s, the winery moved from Woodburne's Laurelhurst garage to more spacious quarters in Kirkland when it became clear that larger volumes of wine were needed to meet rising demand. In 1979, Master of Wine David Lake was hired to assume winemaker duties. A succession of business park facilities preceded the winery's move in 1989 to its current grand Victorian manor in Woodinville.

## A visit to Columbia Winery

Columbia Winery is located directly across the road from Chateau Ste. Michelle in a magnificent Victorian building where tours of the winemaking facility and tastings of the winery's current releases are conducted by an enthusiastic and well-informed staff. Now the destination for the Spirit of Washington Dinner Train, the gift shop offers a wide assortment of apparel, souvenirs, picnic supplies and other wine kitsch. Also, many events are held at the winery in the spacious banquet facilities. Call for a list of upcoming food and wine events.

## The Wines

The wines produced by David Lake at Columbia have long been recognized as fine quality bottlings which set an example for Northwest style and elegance. Vineyard designated Cabernet, Chardonnay and other varietals have won rave reviews and many awards at festivals and fairs. Innovation with new varietals and techniques are another hallmark of David Lake. A 1994 Pinot Gris, harvested from the Otis Vineyard in the Yakima Valley, was recently added, and both Viognier and Sangiovese are anticipated from the 1995 vintage (from Red Willow Vineyard). Lake's relationship with Red Willow Vineyard and its owner Mike Sauer continues to "bear fruit" in style and quality. Columbia's offering of wines is extensive including nearly all Washington-grown varieties in several different styles.

### Tom Douglas
### Executive Chef / Owner
### Dahlia Lounge, Etta's Seafood,
### The Palace Kitchen

*Tom Douglas started cooking at the Hotel DuPont in Wilmington, Delaware before heading west to Seattle in 1978. Starting with the acclaimed Cafe Sport in 1984, Douglas helped to define the Northwest style, or "Pacific Rim Cuisine" as it is sometimes called. This style of cuisine borrows from a cornucopia of cultures, using the best and freshest ingredients of the Pacific Northwest.*

*In November of 1989, Douglas left Cafe Sport to open the Dahlia Lounge in the heart of downtown Seattle. The popularity of the restaurant grew and wide acclaim for Tom led to his receiving the James Beard Award for Best Northwest Chef in 1994.*

*In February of 1995, Tom and Jackie Cross, his wife and business partner, opened their second restaurant after remodelling the old Cafe Sport location. Etta's Seafood is named after their daughter Loretta and allows Tom to showcase his unique cooking style using the best seafood available.*

*The Palace Kitchen offers the latest perspective on Douglas' creativity. Opened in March of 1996, the Palace offers a menu more rustic in style, with a wood-fired grill offering nightly rotisserie specials. The Palace Kitchen also serves as the commissary for Dahlia Lounge and Etta's. Douglas describes it as his dream kitchen, with baking, prep and butchery for all three restaurants taking place at this site.*

### ❖ A RECIPE FROM TOM DOUGLAS ❖

# Northwest Oysters on the Half Shell with Red Verjus Granita

*Wine Recommendation:* Columbia Pinot Gris

Raw northwest oysters such as Kumomotos, Olympias, Quilcenes, Penn Cove Selects
Crushed ice
For granita:

| | | |
|---|---|---|
| 2 | cups red verjus (unfermented red grape juice) * |
| 1 | Tbs. chopped fresh marjoram |
| 2 | tsp. freshly ground black pepper, or to taste |
| 1/2 | tsp. salt |
| 1/2 | cup simple syrup (equal parts water and sugar, boil together and cool) |
| 2 | Tbs. lemon juice or to taste |

Combine all ingredients for granita. Pour into a shallow metal pan and place in freezer. As mixture freezes, stir with fork several times to create small crystals.

To serve, shuck oysters and place on a bed of crushed ice. Top each oyster with a tiny spoonful of granita.

* verjus can be found at gourmet markets

"I like this granita with oysters because having crushed ice under the shells and a little granita on top makes them super icy cold when you eat them. This granita seems to me to have just the right amount of flavor, slight sweetness, acid, and pepper to complement the oysters and the dark pink color is beautiful in contrast to the pearly gray oysters. It is perfect with a Pinot Gris such as made by Columbia Winery."

*Son and father, Greg and Charles Lill, two of the partners in DeLille Cellars*

# DeLille Cellars/ Chaleur Estate

P.O. Box 2233,
Woodinville, WA 98072
(425) 489-0544
FAX (425) 402-9295
Email: DeLille@compuserve.com

**Tasting Room Hours:** By appointment only.

**Owners:** Partnership
**Winemaker:** Chris Upchurch
**First Year:** 1992
**Winery Capacity:** 13,000 Gallons

**Winery History**

This winery is a partnership between wine lovers Charles Lill and his son Greg with wine marketer Jay Soloff and winemaker Chris Upchurch. Familiarity with many Washington wine grape growers, along with help from consultant David Lake, helped this group procure quality grapes from several important vineyard sources in 1992. A key to their plan, this fruit produced a spectacular first release of Bordeaux-style red wine labelled Chaleur Estate. The beautiful new winery chateau was opened in July of 1995 near Hollywood Corner in Woodinville.

**A visit to DeLille Cellars**

Though the winery is not open to the public on a regular basis, part of the winery facility is rented for private parties as conditions permit. You may also call the winery to be included on their "CEO" newsletter mailing list for news of upcoming releases and special "invitation only" events. A chance to visit the charming estate is an opportunity not to miss.

**The Wine**

DeLille Cellars wines are crafted using fine Bordeaux blends as a model but taking advantage of the best fruit available from the Columbia Valley. Using a substantial amount of new oak, winemaker Chris Upchurch has shown remarkable finesse in not creating overly-oaky wines. The flagship red, Chaleur Estate, is joined by a second label wine named "D2" (partly as a pun after the auto route through Bordeaux's Medoc). A recently added vineyard-designated red is the subtle and elegant Harrison Hill. Most recently the winery has released Chaleur Estate Blanc a white wine blended from Bordeaux varieties Sauvignon Blanc and Semillon.

# DiStefano Wines

12280 Woodinville Dr. NE,
Suite 1
Woodinville, WA 98072
(206) 282-6484
FAX (206) 329-7792

**Tasting Room Hours:** By appointment only

**Owner:** Oregon Methode Champenoise, Inc.
**Winemaker:** Mark Newton
**First Year:** 1984

**Winery History**

Mark Newton's early fame came from his efforts with methode champenoise sparkling wine. Having studied the subject with well-known experts from France and California, he chose Oregon fruit to craft his ripe, full-bodied Brut and Blanc de Noir. Discovering the joy of making still wines in the early 1990s, Mark created the DiStefano label for his Fume Blanc and Cabernet Sauvignon. The Whittlesey Mark sparkling wines will now be bottled under the DiStefano label as well.

**The Wines**

DiStefano sparkling wines follow the tradition of Mark Newton's first bottlings and the small lots of Fume Blanc and Cabernet are also intensely aromatic and full flavored.

## E. B. Foote Winery

9354 - 4th Ave. South
Seattle, WA 98108
(206) 763-9928

**Tasting Room Hours:**
Tuesday and Thursday,
7 PM to 9 PM; Saturdays,
Noon to 4 PM.

**Owners/Winemakers:** Sherrill Miller and
  Rich Higginbotham
**First Year:** 1978
**Winery Capacity:** 5,000 Gallons

**Winery History**
    E. B. Foote Winery was founded in 1978 by
Eugene Foote and is the seventh-oldest winery
in the state. Gene Foote retired in the early
1990s and the current owners took over with
Gene as their consultant. Grapes from the
Yakima Valley are trucked to the South Seattle
industrial location where the crush and
winemaking take place.

**A visit to E. B. Foote Winery**
    Free tasting and tours are offered in the
winery with the owners most frequently your
hosts. Special events include a barrel tasting
the first weekend in May and a Christmas
open house the first weekend in December.

**The Wines**
    Current releases of Chardonnay, Merlot,
Cabernet Sauvignon and Reserve Cabernet
have been well received by consumers and
wine critics alike.

## Facelli Winery

16120 Woodinville-
Redmond Road N.E. #1,
Woodinville, WA 98072
(425) 488-1020
FAX (425) 488-6383

**Tasting Room Hours:**
Noon to 4 PM, weekends
or by appointment

**Owner:** Facelli Family
**Winemaker:** Louis Facelli
**First Year:** 1988
**Winery Capacity:** 12,000 Gallons

**Winery History**
    The history of the Facelli Winery is the
history of its owner. After relocating from

California to Idaho in the early 1970s, Lou
Facelli began making homemade wine from
fruit grown in the area around his new home
of Caldwell. He discovered a passion for
winemaking that led to the bonding of his own
winery. Through an unfortunate turn of
events he was soon left winery-less but much
wiser about the ways of the wine business.
Things are now on an upswing and headed in
the right direction as this talented winemaker
stakes his future on his ability to coax quality
and magic out of a load of grapes. A new label
design in 1995 and a commitment to larger
production keep the operation moving
forward.

**A visit to Louis Facelli Winery**
    Although the winery is not a grand
chateau, there are plenty of reasons to visit the
Facelli family at their business-park winery in
Woodinville. Friendly and insightful tours
and tastings explain traditional winemaking
methods used and the varietal styles offered
for sale.

**The Wines**
    Lou Facelli crafts his wines as each vintage
tells him to. The grapes and wine "speak to
him." Facelli's reds include rich and flavorful
Cabernet Sauvignon and Merlot, and lush and
fruity Pinot Noir and Lemberger. White wine
releases include Fumé Blanc, Chardonnay,
Semillon Reserve and Late Harvest Riesling.

## Firesteed Cellars

1809 7th Ave. Suite 1108
Seattle, WA 98101
(206) 233-0683, FAX (206) 292-2780

    Firesteed Cellars was founded by Howard
Rossbach in 1992 as a "virtual winery,"
contracting grapes with growers and having
them vinified by respected winemakers. The
original Firesteed Pinot Noirs were made from
Willamette Valley grapes in Oregon, but they
were marketed by Rossbach and his firm in
Seattle. Having grown to a production level of
almost 30,000 cases per year, Firesteed is
available around the country. A new venture
in Italy has produced a Firesteed Barbera.

## Hedges Reserve Cellars

195 NE Gilman Blvd.
Issaquah, WA 98027
(425) 391-6056
FAX (425) 391-3827
Web: www.hedgescellars.com

**Tasting Room Hours:** Monday thru Saturday, 11 AM to 6 PM

**Owners:** Tom & Anne-Marie Hedges, Mats Hanzon
**Winemaker:** Steve Lessard
**First Year:** 1990
**Winery Capacity:** 175,000 Gallons

**Winery History**

With a background in international management and a love for fine wine, it's no wonder that Tom Hedges' first transaction in the wine business was providing an affordable red wine blend to a European client. With this initial success, Hedges Cellars has built its reputation on producing principally this one red wine, a blend of Cabernet Sauvignon and Merlot. The 1989 Hedges, the first vintage to be released in the U.S., won a gold medal at the Seattle Enological Society tasting. Subsequent bottlings have been lauded by The Wine Spectator as "best buys." Hedges Cellars recently completed a new winery next to their vineyard site on Red Mountain at the east end of the Yakima Valley.

**A visit to Hedges Cellars**

Hedges new Issaquah tasting room, banquet facility and offices are stylish and well appointed for everyday touring and for special events. Everything from weddings to cooking classes are part of the plan so check with the winery for current happenings. In the Yakima Valley, you can visit the Hedges winery at Red Mountain by appointment.

**The Wines**

Hedges Cellars' Cabernet Merlot is an excellent example of blended red wine in the Columbia Valley style. Barrel-aged for a short time, the wine is approachable on purchase but will gain complexity for one to two years. Red Mountain Reserve is a very limited bottling of the best lots featuring additional barrel-aged character and requiring two to three years

additional bottle age to bring out the distinctive flavor and aroma. An unusual blend of Sauvignon Blanc and Chardonnay named "Fume Chardonnay" has gained a following for its round, flavorful style and its ability to pair with a remarkable variety of foods.

*Hedges Reserve Cellars in Issaquah.*

## Matthews Cellars

16116 140th Pl. NE
Woodinville, WA 98072

(425) 487-9810, Fax (425) 483-1652

**Winemaker:** Matthew Loso
**First Year:** 1993

The winery was founded by Matthew Loso in 1993 and offers a blended Bordeaux-style red and other blended or vineyard-designated wines as opportunity arises. The winemaker's experience came first as a wine steward in the restaurant business and later as cellar worker for several Seattle-area wineries. With several years experience under his belt, Matthew Loso confidently began his own operation. In 1998, Loso acquired an 8-acre site south on 140th Pl. where his new winery and visitors center will be built. Call for an appointment.

**The Wines**

Matthews Cellars Yakima Valley Red Wine continues to impress wine lovers with each new vintage, and Matt's Elerding Vineyard Cabernet Sauvignon has received equally high praise.

## Emily Moore
## Chef at Emily's Kitchen

*Emily Moore has been trained as a chef and as a cellist. She creates veritable symphonies with the imaginative dishes she creates.*

*From her first informal training as the main cook at a British Columbia boarding school, Emily learned the basics and more. Not only responsible for cooking the foods, she was trained to butcher the meat and handled a whole repertoire of pantry and cooking responsibilities.*

*As chef at The Painted Table, she gained international fame and helped put Seattle and the Northwest on the map for culinary achievement. More recently she has consulted on menu development for several restaurants and continued her upscale culinary art as Executive Chef at Theoz.*

*Today, her catering company is in full swing and she teaches classes at Hedges Cellars in Issaquah. As we go to press she has been retained by Six Degrees to help open their new Kirkland restaurant and develop some new menu items.*

### ❖ A RECIPE FROM EMILY MOORE ❖

# Roast Loin of Pork with Sundried Cherries, Sage and Prosciutto

*Serves 4 - Serve with:* Hedges Cabernet-Merlot

| | |
|---|---|
| 1 | Tbs. olive oil |
| 1 | 3 to 4 lb. loin of pork, cleaned |
| 1/3 | cup sundried cherries or sundried cranberries |
| 10 | fresh sage leaves |
| 4 | slices good prosciutto |
| 1-1/2 | cups Hedges Cellars Cabernet-Merlot |
| | kitchen string |
| | salt, white pepper and powdered ginger |

Have your butcher "butterfly" the pork loin to make a flat rectangle of meat about 6 by 8-inches. Soak the sundried cherries in 1/2 cup of Cabernet-Merlot for 10 to 15 minutes, then heat over low flame til just simmering. Cool.

Lay the meat on the work surface with the long end toward you. Season with a mixture of salt, white pepper, and good powdered ginger. Lay the prosciutto flat over the surface of the meat, covering the entire rectangle. Lay sage leaves on top (leave whole) then sprinkle with the cherries. Roll the loin into a tube, beginning with the closest edge (the long side) and rolling away from you. Place seam side down and tie in three or four places with string to hold together. Sprinkle with salt and black pepper.

Heat an oven-proof pan or casserole over medium-high flame. Add olive oil and heat until almost smoking. Put in pork loin and sear on all sides. Pour on remaining wine and roast at 400° F. for 25 minutes or until a meat thermometer registers 120° to 125° F.

Remove from the oven and let rest on a plate for 5 to 10 minutes in a warm place. Replace the casserole on the heat and bring the pan juices to a simmer. Beat in 2 to 4 tablespoons of butter and keep warm. Remove strings from the pork, slice into 1/2-inch slices and serve with the jus spooned over.

## Quilceda Creek Vintners

5226 Old
Machias Rd.
Snohomish, WA
98290
(360) 568-2389

**Tasting Room Hours:** By appointment only

**Owner:** Golitzin Family
**Winemakers:** Alex & Paul Golitzin
**First Year:** 1978
**Winery Capacity:** 3,200 Gallons

### Winery History

Some of Washington's best Cabernet Sauvignon is also the hardest to get. Alex and Paul Golitzin produce just 1,500 cases of this varietal each year and it always sells out before the next vintage is released. The nephew of the late André Tchelistcheff, Alex had constant encouragement from "Uncle André" in his winemaking endeavors after receiving his degree in chemical engineering from U.C. Berkeley. (A winemaking curriculum is almost identical to that of chemical engineers.) Recently retired from Scott Paper Co., he can now devote full time to his love of fine Cabernet. Alex and Jeanette's son Paul, a level-headed young man who has taken to the winemaker role with a passion, is now in charge of day to day winemaking duties for Quilceda Creek.

### A visit to Quilceda Creek Vintners

You may call the winery (at the Golitzin's home just north of Snohomish) to make an appointment to taste and buy some of this excellent wine and to chat with Alex and Paul about matters enological. Their Cabernet is also poured at several local wine events throughout the year.

### The Wines

Alex Golitzin's appreciation for fine wine in the style of famous French chateaux was amplified when his own 1983 Cabernet placed second in a tasting of Bordeaux's finest red wines. Lauded by Robert Parker and others, his wines reflect the best of Washington's Cabernet vineyards with a minimum of oaky intervention. Ripe, supple, structured, and ageworthy.

*Paul and Alex Golitzin of Quilceda Creek*

## Rich Passage Winery

7869 NE Day Road W.,
Bldg. A
Bainbridge Island, WA
98110
(206) 842-1199
FAX (206) 842-8198

**Tasting Room Hours:** By appointment only

**Owners/Winemaker:** Linda & Jeff Owen
**First Year:** 1989
**Winery Capacity:** 1,500 Gallons

### Winery History

Rich Passage is a small, family operation annually producing about 500 cases of Pinot Noir, Chardonnay and Fumé Blanc. All the wines are barrel fermented and aged in small French oak barrels. Owners Linda and Jeff Owen took their home winemaking hobby commercial in 1989 and now occupy the same space where Will Kemper and Andy Thomas began Thomas Kemper brewery!

### A visit to Rich Passage Winery

The quiet business park location halfway up Bainbridge Island (west of the highway) is not particularly romantic, but winemaker Jeff Owen offers his personal insights on wine to those who call for a visit.

### The Wines

Small quantities of Chardonnay, Fumé Blanc and Pinot Noir are produced and are sold mostly at the winery.

## Silver Lake Winery

17616 15th Ave. SE,
Suite 106B,
Bothell, WA 98012
(425) 485-2437

## Silver Lake Sparkling Cellars

17721 132nd Ave. NE
Woodinville, WA 98072
(425) 486-1900
**Email:** info@washingtonwine.com
**Web:** www.washingtonwine.com

**Tasting Room Hours:** Winery, by appointment only; Silver Lake Sparkling Cellars, Daily, Noon -5 PM

**Owner:** Washington Wine & Beverage Co.
**Winemaker:** Cheryl Barber Jones
**First Year:** 1989
**Winery Capacity:** 30,000 Gallons

### Winery History

Silver Lake Winery began life as the producer of Spire Mountain Ciders – apple, pear and other hard cider products which continue to have a strong following of loyal fans. With all the equipment and licenses necessary for winemaking, the owners and winemaker decided to produce some wines from the 1989 vintage. A good crop, a talented winemaker, and the rest was history. Strong marketing efforts and continued high-quality wines are keeping Silver Lake in the limelight.

In 1995 the winery acquired the former French Creek Cellars facility near downtown Woodinville. Finally, with a place to hold events and space for a well-appointed tasting room, Silver Lake is stepping up their local image building and marketing efforts.

### A visit to Silver Lake Winery

The Woodinville location of Silver Lake Sparkling Cellars has been completely remodelled to offer banquet facilities in addition to their tasting room and gift shop. During the warmer months you can enjoy a picnic on the banks of Little Bear Creek under the shade of some ancient Douglas firs.

### The Wines

Silver Lake offers a wide selection of varietals including Chardonnay (regular and reserve), Merlot, Cabernet Sauvignon, Sauvignon Blanc, Dry Riesling, Off-Dry Riesling and Riesling Ice Wine. Sparkling Brut is the bubbly selection offered.

## Soos Creek Wine Cellars

20404 - 140th Ave. SE,
Kent, WA 98042
(253) 631-8775
**Email:** sooscreek @ mindspring.com

**Tasting Room Hours:** By appointment

**Owners:** David & Cecile Larsen
**Winemaker:** David Larsen
**First Year:** 1989
**Winery Capacity:** 2,000 Gallons

### Winery History

David Larsen pursued winemaking as a hobby and avocation for eight years when admiration for several of Washington's boutique wineries specializing in Cabernet inspired him to try his hand at the big red. His first release was a 1989 Cabernet Sauvignon – rich and powerful – made in the winery at his home in Renton. The winery is now located in nearby Kent. David's position in the finance department at Boeing is the stabilizing influence away from the excitement and romance of winemaking. David's wife Cecile and their children all help out in the winery operation.

### The Wines

Soos Creek Wine Cellars intends to produce only Cabernet Sauvignon made in an intense style emphasizing oak aging. Only 100% French oak is used and the wines are aged three years before release. The wine offers aromas of cherries, cassis and barrel toast. The palate is long and rich, demanding further bottle age for maximum enjoyment.

# Vashon Winery

12629 SW Cemetery Rd.
Vashon, WA 98070
(206) 463-2990

**Tasting Room Hours:**
Friday and Saturday
by appointment, 11 AM
to 5 PM

**Owners/Winemakers:**
 Will Gerrior and Karen Peterson
**First Year:** 1990
**Winery Capacity:** 2,300 Gallons

### Winery History
 Will Gerrior and Karen Peterson, husband and wife, began the Vashon Winery inspired by their original contacts with Chalone Winery and Joseph Swan Winery in California. They produce Cabernet Sauvignon from grapes grown at the Portteus Vineyard in Zillah as well as Chardonnay and Semillon.

### A visit to Vashon Winery
 Take the short ferry ride from West Seattle to beautiful Vashon Island and you are transported to a relaxing country atmosphere. Will Gerrior and Karen Peterson graciously welcome you to taste and purchase their wines by appointment on Fridays or Saturdays.

### The Wines
 All wines are handmade and purposely on a small scale. Currently the winery produces about a thousand cases a year.

# Wilridge Winery

1416-34 Ave.
Seattle, WA 98122
(206) 325-3051
FAX (206) 447-0849
**Email:**
PBeveridge@HEWM.com

**Tasting Room Hours:**
 By appointment

**Owner/Winemaker:**
 Paul Beveridge
**Tasting Room Manager:** Lysle Wilhelmi
**First Year:** 1993
**Winery Capacity:** 4,700 Gallons

### Winery History
 Wilridge Winery was born in the cellar of the Madrona Bistro restaurant. This neighborhood gathering spot is now closed but winemaker Paul Beveridge's Cabernet Sauvignon and Merlot live on, crafted in small lots from grapes purchased from select vineyard sites including Klipsun Vineyards on Red Mountain in the Yakima Valley.

### A visit to Wilridge Winery
 The small residential/urban winery is open by appointment where you may meet the winemaker and learn more about the winery. The wines are also in limited distribution in the Puget Sound area. Follow James Street east from I-5 until it becomes Cherry Street, then continue to 34th Ave. Turn left and head north two blocks.

**Scott Samuel and Alison Leber of Brie & Bordeaux**

*From a humble fromagerie in Seattle's Green Lake neighborhood, Alison Leber has created an upscale bistro that challenges every aspect of pricey downtown eateries . . . and with free parking!*

*A background in wine and food, almost unlimited energy, and great people skills enabled Leber to expand her cozy cheese shop and add a staff of talented chefs, helpful waitstaff and dedicated managers to launch Brie & Bordeaux, the bistro.*

*Patrons can still buy fine cheeses and wines from the adjacent shop.*

## ❖ A RECIPE FROM BRIE & BORDEAUX BISTRO ❖

# Duck Confit

*Serves 8 - Serve with* Eyrie 1996 Pinot Gris
or Chinook 1995 Cabernet Franc

| | | | |
|---|---|---|---|
| 8 | each bay leaf | 2 | shallots |
| 12-1/2 | inch cinnamon stick | 1 | Tbs. thyme, fresh |
| 4 | each cloves | 1/2 | tsp. rosemary, fresh |
| 1 | Tbs. black peppercorns | | zest of 1 orange |
| 6 | cardamom pods, green | 8 | duck legs |
| 5 | Tbs. kosher salt | 4 | cups duck fat |
| 5 | cloves garlic | | |

In a saute pan over medium-high heat, toast bay leaf, cinnamon, cloves, black pepper and cardamom until fragrant, about one minute. Be sure to constantly move spices to prevent burning. Coarsely grind the spices and place in a medium bowl with the salt. Finely chop the garlic, shallot, rosemary, thyme and zest and toss all the ingredients together until the mixture is uniform.

Place the duck legs snugly, in a single layer, skin side down in a deep oven-proof baking dish. Spread the spice mixture evenly over the legs. Cover with plastic wrap and refrigerate overnight.

Preheat oven to 250° F. Remove legs from the pan and rinse off the spice marinade under lukewarm water. Place the legs back in the baking dish, skin side up.

Melt the duck fat in a heavy-bottomed sauce pan over medium heat. Pour the fat over the legs being sure to cover them completely. Bake for 2 hours then lower the heat to 195° F. and bake an additional 2 - 3 hours until the meat easily pulls away from the bones and the skin is golden brown. Remove from the oven and cool. Do not take legs out of the fat. Cover and refrigerate. For optimal flavor, age the legs in the fat for at least 3 weeks. Confit will keep, refrigerated and covered with fat up to 6 weeks.

To serve: Remove the number of legs you need from the fat, being careful not to tear any meat off. Heat a nonstick, oven-proof saute pan over high heat. Place legs skin-side-down in pan and sear for 30 seconds. Place in a 375° F. oven until heated through, 5 to 7 minutes. Skin should be very crisp. Carefully remove from the pan and serve.

Serve with seasoned white beans or a salad of bitter greens dressed with an herbed vinaigrette. Note: ask your local butcher or grocery store about special ordering duck legs and duck fat if it is not readily available.

# SEATTLE AREA DINING

## Anthony's HomePorts

Multiple Seattle-area view locations: Shilshole Bay (206) 783-0780, Kirkland (425) 822-0225, Edmonds (425) 771-4400, Seattle - Pier 66/Bell Street Diner (206) 448-6688. "Fresh fish daily" is Anthony's motto and they back up the claim with wild salmon, halibut, Dungeness crab, oysters and more. Superb preparations, great selection of NW wines. Moderate. Also don't miss their Chinooks at Salmon Bay at Seattle's Fishermen's Terminal (206) 283-HOOK. (See recipe, page 43)

## Brie & Bordeaux Bistro

2227 N. 56th, (206) 633-3538  Lunch T-F, 11:30 to 2:30; dinner, T-Sat, 5:30 to 9; brunch, S/S 9 to 3.  Alison Leber moved her popular Green Lake-area wine and cheese shop into larger quarters and added this upscale bistro. The staff is tip-top, chef Scott Samuel is creative yet sensible, the wine glasses are Riedel crystal and everything on the menu is tempting. Friday and Saturday price-fixed dinners give the chef and his staff a chance to spread their wings and fly.  A recent visit uncovered Brie ice cream for dessert - a cheese lover's dessert dream come true.  Also try lunch or B & B's "rockin" brunch. (See recipe on page 41.)

## Cafe Juanita

9702 NE 120th Pl., Kirkland  (425) 823-1505 The home of Cavatappi Winery, Cafe Juanita specializes in Northern Italian cooking. Chef John Neumark and owner Peter Dow work together to make sure everything is just so. Pastas, meats, seafood, delicious sauces, fresh rosemary rolls and tempting desserts. Dinner only. (See recipe on page 29.)

## Canlis

2576 Aurora Ave. N., (206) 283-3313  We know a hip, recent college graduate who says of Canlis, "I've been going to Canlis for years with my dad and my grandfather. So what? The food is great, they remember my name and the valet always brings us the right car!" As Seattle's younger generation settles into steady jobs (and steady income) they discover that impeccable service, exquisite cuisine and elegant atmosphere are worth the price.  The wine program – currently under the eye of sommelier Rob Bigelow – is superb and award winning. Greg Atkinson joins Rocky Toguchi in the kitchen to make great food even greater. Chris and Alice Canlis look the part, as they welcome guests to their Seattle landmark. (See recipe on page 145.)

## Elliott's Oyster House

Downtown Seattle, Pier 56, (206) 623-4340. Fine seafood served at the center of Seattle's busy waterfront. Enjoy Northwest wines and seafood-friendly microbrews with attentive and well-informed staff. Cracked crab service is fun and unique. Oyster selection is always tempting for half-shell aficionados. Moderate to expensive. (See recipe on page 73.)

## Flying Fish

2234 1st Avenue, (206) 728-8595  Christine Keff made it in New York, traveled the world, then came to the Seattle area to fulfill a dream. Her experiences in Asia combined with her love of fresh Northwest seafood spawned Flying Fish in 1995.  Rave reviews followed and the place has been crowded ever since. Thai crab cakes, seafood spring rolls, whole fried snapper, and Thai Curry Sea Scallops (recipe on page 157!) are just a few of the Asian offerings. Other fare is equally creative and tasty. The wine list offers plenty of choices from the Northwest and beyond.

## Kaspar's

2701 1st Ave., (206) 441-4805  Kaspar and Nancy Donier present some of Seattle's finest, innovative cuisine – created by Kaspar featuring seasonal local ingredients in delicious adaptations of continental style. Nancy keeps the front of the house in order with help from one of Seattle's most courteous and helpful staffs. Good NW wine selection.

## Macrina Bakery & Cafe

2408 1st. Avenue, (206) 448-4032  Stop by for a latte and pastry, a loaf of bread or dessert to take home. It's all great. See recipe page 65.

## The Metropolitan Grill

820 - 2nd Ave., (206) 624-3287  Voted one of America's top ten steak houses, The Met Grill offers the red wine lover a place to indulge the fantasy of thick, juicy cuts of the finest aged beef and other carnivore's delights. Enjoy a superb list of red wines from local wineries.

## The Golden Goat

14471 Woodinville-Redmond Rd. (at Hollywood Corner area) (425) 483-6791  Owner/ chef Jeff Boswell presides over the neighborhood cafe to Woodinville's wine country. Innovative and traditional preparations of pasta, chicken, lamb and other dishes keep the locals coming back. Award-winning wine list.

### Executive Chef Kelly Degala
### Anthony's Restaurants

*Operating their own wholesale seafood company, Anthony's buys their seafood directly from fishermen in Alaska and other prime fishing locations. Serving the freshest wild Chinook salmon, halibut and Northwest shellfish at a dozen view locations throughout the Puget Sound region, Anthony's is a favorite stop for out-of-town visitors and local residents alike.*

*Executive Chef Kelly Degala invites you to bake up this tasty oyster dish that highlights fresh Pacific oysters from Puget Sound.*

# Baked Oysters with Beurre Blanc

### Serves 2 - Serve with King Estate Reserve Pinot Gris

| | |
|---|---|
| 6 | each oysters in the shell (Pacifics) |
| 4-1/2 | oz. spinach saute (recipe follows) |
| 3 | tsp. tomato, diced and seeded |
| 1-1/2 | oz. beurre blanc (recipe follows) |
| 3/4 | tsp. gremolata (recipe follows) |

Prepare spinach saute, beurre blanc and gremolata for assembly. Shuck and remove oysters from shells making sure there are no shell fragments left in the shell. Place 3/4 oz. spinach saute in shell. Set oyster in middle of the spinach. Sprinkle 1/2 tsp. tomato on oyster. Top oysters with 2 tsp. beurre blanc, then 1/8 tsp. gremolata on each. Bake oysters at 375° F. for 3-5 minutes until hot. Serve on bed of sea salt accompanied with garlic toast points.

## Spinach Saute

| | |
|---|---|
| 12 | oz. washed spinach, no stems |
| 1 | oz. olive oil |
| 1/8 | tsp. kosher salt |
| | pinch ground black pepper |
| 4 | tsp. Anisette |
| 1 | tsp. shallots, finely minced |

Over medium heat, add oil and shallots, saute for about 1 minute. Add spinach, Anisette and saute until leaves are wilted slightly and bright green. Note: this is a quick process and too long of cooking time will overcook the spinach. Season, drain and set aside to cool.

## Beurre Blanc

| | | | |
|---|---|---|---|
| 3 | Tbs. shallots, finely minced | 2 | oz. heavy cream |
| 1/2 | tsp. lemon juice, fresh squeezed | 16 | oz. unsalted butter |
| 3 | oz. white wine | 1/4 | tsp. kosher salt |

Combine shallots, lemon juice and white wine in small saucepan. Reduce by 50%. Strain. Return liquid to sauce pan and add cream. Working on and off the heat, whisk in butter in small pieces to form emulsion.

## Gremolata

| | | | |
|---|---|---|---|
| 1 | cup parsley, finely minced | 1 | tsp. black pepper |
| 4 | tsp. garlic, finely minced | 4 | tsp. lemon zest |
| 2 | tsp. kosher salt | | |

Chop all ingredients together until finely minced and well mixed.

## SEATTLE AREA RESTAURANTS

### Palace Kitchen

2030 5th Avenue, (206) 448-2001
www.tomdouglas.com Tom Douglas' Palace
Kitchen is as close as Seattle comes to a bar
and grill. Not a restaurant with a bar in
another room but a big, noisy "Gimme a
double martini. Up." sort of place with sassy –
yet accommodating – staff and hunks of
delicious meat from the applewood grill. The
place is not for everyone, but Douglas' good
friend Michael Teer of Pike & Western Wine
Merchants has counseled his friend to have a
wine for everyone. Good list, reasonably
priced, fun to sample. (Enjoy Tom's recipe for
oysters on the half shell on page 31.)

### Ray's Boathouse

6049 Seaview Ave. NW, (206) 789-3770
www.rays.com Enjoy the superb seafood
creations of chef Charles Ramseyer at a Seattle
landmark while watching the boats on
Shilshole Bay. Innovative preparations and
friendly waitstaff make for memorable visits.
Impressive offering of Northwest wines on the
restauant list and great winemaker dinners are
presented in the Northwest room each month.
(See recipe on page 47.)

### Rover's Restaurant

2808 E. Madison, (206) 325-7442, Chef Thierry
Rautureau was co-recipient of the James Beard
Award for Best Northwest Chef in 1998. This
latest kudo is the crowning touch to the many
fine reviews and accolades received by
Rover's. Rautureau's French training and
allegiance to classical cooking styles serve to
make the most out of the freshest local
ingredients. The wine list is outstanding as
one would expect of this level of excellence.
Check out the Rover's web site at www.rovers-
seattle.com. (Thierry's recipe for Ellensburg
lamb loin is on page 45.)

### Spirit of Washington Dinner Train

1-800-876-7245, A great outing for visitors and
curious locals, the train travels between
Renton and Columbia Winery in Woodinville
offering views of Lake Washington, Seattle's
skyline and other eastside points of interest.
Delicious meals are prepared by Schwartz
Brothers' Gretchen's Of Course Catering.
Moderate to expensive.

## SEATTLE AREA ACCOMMODATIONS

Included here is a brief selection of
lodgings that are among the finest available.
Other less expensive offerings abound
including some near the eastside wine country
(Marriott Residence Inn, (425) 485-3030 or
Wyndham Garden, (425) 485-5557) The local
Bed & Breakfast Association, (206) 784-0539
offers homey suggestions.

### Sheraton Seattle Hotel & Towers

1400 Sixth Ave., (206) 621-9000 The reputation of Fullers restaurant alone should be
enough to coax a weary traveller into this
delightful hotel. The hotel staff makes a
similar effort to cater to the needs of each and
every guest. Reserve a Tower room for added
amenities and a great view.

### The Salish Lodge

P.O. Box 1109, Snoqualmie, WA 98065 (425)
888-4230 The Salishan Resort folks took over
the former Snoqualmie Falls Lodge and added
a 91-room "country inn" that looks remarkably
like a fancy hotel. Great winemaker dinners
and other culinary extravaganzas take place in
the restaurant.

### The Hotel Vintage Park

1100 5th Avenue, (206) 624-8000 The idea of a
wine-themed hotel was long overdue and
Kimco Hotels have thoughtfully provided one
in Seattle and one in Portland. Each room is
named for a Washington winery or vineyard
and Tulio Ristorante serves delectable Italian
specialties.

❖ A RECIPE FROM ROVER'S ❖

# Ellensburg Lamb Loin with Bing Cherry Sauce and Nectarine Chutney

### Serves 4 - Serve with DeLille Cellars D2

lamb loin (about 24 oz., boned out and silver skin out)
lamb bones (broken into small pieces)
1   carrot, diced small
6   shallots, chopped
1   garlic clove, chopped
2   cups Bing cherries, pitted, diced small
5   thyme sprigs
3   bay leaves
3/4 cup raspberry vinegar
3   cups lamb stock (can substitute veal stock)

1/4 cup sugar
4   ounces water
4   Tbs. raspberry vinegar
4   Tbs. butter

Brown lamb bones in a hot pan, add and color carrot, shallots and garlic. Once roasted, add the vinegar and reduce it by 3/4. Add cherries, cook for a few minutes, then add the lamb stock and herbs and reduce by 2/3.

In a hot saute pan, sear the lamb loin, then finish in the oven at 375° a few minutes until pink. Let the loin rest for at least 5 minutes, then slice it.

Make a caramel of the sugar and water and finish it with raspberry vinegar, add to the sauce, strain it and finish with butter.

Serve hot on the sliced lamb loin.

## For the chutney

4   nectarine halves
1   red onion, diced small
2   oz. red wine vinegar

In a hot saute pan put the onion, nectarine and red wine vinegar. Cook slowly for about 5 minutes and put aside. Serve warm next to the lamb.

© 1993 Thierry Rautureau

## Rover's Owner/Chef
## Thierry Rautureau

*Award-winning chef Thierry Rautureau was born in the Muscadet region of France in the town of Saint Hilaire de Loulay. His parents were farmers in a community where "cows and chickens outnumbered people." Seasonal cooking came naturally as the family cooked only what they grew on their farm.*

*Thierry started a cooking apprenticeship at age 14 in Anjou and continued his traditional French culinary training until the age of 20 when he came to the U.S. and worked for several restaurants before coming to Seattle and taking over Rover's in 1987.*

*His philosophy of "starting with freshness and treating all ingredients with attention" is a building block for the superb "Northwest contemporary cuisine with a French accent" that is the hallmark of a meal at Rover's.*

*Awards and accollades for Thierry and Rover's include his selection as co-winner for Best Northwest Chef by the James Beard Foundation in 1998 and selection of Rover's as the number one area restaurant by Gourmet Magazine. Seattle Magazine named Rover's Restaurant of the Year in 1998 and Nation's Restaurant News inducted Rover's into the Fine Dining Hall of Fame along with only nine other restaurants across the country.*

# SEATTLE AREA WINE & SPECIALTY SHOPS

## McCarthy & Schiering Wine Merchants

Queen Anne Ave. N, (206) 282-8500, also in the north end at 6500 Ravenna Ave. NE (206) 524-9500. Dan McCarthy and Jay Schiering have a loyal following owing to their sound wine advice. Tastings on Sat. T-F, 11-7, Sat 'til 6.

## Pike & Western Wine Merchants

Pike Pl. at Virginia St. (206) 441-1307 Michael Teer and his helpful staff share their expertise at this popular Pike Place wine shop. Extensive NW section. Frequent dinners and tastings. M-F, 9:30-6:30, Sa 9-6.

## Champion Wine Cellars

108 Denny Way, (206) 284-8306 Stephanie & Emile Ninaud's cozy bottle shop features a great selection of wines from around the world. Just north of Denny Regrade.

## Brie & Bordeaux

2227 N. 56th, (206) 633-3538 Alison Leber operates this charming fromagerie and wine shop near Green Lake offering a great selection of cheeses, selected fine wines & superb catering. The wine and cheese shop is adjacent to her acclaimed bistro of the same name.

## Eastside - Bellevue, etc.

### The Grape Choice

220 Kirkland Ave. - Kirkland, (425) 827-7551 Fine wines, beers and foods in this wine shop near Moss Bay. Open daily, 10 AM to 9 PM.

### La Cantina Bellevue

10218 NE 8th - (425) 455-4363, A cozy wine shop just across N.E. 8th from Bellevue Square Mall. Nice selection of wines and expert advice on wine selection and food pairings.

### Northwest Cellars

136 Railroad Ave. N. - Snoqualmie - (800) WINES-01, (425) 888-6176 Scott and Deborah Williams' mail order business of specialty food and wine baskets has grown to include wine tasting, select fresh baked goods, picnic fare and more!

# SEATTLE AREA ACTIVITIES

## Seattle Parks

Located in the city itself are dozens of parks and playgrounds. Check out: Greenlake Park, Volunteer Park on Capitol Hill (enjoy the conservatory here), Gasworks Park (north shore of Lake Union), Golden Gardens beach on Shilshole Bay.

## Woodland Park Zoo

NE 50th St. at Phinney - This is one of our country's most lauded zoos with natural habitats for hundreds of species of animals and birds. The Thai logging camp elephant exhibit and the Alaska Tiaga exhibit are the frosting on the cake.

## Pike Place Farmer's Market

Great restaurants, streetcorner singers, crafts and the west's finest collection of vendors offering all manner of produce and proteins from Mother Earth to you!

## The Seattle Waterfront

Get your hands on a starfish at the Seattle Aquarium on Pier 59 or enjoy fish and chips or fish tacos at the Bell Street Diner on Pier 66. Lots to do and see for young and old.

## The Space Needle at the Seattle Center

Kids are thrilled by the ride to the top and both adults and kids love the view.

## Eastside

### Marymoor Park

Redmond's favorite park is a huge place with areas set aside for everyone. Bring the kids, the dog, the frisbee, soccer ball, etc.

### Sammamish River Bike Trail

The Sammamish Slough Greenbelt offers this trail from Woodinville to Redmond. One access point is just east of Ch. Ste. Michelle off Hwy. 202. The whole family can tour the Red Hook Brewery after the ride!

## Charles Ramseyer, Chef
## Ray's Boathouse

*Ray's Boathouse on Shilshole Bay in Seattle has been at the forefront of Northwest seafood since it opened in its current iteration in 1973. Spectacular views of Puget Sound and the Olympic Mountains complement fresh seafood and the superb selection of NW wines. Ray's Boathouse and Ray's Cafe are open every day, and Ray's offers catering services on site and off.*

*Executive Chef Charles Ramseyer came to Ray's in 1993 after nearly two decades of cooking in fine restaurants around the world. He's continued to cultivate his passion for deliciously simple and unusual pairings of the natural flavors and local ingredients of the Pacific Northwest.*

### ❖ A RECIPE FROM RAY'S BOATHOUSE ❖

# Alaska Weathervane Scallops
## with Sundried Tomato Cream & Potato Thyme Crisps

Serves 4 as an appetizer
Serve with Columbia Crest Chardonnay

### Scallops
12 medium-sized Weathervane Scallops (1 oz. each)
1 Tbs. olive oil

### Sauce
3 whole shallots, diced
1/2 cup Columbia Crest Chardonnay
1 oz. sundried tomato, drained and sliced
1 Tbs. fresh basil, chopped
4 sprigs fresh basil (reserve for garnish)
1 cup heavy cream
3 Tbs. unsalted butter, divided

### Potato Crisps
1 large Russet potato
1 Tbs. fresh thyme, chopped
2 cups peanut oil for frying
1 Tbs. unsalted butter
  salt and pepper to taste

**For Potato Crisps** Heat oil to 300° F. in heavy saucepan. Peel potato and slice paper thin into 24 slices. Blanch potato slices in hot oil for 20 seconds. Drain on paper towels until cool. Preheat oven to 300° F. Butter a cooking sheet and lay 12 potato slices on sheet. Sprinkle fresh thyme and salt and pepper to taste on each slice. Layer a second potato slice on top of the seasoned potato slices, forming 12 packets. Bake potato packets for 5 - 7 minutes until golden brown and crisp around the edges. Cool to room temperature, do not refrigerate.

**For Sauce** In heavy saucepan, melt 1 tablespoon butter over medium heat. Add shallots and cook until translucent, but not brown, about 1 minute. Add Chardonnay, sundried tomato and chopped basil. Reduce over medium heat for 5 minutes; add heavy cream. Reduce for 5 minutes and remove from heat. Divide remaining 2 tablespoons butter into three pieces. Slowly whisk butter into sauce, one piece at a time. Butter should be fully incorporated into sauce before adding next piece. Cover finished sauce and keep in a warm place.

**For Scallops and Presentation** Blot scallops with paper towels. Season lightly with salt and pepper. Heat olive oil in heavy frying pan until hot but not smoking. Add scallops and sear on each side for approximately 30 seconds until lightly firm to the touch. Divide the sauce equally among four plates. Arrange three potato crisps on each plate, laying the narrow end of each crisp in the center of the plate to form a "flower." Place 3 scallops in the center of the plate and garnish with the reserved basil sprigs.

# SEATTLE AREA MICROBREWERIES

The Seattle area has more microbreweries and brewpubs than any other Northwest city – except Portland! Oh well, some of the Northwest's finest producers are here as well as many superb ale houses and brewpubs. Let's start with the breweries.

## Hale's Ales Microbrewery

4301 Leary Way N.W., Seattle (206) 706-1544. Expanding from the original western Washington location in Kirkland in 1995, Hale's Ales now has a larger, state-of-the-art facility in Seattle with a large brewpub, gift shop and everything. Most of Hale's ale styles are variations on pale ale, offering subtle differences for the discriminating ale aficionado: American Pale Ale, Honey Wheat, India Pale Ale, Amber Ale and the famous Wee Heavy.

## Hart Brewing Company - Pyramid Ales

91 Royal Brougham and 1201 First Ave. S. (right by the Kingdome) - (206) 682-8322. This fancy taproom and brewery opened in 1994 to the cheers of beer lovers and sports fans alike. An exquisite bar and eatery offers views to the brewing operation which is the "show" brewery. The production brewery is at a more industrial location. Also the home of Thomas Kemper Brewery which is also owned by Hart Brewing. As far as the Pyramid Ales go, try the delicious Hefe Weizen, Wheaten Ale, Apricot Ale and Espresso Stout. And have a bite to eat, the food here is great!

## Mac & Jack's Brewery

Redmond (425) 868-4778. Malcolm Rankin (Mac) and Jack Schropp turned their homebrewing hobby into a business producing 500+ barrels of pale ale, amber ale, hefe weizen, Blackjack Porter and Afrikan Amber (dry hopped). While they have no tourist facilities, you can find their brews at local ale houses. A new location is being negotiated at press time which will have a tasting room and eventually a brew pub. Call the brewery for an update and current availability at restaurants, ale houses and taverns.

## Maritime Pacific Brewing Co.

1514 NW. Leary Way, Seattle - (206) 782-6181. This great little brewery in Ballard offers a superb line of hand-crafted ales and a wide selection of seasonal brews. The regular lineup includes Flagship Red Ale, Nitewatch Dark Ale, Islander Pale Ale, Clipper Golden Wheat and Salmon Bay Bitter. Both regular and seasonal brews (as well as T-shirts, caps, and trinkets) are available at the brewery store open 8:30 AM to 6 PM, M-F; and 11 AM to 6 PM on Saturday. Brewery tours are offered Saturdays at 1, 2, 3 and 4 PM.

## Pike Place Brewery

1432 Western Ave., Seattle - (206) 622-3373. A fixture in the lower level of the Pike Place Market for years, Pike Place Brewery has expanded its Liberty Malt Homebrewers Supply into a storefront at 1419 First Ave. where you can sample the ales and take a tour of the Northwest Brewing Museum downstairs. East India Pale Ale, regular Pale Ale, Porter and Stout are favorite brews.

## Redhook Brewery - Seattle

3400 Phinney Ave. N., Seattle - (206) 548-8000. Like a 14-year-old trick or treating, Redhook is getting a little big to be calling itself a microbrewery. Retreating to the name "craft brewery" this company is still the original and the best of the Seattle-area breweries. The facility occupies the streetcar barn of the old Seattle Electric Company in Fremont (circa 1905). The delightful Trolleyman Pub sets a standard for comfort, good food and an overall great place to drink beer. The brewery's ESB, Wheathook, Blackhook Porter and a changing line of Blue Line special seasonal beers make for a great selection. A nice selection of logo wear and beer to go are added attractions. Tours available.

## Redhook Brewery - Woodinville

14300 NE 145th, Woodinville - (425) 483-3232. Redhook's new state-of-the-art production facility in the eastside wine country opened in 1994 and includes the delightful Forecaster's Public House and a huge beer garden for outside sipping in summer. The dramatic modern architecture of the building is striking against the more pedestrian structures that dot the surrounding landscape, but local beer aficionados flock to the pub each evening to slurp their favorite Redhook suds. The Sammamish Slough bike trail rides right by the beer garden so a lot of two-wheelers take a detour for a pint after their ride. Tours of the facility are offered on weekends. The large Weatherman's Banquet Room is available for large parties or receptions.

## Bigtime Brewery & Alehouse

4133 University Way NE, (206) 545-4509. Fresh beers brewed on premises plus inexpensive pub grub tailored for the college set. Try the Coal Creek Porter.

## Blue Star Cafe & Pub

4512 Stone Way NE, (206) 548-0345. Another damn fine restaurant masquerading as a pub. Good food needs good beer—choose from 20 micros on tap.

## College Inn Pub

4006 University Way NE, (206) 634-2307. A sentimental favorite where the author has won many a dart game and enjoyed too many plates of nachos. Hiccup!

## Cooper's Alehouse

8065 Lake City Way NE, (206) 522-2923. Bring your darts and your softball team and a thirst for microbrewed beer and a hunger for beer batter fish n' chips.

## The Latona

6423 Latona Ave. NE, (206) 525-2238. Just up the hill from Greenlake featuring great micros, live jazz/rock. A Northwest classic neighborhood pub.

## Murphy's Pub

1928 N 45th, (206) 634-2110. In the heart of Wallingford, Murphy's is a classic Irish pub offering a fine pint of Guinness or your choice of a dozen other brews.

## Hilltop Ale House

Queen Anne Ave at McGraw. (206) 285-3877 Dedicated to providing a wide selection of brews, the food here is outstanding. Enjoy a seat in the garden out back.

## Eastside

### Canyon's Restaurant and Tap Room

22010 17th SE, Bothell, (206) 485-3288. Get into some spicy southwestern fare and a pint of microbrew. Not far from the Woodinville wine country.

## The Pumphouse Tavern/Restaurant

11802 NE Eighth, Bellevue, (206) 455-4110. A sports bar and burger joint that also happens to serve a great selection of fine microbrews.

## The Roost

120 Gilman Blvd., Issaquah (206) 392-5550. A fine restaurant enjoying a reputation as a great beer drinker's bar.

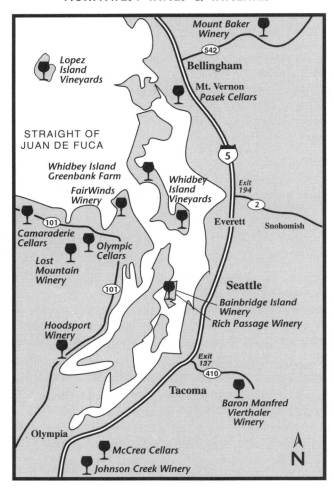

Mount Baker
Winery

542

Bellingham

Mt. Vernon
Pasek Cellars

STRAIGHT OF
JUAN DE FUCA

5

Whidbey Island
Greenbank Farm

FairWinds
Winery

Whidbey
Island
Vineyards

Exit
194

2

Everett        Snohomish

Camaraderie
Cellars

101

Olympic
Cellars

Lost
Mountain
Winery

101

Seattle

Bainbridge Island
Winery
Rich Passage Winery

Hoodsport
Winery

Exit
137

410

Tacoma

Baron Manfred
Vierthaler
Winery

Olympia

McCrea Cellars

Johnson Creek Winery

N

Lopez
Island
Vineyards

# Olympic Peninsula &
# Greater Puget Sound Wine Touring

As you leave the greater Seattle metropolitan area of Western Washington, the wineries become fewer in number and much further apart. It's time to commit a weekend and visit some of Washington's most scenic areas and include stops at some unique winery facilities.

### Olympic Peninsula

Leaving Seattle via the Winslow Ferry you can start your tour by visiting **Bainbridge Island Winery** just before lunch (see Seattle area listings) or plan a picnic beside their vineyard. Continue north on Highway 305 to cross the Hood Canal Bridge to the Olympic Peninsula. Continue north on Highways 104 and 101 to enter Sequim, home of **Neuharth Winery**. Just east of "downtown" Sequim take the southward turn to head up into the mountains to visit **Lost Mountain Winery**. Prior arrangements are necessary unless you plan your trip during their annual month-long "open winery" each June. Port Angeles is home to **Camaraderie Cellars**, open by appointment only.

On your way back, visit Port Townsend to seek out **Fair Winds Winery** then follow Highway 101 south along Hood Canal to **Hoodsport Winery**.

### North Puget Sound

Enjoy the island life, Washington style, by taking the ferry from Mukilteo to Whidbey Island for visits to **Whidbey Island Vineyards** and **Whidbey Island Greenbank Farm**. Be sure to allow time to visit Langley, Penn Cove and Coupeville as you drive north. After you cross Deception Pass you can return to

Interstate 5 to visit Bellingham and **Mount Baker Vineyards** in the Nooksack Valley. An alternate plan would be to time your visits to make the Anacortes Ferry to rustic **Lopez Island** to visit the winery of the same name.

### Olympia Wine Touring

Near Olympia and in the scenic Skookumchuck Valley further south, you can visit **McCrea Cellars** (open by appointment) and **Johnson Creek Winery** at Alice's Restaurant dinner house near Tenino.

## Camaraderie Cellars

334 Benson Road, Port
Angeles, WA 98362
(360) 452-4964

**Owner/Winemaker:**
Don Corson
**First Year:** 1992

### Winery History

Camaraderie Cellars is located on the scenic Olympic Peninsula in the shadow of the majestic Olympic Mountain ridges. The winery's first commercial vintage was in 1992 with an emphasis on limited production of premium Cabernet Sauvignon.

### A visit to Camaraderie Cellars

The small winery building with a view of the Olympic Mountains is located just west of Port Angeles, 1/4 mile south of Highway 101. Please call ahead for an appointment to visit.

### The Wines

Grapes for the Cabernet Sauvignon of Camaraderie Cellars come from many prestigious vineyards in Eastern Washington. First releases have proved that the fine red wines will stand with the best the Northwest has to offer. Very limited.

## FairWinds Winery

1924 Hastings Ave. W.
Port Townsend, WA 98368
(360) 385-0503

**Tasting Room Hours:**
Weekends, 1 to 5 PM

**Owners:** Michael Cavett,
Judy Cavett, Harry Dudley,
Zoe Ann Dudley
**Winemaker:** Michael Cavett
**First Year:** 1993

### Winery History

Michael Cavett and co-owner Harry Dudley worked together in the Coast Guard until they retired in 1991. Together they purchased property in the rural area southwest of Port Townsend where FairWinds Winery grew out of a dream and into a converted barn. Buying grapes from Eastern Washington and crafting the wines by hand, the duo offer Cabernet Sauvignon, Lemberger and Gewurztraminer.

### A visit to FairWinds Winery

The tasting room is open Saturday and Sunday from 1 to 5 PM in the corner of the winery. Enjoy this opportunity to discuss the wines with one of the owners.

### The Wines

The rustic bottlings produced at FairWinds Winery cry out to accompany food and the reds can often benefit from a year or two additional bottle age to smooth them out a bit.

# Hoodsport Winery

N 23501 Highway 101
P.O. Box 597
Hoodsport, WA 98548
(360) 877-9894
FAX (360) 877-9508
**Email:** hoodsport@hctc.com

**Tasting Room Hours:** Daily, 10 AM to 6 PM

**Owners:** Edwin R. and Peggy J. Patterson,
Majority Shareholders
**Winemaker:** Brent Trela
**First Year:** 1978
**Winery Capacity:** 38,000 Gallons

### Winery History

The first bottlings produced at Hoodsport Winery were fruit wines vinted by the Patterson family on a small scale. These flavorful wines were sold at the highway-side winery to local residents and interested passers-by. The success of Hoodsport's aromatic raspberry wine propelled the winery into large scale production of both fruit wines and varietal grape wines.

Each October the winery hosts the annual grape picking party on Stretch Island where their vineyard of "Island Belle" grapes is harvested with friends and fellow wine lovers. This grape variety was created on Stretch Island by early grape growers around the turn of the century. Some of the vines harvested today are upwards of 70 years old.

### A visit to Hoodsport Winery

The location of Hoodsport Winery on Hwy. 101, makes it a popular stop for vacationers who would like a look at a winery and a taste of wine. Hood Canal is popular with scuba divers and water skiers, as well as those seeking the famous shrimp and oysters that do so well in the area. Chocolate Truffles filled with Hoodsport's Raspberry Wine are also offered for sale.

### The Wines

Hoodsport's fruit wines are hard to find except at the winery as is the Island Belle wine. Take the opportunity to sample these specialties when you visit. Hoodsport has also become well known for their Chardonnay Sauvignon Blanc, Lemberger-Cab, Gewurztraminer, Merlot, and other grape varietals.

# Johnson Creek Winery

19248 Johnson Creek
Rd. S.E.
Tenino, WA 98589
(360) 264-2100
**Owner & Winemaker:**
Vincent de Bellis, Sr.
**First Year:** 1984

### Winery History

Ann and Vince DeBellis' Alice's Restaurant and Johnson Creek Winery offer unique perspectives on country life in the Skookumchuck Valley. A small vineyard is planted next to the restaurant, but most grapes come from Eastern Washington.

### A visit to Johnson Creek Winery

The best way to visit Johnson Creek Winery is to call and make dinner reservations at Alice's Restaurant. The delicious, five-course meal is reasonably priced and includes a winery tour and tasting of Johnson Creek's wines before dinner. Access to the facility is via Washington Highway 507.

### The Wines

Johnson Creek Cabernet Sauvignon, Lemberger, Blush Riesling, Chenin Blanc and Chardonnay are available at the restaurant or by special appointment with the owner.

# Lopez Island Vineyards

Rt. 2, Box 3096 -
Fishermans Bay Road
Lopez Island, WA 98261
(360) 468-3644
FAX (360) 468-3073
**Email:** lopezvineyards@
yahoo.com
**Web:** www.civicnet.org/webmarket/

**Owners:** Brent Charnley, Maggie Nilan
**First Year:** 1990
**Winery Capacity:** 4,000 Gallons
**Tasting Room Hours:** Summer: Wednesday through Sunday, Noon to 5 PM,
Winter: Friday & Saturday, Noon to 5 PM
Closed Christmas through March 1st.
Tasting fee: $1.00

## Winery History

Lopez Island Vineyards is a small family-run winery, growing grapes and making wine in the San Juan archipeligo. The vineyard consists of unique, high quality varieties (certified organically grown), selected for growing in the rain shadow of the Olympic Mountains. Also produced are wines from well-known grape varieties grown in Eastern Washington. The owners invites you to the small stone and timber winery for a tasting and a visit. Take the Anacortes ferry (or east from Victoria, B.C.) and follow the road southwest from the ferry dock to Fishermans Bay Road.

## The Wines

Brent Charnley, as winemaker for Mount Baker Vineyard in the mid-1980s, learned the making of Madeleine Angevine and Siegerrebe. His lineup at Lopez Island Vineyards also includes Merlot, Cabernet-Merlot and Chardonnay made from grapes grown in Eastern Washington. Apple-pear and blackberry fruit wines are also produced.

# Lost Mountain Winery

3174 Lost Mountain Rd.
Sequim, WA 98382
(360) 683-5229
FAX (360) 683-2202
**Email:** wine@olypen.com
**Web:** www.lostmountain.com

**Tasting Room Hours:**
Last week of June and first week of July, 11-5

**Owners:** Steve & Sue Conca
**Winemaker:** Steve Conca
**First Year:** 1982
**Winery Capacity:** 4,000 Gallons

## Winery History

Romeo Conca remembered fondly the wines he made with his father (a famous chef) during his boyhood in Connecticut. These were red wines of Italian style, strong in flavor and rich in body and texture. Those wines were the wines that Romeo produced at Lost Mountain Winery. Romeo passed away in 1997 and is missed by all who knew him for his wisdom, his gentle manner and his love of

*In memory of Romeo Conca who died in 1997. A lover of fine wine, classical music and good food. A great human being and gentle soul.*

good food and wine. The Conca family continues to operate the winery with son Steve doing the winemaking and Sue Conca operating the tasting room during the annual open winery each summer.

## A visit to Lost Mountain Winery

Set well back in the forested foothills of the Olympic Mountains, the winery occupies the basement of the Conca home. It is here that wine is made from grapes purchased in California and Eastern Washington. Birdwatchers should bring their binoculars along to check out the local fauna.

Just west of the Dungeness River turn south off Hwy. 101 onto Taylor Cutoff Road. Head toward the hills turning right just before you descend to the fish hatchery. Watch for Lost Mountain Road as you ascend from the valley then watch for the address at the driveway.

## The Wines

Rich red wines from local and California grapes are the hallmark of Lost Mountain Winery. Pinot Noir, Barbera and other blends are great accompaniments to hearty meals.

# McCrea Cellars

13443-118th Ave. SE
Rainier, WA 98576
(360) 458-9463

**Tasting Room Hours:**
By appointment

**Owner & Winemaker:**
Douglas McCrea
**First Year:** 1988
**Winery Capacity:** 2,000 Gallons

**Winery History**

Barrel-fermented Chardonnay and red wines produced from Rhone varietals Grenache and Syrah are the emphasis at this small winery.

Doug McCrea strives to achieve elegance, balance and richness in his wines by carefully nurturing the essence of each vineyard's unique fruit flavors. In 1994 the winery relocated to a lovely rural site southeast of Olympia with a stunning view of

*Doug McCrea embracing two passions*

Mt. Rainier. A delightful afternoon's journey to this often unexplored area of Puget Sound awaits the wine enthusiast. Tours and tastings available by appointment.

**The Wines**

Doug McCrea crafts his unique varietals by traditional, labor-intensive methods. Production is small and distribution is limited but his wines are worth seeking out. Rich Syrah red wine is complemented by his barrel-fermented Chardonnays and his newest passion, Viognier.

# Mount Baker Winery

4298 Mt. Baker Hwy.
Deming, WA 98244
(360) 592-2300
(360) 592-2526

**Tasting Room Hours:**
Daily, 11 AM to 5 PM
$1.00 tasting fee refundable with purchase

**Owner:** Randy Finley
**Winemaker:** Maitland Finley
**First Release:** 1982
**Winery Capacity:** 100,000 Gallons

**Winery History**

The long, mild growing season of Washington's Nooksack Valley provides a perfect microclimate for the growing of Mount Baker Vineyards' favored varietals. Experimentation by viticulturalist Albert Stratton with over 100 varietals led to the planting of Chardonnay, Gewurztraminer, Madeline Angevine, Muller-Thurgau, Pinot Noir, Sauvignon Blanc and others.

Current owner Randy Finley brought new life to the winery when he took over some years ago and now offers culinary events that feature Mount Baker wines. Call the winery for details of upcoming opportunities to visit and participate in these special dinners.

**A visit to Mount Baker Vineyards**

The drive to Mount Baker from Interstate 5 serves to soothe the soul as one passes from freeway construction and growing clusters of condominiums to rural residences and finally to the quiet of farm and field disturbed only by the sound of birds and the rush of the Nooksack River. Bring your picnic lunch to enjoy on the deck or under the spreading cedar trees nearby.

**The Wines**

A wide variety of wines includes mainstream varietals like Chardonnay, Cabernet and Merlot as well as unusual varieties like Chasselas. Madeleine Angevine, Siegerrebe, Lemberger, assorted blends, and fruit and berry wines round out the lineup for tasting. Some truly unique wines are offered that pair very well with specific types of foods.

# Olympic Cellars

255410 Highway 101
Port Angeles, WA 98362
(360) 683-9652, (360) 452-0160

**Tasting Room Hours:** Daily, 9:30 AM to
5:30 PM. Tours and groups by appointment.
**Owners/Winemaker:** Dan Caudill
**First Year:** 1979
**Winery Capacity:** 4,400 Gallons

### Winery History

Gene Neuharth came north from California
to retire from the grape growing business only
to find himself making homemade wine and
then opening a winery. Current production
from Washington-grown grapes is continuing
after Gene Neuharth's death in 1994.
Neuharth's close friend and associate Dan
Caudill operates the winery and tasting room.

### A visit to Olympic Cellars

The winery relocated in 1997 from the
eastern edge of downtown Sequim to a
picturesque 1890s dairy barn on the south side
of Highway 101 halfway between Sequim and
Port Angeles. The selection of wines for tasting
echoes the winery's slogan of producing "fine
dinner wines," dry or almost dry wines to
complement seafood or meats.

### The Wines

Olympic Cellar's proprietary "Dungeness"
table wines—red, white and rosé—provide full
flavor and a balanced palate to accompany
almost any meal and are great values.

# Pasek Cellars

511 South 1st
Mt. Vernon, WA 982
(360) 336-6877

**Tasting Room Hours:**
Tuesday thru Saturday,
11 AM to 6 PM
Sunday, Noon to 5 PM
Closed Mondays

**Owners/Winemakers:** Gene & Kathy Pasek
**First Year:** 1996

### Winery History

This small operation in the Skagit Valley
specializes in aperitif and dessert style wines
made from local fruit and grapes.

### A visit to Pasek Cellars

Located in downtown Mount Vernon just
off I-5, you can stop in and taste the wines and
visit with the winemaker, Gene Pasek.

### The Wines

Currently available are Gewurztraminer,
Cabernet Sauvignon (24% Merlot), Cabernet
Port, Cherry Wine, Raspberry Dessert Wine,
Blackberry Dessert Wine and Blackberry
Liqueur.

# San Juan Vineyards

2000 Roche Harbor Road
P.O. Box 1127
Friday Harbor, WA 98250
(360) 378-9463
FAX (360) 378-3411
**Email:** sjvineyards@rockisland.com
**Web:** www.rockisland.com/~sjvineyards

**Tasting Room Hours:** 10 AM to 7 PM daily

**Owners:** Steve & Yvonne Swanberg,
Tim Judkins
**First Year:** 1997

### Winery History

From a popular wine shop in Friday
Harbor where custom bottled wines were sold
under the San Juan Cellars label, comes this
new producing winery planning their first
crush from purchased fruit in 1998 and from
the harvest of their own vineyard in 2000.

### A visit to San Juan Vineyards

Located three miles from Friday Harbor on
Roche Harbor Road, the tasting room is in a
renovated, turn-of-the-century schoolhouse.
Gourmet foods, gifts and other wine-related
items are for sale.

### The Wines

Formerly produced by another Washington
winery, the wines of San Juan Vineyards will
soon be produced by the new owners. A
winery building is on the drawing boards for
imminent construction.

# Baron Manfred Vierthaler Winery

17136 Hwy. 410 East
Sumner, WA 98390
(360) 863-1633

**Tasting Room Hours:** Daily, 11 AM to 10 PM

**Owner/Winemaker:** Manfred J. Vierthaler
**First Year:** 1976
**Winery Capacity:** 40,000 Gallons

## Winery History

The Manfred J. Vierthaler Winery stands as a local landmark above the Puyallup Valley, a monument to strong will and over two decades of hard work to make a business succeed. The winery's owner and winemaker has forged a place in the local community by offering a wide variety of wines to travelers heading to Chinook Pass from Tacoma and Seattle.

The Swiss-style chalet is home to the Vierthaler Winery and also to the Vierthaler's Roofgarden Restaurant. Restaurant fare is of widely varying origin – everything from traditional German dishes to hippopotamus and wild boar. The tables are arranged to make the most of the view of the Puyallup Valley below.

## A visit to Manfred Vierthaler Winery

The winery tasting room is located in the restaurant lobby where visitors may sample and purchase the wines.

## The Wines

Manfred Vierthaler's wines follow a non-Northwest tradition of being named for internationally famous wine regions as well as varietal grapes. Chablis, Cream Sherry, Burgundy and Rhine are presented alongside Riesling and Chardonnay.

# Whidbey Island Greenbank Farm

765 E. Wonn Road
Greenbank, WA 98253
(360) 678-7700

**Tasting Room Hours:** 10 AM to 5 PM daily

**Owners:** Non-Profit Corporation in partnership with the Port of Coupeville, Island County
**First Year:** 1997

## Winery History

Located on Whidbey Island, this loganberry farm-turned-winery was opened to public visits in 1985 by Stimson Lane Wine & Spirits. The historic buildings date back to the turn of the century when school was held for local youngsters in the farm's barn. The first loganberry vines were planted in the 1940s and the predecessor of Chateau Ste. Michelle used the fruit from these vines for winemaking for several decades. In September of 1997, the property was sold to local ownership with wine production of the Whidbey's brand Port and Loganberry liqueur being shifted to another Stimson Lane winery. Wines under the Whidbey Island Greenbank Farm label are custom bottled by another winery.

## A visit to Whidbeys

A scenic ferry ride from Mukilteo to Clinton and a short drive up the island leads to the visitor center at Whidbey Island Greenbank Farm. The property includes delightful picnic opportunities on the landscaped grounds. The annual Loganberry Festival (last two weekends in July) and other special events are planned.

## The Wines

With the change of management the wines are custom bottled at another winery. Fruit wines of loganberry, raspberry and rhubarb as well as vinifera wines of Merlot, Chardonnay, and others are offered.

## Whidbey Island Vineyard

5237 So. Langley Rd.
Langley, WA 98260
(360) 221-2040

**Tasting Room Hours:**
Thursday through
Sunday, Noon to 5 PM
$1.00 tasting fee

**Owners:** Gregory & Elizabeth Osenbach
**Winemaker:** Greg Osenbach
**First Year:** 1991
**Winery Capacity:** 1,200 Gallons

**Winery History**

Scenic Whidbey Island offers many things to visitors and residents alike. The natural beauty of this jewel of Puget Sound is undeniable and the historical and cultural aspects of the small island communities are unique and interesting. Langley, with its artists, booksellers and small cafes, offers an intellectual side to island life and it is here that Whidbey Island Winery follows the example of other Puget Sound area wineries in growing locally suitable grapes for estate-bottled wines. Owners Greg and Elizabeth Osenbach find the area a perfect place to raise their family and operate the winery.

**A visit to Whidbey Island Vineyard**

The distinctive red barn of Whidbey Island Winery is unmistakable along Langley Road. A picnic area adjacent to the winery building offers a tranquil view of the vineyard and a decades-old apple orchard.

**The Wines**

A proprietary "Island White" blend is a refreshing sipping wine – well balanced and characterful. Pleasant versions of Siegerrebe, Madeleine Angevine are available as well as Rhubarb wine and a Lemberger made from grapes grown in Eastern Washington. A ripe and fruity Cabernet Sauvignon is also made.

# OLYMPIC PENINSULA & PUGET SOUND ACCOMMODATIONS

## Manor Farm Inn

**Poulsbo,** 26069 Big Valley Road off Hwy. 3, Poulsbo, WA 98370 (360) 779-4628 Country charm with city amenities and livestock to boot! Jill Hughes offers guest rooms with private baths, cottages for more privacy and conference facilities. In addition, the restaurant on the premises is one of the finest on the Peninsula. Strolling the working farm, relaxing in the hot tub and enjoying a leisurely breakfast are but a few of the temptations.

## The James House B & B

**Port Townsend** – 1238 Washington St., Port Townsend, 98368, (360) 385-1238 A collection of 12 rooms beautifully furnished in Victorian style, some with private bath, some with a terrific view of Puget Sound, some with both. Continental breakfast. Children over 12 only, no pets.

## Fort Worden State Park

**Port Townsend** – (360) 385-4730 For the budget conscious, or those with a large family, this is the place to stay. Accommodations range from restored multi-bedroom homes (officers quarters) to youth hostel dormitories to campsites and trailer/RV hookups. Bring the kids and the dog.

## The Inn at Langley

**Whidbey Island** - 400 - 1st St., (P.O. Box 835), Langley, WA 98260 (360) 221-3033 Exploring the quaint shops in Langley, visiting nearby wineries or simply relaxing and enjoying the view of Saratoga Passage, The Inn at Langley can be your convenient base of operations. Muted Northwest decor accents 24 guest rooms featuring fine views and fireplaces. Dinner is offered in the Inn's dining room on weekends.

## Groveland Cottage B & B

**Sequim** - 1673 Sequim-Dungeness Way, Dungeness, WA 98382 - (360) 683-3565 On the road that eventually leads to the Three Crabs restaurant, Groveland Cottage is close by to the activities of the area, but removed from the hustle and bustle of Highway 101. An expanded beach house circa 1900, the charm of the place has survived despite modernizing of facilities. Owner Simone Nichols keeps the guests coming back with delicious food and service.

## Oyster Creek Inn

190 Chuckanut Drive, Bow, WA 98232, (360) 766-6179  Doug Charles keeps the seafood fresh and the preparations original at the Oyster Creek Inn.  Famous for their superb selection of Northwest wines.  Lunch and dinner daily.

## Friday Harbor House

130 West St., Friday Harbor  (360) 378-8455 This fancy inn is popular with well-heeled tourists for its soothing accommodations and superb dining.  The dishes are creative and the service is friendly.

## The Star Bistro

201-1/2 First St., Langley, (360) 221-2627 Located above the Star Store on Langley's fashionable First Street, you can enjoy a burger or a caesar salad or something fancier if the mood strikes.  The weekend scene is busy but worth the wait.  Check the sunny deck if you need a few rays.

## Trattoria Giuseppe

4141 E. Hwy. 525, Langley (360) 341-3454 Highly recommended by local winery owners, the Trattoria Giuseppe offers creative Italian dishes that take advantage of local seafood (Penn Cove mussels, salmon and shrimp). Enjoy a local wine with your lunch or dinner.

## The Doghouse

North end of First Street above the water.  This pub/burger joint is a little rough around the edges for the likes of the Langley landed gentry but you can get a delicious sandwich or fish and chips to pair with a local microbrew or glass of local wine.  View tables go early.

## Gail's

Lopez Island, (360) 468-2150  For a restaurant in an out-of-the-way location, Gail's offers superb cuisine and an unmatched wine list (recently awarded by The Wine Spectator!). Lunch is served every day, dinner Thurs. thru Sun.  Deli and retail outlet are next door.

## ★ ★ ★ Northwest Legends of Food & Wine ★ ★ ★

### ❖ A RECIPE FROM DOUG CHARLES ❖

### Doug Charles
### Oyster Creek Inn

*"Wine is food, not some out of world experience.  What is important is what YOU like.  If this means Leonetti with frozen pizza, all the better."*

*Doug Charles has hosted some of the area's finest red wine extravaganzas at the Oyster Creek Inn on Chuckanut Drive.  This modest dinner house has a superb wine collection at very reasonable prices.  Make reservations or drop in if you're out for a drive and you can enjoy fresh seafood and other delicious choices with attentive service and a nice forest view to the bay.*

## Chocolate Dipped Spearmint Leaves

Dessert or Snack
Wine Recommendation: Washington Cabernet Sauvignon

20-50  organically grown spearmint leaves - washed and dried
2  lbs. semi-sweet chocolate

Break chocolate into 1-inch pieces and melt in a double boiler over hot water.  Do not let steam into the chocolate!

When just melted, remove from the heat and dip each leaf into chocolate while holding the stem end.  Lay out on wax paper to cool, then munch while sipping Cabernet!

## Puget Sound Microbrews

Something about being near the water inspires people to drink beer—and to brew beer! The Greater Puget Sound area offers several interesting regional breweries and lots of fun places to slurp up some suds with a tasty meal.

## Breweries/Brewpubs

### Anacortes Brew House

320 Commercial Ave., Anacortes (360) 293-2444. Both ales and lagers are brewed here by talented brewmeister Paul Wasik. The demand for craft-brewed beer became apparent the minute Paul and his partner Linda Spricher opened their doors in 1994. The pub serves a full menu including tasty pizza from a wood-fired oven. Six handles provides a wide range of brews for beer lovers to choose from. Open daily.

### Boundary Bay Brewery

1107 Railroad Ave., Bellingham (360) 647-5593. Edward Bennett is the proprietor and brewer at this brewpub across the street from the Bellingham farmers market. Conceived as much as a restaurant as a brewery, the kitchen uses fresh ingredients from the market to prepare dishes that pair with Pale Ale, Bitter, Amber Ale, Scotch Ale and Porter. Open daily.

### Fish Brewing Company

515 Jefferson St. SE, Olympia (360) 943-3650. Crayne and Mary Horton began this operation in 1993 and have gained a wide following for their delightful Fish Tale Ales. From a smoky-peat flavored Scotch Ale to more traditional pale and amber styles, they offer quality craft beers to the discriminating Northwest market. The Fishbowl Pub in Olympia has become a mecca for local beer aficionados.

### Orchard Street Brewery

709 W. Orchard Dr., Bellingham (360) 647-1614. Christian Krogstad crafts the beers and chef Chad Clarke presides over the wood-fired oven to provide the delightful and creative food offerings at this charming taproom. Whether you slurp the Orchard Street Amber, Porter, Rye Ale or hoppy Pale Ale, you'll enjoy the quality beer and the ambiance. Just south of Bellisfair Mall off Guide Meridian.

### Skagit River Brewing Company

404 S. Third St., Mount Vernon (360) 336-2884. Already regionally famous for their Dutch Gold Lager ("smooth, malty taste and mild hop flavor") and the Steelie-Brown Ale ("medium bodied nut brown ale with hints of oats and roasted barley") Charlie Sullivan and Scott Price are dedicated to quality rather than quantity. The facility opened in 1994 and is already brewing at capacity to keep up with demand.

### Whidbey Island Brewing Co.

630 2nd St., Langley (360) 221-8373. Jim Grimes opened his brewery and taproom in the old Langley Lumber Company building just up the hill from Langley's main street. A wide selection of ales is brewed for distribution to local and regional accounts including Langley Light, Whidbey Amber, Bayview Blackberry Ale, Island Stout and a refreshing root beer. Taproom opens at noon every day.

## Olympic Peninsula

### Fort Worden State Park

**Port Townsend** - Let the kids run wild on the sand dunes and play in the old gun emplacements while mom and dad surf-fish or bask in the sun. Clean restrooms, a little grocery store and an aquarium and camping . . .

### Port Townsend Shopping

Dozens of shops are eager to take your money for antiques, trinkets, cards, shirts, wine, everything under the sun. When you're shopped out, grab a sandwich or a snack at one of the delis and restaurants that line Water Street.

### Olympic Game Farm

**Dungeness** - Zebras and Tigers and Bears, oh MY! Check out these and other wild animals at close range and enjoy the performing bears and the kids petting farm.

### Dungeness Spit Wildlife Area

If you enjoy birdwatching and your kids enjoy beachwalking then bring your binoculars and tennis shoes for this fantastic natural seabird habitat. No dogs allowed - they chase the birds.

### Olympic Rain Forest

With more than 140 inches of rain a year, the forest is thick and mossy. A natural wonder not to be missed, this is the only rain forest in the U.S. The Hoh Rain Forest Park is reached by following Highway 101 south from Forks.

### Hurricane Ridge

South of Port Angeles exit is clearly marked from Hwy. 101. This drive up into the Olympic Mountains offers spectacular panoramic views of wild flowers and the Strait of Juan de Fuca in summer and snowy vistas of cross country skiers in the winter. Check your anti-freeze level in either season because the elevation gain can cause boil-overs.

## Puget Sound Highlights

### San Juan Islands

There is so much to do and see in the San Juans that whole books are written about it. Charter a boat to cruise the archipelago or drive on the ferry to San Juan, Lopez or Orcas Islands - either way you can whale watch, bicycle on quiet back roads, shop for local crafts, or even climb a mountain.

### Skagit Valley Tulip Festival

Mt. Vernon - In the springtime, the tulips and daffodils bloom in profusion at the low-lying bulb farms just a few miles off I-5. Take a tour and buy a bouquet!

### Washington Park

Anacortes - This partly developed, partly wilderness peninsula offers picnicking, boat launch, beach and wildlife watching (the four-footed kind!) Drive out past the San Juan ferry terminal.

### Point Defiance Zoo and Aquarium

Tacoma - Drive out Highway 16 to Pearl Street to reach this world-renowned zoological garden and aquarium. Lots of open space for picnicking, access to the water at several spots. New Anthony's Restaurant on the pier.

**Jon Rowley**
**Jon Rowley & Associates**

*I first saw Jon Rowley about a dozen years ago on television helping Julia Child onto a fishing boat to go catch a salmon somewhere in Puget Sound or the Strait of Juan de Fuca. Jon was embarking at that time on his career as a "dating service for Northwest seafood."*

*Since then Jon has helped the seafood industry promote the fine quality fish and shellfish that are available from the West Coast and specifically the Northwest. He has worked with the Oregon Wine Advisory Board to help establish Pinot Noir as a delicious accompaniment to salmon and he established the Pacific Coast Oyster Wine Competition in cooperation with the Washington Wine Commission.*

*Getting the word out that Northwest seafood and Northwest wines are perfect partners has been a passion with Jon and he has truly risen to the occasion. He also enjoys the superb fruits, vegetables and wild foraged mushrooms of Washington and Oregon.*

## ❖ A RECIPE FROM JON ROWLEY ❖

## *Jon Rowley on Salmon*

The annual mid-May to mid-June arrival of fat-bellied king salmon from Alaska's legendary Copper River has become a kind of Northwest religion. When we're talking the world's best eating salmon, look for a preparation that lets the inherent goodness of the fish come through. This recipe is so simple it hardly deserves to be called a recipe, yet it captures the flavor and juicy succulence of the fish perfectly. When purchasing Copper River king salmon steaks, the larger the fish, the better. A one-inch steak from a 25 lb. king is enough for two people; a steak from a 50 lb. king will feed four. The wider the belly flap, the better the eating.

## Seared and Roasted Copper River King Salmon Steak

Copper River king salmon steaks
2  Tbs. very good quality olive oil
   sea salt to taste
   pepper to taste (optional)

Preheat oven to 250° F.

Heat olive oil in black iron skillet (or other oven-proof skillet) until almost smoking. Sear steaks on both sides until burnished.

Season with sea salt and pepper. Place skillet in oven to finish cooking at 250° F. for approximately 15 minutes.

Serve with fresh Washington asparagus, wild morel mushrooms and Oregon Pinot Noir.

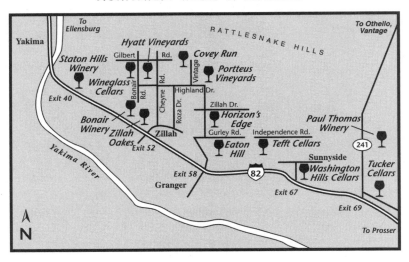

## Yakima Valley Touring – West End

A tour through the Yakima Valley is a wonderful introduction to the origin of Washington State's agricultural bounty. As you travel the main highway, Interstate 82, and as you wander the myriad back roads, you discover orchards, vineyards, hop yards, fields of mint, onions and other row crops. Roll down the car window and take a deep whiff of country air.

Making sure you don't miss a chance to visit **Grant's Ale Brewery** in downtown Yakima, the west end tour begins at **Staton Hills Winery** near Wapato. Striking architecture and a picture-perfect vineyard are a grand introduction to the valley.

The Zillah area wineries have nicknamed their circuit "the Zillah Fruit Loop" which includes referrals to places where you can purchase apples, cherries, pears, peaches and other produce. The wineries are literally too numerous to catch in one day so space out your visit with a nice lunchtime picnic, an afternoon siesta then dinner after your last stop.

From west to east in the Zillah area you'll enjoy visiting: **Zillah Oakes Winery, Bonair Winery, Wineglass Cellars, Hyatt Vineyards, Covey Run Winery, Portteus Winery, Horizon's Edge** and **Eaton Hill Wineries**. Each stop is just a mile or two apart and directional signs point the way in most cases.

Slightly further east, the mid-valley wineries range from some of the valley's oldest wineries to the very newest. Old wine touring hands will be sad to learn that **Stewart Vineyards Winery** is no longer in operation, but across the highway near the tiny town of Outlook is **Tefft Cellars** located on Independence Road. Pam and Joel Tefft also operate the Outlook Inn B & B at the winery site.

In Sunnyside proper, look up **Washington Hills Cellars** and **Tucker Cellars**. Washington Hills is home to their namesake brand and also to the **W. B. Bridgman brand** and **Apex** ultra premium brand. At the east end of town, the Tucker Farms produce market is adjacent to the winery and provides a chance to select some succulent tomatoes, fruits or fresh corn for later enjoyment. South of exit 67, don't miss **Dairy Fair**, a unique cheesemaking facility with dairy product sampling and a deli-restaurant. The **Paul Thomas Winery** production facility currently offers no tours or tasting, but visitors are encouraged to sample their wines at the Zillah Oakes facility (both wineries are owned by Associated Vintners).

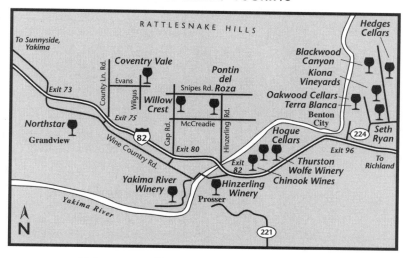

## Yakima Valley Touring – East End

Touring eastward you'll continue to enjoy vistas of vast vineyards, many of them concord grapes used in the production of grape juice. If you happen to be traveling during September or October, roll down your car window for the aroma of Welches!

**Chateau Ste. Michelle's** historic winery in Grandview has been operating continuously since 1937. Today, their Canoe Ridge Estate along the Columbia River has taken over red wine production for the Chateau Ste. Michelle brand. The Grandview winery is now used for a special project called Northstar with California winemaker Jed Steele joining CSM winemaker Gordie Hill in crafting ultra premium reds. No tours or tasting.

Just east in Prosser no fewer than six wineries await your inspection. On the southwest side, **Yakima River Winery** is a short drive out North River Road. A few miles north of I-82 on Hinzerling and Gap Roads, visit **Pontin del Roza winery** and the new **Willow Crest** facility.

Not far from downtown Prosser are Hinzerling Winery, Chinook Wines, Hogue Cellars and Thurston Wolfe Winery. Mike Wallace at **Hinzerling Winery** was an area pioneer and is working on his third decade of operation. Clay Mackey and Kay Simon welcome visitors to **Chinook Wines** tasting room on Wine Country Road, a small but exceedingly friendly operation hosted by two of Washington's most knowledgeable wine/grape scientists. Further east on Wine Country Road is **Hogue Cellars** winery. You can sample Hogue's wines and also try some of the preserved fruits or vegetables from Hogue Ranches. **Thurston Wolfe Winery** is right next door. While you're in town, don't miss the **Chukar Cherry Company Store**.

Travel east on I-82 from Prosser about 14 miles to the Benton City exit where you follow signs to Highway 224 to Richland. **Oakwood Cellars** and the new **Terra Blanca Vintners** await you on Demoss Road, and up the highway, a short drive down Sunset Road leads to four wineries operating on Red Mountain. **Seth Ryan**, **Kiona Vineyards**, **Hedges Cellars** and **Blackwood Canyon** share this unique microclimate, an area well known for the production of intense and flavorful Cabernet, Merlot and other wines.

While you're at Red Mountain be sure to ask someone to point out the different vineyards here that have helped make Washington wine famous. **Klipsun Vineyard** is on the west ridge, **Kiona Vineyard** is just east, **Ciel du Cheval** is east across Sunset Road and **Taptiel Vineyard** is at the end of the road up toward the mountain.

# Blackwood Canyon

Rt. 2, Box 2169H, Sunset Road
Benton City, WA 99320
(509) 588-6249, FAX (509) 588-5195

**Tasting Room Hours:** Daily, 10 AM to 6 PM

**Owner & Winemaker:** Mike Moore
**First Year:** 1983
**Winery Capacity:** 30,000 Gallons

## Winery History

Mike Moore of Blackwood Canyon continues on the road back from the disastrous fire of 1985 that destroyed his winery building and thousands of gallons of wine. At the replacement building, visitors experience unique tasting sessions.

## A visit to Blackwood Canyon Winery

Out Sunset Road past the entrance to Kiona Vineyards, a left turn leads to Blackwood Canyon Winery perched on the edge of the ridge. Winemaker/owner Mike Moore is often on hand to explain his philosophies about winemaking and grape growing while serving mostly older vintages.

## The Wines

From the promising start in the 1980s, Blackwood Canyon wines have yet to achieve the quality promised by those early efforts.

# Bonair Winery

500 S. Bonair Rd.
Zillah, WA 98953
(509) 829-6027,
FAX (509) 829-6410
Email: bonairwine@aol.com
Web: bonairwine.com

**Tasting Room Hours:** Daily, 10 AM to 5 PM

**Manager:** Shirley Puryear
**Winemaker:** Gail Puryear
**First Year:** 1985
**Winery Capacity:** 20,000 Gallons

## Winery History

After a number of years in California, Gail and Shirley Puryear returned to their native Yakima Valley to grow grapes and make wine. The dream that began on the outskirts of Zillah in 1979 is now a full-blown reality with Bonair wines regularly winning awards and the tasting room brimming with interested visitors. A home winemaker for more than a decade, Gail traded in his carboys for stainless steel tanks and French oak barrels in 1985. Expansion of both winery and vineyard have kept pace with production and sales. Celebrating a decade of operation in 1995, the winery offers a great visit to Northwest wine lovers.

## A visit to Bonair Winery

One of the most friendly tasting-room welcomes you'll ever receive comes from Shirley Puryear at Bonair. Her enthusiasm for the wines and winery operation are high, and her interest in every visitor makes everyone feel at home. Enjoy your picnic in the shady gazebo or outside with a view of Mount Adams.

## The Wines

Bonair Winery enjoys a reputation for rich and flavorful Chardonnay and Cabernet Sauvignon with several vineyard-designated bottlings often available. Cabernet is in short supply and is sold mostly at the winery. Barrel-fermented Dry Riesling has become a favorite in recent years complementing the Johannisberg off-dry bottling. Sunset blush wine and Bonnie Bonair red are popular picnic wines with winery visitors.

## Leslie Mackie
### Owner, Macrina Bakery

*"Simplicity . . . creating flavor with wonderful raw ingredients, textures and cooking procedures; not lots of different ingredients."* With these words Leslie Mackie defines her philosophy of baking (and cooking in general).

*Her delightful artisan bakery in Seattle's Belltown, Macrina Bakery & Cafe, is a popular stop for knowing souls who crave the finest breads, tarts and pastries.*

*Leslie opened Macrina after being the head baker at the breakthrough Grand Central Baking Company in Pioneer Square. An expert at the fine art of leavened dough, she has now assembled a dedicated staff to help her meet the demand of dozens of Seattle's finest restaurants, fine-food markets, and the fans who come to her First Avenue location each day for their daily bread. Leslie was featured in the PBS series* Baking with Julia *and in the accompanying cookbook.*

*This pear and blue cheese tart can be served as an appetizer or dessert, and Leslie recommends Kay Simon's rich and fruity Merlot as an accompaniment.*

*Look for Macrina Bakery in the Specialty Shop section of the Seattle Wine Touring portion of this book.*

❖ A RECIPE FROM MACRINA BAKERY ❖

# Savory Poached Pear and Oregon Blue Cheese Tart

*4 servings - Wine Recommendation: Chinook Merlot*

## Crust

| | |
|---|---|
| 12 | oz. pastry flour - all purpose |
| 1/2 | Tbs. salt |
| 3 | oz. cold butter, cut into small pieces |
| 5 | oz. vegetable shortening |
| 1/2 | cup cold water |

Combine flour and salt. Cut in butter with two forks until texture is a coarse crumb. Add the shortening in small pieces, when the mixture begins to look wet or shiny add water all at once. Mix until dough is wet. Scoop into plastic wrap and chill for 2 hours.

## Poached Pears

| | |
|---|---|
| 2 | medium sized ripe Anjou pears |
| 2 | cups medium bodied red wine (preferably the small leftovers at the end of a few evenings of wine!) |
| 1/4 | cup sugar |
| 1/8 | tsp. ground cloves |
| 3 | sprigs fresh thyme |

Peel and core pears. Bring wine, spice and sugar mixture to a boil and cook for 5 minutes. Poach pear halves at a simmer until tender.

| | |
|---|---|
| 2 | oz. Oregon Blue Cheese |
| 1/4 | cup walnuts, coarsely chopped |

## To Assemble

Slice poached pears about 1/4-inch thick. Roll chilled dough out to make an 8-inch circle. Place dough on parchment-lined baking sheet. Lay sliced pears on dough leaving a 1-1/2-inch border. Sprinkle with half of the cheese. Lay another layer of pears. Bring up the edges of the pastry to make a free-form tart. Eggwash exposed pears and top with remaining cheese and walnuts. Chill for 30 minutes in refrigerator. Bake at 350° F. for 20 minutes until golden brown. Best served warm or at room temperature.

## Chinook Wines

Wine Country Road at
Wittkopf Road
P.O. Box 387, Prosser,
WA 99350
(509) 786-2725
Fax (509) 786-2777

**Tasting Room Hours:**
May through December, Saturday and Sunday,
Noon to 5 PM. Tours and tour groups by prior
appointment only.

**Owners/Winemakers:**
Kay Simon and Clay Mackey
**First Year:** 1983
**Winery Capacity:** 7,000 Gallons

**Winery History**

Chinook Wines was born of the union
between an enologist and a viticulturist. The
winemaker, Kay Simon, is one of the most
experienced in the Northwest with over a
dozen successful harvests to her credit while
her equally-talented husband, Clay Mackey,
works with growers and consults on vineyard
management. Kay and Clay were married in
August of 1984 on a date that celebrated the
release of the first Chinook wine. The
operation occupies several renovated farm
buildings with just enough capacity for the
owners to handle all production.

**A visit to Chinook Winery**

This visit is a must for serious wine lovers.
The two owners are not only charming and
friendly but hold a wealth of knowledge about
all aspects of wine, both art and science. The
picnic area under a spreading oak tree invites
the visitor to relax on the lawn after a taste of
Chinook's wines in the tasting room.

Take exit 82 from I-82 and head east on
Wine Country Road. Chinook is on the right.

**The Wines**

Kay Simon and Clay Mackey craft
Chardonnay, Sauvignon Blanc and Semillon in
a dry style that is a wonderful complement to
food. Chinook Merlot, Cabernet Sauvignon
and Cabernet Franc are deliciously fruity and
full with a hint of oak, great food wines, but
are always in short supply.

*Winemaker Kay Simon is often on hand at the cozy Chinook tasting room on Wine Country Road.*

## Coventry Vale Winery

Wilgus & Evans Road
P. O. Box 249
Grandview, WA 98930
(509) 882-4100

**President:** Reed McKinley
**Winemaker:** Tom Sans Souci
**First Year:** 1983
**Winery Capacity:** 1,000,000 Gallons

**Winery History**

Originally known in the Northwest wine
industry as a "custom crush" facility, Coventry
Vale produces wine for many Yakima Valley
and Columbia Valley wineries who do not
have the tank space for their own winemaking
efforts.

Forests of stainless steel tanks and rows of
barrels fill the building located north of
Grandview. No wine is available for tasting
and no regular tours are offered. Appoint-
ments can be made on a limited basis to look
through the facility.

*Clay Mackey at the grill as Travel Editor Stephen Gaddis looks on.*

## Clay Mackey, Kay Simon Chinook Winery

Clay Mackey and Kay Simon, husband and wife, vineyardist and winemaker, master of the grill and mistress of the kitchen. Kay is a superb baker who creates delicious fresh breads, rolls, tarts and other hearthside temptations. Clay produces delicious grilled lamb, vegetables and other delights from his barbecue in the side yard of the Chinook tasting room.

As a lover of fine chevre, Kay loves to cook with the earthy, pungent cheese. This rich and healthful appetizer will make you run out to your favorite cheesemonger and seek out some Rollingstone Chevre of your own to pair with Chinook's crisp and elegant Sauvignon Blanc. The Rollingstone Chevre dairy is in Parma, Idaho just an hour west of Boise.

### ❖ A RECIPE FROM CHINOOK WINES ❖

# Chevre and Sundried Tomato Tart

*8 servings*
*Wine Recommendation: Chinook Sauvignon Blanc*

## Crust

| | |
|---|---|
| 2 | Tbs. + 1 tsp. olive oil |
| 2/3 | cup yellow cornmeal |
| 1/3 | cup all-purpose flour |
| 1 | Tbs. sugar |
| 1/4 | tsp. salt |
| 1/4 | tsp. baking powder |
| 4-5 | sundried tomatoes, drained of oil and diced |
| 1/2 | cup buttermilk |
| 1 | egg |
| 1 | clove of garlic, minced |

Use 1 teaspoon of olive oil to grease a 7 x 11-inch or 9-inch square pyrex pan. Combine remaining 2 tablespoons oil, egg and buttermilk, and beat with a fork in a small bowl. Combine remaining ingredients in a mixing bowl then blend in egg/buttermilk combination quickly. Do not overbeat. Pour crust batter into pyrex pan and bake at 375° F. for 8 to 10 minutes. Remove from oven and spread with:

## Filling - Mix together until well-blended.

| | |
|---|---|
| 2 | oz. nonfat cream cheese |
| 4 | oz. Rollingstone fresh chevre (goatsmilk cheese) |
| 1 | egg |

Spread evenly on baked crust and garnish with:

| | |
|---|---|
| 2-3 | thinly sliced baby zucchini |
| 1 | Tbs. freshly grated Parmesan cheese |
| 2 | tsp. finely chopped herb of choice (Suggest basil or thyme) |

Return to oven for an additional 10 minutes of baking time. Serve slices of tart, warm or chilled with a glass of Chinook Sauvignon Blanc.

## Covey Run Wines

1500 Vintage Rd.
Zillah, WA 98953
(509) 829-6235, FAX (509) 829-6895

**Tasting Room Hours:** Mon. thru Sat.,
10 AM to 5 PM; Sunday, Noon to 5 PM

**Owners:** Associated Vintners
**Winemaker:** David Crippen
**First Year:** 1982
**Winery Capacity:** 90,000 Gallons

### Winery History

The Quail Run Vintners winery began in 1980 as a partnership of fruit growers diversifying into winegrapes. Vineyards were planted, the grapes flourished and the rest would have been history save a minor disruption by California's Quail Ridge who squawked about name similarity and forced the change of Quail Run's label to Covey Run. But the wine behind the label didn't suffer and today winemaker David Crippen crafts a wide range of varietals including some spectacular reserves. In 1997 Covey Run was acquired by Associated Vintners, parent corporation of Columbia Winery. Sharing the resources of a central promotion and sales staff makes sense for a medium sized winery.

### A visit to Covey Run

Visiting the Covey Run Winery outside of Zillah is a treat. The expansive decks and patios overlook the vineyards and provide an excellent opportunity to picnic. Inside the spacious tasting room, large windows look down into the winery.

Find the winery by traveling north out of Zillah on 5th or on Cheyne Road, take a right on Highland Drive and follow to a left on Vintage Road.

### The Wines

Varietals offered by Covey Run include Merlot, Cabernet Sauvignon, Chardonnay, Lemberger, Fume Blanc, Chenin Blanc and others. Riesling dessert wines and the reserve bottlings of Chardonnay have been especially good.

*Kurt Krause and Covey Run winemaker David Crippen at the winery.*

## Eaton Hill Winery

Route 1, Box 1117,
Gurley Road
Granger, WA 98932
(509) 854-2220

**Tasting Room Hours:** Daily, 10 AM to 5 PM
Closed Thursdays

**Owners:** Edwin & JoAnn Stear
**Winemaker:** Gary Rogers
**First Year:** 1988

### Winery History

Scientist Edwin Stear has extensive background and experience in the business of technology and its application to the real world. Currently serving in several capacities at the University of Washington, he finds relaxation in the Yakima Valley by restoring the 90-year-old Rinehold homestead.

A former fruit and vegetable cannery on the homestead was transformed into Eaton Hill Winery in 1988. Gary Rogers and his wife Arlene are your hosts in the tasting room.

### A visit to Eaton Hill Winery

Not far from I-82 exit 58, around Punkin Corner on Gurley Road, is Rinehold Cannery Homestead and Eaton Hill Winery.

### The Wines

A range of varietal wines are produced including Semillon, Chardonnay, Cabernet Sauvignon and others. A fruit wine crafted from Rainier cherries is an unusual treat.

*Hedges Cellars on Red Mountain*

wineries. Since it is mostly a production facility, an appointment is required for a visit. The winery participates, however, in the April barrel tasting weekend and is open during Catch the Crush in October. Call for details.

**The Wines**

Hedges Cellars' Cabernet Merlot is an excellent example of blended red wine in the Columbia Valley style. Barrel-aged for a short time, the wine is approachable on purchase but will gain complexity for one to two years. Red Mountain Reserve is a very limited bottling of the best lots featuring additional barrel-aged character and requiring two to three years additional bottle age to bring out the distinctive flavor and aroma. An unusual blend of Sauvignon Blanc and Chardonnay named "Fume Chardonnay" has gained a following for its round, flavorful style and its ability to pair with a remarkable variety of foods.

# Hedges Cellars

53511 North Sunset Rd.
Benton City, WA 99320
(509) 588-3155
FAX (509) 588-5323
Web:
www.hedgescellars.com

**Tasting Room Hours:** By appointment

**Owner:** Tom & Anne-Marie Hedges,
Mats Hanzon
**Winemaker:** Steve Lessard
**First Year:** 1990
**Winery Capacity:** 175,000 Gallons

**Winery History**

The Hedges Cellars winery continues to build on the recognition gained from their fine Cabernet-Merlot blend that launched the brand in 1991. Early-drinking, fruity, and value-priced, the wine gained immediate attention from wine lovers and media alike. Today, Hedges wine is made in the winery headquarters on Red Mountain next to the Hedges vineyard. The main tasting room is at Hedges Reserve Cellars in Issaquah, convenient for Puget Sound area residents.

**A visit to Hedges Cellars at Red Mountain**

The striking winery building is north on Sunset Road past Seth Ryan and Kiona

# Hinzerling Vineyards

1520 Sheridan
Prosser, WA 99350
(509) 786-2163
FAX (509) 786-2163
Email: hinzwine@quicktel.com

**RAINY DAY FINE TAWNY PORT**

WASHINGTON STATE

**Tasting Room Hours:** Daily, 11 AM to 5 PM

**Owner:** The Wallace Family
**Winemaker:** Mike Wallace
**First Year:** 1976
**Winery Capacity:** 10,000 Gallons

**Winery History**

More than two decades of winemaking and grape growing sets Hinzerling Vineyards apart from almost every other winery in the state. The winery was begun by Mike Wallace, a pioneer in the new era of Washington viticulture in the early 1970s.

A 25-acre vineyard was planted north of Prosser with the purpose of eventual production of fine table wines. The first wine was made in 1976 and Hinzerling Vineyards was begun (the name was taken from Prosser-area pioneers and the road where the vineyard was

*Continued on next page*

planted). The winery changed hands for a short period during 1988 and 1989 but the Wallace family is back in control with Mike once again at the winemaking helm.

### A visit to Hinzerling Vineyards

Visiting the winery presents an opportunity to purchase some of the sought after Hinzerling 'library' Cabernet Sauvignon and other wines from vintages past. Tasting and brief tours of the small winery are offered by family members in the cellar. Write or call the winery for their newsletter detailing upcoming events.

### The Wines

The Hinzerling Winery reputation was made on Cabernet Sauvignon but currently the production also includes several Port-style wines and a variety of Sherries.

# The Hogue Cellars

P.O. Box 31
Lee Rd. at Wine Country Rd.
Prosser, WA 99350
(509) 786-4557
FAX (509) 786-4580
Web: www.hogue-cellars.com

**Tasting Room Hours:**
Daily, 10 AM to 5 PM

**Owner:** Mike Hogue
**Winemaker:** David Forsyth
**First Year:** 1982
**Winery Capacity:** 1,000,000+ Gallons

### Winery History

As a well-established Yakima Valley farming family, the Hogues founded their winery, The Hogue Cellars, in the early 1980s and gained immediate attention with several award-winning wines. The source for many of the grapes that go into The Hogue Cellars wines are the Hogue Ranches – a 1,200 acre farm that has been producing for the Hogue family since the 1950s. Grape acreage planted since the 1970s totals 400 acres of premium varietals. Winemaker Rob Griffin guided Hogue's operation until 1990 when he left to pursue his Barnard Griffin label. Talented David Forsyth is the creative force behind the current releases of The Hogue Cellars wines. A

new winery production building was added in 1990-91 to increase the capacity of the Hogue operation.

### A visit to Hogue Cellars

The current winery and tasting room just northeast of Prosser are a must for wine tourists in the area. An attractive tasting bar and gift shop are handled by experienced and friendly personnel. The Hogue Ranches preserved fruits and vegetables are also available to sample (and buy) in the Hogue Cellars' tasting room.

The Hogues are literally the "first family" of Prosser with patriarch Wayne Hogue holding the office of mayor of this thriving agricultural community. Several times a year the winery hosts special celebrations with music, barbecues, and other entertainment for wine lovers who venture out to Prosser.

### The Wines

Each *Fruit Forward* varietal offering from the Hogue Cellars is cleanly made and features appropriate character in both aroma and flavor. Chardonnay, Fume Blanc, Dry Chenin Blanc, Semillon, and Semillon-Chardonnay are superb food wines with crisp acidity and bright, fresh flavors. Off-dry sipping wines include Gewurztraminer, Chenin Blanc and Johannisberg Riesling. Cabernet-Merlot is the red wine contributor to this price tier and a Late Harvest White Riesling is also offered.

At a higher price, the Hogue Cellars *Barrel Select* wines offer greater complexity and concentration of flavor. Chardonnay, Cabernet Sauvignon and Merlot bring strong varietal notes and toasty-oaky character.

The relatively new *Genesis* brand includes unusual varietal wines and wines made with particular character that the winery finds appealing. Look for Lemberger (with the added Germanic prefix *Blau Franc*), Cabernet Franc, Barrel Fermented Semillon and Syrah. Also in this category are a vineyard designated Chardonnay, and a Merlot and Cabernet Sauvignon.

Hogue Cellars wines are among the best values in Northwest wine and offer consistent quality and varietal character.

# Horizon's Edge Winery

4530 East Zillah Drive
Zillah, WA 98953
(509) 829-6401
Email: yvwine@aol.com

**Tasting Room Hours:** Summer: daily, 11 AM to 5 PM; Spring: Friday thru Monday only; Winter by appointment

**Owners:** Tom Campbell & Hema Shah
**Winemaker:** Tom Campbell
**First Year:** 1984
**Winery Capacity:** 13,000 Gallons

### Winery History

Tom Campbell set his sights on winemaking and never looked back. After finishing his studies at U.C. Davis in 1979, Tom worked for Jekel Vineyards in California before relocating to the Yakima Valley. No fewer than four local wineries benefited from his services between 1981 and 1985 when Tom struck out on his own and bonded Horizon's Edge Winery just east of Zillah.

### A visit to Horizon's Edge

The winery building stands out behind Tom Campbell's house. From the second floor tasting loft in the winery you enjoy samples of Horizon's Edge wines as you admire the namesake view across the top of an apple orchard to Mount Rainier and Mount Adams. The owners invite visitors to stroll through the vineyard or to enjoy a picnic under the grape arbor. Find the winery east of Zillah near the corner of Thacker Rd. and East Zillah Dr.

### The Wines

Tom Campbell's Chardonnay and Cabernet Sauvignon have found many followers. One of the few remaining producers of quality Muscat Canelli, Horizon's Edge offers a dry version and a sweet dessert style. A Cream Sherry and Pinot Noir Port are also made.

*One of the decorative antiques that surround the Hyatt Vineyards picnic area.*

# Hyatt Vineyards

2020 Gilbert Road
Zillah, WA 98953
(509) 829-6333
FAX (509) 829-6433
**Email:** wine @hyattwines.com
**Web:** www.hyattwines.com

**Tasting Room Hours:** Daily, 11 AM to 5 PM, closed during January

**Owners:** Leland & Lynda Hyatt
**Winemaker:** Ray Sandidge
**First Year:** 1987
**Winery Capacity:** 45,000 Gallons

### Winery History

Leland and Lynda Hyatt began their adventure with grape growing in the Yakima Valley in the early 1970s growing concord grapes for the local juice plant. Wine grape growing followed as they planted a vineyard on a site near Zillah that had been pointed out to them by Dr. Walter Clore. The winery was opened in 1987 and today Ray Sandidge handles the winemaking duties.

### A visit to Hyatt Vineyards Winery

The short drive north of Bonair Winery (take either Bonair or Cheyne Road) leads to the Hyatt winery on Gilbert Road. The beautifully manicured picnic area has a panoramic view across the valley to Mount Adams and Mount Rainier.

### The Wines

Hyatt Vineyards' wines have continued the award-winning ways of wines made by other wineries using Hyatt grapes. Look for the superb Hyatt Merlot and late harvest wines of Riesling and Black Muscat.

## Kiona Vineyards Winery

44612 N. Sunset Road
Benton City, WA 99320
(509) 588-6716

**Owners:**
The Williams Family
**Winemaker:** Scott Williams
**Winery Capacity:** 30,000 Gallons
**Tasting Room Hours:** Daily, Noon to 5 PM

### Winery History

John Williams and Jim Holmes let their hobby run wild in the late 1970s and created a Washington wine success story. These two metallurgical engineers from Westinghouse Hanford produced wine in Jim's garage-turned-winery in Richland and then aged and bottled it in the basement of John's home-turned-winery in the Kiona (pronounced Ki o´ nah) hills near Benton City. Kiona's vineyards are located behind the Williams home on the lower slopes of Red Mountain with a wide variety of grapes planted: Chardonnay, Chenin Blanc, White Riesling, Cabernet Sauvignon, Lemberger and Merlot. Before the winery began, these grapes were sold to other wineries and made many award-winning wines. Most of the grapes now go into wines sold under the Kiona label.

Scott Williams, the son of John and Ann, is a tireless general manager for the winery. Hands-on experience has provided him with insights into the realities of winemaking and grape growing. The 1990s have seen some changes in winery ownership with the Williams family becoming sole owner of both winery and vineyard. The nearby Red Mountain vineyard named Ciel du Cheval has also been acquired by the Kiona clan. A new winery building just up the hill from the tasting room offers increased capacity for the future.

### A visit to Kiona Vineyards Winery

To find Kiona, take exit 96 from I-82 and follow the signs for Highway 224 which leads you up to Sunset Road. At Kiona, picnickers enjoy the grassy picnic area as both sun worshippers and the adjacent grape vines soak up heat units in the warm summer sun. Wine lovers appreciate the comprehensive sampling of Kiona wines offered in the tasting room.

**The Wines**

Rich, toasty Kiona Chardonnay is a favorite with many wine tasters, and several red wines offer powerful statements about the superb fruit of Red Mountain. Cabernet Sauvignon from the estate vineyard is a prize specimen of rich, ripe fruit framed by toasty qualities imparted by American and French oak aging. Merlot and other white varietals are equally tasty, but eclipsing nearly all of the Kiona wines are the spectacular late harvest and ice wines crafted from Riesling, Gewurztraminer and Chenin Blanc. These sweet treats stand with pride next to the finest international late harvest offerings.

## Northstar

205 W. 5th
Grandview, WA 98930

**Owners:** Stimson Lane Vineyards & Estates
**Winemaker:** Jed Steele, Gordy Hill
**First Year:** 1994

### Winery History

The smallest and oldest of Stimson Lane's Northwest wine operations, Grandview has the historical significance of being the oldest operating winery in Washington State. The building was bonded as a winery in 1937 and until 1994 produced most of Chateau Ste. Michelle's red wines. The new state-of-the-art red wine facility at Canoe Ridge near the Columbia Crest winery now handles this duty.

Well-known California winemaker Jed Steele is now involved in a collaborative effort which utilizes this historic facility as well as the talents of longtime Stimson Lane winemaker Gordy Hill. Northstar is the brand name for the initial release of Merlot.

### A visit to Northstar

The winery is no longer open to the public and the Northstar wine is extremely limited. The Northstar Merlot is offered at $50 per bottle in selected markets.

*Chef Andy Juhl teaching a class on salmon on the pier at Elliott's.*

## Andy Juhl
## Elliott's Oyster House

*For several years the Paul Thomas Winery and Elliott's Oyster House has had a special tasting with winemaker Mark Cave, Elliott's Manager Kevin Shoemaker, Chef Andy Juhl and other employees and wine fans to select the blend for that vintage of Elliott's Oyster Wine produced by Paul Thomas Winery. Simply selecting the best blend to accompany oysters on the half shell is the duty at hand. Various blends of Sauvignon Blanc, Gewurztraminer, Riesling and other varietals have been selected depending on the vintage.*

*Since you can enjoy oysters on the half shell with Elliott's Oyster Wine at the restaurant, Chef Juhl and Consolidated Restaurants Sally McArthur invite you to enjoy this Copper River salmon recipe with your favorite Northwest Pinot Noir in the spring.*

### ❖ A RECIPE FROM ELLIOTT'S OYSTER HOUSE ❖

## Oysters on the Half Shell

*Wine Recommendation: Elliott's Oyster Wine (at the restaurant on Pier 56, of course!*

## Copper River Salmon with
## Cherry and Black Pepper Pinot Noir Glaze

*Serves 4. Wine Recommendation: Northwest Pinot Noir*

### Pinot Noir Glaze

- 1/2 cup dried Montmorency (sour) cherries
- 1-1/2 cups Pinot Noir
- 1 tsp. conrstarch, dissolved in 2 Tbs. of water
- 1/4 tsp. Glace de Viande or beef bouillon base
- 1/4 tsp. kosher or sea salt
- 1/4 tsp. fresh ground black pepper
- 1 Tbs. softened butter

Place dried cherries and the wine in a small saucepan. Bring to a boil, turn off the heat, and allow cherries to infuse in the wine for one hour. Strain and reserve half of the cherries. Place the juice in small saucepan and whisk in dissolved cornstarch. Add Glace de Viande, salt and pepper, and bring to a boil, whisking constantly until sauce thickens. Remove from heat and whisk in butter. Stir in reserved cherries. Hold warm.

### To cook and glaze salmon

- 4 6-8 oz. filets of fresh Copper River King Salmon
- 4 tsp. pure olive oil
- 1 tsp. kosher or sea salt mixed with
  1/4 tsp. fresh ground black pepper

Coat each filet with 1 teaspoon olive oil and season with salt and pepper. Place on seasoned grill on the barbecue or broil in the oven for approximately 4 minutes per side. Arrange filets on warm dinner plates and diagonally nap each with 1/4 cup of sauce. Enjoy!

# Oakwood Cellars

40504 N. Demoss Road
Benton City, WA 99320
(509) 588-5332
**Email:** oakcellars@aol.com

**Tasting Room Hours:**
Weekends, 12 to 6 PM

**Owners:** Bob and Evelyn
Skelton
**Winemaker:** Bob Skelton
**First Year:** 1986
**Winery Capacity:** 6,000 Gallons

### Winery History

Bob and Evelyn Skelton pursue the French family-style winery tradition. The two winery owners visit Europe every few years to compare winemaking techniques at wineries in France and Germany. Insights gained in Chablis shed some new light on Chardonnay production while discussions with German producers of Lemberger offered comparisons of red wine style.

### A visit to Oakwood Cellars

The two owners of Oakwood Cellars are your hosts in their cozy tasting room. Exit 96 from I-82 leads you onto Highway 224 where a left turn onto Demoss Road leads to Oakwood Cellars.

### The Wines

Bob Skelton's winemaking efforts are consistent and improving with each vintage. Chardonnay, Semillon, Riesling and Muscat are enjoyable white wines, while Cabernet Sauvignon, Merlot and Lemberger tempt red wine aficionados.

# Paul Thomas Winery

2310 Holmason Rd.
Sunnyside, WA 98944
(509) 837-5605
FAX (509) 837-5612
**Email:**
ptwinery@bentonrea.com

**Owners:** Associated Vintners, Inc.
**Winemaker:** Mark Cave
**First Year:** 1979
**Winery Capacity:** 500,000+ Gallons

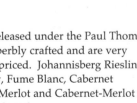

### Winery History

This production facility opened in 1995 with the purpose of increasing the production of the popular Paul Thomas line of varietal and fruit wines made by Mark Cave. Associated Vintners built the winery on the site of the original Phil Church Vineyard.

### A visit to Paul Thomas Winery

It is easier to visit the Zillah Oakes/Paul Thomas tasting room off exit 52 in Zillah (open daily, 10 AM to 5 PM) than to get an appointment to look through the huge winery on the outskirts of Sunnyside. There are no visitor facilities at present and a tasting room is not planned for the immediate future.

But Mark Cave is such a darned nice guy! (You can meet him at Enological festivals and winemaker dinners throughout the Northwest to enjoy his superb wines and his dry sense of humor.)

### The Wines

Wines released under the Paul Thomas label are superbly crafted and are very attractively priced. Johannisberg Riesling, Chardonnay, Fume Blanc, Cabernet Sauvignon, Merlot and Cabernet-Merlot are widely distributed.

# Pontin del Roza

35502 N. Hinzerling Rd.
Prosser, WA 99350
(509) 786-4449

**Tasting Room Hours:** Daily,
10 AM to 5 PM

**Owner:** Pontin Family
**Winemaker:** Scott Pontin
**First Year:** 1984
**Winery Capacity:** 15,000 Gallons

### Winery History

Nesto Pontin (pronounced pon teen´) has farmed along the Roza Canal for over 30 years and his father before him arrived in the Yakima Valley in the 1920s. Nesto's son Scott began the family winery with other family members helping out.

### A visit to Pontin del Roza

The winery is located north of Prosser on Hinzerling Road just a short 10 minute drive from I-82 (take exit 80, Gap Road). A large tree shades an inviting, grassy picnic area.

### The Wines

Cabernet Sauvignon, Chardonnay and other traditional Washington varietals are available. Pinot Gris is also made.

# Portteus Winery

5201 Highland Drive
Zillah, WA 98953
(509) 829-6970
FAX (509) 829-5683
**Email:** port4you@aol.com

**Tasting Room Hours:**
Daily, Noon to 5 PM,
Feb.15 to Dec. 1

**Owner:** Paul Portteus III & Jr.
**Winemaker:** Paul Portteus III
**First Year:** 1987
**Winery Capacity:** 10,000 Gallons

### Winery History

Paul Portteus, III was given a birthday present on his 21st birthday that would change his life. A box of 21 different wines from around the world began his appreciation of fine wine. Purchase of vineyard land near Zillah in 1980 was motivated by this evolving interest. Today, over a decade of grape-growing has Paul convinced that the land he farms is the finest vineyard land in the state. Some of his vineyard's harvest is sold, but a wide array of Portteus wines are produced from estate grapes.

### A visit to Portteus Winery

At the east end of Highland Drive, an orchard-lined driveway heads north toward the Rattlesnake Mountains and leads to the Portteus vineyards and winery. The tasting bar is in the winery building affording a glimpse at the tools of the winemaking trade. Paul and his wife Marilyn host the tasting room.

### The Wines

Portteus wines are hearty in style and richly structured for the long haul. Enjoy the powerful Cabernet, spicy Zinfandel (the first in Washington), ripe and fruity Merlot or toasty Chardonnay.

# R.L. Wine Co.

Office: 3051 42nd Ave. W.
Seattle, WA 98199
(206) 283-7688
FAX (206) 283-7684

**Owner:** Randy Leitman
**Winemaker:** Consultant
**First Year:** 1994

### Winery History

Randy Leitman produces his "negociant" wine under the randall harris label and sells it to wine retailers and restaurants in the Northwest and in California. His Merlot-Cabernet and Chardonnay are clean, varietally-true examples and are sought out by many wine lovers for their value. Current vintages have been produced at Washington Hills Cellars in Sunnyside. There is no tasting room to sample the wines, but Randy sometimes enters them in the Enological Society wine festival held each summer in Seattle where you can seek him out and taste the current releases.

# Seth Ryan Winery

Mail:
681 South 40th
West Richland, WA
99352
Winery: Sunset Road
Benton City, WA 99320
(509)588-6780

**Tasting Room Hours:** Weekends in summer, 11 AM to 6 PM; winter, Noon to 5 PM

**Owners/Winemakers:** Brodzinski and Olsen Families
**First Year:** 1986
**Winery Capacity:** 40,000 Gallons

### Winery History

The proximity to the wine country is luring more and more Richland scientists into the winemaking avocation. Ron and Jo Brodzinski along with Khris Olsen and his father Robert are the owners of the small winery operation that began in the Brodzinski family garage but now occupies a new winery building on Sunset Road near Red Mountain.

### A visit to Seth Ryan winery

The Sunset Road winery facility brought Seth Ryan wines to the public. Plans for the site include additional visitor amenities.

### The Wines

The winery goal at Seth Ryan is to consistently make quality wines specializing in German-style Gewurztraminer and Riesling, "unique" Chardonnay, Cabernet Sauvignon, Cabernet Franc and Merlot. Chardonnay is barrel fermented to produce a "gorgeous floral nose and superb balance."

# Staton Hills Winery

71 Gangl Road
Wapato, WA 98951
(509) 877-2112
**Email:** shwine@ibm.net

**Tasting Room Hours:**
Daily, 11 AM to 5:30 PM;
winter: Noon - 5 PM

**Owners:** Investor Group
**Winemaker:** Jamie Meves
**First Year:** 1984
**Winery Capacity:** 200,000 Gallons

*Staton Hills Winery near Wapato, Washington.*

### Winery History

When David and Susanne Staton moved to the Yakima Valley in 1976 there were just the beginnings of a Yakima Valley wine industry. They planted test blocks of vinifera grapes near their orchards and started laying out plans for a first class winery to make first class wines.

The dream became a reality in 1985 with the construction of a striking cedar and glass building just off I-82 east of Yakima. The 4,000 square foot visitor facility features a huge native-rock fireplace set across the room from the long tasting bar. Two story windows provide a spectacular view of the Yakima Valley with Mount Adams in the distance. The winery is now owned by investors other than the Statons, and this group is overseeing progress in both winemaking and sales.

### A visit to Staton Hills Winery

The close proximity of Staton Hills to Yakima and particularly to I-82 (exit 40) insures that almost every wine-loving tourist will not get lost finding the place. The winery has provided a first-class facility and the tasting room staff is friendly and informative. A nice selection of wine-related gifts is a plus.

### The Wines

Staton Hills' current production focuses on red wine. Cabernet Sauvignon and Merlot account for 85% of the production and are joined by small quantities of Pinot Noir, Chardonnay and Fume Blanc. The blends of the flagship red wines are tuned to the character of the northern Yakima Valley vineyard sites. Staton Hills Port is available at the winery only.

*Joel Tefft of Tefft Cellars.*

## Tefft Cellars

1320 Independence Rd.
Outlook, WA 98938
(509) 837-7651
FAX (509) 839-7337
**Email:**
tcwinery@aol.com

**Tasting Room Hours:** Friday through Sunday, Noon - 5 PM
Closed December 1 through April 1.

**Owners:** Joel & Pam Tefft
**Winemaker:** Joel Tefft
**First Year:** 1990
**Winery Capacity:** 1,000 Gallons

**Winery History**

Joel and Pam Tefft are in love with Yakima Valley winemaking. Leaving more lucrative fields to pursue the dream of owning their own winery, Joel gained experience as cellarmaster for Hyatt Vineyards and made wine at Stewart Vineyards while operating his own venture simultaneously.

**A visit to Tefft Cellars**

On your way from the Zillah area to Sunnyside, you'll find Tefft Cellars on Independence Road in the community of Outlook. The Tefft vineyard is neatly laid out in front of the winery and home of Joel and Pam Tefft who are your enthusiastic hosts on weekend afternoons.

By the way, Pam and Joel also operate the Outlook Inn Bed & Breakfast at the winery and are well known for hosting special dinners and other fun wine country events.

**The Wines**

Serious wine lovers are sometimes taken aback at the unusual wines offered by Tefft Cellars. Late harvest Chardonnay, Cabernet Champagne and Sweet Nebbiolo are not commonly found. These wines and other more traditional bottlings are, however, well made and have attracted a loyal following.

## Terra Blanca

34715 N. DeMoss Rd.
Benton City, WA 99320
(509) 588-6082
FAX (509) 588-2634
**Email:**
kpilgrim@terrablanca.com
**Web:**
www.terrablanca.com

**Tasting Room Hours:** Daily, Monday thru Friday, Noon to 6 PM; weekends, 11 to 6.

**Owner/Winermaker:** Keith Pilgrim
**First Year:** 1993
**Winery Capacity:** 160,000 gallons

**Winery History**

Keith Pilgrim was trained as a geologist at U.C. Davis and, since he enjoyed drinking wine, became interested in the winemaking program. Working as a geologist for several years, Pilgrim gradually discovered that his true love was wine and he began a search throughout the west for a place to build his winery. The search ended at Red Mountain at the east end of the Yakima Valley in 1992 and he since has planted vines and created underground storage caves for Terra Blanca.

**A visit to Terra Blanca**

Take exit 96 from I-82 and follow the signs for Highway 224. Turn left on DeMoss Road and proceed ahead to the winery which is on your right. Currently, wine tasting is offered in the Pilgrim home adjacent to the winery. Keith will take visitors on tours as time and schedule permit.

**The Wines:**

A wide selection of varietal wines and blends have been released. Cabernet Sauvignon, Merlot and Chardonnay are accompanied by a white blend, a red blend and several late harvest wines. Not tasted.

*Becky Yeaman and Wade Wolfe*

# Thurston Wolfe Winery

3800 Lee Road, Suite C
Prosser, WA 99350
(509) 786-3313

**Tasting Room Hours:** April thru November, Friday thru Sunday: 11 AM to 5 PM

**Owners:** Wade Wolfe & Becky Yeaman
**Winemaker:** Wade Wolfe
**First Year:** 1987
**Winery Capacity:** 1,600 Gallons

## Winery History

Wade Wolfe is no stranger to the Washington wine industry. His two-decades as vineyard manager and consultant have been well spent learning the finer points of grape growing and winemaking. Now general manager at the Hogue Cellars, Wade and his wife Becky continue their own personal label with the hallmark bottlings of personal varietal favorites.

## A visit to Thurston Wolfe

The Thurston Wolfe winery and tasting room relocated to Prosser in the fall of 1995. The new tasting room is 100 yards east of the Hogue Cellars on Lee Road. Your tasting room hosts are often the winery owners who are both charming and informative.

## The Wines

The Thurston Wolfe tradition of crafting unique dessert wines and selected table wines continues. Two styles of Port are offered, and Lemberger and Pinot Gris are recent bottlings.

# Tucker Cellars

70 Ray Road
(on Highway 12)
Sunnyside, WA 98944
(509) 837-8701
**Email:**
wineman@televar.com
**Web:** www.business-link/tucker/

**Tasting Room Hours:** Daily, 9 AM - 4:30 PM

**Owners:** Dean & Rose Tucker
**Manager/Winemaker:** Randy Tucker
**First Year:** 1981
**Winery Capacity:** 30,000 Gallons

## Winery History

The history of Tucker Cellars goes back almost 50 years when some of the first vinifera (winegrape) plantings in the Yakima Valley were made by William Bridgman. Dean Tucker's father had brought his family out from Nebraska during the depression and was exposed through Bridgman to vinifera grapes and winemaking. This early education planted a seed in the Tucker family that would bear fruit in the early 1980s when Tucker Cellars winery became a reality. Already well-known for their fresh fruit and produce market on Highway 12 east of Sunnyside, the Tuckers expanded into the wine business making award-winning Riesling and Chenin Blanc wines from the 1981 crush.

## A visit to Tucker Cellars

Don't get the idea that the Tuckers are going out of the fruit and produce business! Carrots, asparagus, fresh corn and other crops are right there for sale—fresh and in-season—next to the winery tasting room. Take exit 69 or 73 to Highway 12. During the Yakima Valley Barrel Tasting weekend they have quite a hootenanny at the winery.

## The Wines

Tucker Cellars produces some of the Valley's most consistent sipping varietals including a refreshing Johannisberg Riesling and a Chenin Blanc with a touch of sweetness. Red varietals and reserve Chardonnay are available at the winery only.

# Washington Hills Cellars

111 East Lincoln Ave.
Sunnyside , WA 98944
(509) 839-9463
FAX (509) 839-6155
**Email:** wahills@quicktel.com
**Web:**
www.washingtonhills.com

**Tasting Room Hours:** Daily, 10 AM - 5:30 PM

**Owners:** Harry Alhadeff, Pres.
**Winemaker:** Brian Carter
**First Year:** 1990
**Winery Capacity:** 200,000 Gallons

*Partners Brian Carter and Harry Alhadeff of Washington Hills Cellars/Apex.*

## Winery History

The principals involved in Washington Hills Cellars are two of Washington's most well-known wine men. Brian Carter has consistently demonstrated the ability to make the finest wine possible from Northwest grapes and his partner, Harry Alhadeff, has a wide reputation as an innovative and competitive wine marketer. First utilizing custom crush facilities to create their initial bottlings, Washington Hills acquired the Sunnyside facility a few years later. Three lines of varietals satisfy the premium and super-premium market tiers and both labels have been consistent winners of medals in local and national wine judgings.

## A visit to Washington Hills Cellars

The old Carnation Dairy plant has never looked better with a bright tasting room and gift shop and a courtyard complete with umbrella'd picnic tables for an alfresco snack. The tasting room employees are both friendly and well-informed about the wines.

## The Wines

The Apex brand of ultra-premium varietals includes a tempting Chardonnay along with Cabernet Sauvignon, Merlot, Late Harvest Riesling, Pinot Noir, Barrel Fermented Gewurztraminer and a white blend named Montage. Washington Hills wines include a wide selection of varietal offerings and the W. B. Bridgman wines – which include the winery's unusual varietals of Cabernet Franc, Lemberger and Syrah – are nearly always award winners.

# Willow Crest Winery

13570 Snipes Road
Prosser, WA 99350
(509) 786-7999

**Tasting Room Hours:**
Weekends, 10 AM to 5 PM,
President's Weekend
through Thanksgiving

**Owners/Winemakers:** David & Kathy Minick
First Year: 1997

Among the Yakima Valley's newest wineries, Willow Crest is the project of a young family who have been growing grapes for others for over a decade and wanted to see the end product vinted by their own hands. David and Kathy Minick are self-taught winemakers who are producing small amounts of Pinot Gris, Gewurztraminer, Cabernet-Merlot and late harvest styles.

The small picnic area in the vineyard has a great view and is a great place to enjoy an alfresco snack with a glass of wine.

# Wineglass Cellars

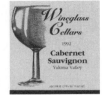

260 N. Bonair Rd.
Zillah, WA 98953
(509) 829-3011
FAX (509) 829-6666
**Email:** davidlowe@ibm.net

**Tasting Room Hours:**
Friday through Monday: 10:30 AM to 5 PM

**Owners:**
   David and Linda Lowe
**Winemaker:** David Lowe
**First Year:** 1994
**Winery Capacity:** 6,000 Gallons

**Winery History**

David Lowe enjoys the pleasures of wine when not at his regular job in the computer industry and, with his wife Linda, decided to open Wineglass Cellars at their home near Zillah. Their cozy winery building is on Bonair Road beckoning weekend wine country visitors to stop by and sample the latest releases.

**A visit to Wineglass Cellars**

The Lowes have jumped into the winery game with both feet and are very enthusiastic when hosting visitors. Fastidious winemaking has resulted in very high quality wines that the owners are proud to pour and discuss with visitors. A $1.00 fee is charged to sample reserve wines. Follow Bonair Road north from Bonair Winery or other points along the cross-roads.

**The Wines**

Ripe, barrel-fermented Chardonnay has been popular with wine lovers offering notes of tropical fruit and butterscotch. Superb Merlots and Cabernet Sauvignons have proven most successful with many awards and compliments from the Northwest wine press. A winery to watch in the future.

# Yakima River Winery

1657 North River Rd.
Prosser, WA 99350
(509) 786-2805
FAX (509) 786-3203
**Email:** yakimawine
@quicktel.com

**Tasting Room Hours:** Daily, 10 AM - 5 PM
Winter hours: please call ahead

**Owners:** John & Louise Rauner
**Winemaker:** John Rauner
**First Year:** 1978
**Winery Capacity:** 78,000 Gallons

**Winery History**

John and Louise Rauner came out to Washington in the mid-1970s with winemaking in mind. It didn't take long for John to catch on to the ins and outs of enology and he bonded Yakima River Winery in 1978. Throughout the years, John Rauner has produced many styles of Northwest wine ranging from his first crisp-and-clean white wines to hearty Cabernet and Merlot and, more recently, to other Bordeaux varieties and Port.

**A visit to Yakima River Winery**

Find Yakima River Winery by heading west from Wine Country Road in Prosser (the turn is just west of the Yakima River bridge) on North River Road. A couple of sharp turns along the way are well marked. John and Louise Rauner are your hosts for enjoyable tastings of the winery's selections. John really puts his all into the special events held at the winery. During the April barrel tasting tour and on Thanksgiving weekend he offers special vertical tastings of Cabernet and Merlot, respectively.

**The Wines**

Yakima River currently produces Cabernet Sauvignon, Cabernet Franc and Merlot as well as Rendezvous, which is 100% Lemberger. Fume Blanc, Pinot Gris and Riesling are offered, and several late harvest wines are joined by "John's Port."

*Author Chuck Hill with Wil Masset of Birchfield Manor*

### ❖ A RECIPE FROM BIRCHFIELD MANOR ❖

## Birchfield Manor's Eastern Washington Roast Rack of Lamb

Serves 2

*Wine Recommendation:*
Wineglass Cellars Reserve Merlot

### Wil Masset
### Birchfield Manor Restaurant
### Birchfield Manor B & B

*A Yakima Valley institution for well over a decade, Birchfield Manor offers French country dining in a converted house just east of town. European-trained Wil Masset and his wife Sandy welcome each guest to two evening seatings in the tiny entryway of the restaurant. This hospitality continues throughout the meal as the well-trained waitstaff informs each diner of the menu choices and the specialties of the night. Elegance and decorum prevail.*

*Maintaining the high standards that make Birchfield Manor a perennial favorite with wine country visitors is a passion with the owners. The wine selections are splendid and are offered at very reasonable prices. A number of imported wines give the adventurous dining group a chance to compare local favorites with some of Europe's fine bottlings.*

*Several B & B rooms are just upstairs from the restaurant and have use of the swimming pool that shimmers enticingly in the restaurant garden.*

rack of lamb, frenched
salt and freshly ground black pepper

1   tbs. apple concentrate (thawed frozen apple juice concentrate)
1   tbs. brown sugar
2   tbs. soy sauce
2   tbs. dijon-style mustard
1   tbs. olive oil
1   tsp. minced garlic

Brown lamb rack in skillet over high heat. Place in roasting pan and baste with sauce.

Roast in 400° F. oven until internal temperature of lamb is 130° F. for rare.

Let rest 10 minutes in a warm place and baste again. Slice rack between bones and enjoy!

## Zillah Oakes Winery

1001 Vintage Valley
Parkway
Zillah, WA 98953
(509) 829-6990
FAX (509) 829-6895

**Tasting Room Hours:** Daily, 10 AM - 5 PM

**Owner:** Associated Vintners
**Winemaker:** David Crippen

**Winery History**

"Shortly after the turn of the century, when both railroads and irrigation systems were first being established in the Yakima Valley, Mr. Walter Granger became entranced by the beauty of the daughter of the local railroad manager, a Mr. Oakes. Mr. Granger asked Mr. Oakes if he could name the township he was surveying at the time after his daughter, seventeen-year-old Zillah. Mr. Oakes gave his permission, and the town of Zillah was born." With the coming of Zillah Oakes (the winery),

Miss Zillah has now been honored with her own enological namesake! The winery itself was originally spun off as another brand and outlet for Covey Run winery. The location right at the freeway exit has obvious marketing value and the new owners (Associated Vintners bought this brand / winery in 1997) are using it to the fullest.

**A visit to Zillah Oakes**

The freeway-side location of the Zillah Oakes facility is a natural draw for tourists not keen on venturing into the foothills. The tasting room and gift shop make for a pleasant visit where you can taste wines from several Asociated Vintners-owned properties.

**The Wines**

Many of Zillah Oakes wines are made with beginning consumers in mind - slightly off-dry and very easy to drink. Some varietals are offered under this label that are not produced at any other winery including Aligote. The varietal mix may change with the new ownership.

# YAKIMA VALLEY ACCOMMODATIONS

### Yakima Rio Mirada Best Western

1603 Terrace Heights Dr. 98901 (509) 457-4444
- Every room has a view of the river with balcony, queen beds, TV. Spa and heated pool. Exit 33 off I-82.

### Cavanaugh's at Yakima Center

607 East Yakima Ave., Yakima, 98901
1-800-THE INNS Cavanaugh's quality accommodations are well known throughout Eastern Washington. Nicely appointed rooms, two outdoor pools.

### Sunnyside Inn B & B

800 East Edison, Sunnyside (509) 839-5557 All private baths, jacuzzi tubs, phones, TV. A great find in a cozy, older home!

### Apple Valley Motel

Grandview - Highway 12, (509) 882-3003
Queen beds, swimming pool, cable TV. Some kitchens. Clean and comfortable. Bargain rates.

### Best Western Prosser Inn

225 Merlot Drive (Exit 80), (509) 786-7977, (800) 688-2192 Just off the freeway and offering all the amenities a wine lover could want in a convenient, wine country motel. Pool, spa, free continental breakfast.

### Wine Country Inn B & B

Prosser, 104 - 6th St., (509) 786-2855 An older home remodelled into a B & B with a beautiful riverside setting. Gourmet country breakfast.

### The Barn

490 Wine Country Road, Prosser, (509) 786-2121 This combination motel, RV park and restaurant is an institution in Prosser. A little more country and western than classical wine country.

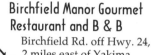

## Birchfield Manor Gourmet Restaurant and B & B

Birchfield Rd. off Hwy. 24, 2 miles east of Yakima (509) 452-1960 Wil & Sandy Massett operate this elegant dinner house featuring multi-course dinners in a pleasant country farmhouse east of town. Extensive wine list of local and international bottlings. Reservations required. Weekends only. Their B & B is right upstairs! (See recipe on page 80.)

## Gasparetti's

1013 North 1st, Yakima (509) 248-0628 Fine Northern Italian cuisine in a restaurant that can handle both families with kids and fancy food critics from the big city. Delicious specialties.

## The Greystone Restaurant

5 N. Front St., Yakima (509) 248-9801 One of Yakima's finest restaurants with delicious specialties (duck and lamb are superb) and a broad selection of favorites. Wine list is extensive and reasonable! This is where the older locals come for cocktails while the younger locals are across the street at Grant's having a brewski.

## The Brewery Pub

25 N. Front, Yakima (509) 575-2922 Visit the home of Grant's Ale and have a pint and a pasty! Enjoy fresh cask-conditioned ales. Sample the beers and play some darts . . . steel points, the real ones.

## Deli de Pasta

7 N. Front St., Yakima (509) 453-0571 Tasty Italian specialties are made on the premises. Great desserts and a nice selection of local wines. Dine in or carry out for picnics.

## El Ranchito Restaurant, Gift Shop and Tortilla Factory

1319-1st Ave., Zillah (509) 829-5880 Even with continuous publicity El Ranchito remains humble and homey. The food is authentic Mexican, the gifts are authentic, everything is aimed at the local Latino population. An experience that is more than a meal! No beer or wine is served in the fast-food style restaurant.

## The Squeeze Inn

611 1st Ave., Zillah, (509) 829-6226, A favorite with locals for steaks, seafood and prime rib. Wine, beer and cocktails are available for your afternoon or evening refreshment.

## Taqueria La Fogata

1300 Yakima Valley Highway, Sunnyside (509) 839-9019 Enjoy Mexican food in its native style. All the regulars plus the specialties you won't find at a local taco stand.

## Dykstra House

114 Birch Ave., Grandview (509) 882-2082 A restored home in Grandview's quiet residential area is the setting for tasty lunches (M-F) and dinners (Fri., Sat.) featuring fresh local ingredients and Yakima Valley wines.

## The Blue Goose

306-7th St., Prosser (509) 786-1774 A wine-knowledgeable staff, ample portions and a varied menu keep locals and visitors coming back to The Blue Goose. Outside patio. "The largest selection of local wines in the valley."

# YAKIMA VALLEY ACTIVITIES

## Picnicking and Camping

Your best bet may be the campground along the Yakima River on Highway 821 between Yakima and Ellensburg (camping), the Riverfront Park in Prosser and the Prosser city park (picnicking). In Yakima, the State Park and KOA are just across the river from town.

## A note about picnicking

Most area wineries offer picnic tables and encourage visitors to enjoy their lunch or snacks on their grounds. Staton Hills, Covey Run and Kiona Vineyards are among the best. Kay and Clay at Chinook offer a shady picnic area under the oak tree out back.

## Yakama Nation Indian Cultural Center

Highway 97 - Toppenish - Devoted to the history of the Yakima Indian Nation, the Indian Cultural Center features extensive exhibits illustrating the history of the area and the culture of the native inhabitants.

## Donald Fruit & Mercantile

Exit 44 from I-82 at Donald, (509) 877-3115 This farmer-owned general store and fruit market offers unique gifts, fresh produce, delicious fresh fruit sundaes in season.

## The Picket Fence Antiques & Sweet Shoppe

Yakima Valley Highway between Cheyne Road and Roza in Zillah. Enjoy traditional sweets and unique country gifts.

## Sunnyside Museum

704 S. 4th - A nice collection of pioneer artifacts documenting the settlement of the Yakima Valley. (Park nearby at W. Edison St.)

## Dairy Fair

400 Alexander Rd., Sunnyside  Darigold Dairy's newest cheese plant with self-guided tours, cheese tasting, gift shop, deli and ice cream.

## Benton County Historical Museum, Prosser City Park

Prosser  7th St. at Paterson Drive - Museum, shady play area, picnic tables.

## Chukar Cherry Store

Prosser - 320 Wine Country Rd. - Open daily - (509) 786-2055  Gourmet dried cherries and berries from local harvests, some coated with chocolate, some sweetened . . . all delicious! This Yakima Valley success story has blossomed into a worldwide endeavor celebrating the joys of fruit. The tasting room offers not wine but samples of the various dried fruits, as well as cookbooks, souvenirs, jams, whatta great place!

## Prosser Farmers' Market

Every Saturday, June through October, 8 AM to 1 PM at the Prosser City Park, 7th & Sommers. Fresh fruits and vegetables, craft items, baked goods.

# NORTHWEST MICROBREWS - YAKIMA

## Grant's Ale (Yakima Brewing Co.)

32 North Front St., Yakima  (509) 575-1900 From the first release of Grant's Scottish Ale in the early 1980s, Grant's has continued to be a leader in Northwest microbrewing. The original brewery was in cramped quarters in a portion of the historic Yakima Opera House. The building's recent use as a moving and storage warehouse proved beneficial to the fledgling Grant's since the large fur vault was temperature and humidity controlled. The first fermentation tanks were placed in this narrow space and the brew kettle and grain mill were in improvised spaces in the attic and adjacent offices. The business has grown exponentially since those days and the once tiny taproom now occupies the former railroad depot across the street. Stop in daily for fresh ales, terrific pub food and a game of darts. A larger commercial production facility has been built off-site to accommodate the much-larger volumes now produced.

**Bert Grant
Founder: Grant's Ales**

*Arguably the founder of the craft beer movement in Washington State, Bert Grant rolled out his first barrels of Grant's Scottish Ale in 1981 and has continued to be on the cutting edge of microbrewing ever since. This statement is made with the caveat that one is speaking of traditional brewing styles. The brewery has never turned out flavored "berry beers" or other oddities, but has instead relied on the public's demand for quality ales and hard cider crafted in the European style. As for food-friendliness, the brewery staff feels that distinctive beers like Bert Grant's ales pair as well as, or better than, wine with many foods.*

## ❖ RECIPES FROM GRANT'S ALE PUB ❖

## Grant's Brewery Pub Artichoke-Crab Dip

Serves 4 - Recommended accompaniment: Grant's Ale

| | |
|---|---|
| 1 | 14 oz. can artichoke hearts, drained |
| 4 | large cloves garlic, minced |
| 1/2 | cup plus 2 tablespoons finely grated Parmesan or Romano cheese |
| 1 | Tbs. lemon juice |
| 1/4 | cup mayonnaise |
| 1/4 | cup cream cheese, softened |
| 2 | Tbs. bread crumbs |
| 1/2 | cup crab meat |
| 1/4 | cup Grant's Hefeweizen |

Chips, crackers or raw vegetables for dipping

Finely chop artichoke hearts or run through a food processor along with the garlic using the steel chopping blade. Combine the 1/2 cup cheese, lemon juice, mayonnaise and cream cheese. Mix well with the artichoke/garlic mixture. Fold in crab meat. Put mixture into a 1 quart casserole dish and sprinkle top with bread crumbs and remaining cheese. Bake at 375° F. for 20 minutes. Serve with chips, vegetables, crusty French bread or crackers.

## Bert Grant's Pub Fish & Chip Batter

| | |
|---|---|
| 1-1/4 | cups all purpose flour |
| 1/2 | Tbs. baking powder |
| 1/2 | Tbs. salt |
| | dash Tabasco sauce |
| 1/3 | cup salad oil |
| 3/4 | cup Grant's Scottish Ale |
| 24 | oz. cod, cut up into 2 oz.pieces |

Mix together dry ingredients. Add the Tabasco and the salad oil to the dry ingredients and mix well. Slowly add the Grant's beer to the mixture. You don't want the batter too runny. Dip the cod in the batter and let the excess drip off fish. Deep fry fish in oil at 360° F. until golden brown (3 to 5 minutes depending on the size of the fish pieces).

Serve with French fries, lemon wedge, and your favorite tartar sauce.
Serves 4

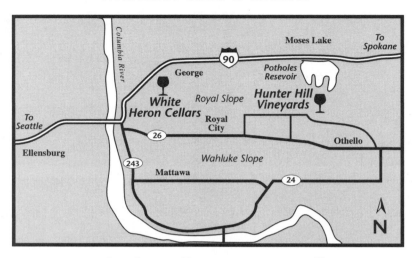

## Columbia Valley Touring – North

Most of the North Columbia Valley is off the major path of tourism in Washington State. Travelers zip by on I-90 on their way to Spokane or roar north past Wenatchee to take in the Lake Chelan and Sun Lakes resorts. The attraction of wine touring the desolate miles of sage brush punctuated by an occasional winery or small town is minimal. The demise of several North Columbia Valley wine operations will thus not surprise you.

Cascade Mountain Cellars in Ellensburg and Wenatchee Valley Vintners in East Wenatchee both succumbed to lack of wine sales to keep their businesses going. Champs de Brionne— a larger and better financed operation—couldn't decide if the concerts in the Gorge were good for wine business or if the wine business was good for the concerts. New management for the concert site decided the question, and the winery expired while the concerts have become nationally famous.

Grape growing, on the other hand, on the Wahluke and Royal Slopes is still an ongoing and successful venture. Several large vineyards supply wine grapes to Yakima Valley wineries and to wineries in Spokane and the Tri-Cities. Two wineries are still open for business in this area.

Cameron and Phyllis Fries operate **White Heron Cellars** just off I-90 in the town of George, where they are visited by cross-state travelers (many are regular customers!) who enjoy the wines of Cameron's making. A nice stop on the long drive to Spokane.

Near the Potholes Recreation Area, hunters and fishermen have kept things lively for Art Byron's **Hunter Hill Vineyards**. New roads and RV parking at the winery have increased the attraction for this detour from the sporting business at hand.

# COLUMBIA VALLEY WINERIES

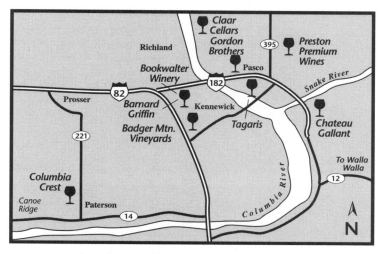

## Columbia Valley Touring – Tri-Cities

The South Columbia Valley has a larger population to support local wineries and offers more amenities to tourists who are passing through or are coming for an escape from damp weather. Most of the wine operations are clustered around the Tri-Cities of Richland, Pasco and Kennewick.

Between Richland and Kennewick Gerry, Jean and John Bookwalter operate **Bookwalter Winery** not far from the highway and also near the Columbia Center area where restaurants, hotels and other activities abound.

In 1997 Rob Griffin completed construction of his new facility for **Barnard Griffin Winery** located just across the road from Bookwalter. Stop by and enjoy this "two-fer" on the same corner.

In Kennewick, **Badger Mountain Vineyards** is making organically-grown varietals for the namesake label and also additional wines under the Powers label. The tasting room is open daily, tours by appointment.

East across the river and heading from north to south, you'll first find **Gordon Brothers Cellars** open daily at their new facility just off I-182. **Preston Premium Wines** is just north of Pasco on Highway 395. The large park at the winery is a great picnic stop and the Preston family offers a nice, self-guided tour of the winery facility. Open daily. In downtown Pasco, **Tagaris Winery** offers their wines for sale at a small retail outlet.

South on I-182 and up Highway 124, **Chateau Gallant** is within duck-calling distance of McNary Wildlife Refuge. Enjoy a view of seasonally migrating waterfowl but the winery tasting room is now closed indefinitely.

Interstate 82 runs from Kennewick to the Columbia River making a quick drive through the wheat fields to visit the Northwest's largest winemaking facility, **Columbia Crest Winery** near Paterson. Columbia Crest is magnificent. The winery tour is awe-inspiring and tourist amenities are first rate.

# Badger Mountain Vineyard

1106 S. Jurupa
Kennewick, WA 99338
(509) 627-4986
FAX (509) 627-2071
**Email:** bmvwine@aol.com
**Web:** badgermtnvineyard.com

**Tasting Room Hours:** Daily, 10 AM to 5 PM.

**Owners:** Bill Powers, Tim DeCook
**Winemaker:** Greg Powers
**First Year:** 1987
**Winery Capacity:** 200,000 Gallons

### Winery History

Badger Mountain Vineyard staked its claim to fame on organically grown grapes and is proud to be one of the first Northwest wineries to produce a line of organically-grown wines. Owners Bill Powers and Tim DeCook have moved their wine into foreign markets and offer a wide selection of varietals.

### A visit to Badger Mountain Vineyard

This operation is tucked away in the hills near the back side of Kennewick. Take exit 109 from Highway 82, turn left on Leslie Road then left again on Rachel Road. You wind through a mile or so of residental area as you climb the hill to Badger Mountain.

### The Wines

Chardonnay, Gewurztraminer, White Riesling, Chenin Blanc, Cabernet Franc and a blend named Seve are produced as organic wines under the Badger Mountain label from 76 acres of estate vineyard. Additional varietals are produced under the Powers label.

# Balcom & Moe

2520 Commercial Ave.
Pasco, WA 99301
(509) 547-7307
**Email:** balcom@owt.com
**Web:**
www.nwwines.com/balcom/

**Owner:** Balcom & Moe, Inc.
**Winemaker:** Maury Balcom
**First Year:** 1985
**Tasting Room Hours:** Not open to the public.

### Winery History

From grape grower to winemaker was a popular transition in the Columbia Valley during the 1980s. Maury Balcom of Balcom & Moe Winery waited 15 years after planting winegrapes at Balcom & Moe Farms to ferment some of his harvest instead of selling all of it to other wineries. The original label name of Quarry Lake referred to a nearby shallow lake where a larger winery facility was once planned. The current business park location provides for wine aging and storage.

### The Wines

Under the Balcom & Moe label small lots of Cabernet Sauvignon, Merlot, Chardonnay and Sauvignon Blanc are produced and continue the high quality of the original Quarry Lake bottlings.

# Barnard Griffin

878 Tulip Lane
Richland, WA 99352
(509) 627-0266
FAX (509) 627-7776
**Web:**
www.barnardgriffin.com

**Tasting Room Hours:** Daily, 10 AM to 6 PM.

**Owners:** Deborah Barnard and Rob Griffin
**Winemaker:** Rob Griffin
**First Year:** 1983
**Winery Capacity:** 75,000 Gallons

### Winery History

So why would a winemaker take up winemaking as a hobby? That question might have occurred to Rob Griffin and Deborah Barnard sometime during Rob's tenure as general manager for The Hogue Cellars. He worked hard creating a popular style for Hogue and separately crafted his own brand where he alone controlled the stylistic appeal. Barnard Griffin winery was never intended as a hobby and now Rob has left Hogue to pursue the success of his well-established brand. Rob and Deborah sometimes pour their wines at enological festivals and fairs as production levels permit.

### The Wines

Clean varietal character and insightful handling of barrel fermentation and oak aging make Rob Griffin's wines among the most enjoyable of Washington bottlings. Merlot, Cabernet Sauvignon, Fume Blanc, Semillon and Chardonnay each offer the consumer ripe, fruity character and superb food pairing qualities. Wines are sometimes in short supply, especially in vintages where certain varietals suffer from low crop yields. Watch for reserve wines that are especially characterful.

# Bookwalter Winery

710 S. Windmill Rd.
Richland, WA 99352
(509) 627-5000
FAX (509) 627-5010
**Email:**
bookwine@owt.com
**Web:** www.nwwines.com/bookwalter

**Tasting Room Hours:** Daily, 10 AM - 5 PM
Tours Available

**Owners:** Jerrold, Jean & John Bookwalter
**Winemaker:** Jerry Bookwalter
**First Year:** 1983
**Winery Capacity:** 30,000 Gallons

## Winery History

After graduating from U. C. Davis in 1963, Jerry Bookwalter managed orchards and vineyards in California. In 1976, he moved north to Washington where he was general manager of Bacchus and Dionysus Vineyards for Sagemoor Farms until 1983.

A belief in the quality of Washington wines and the dedication to produce only small lots of quality wines led to the bonding of Bookwalter Winery in 1984. Bookwalter wines do well in competitions but more importantly for Jerry, they are well liked by consumers. New winery quarters just off Highway 182 in Richland were completed in 1993.

## A visit to Bookwalter Winery

The new Bookwalter location at the corner of Windmill Rd. and Columbia Dr. offers easy access to wine lovers traveling between Yakima and the Tri-Cities. The cozy tasting room and informal tour make for an interesting and educational stop.

*The Bookwalter Winery near Richland, Washington.*

## The Wines

Clean and crisp whites and rich, fruity reds are the Columbia Valley style of Bookwalter Winery. Cabernet, Merlot, Chardonnay, Chenin Blanc, Muscat Blanc and Riesling are frequent medal winners, as is Bookwalter's Red Table Wine.

# Canoe Ridge Estate

Highway 14, 11 miles west of Paterson
**Owners:** Stimson Lane Vineyards & Estates
**Winemaker:** Charlie Hoppes
**First Year:** 1994

## Winery History

Not to be confused with the Chalone Group's venture (see Walla Walla area listings), this is the new red wine facility for Chateau Ste. Michelle. Built here in 1993 for convenient access to their extensive new Canoe Ridge vineyards, the winery is a production facility only, offering no tourist amenities. Impressive and well organized, the winemakers of Chateau Ste. Michelle were given a free hand to create a winery that offered maximum flexibility for wine production. No tourist facilities available.

## Chateau Gallant

S. 1355 Gallant Rd.
Pasco, WA 99301
(509) 545-9570
FAX (509) 547-1768

**Owners:** David &
Theresa Gallant
**First Year:** 1987
**Winery Capacity:** 10,000 Gallons

**Winery History**

Chateau Gallant planted their first vineyards in 1972, followed by additional plantings in later years for a current total of 25 acres. The facility is located on the edge of the McNary Wildlife Refuge providing a year-round display of waterfowl using the slough for rest stops on their annual migrations.

**A visit to Chateau Gallant**

The Gallant Winery is located a short drive up Highway 124 from its junction with I-182 and then right, down Gallant Road. As press time approaches, tasting room is closed and the owners are currently selling their grape production to other wineries.

## Claar Cellars

1081 Glenwood Road
Pasco, WA 99301
(509) 266-4449
FAX (509) 266-4444

**Owners:** Bob & Christa
Whitelatch
**First Year:** 1997

**Tasting Room Hours:** Weekdays, 10 AM to 2 PM; weekends, 11 AM to 5 PM.

Bob and Christa Whitelatch farm an 80-acre site overlooking the Columbia River, just north of Pasco. Christa's father, Russell Claar, planted the first winegrapes there in 1980. The winery plans on producing Chardonnay, Riesling, Merlot and Cabernet Sauvignon.

From I-182, take exit 9 and follow Road 68 and Taylor Flats Road north to Eltopia West Road (turn left) and head west for a left turn on Glenwood Road. Eltopia West Road may also be reached directly from I-395.

*Columbia Crest Winery in Paterson, Washington*

## Columbia Crest Winery

P.O. Box 231
Paterson, WA
99345-0231
(509) 875-2061
(Located on
Highway 221.)

**Tasting Room Hours:** Daily, 10 AM - 4:30 PM

**Owners:** Stimson Lane Vineyards & Estates
**Winemaker:** Doug Gore
**First Year:** 1985
**Winery Capacity:** 1,000,000 Gallons+

**Winery History**

Columbia Crest began life as Chateau Ste. Michelle's River Ridge winery, created to handle most of the thousands of tons of grapes processed by Washington's largest winery group each year. It soon became clear that the winery could use it's own identity and in 1985 Columbia Crest, the wine and winery, were born. An individual winemaking style and unique market niche for value and quality have propelled Columbia Crest into the 1990s wine limelight.

**A visit to Columbia Crest**

Columbia Crest is without question one of the most impressive wineries in the Northwest. The huge complex houses more than a million gallons of wine plus first-rate tourist facilities. The landscaping around the winery includes acres of manicured lawn for impromptu picnics and a delightful duck pond. A courtyard by the entrance is furnished with café tables for more formal snacking. The lobby of the winery is furnished with tapestries, antiques and immaculate decor at every turn. A self-guided tour is available daily to direct the visitor through all the important production areas of the facility and more complete guided tours are offered on weekends. The well-appointed tasting room provides samplings of Columbia Crest wines, and the gift shop is well stocked for picnickers and souvenir hunters. The half hour drive from Prosser or Kennewick is time well spent to see the Northwest's largest wine facility.

Follow Highway 221 up from I-82 at Prosser over the hill and down to the Columbia River. Alternately, take I-82 from Kennewick to Highway 14 and head west to Paterson.

### The Wines

Columbia Crest winemaker Doug Gore does a tremendous job of putting great value into every Columbia Crest bottle. The wines are true to varietal type and are enjoyable accompaniments to food. Select from a wide range of varietal bottlings with confidence – Chardonnay, Merlot, Cabernet Sauvignon and Semillon-Chardonnay are featured. Barrel Select bottlings offer greater depth of complexity and power.

# Domaine Ste. Michelle

P.O. Box 231
Paterson, WA 99345

**Owners:** Stimson Lane Vineyards & Estates
**Winemaker:** Rick Casqueiro
**First Year:** 1985
**Winery Capacity:** 1,000,000 Gallons+

### Winery History

Domaine Ste. Michelle is the brand of sparkling wines produced by Stimson Lane Vineyards & Estates, the offshoot of a sparkling wine program begun by Joel Klein in the mid-1970s. The first sparkling wines were released under the Chateau Ste. Michelle label but the ambitious production levels now attained make the first effort seem almost like a small experiment.

When Stimson Lane made a firm commitment to establish a sparkling wine brand in the late 1980s, the wine that launched this success was dubbed "Champagne Brut" and was released in 1990. Taking advantage of a popular price point (under $10 per bottle when on sale during the holidays), Domaine Ste. Michelle captured a goodly share of the local bubbly market. Over the last few years several cuvees have been tried that have met with moderate success. Currently the brands are: Cuvee Brut, Blanc de Blanc and Extra Dry.

The wines are produced by the traditional Methode Champenoise where the wine is refermented in the bottle to produce the bubbles. Winemaker Rick Casqueiro came on board in 1996 to handle the production of Domaine Ste. Michelle wines. His nearly 20 years experience at Weibel Champagne Cellars in California certainly qualifies him for the job.

### A visit to Domaine Ste. Michelle

The wines for this brand are made at the sprawling Columbia Crest facility in Paterson (also owned by Stimson Lane Vineyards & Estates), and on the weekend guided tours there you might get a glimpse of the sparkling wine production area. The wine is generally not poured in the tasting room.

### The Wines

While not measuring up to the finest French Champagnes, these are certainly serviceable sparklers that hold their own at weddings, New Year's celebrations and boat christenings. Cuvee Brut is lean and clean with a fine bead of bubbles, crisp on the finish and reminiscent of citrus. Blanc de Blanc is more crisp apple-pear in style with a little more yellow color and slightly more body than Cuvee Brut. Almost 2% residual sugar exemplifies the goal with Extra Dry featuring more body and more fruity character.

## Gordon Brothers Cellars

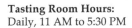

5960 Burden Road
Pasco, WA 99301
(509) 547-6331
FAX (509) 547-6305
**Email:** grdnbrs@owt.com
**Web:** www.nwwines.com/
gordonbros

**Tasting Room Hours:** Daily, 11 AM
to 5 PM

**Owners:** Jeff & Bill Gordon
**Winemaker:** Marie-Eve Gilla
**First Year:** 1983
**Winery Capacity:** 23,000 Gallons

### Winery History

Jeff and Bill Gordon have been growing
grapes since 1980 at their vineyard site east of
Pasco above the Snake River. This is the tame
part of the river where broad, fertile banks
have been formed and flooding is controlled
by several dams. With the coming of dams
also came irrigation for potatoes and other row
crops - an important part of the Gordon
Brothers farming efforts.

Much of the wine grape crop is sold to
Spokane, Walla Walla and Tri-Cities area
vintners who have been steady customers since
the 80-acre vineyard came into bearing in 1982.
Roughly 20% of the harvest is vinified for the
Gordon Brothers label. In 1995, a new winery
facility was built in Pasco.

### A visit to Gordon Brothers Cellars

The new Gordon Brothers winery is located
just off Interstate 182 north of Pasco. Take the
Road 68 exit and head north 1/4 mile to
Burden Road, turn right and head to the
winery. The new facility offers daily tasting of
the Gordon Brothers wines and a banquet/
meeting room that can be rented for special
events. With the increased capacity of the
facility, Jeff Gordon hired winemaker Marie-
Eve Gilla for the 1996 harvest.

### The Wines

The power of Chardonnay has moved
Gordon Brothers' reserve bottling into the top
echelon at many wine competitions - rich and
buttery, with a long finish of vanilla and apple.

Jeff Gordon's Merlot has also been a gold-
medal-regular, brimming with ripe berry fruit
and toasty nuances of American oak. A very
impressive Cabernet Sauvignon is also
produced. A new addition is the winery's
"Tradition," a meritage blend of red varietals.

## Hunter Hill Vineyards

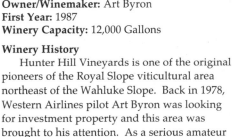

2752 W. McMannaman Rd.
Othello, WA 98344
(509) 346-2736

**Tasting Room Hours:**
Daily, 11 AM to 5:30 PM

**Owner/Winemaker:** Art Byron
**First Year:** 1987
**Winery Capacity:** 12,000 Gallons

### Winery History

Hunter Hill Vineyards is one of the original
pioneers of the Royal Slope viticultural area
northeast of the Wahluke Slope. Back in 1978,
Western Airlines pilot Art Byron was looking
for investment property and this area was
brought to his attention. As a serious amateur
winemaker Art saw more potential in the land
than just a tax deduction. Twenty-eight acres
of vineyard were planted in 1981 and 1982 and
the first commercial harvest came in 1984.

### A visit to Hunter Hill Vineyards

Art Byron doesn't worry about attracting
wine tasters to his new winery since the area
just north of the Royal Slope is a recreational
heaven for fishermen, hunters, wildlife
enthusiasts and boaters—all of whom Art
hopes will take the short side trip to visit
Hunter Hill Vineyards. A picnic area and RV
parking are adjacent to the winery to further
encourage wine-loving visitors to stay awhile.
From Hwy. 26 turn north at milepost 25 and
turn right on Road 12 SE. Head east to winery.

### The Wines

Hunter Hill produces Chardonnay, Chenin
Blanc, Muscat Canelli, Dry Riesling,
Johannisberg Riesling, Merlot, Cabernet
Sauvignon, Meritage and Lemberger.

## Preston Premium Wines

502 E. Vineyard Dr., Pasco, WA 99301
(509) 545-1990, FAX (509) 545-1098

**Tasting Room Hours:** Daily, 10 AM to 5:30 PM, Closed on major holidays.

**Owners:** Preston Family
**Winemaker:** Brent Preston
**First Year:** 1976
**Winery Capacity:** 180,000 Gallons

**Winery History**

Preston Premium Wines is a Columbia Valley institution that began in the earliest days of Washington's modern wine history. In 1972 Bill Preston planted 50 acres of wine-grapes along Highway 395 and later hired Rob Griffin to make his first wines. The widely acclaimed first releases from Preston began a tradition that continues to this day, and helped create a positive image of Washington's fledgling wine industry. Preston family members now handle all aspects of operating the state's largest family-owned winery.

**A visit to Preston**

A short drive north of Pasco, the Preston vineyard and winery are a dramatic sight on the east side of Highway 395. The parklike picnic area invites visitors to relax and "stay awhile" and the unique, second-story tasting room offers views of the vineyard along with wine tasting. The addition of a large gazebo overlooking the koi pond has added even more enticement to linger. The winery sponsors special events that include a chili cook-off, kite fly-in, model boat races and other fun activities.

**The Wines**

Preston has long offered a broad range of varietals from refreshing, off-dry whites to crisp Fume Blanc and Chardonnay to hearty oak-aged reds. Recent vintages of Cabernet and Merlot have shown great character in a powerful, toasty style. Rich and buttery Chardonnay is often a favorite with many wine tasters.

*Preston Winery north of Pasco, Washington.*

## Snoqualmie Winery

P.O. Box 231
Paterson, WA 99345-0231

**Owners:** Stimson Lane Vineyards & Estates
**Winemaker:** Joy Andersen
**First Year:** 1983
**Winery Capacity:** 1,000,000 Gallons+

**Winery History**

Where do I begin? Snoqualmie Winery has just about the most colorful and intriguing history of any Northwest winery, yet every-thing seems to have turned out O.K. in the end. Founded by Joel Klein (Chateau Ste. Michelle's first winemaker at the Woodinville facility), in the early 1980s, with an investor group who put together a nifty winery-for-show on a hill near the town of Snoqualmie. A working winery was later added by acquiring the former F. W. Langguth facility in Mattawa.

Klein eventually left the group and Mike Januik (Chateau Ste. Michelle's current winemaker) came in to make wine for a couple of vintages. Mike was hired by Chateau Ste. Michelle and then Stimson Lane Vineyards and Estates bought the working Snoqualmie facility and continued the brand by having talented Joy Andersen make wine mostly at the Columbia Crest facility where the wine is currently produced.

Got that? O.K. Then Stimson Lane closed the facility at Snoqualmie (the town) as it was leased and the lease was up. So the tasting

*Continued on next page.*

room is now gone but the brand carries on with a spiffy new label added in 1998.

No place to visit – well, you can visit Columbia Crest where the wine is made, but they don't *pour* Snoqualmie wine there – but the wine is still good and it's available in many locations around the country. Whew!

### The Wines

Cabernet-Merlot, Lemberger, Chardonnay, Muscat and Fume Blanc were the usual wines bottled under the Snoqualmie label but with changes as we go to press, watch for the release of superb, reserve-style bottlings.

## Tagaris Winery

P.O. Box 5433, Kennewick, WA 99336
Retail Store: 1625 'A' St., Unit E,
Pasco, WA 99301
(509) 547-3590

**Owner:** Michael Taggares
**First Year:** 1987
**Retail Store Hours:** Monday thru Friday, 8 AM to 5 PM

### Winery History

Michael Taggares is the proprietor of Taggares Vineyards located northeast of Othello near 'Radar Hill.' A very successful farming family, Taggares is also a familiar name as you drive through the Yakima Valley. Many acres of Concord grapes have been producing for this enterprise for decades.

The spelling of the winery's name is the original Greek spelling of Michael Taggares' name. His grandfather Peter, like many immigrants with a limited command of English, had his name spelled incorrectly at Ellis Island upon his arrival in 1911.

### A visit to Tagaris Winery

The winery sales office is open weekdays from 8 AM to 5 PM.

### The Wines

The first Tagaris Winery wines included Chenin Blanc, Johannisberg Riesling and Sauvignon Blanc. In addition to the above varietals, Chardonnay, Late Harvest Riesling, Pinot Noir, Cabernet Sauvignon and sparkling wine are now made.

## White Heron Cellars

101 Washington Way N.
George, WA 98824 •
(509) 785-5521

**Owners:** Phyllis & Cameron Fries
**Winemaker:** Cameron Fries
**First Year:** 1990
**Winery Capacity:** 3,500 Gallons
**Tasting Room Hours:** Wednesday thru Sunday, Noon to 5 PM.

### Winery History

Both Washington natives and graduates of Pacific Lutheran University in Tacoma, Phyllis and Cameron Fries relocated to Switzerland for five years so that Cameron could study winemaking. Upon their return to Washington, Cameron served as winemaker for two Washington wineries prior to establishing his own operation in 1990.

### A visit to White Heron

Located just off Interstate 90 in George, White Heron's facility is a converted gas station on a quiet back street. Phyllis and Cameron have spruced up the place and enjoy pouring their wines for interested visitors. Dispensing humor along with fine wine, they makes fast friends with all who stop by. White Heron makes a great midpoint rest on the long drive to Spokane, or an interesting side-visit if you're heading to a concert at the Gorge.

### The Wines

The winery's vineyard near Trinidad (above the Columbia Gorge near Crescent Bar) produces some of the grapes for White Heron wines. Additional fruit is purchased from Yakima Valley vineyards. Pinot Noir, Dry Riesling and a Bordeaux-style red blend named Chantepierre are the wines produced.

# COLUMBIA VALLEY ACCOMMODATIONS

Waterlogged winelovers seeking a sunny vacation can escape to the sun-drenched Columbia Valley to bake away their cares and troubles. Special events, water sports and a dozen wineries are an extra incentive to put away the umbrella and head east of the Cascades.

## Cavanaugh's Motor Inn
1101 N. Columbia Center, Kennewick - 1-800-THE INNS   Quality accommodations with nice rooms, pool and spa, children's play area. Good Northwest wine list in Cavanaugh's Landing restaurant.

## Red Lion Hanford House
802 George Washington Way, Richland - (509) 946-7611  The swankiest hotel in Richland with a pleasant center courtyard and an elegant dining room.

## Red Lion Pasco
2525 N. 20th, Pasco - (509) 547-0701  Close to the Pasco-area wineries and to the Pasco airport. Just off the freeway you'll find this well-planned and well-staffed Red Lion with swimming pools, nice restaurant. Golf course adjacent.

## Clover Park Quality Inn
435 Clover Island off Columbia Dr., (509) 586-0541 - Located on an island at the Kennewick side of the Columbia River, this inexpensive alternative to the Hanford House and Red Lion in Pasco is popular for its view rooms.

# COLUMBIA VALLEY DINING

## Emerald of Siam
1314 Jadwin, Richland - (509) 946-9328  When this restaurant opened, a cheer went up from many folks who had been yearning for great Thai cooking. Located in a converted storefront on Richland's back street. NW wine list and imported Thai beer are offered.

## Vannini's Italian Restaurant
1026 Lee Blvd., Richland - (509) 946-4525  This name rings a bell up and down the valley for lovers of Italian cuisine. This latest Vannini's offers out-of-the-ordinary cuisine and both Italian and local wine selections in a converted railroad dining car.

## Giacci's
94 Lee Blvd., Richland - (509) 946-4855 - Italian deli and restaurant.  Lunch served Mon. - Sat., Dinner served Fri. and Sat. Good wine list.

## Cedars Pier One
Clover Island, Kennewick - (509) 582-2143 - Hard to find in the arid plateau of Eastern Washington, this waterfront view restaurant offers a variety of traditional fare but excels in beef and stick-to-your-ribs accompaniments. Ostrich has made it onto the menu recently offering some of beef's flavor without the fat.

# COLUMBIA VALLEY ACTIVITIES

## Columbia Park - Kennewick
This greenbelt runs along the Columbia River for several miles with various recreational opportunities spread out along the way. Also a nice place for morning or evening strolls with a river view.

## Tri-Cities Air Show
Scheduled in late June or early July, this is always a real kid-pleaser. Noise, planes, military vehicles.

## Columbia Center Mall
Just off the freeway in Kennewick.

## Columbia Cup Hydroplane Race
Late July or early August and the Thunder-on-the-Columbia comes to town for a wild time by the river. Many nearby residents come to town to enjoy this event with their families.

## Hanford Science Center
In downtown Richland, this interpretive center has many interesting displays on the history of nuclear power. To get closer to the action, you can tour the WPPSS Plant 2 or the Westinghouse Fast Flux Test Facility.

# NORTHWEST WINES & WINERIES

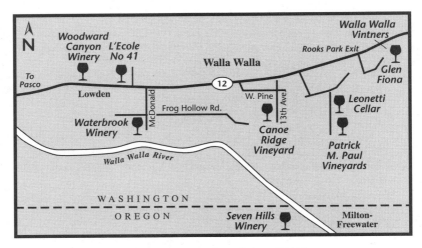

## WALLA WALLA AREA TOURING

Never will you feel so at home as you do in Walla Walla. The shady, tree-lined streets seem to bring back memories of wherever you grew up and the soda shop on the corner still makes a great hamburger. Out in the Walla Walla Valley, next to the onion fields and historical markers, the wineries await.

Starting in the small farming town of Lowden, your first stop is **Woodward Canyon Winery** across the road from the grain elevator. An insightful tasting room host pours Woodward Canyon's wines for interested wine lovers daily. Next door, **L'Ecole No 41** operates out of the converted Lowden Schoolhouse with proprietors Marty and Megan Clubb often on hand to explain the history and future of this unique winery.

Just east of Lowden on Highway 12 is the right turn on McDonald Road for **Waterbrook Winery**. The winery is open for tasting most days from Noon to 5 PM. Schedules change so if you're coming a long way to visit, call ahead to ensure someone is there to meet you.

**Canoe Ridge Vineyards** opened in 1995 in the old Walla Walla Railway engine house on 13th St. in west Walla Walla. If you're coming into town from the west, take the first Walla Walla exit onto Pine Street then watch for your right turn onto 13th. The huge brick building a few blocks south on your right is the winery and the cozy tasting room building is adjacent.

On the east side of residential Walla Walla are **Leonetti Cellar** and **Patrick M. Paul Vineyards**. Leonetti Cellar is currently not open to the public since their wines are sold out upon release. Patrick M. Paul winery is open by appointment and for the annual open houses held twice a year.

**Seven Hills Winery** is located in down-town Milton-Freewater, Oregon reached from Walla Walla by taking Highway 11. The winery is open during the May and September open houses or by appointment.

# Canoe Ridge Vineyard

1102 West Cherry St.
P.O. Box 684
Walla Walla, WA 98362
(509) 527-0885
FAX (509) 527-0886
**Email:** canoerdg@bmi.net
**Web:** www.chalonewinegroup.com

**Tasting Room Hours:** Monday through Friday, 11 AM to 4 PM; weekends, 11 AM - 5 PM

**Owner:** Corporate Partnership
**Winemaker:** John Abbott
**First Year:** 1994
**Winery Capacity:** 60,000 Gallons

**Winery History**

An investment in vineyard land by a partnership headed by California's Chalone Group has finally born fruit and established a winemaking beachhead in Walla Walla. The 700-acre Canoe Ridge Vineyard is located just east of the Chateau Ste. Michelle venture of nearly identical name – Canoe Ridge Estate – along the Columbia River near Columbia Crest winery. The grapes are brought to the Walla Walla winery and vinified by talented winemaker John Abbott (formerly at Acacia winery in California). The first released vintages of Merlot and Chardonnay were in 1994 though production levels became more significant in 1995.

**A visit to Canoe Ridge Vineyards**

The winery for this new venture was created from the shell of the historic Walla Walla Railway Engine House just west of downtown. The cavernous brick and beam structure is both picturesque and utilitarian, as the large tanks and racks of barrels stand where similarly monolithic iron horses once puffed and snorted. A cozy visitor center is next door to provide a warm welcome to visiting wine lovers. Manager Molly Galt and winemaker John Abbott are Northwest natives and share great enthusiasm for the project.

**The Wines**

Merlot, Chardonnay and Cabernet Sauvignon are the varietals of choice with reserve wines produced occasionally. Small lots of other varietals are also made.

*Winemaker John Abbott of Canoe Ridge Vineyard.*

# Dunham Cellars

Lowden, WA 99360

**Owner/Winemaker:**
Eric Dunham
**First Year:** 1995

Eric Dunham has been the assistant winemaker at L'Ecole No 41 for several years and jumped in to make small lots of his own Cabernet in 1995 and 1996. The wines are very good and Eric is moving forward with a winery facility of his own in Lowden. Watch for his opening in 1999. In the meantime, Eric can be reached at L'Ecole.

# Glen Fiona

Rt. 4, Box 251-AA
P.O. Box 2024
Mill Creek Road
Walla Walla, WA 99362
(509) 522-2566
FAX (509) 522-1008

**Tasting Room Hours:** Three winery open houses, second weekends of May, September, and December, call for info.

**Owner/Winemaker:** Berle "Rusty" Figgins
**First Year:** 1995

The brother of Gary Figgins of Leonetti Cellar fame is the man behind Glen Fiona, producer of Rhone varietals. Named for the Gaelic phrase for "Valley of the Vine" Glen Fiona is located in the carriage house on the

*Continued on next page.*

historic Kibler-Finch Homestead east of Walla Walla on Mill Creek Road. Varietals of Syrah, Grenache, Cinsault and Viognier are made. Take the Rooks Park exit from Hwy. 12 and follow to Mill Creek Road (take a left).

## L´Ecole No. 41

P.O. Box 111
41 Lowden School Rd.
Lowden, WA 99360
(509) 525-0940
FAX (509) 525-2775

**Tasting Room Hours:** Wednesday thru Sunday, 11 AM to 4 PM (by appointment during the winter months)

**Owners:** Martin & Megan Clubb
**Winemaker:** Marty Clubb
**First Year:** 1983
**Winery Capacity:** 10,000 Gallons

### Winery History

A Walla Walla native with family going back several generations, Baker Ferguson and his wife Jean saved a valley landmark by converting it into a winery. The old Lowden Schoolhouse, constructed in 1915, now features stainless steel fermenters and barrel storage in the basement auditorium and cafeteria. The main floor of the school is a winery reception area and combination tasting room and banqueting hall. Baker and Jean turned over operation of the winery to their daughter and son-in-law in 1989.

Marty Clubb now uses his chemical engineering degree for a slightly different purpose than he perhaps intended, but his zeal for the wine business is equalled only by his innate talent in crafting ripe and structured red wines that have won him praise worldwide.

### A visit to L´Ecole No 41

The transformation of Lowden School-house into the L´Ecole winery makes for a fun look around. The owners or their assistants provide information on the wines available for tasting and also on local history and things to do. A custom restaurant-for-hire operates in the large classroom by prior arrangement.

### The Wines

Learning the art of winemaking with

hands-on experience, Marty Clubb has shown great insight into the handling of grapes from several area vineyard sources. His vineyard designated wines and proprietary blends have helped him create a demand for L'Ecole No 41 red wines that has eclipsed anything that went before. Merlot and Semillon are the winery's principal focus, but other varietals are also produced with great success.

## Leonetti Cellar

1321 School Ave.
Walla Walla, WA 99362
(509) 525-1428
FAX (509) 525-4006

**Tasting Room Hours:** None

**Owners:** Gary & Nancy Figgins
**Winemaker:** Gary Figgins
**First Year:** 1977
**Winery Capacity:** 12,000 Gallons

### Winery History

With the success that Gary Figgins has enjoyed as a maker of fine Cabernet Sauvignon and Merlot, many winemakers might have secured a loan and expanded production by 100 times to cash-in on the reputation. Gary hasn't done that because he realizes the quality of his wine depends on the grapes he uses and the best quality grapes are in short supply. So with small harvests from his own vineyard and select lots from other growers, Gary hand crafts rich red wines in his small winery in Walla Walla. The larger winery building added in 1988-89 helps Leonetti Cellar keep up with the demand.

A fascination (bordering on fanaticism) with oak and oak barrels consumes much of Gary Figgins free time. His quest to further understand the barrel-aging process and the flavor nuances imparted by various oak types have led to experiments with locally-grown oak and different methods of coopering (barrel-making).

### A visit to Leonetti Cellar

It is difficult to visit Leonetti Cellar. The increasing success of their wines and increasing national exposure have overwhelmed the

*Leonetti Cellar winery in Walla Walla, Washington.*

augment the small quantity of local grapes. The 1996 Merlot from Leonetti Cellar was consequently labelled with "American" as the appellation. To some wine critics this was an opportunity to point out that the wine quickly sold out anyway, implying the quality was lacking and customers just bought for the label. We feel that Gary Figgins did what he felt best given the circumstances and that the wine stands alongside other Leonetti bottlings with no decrease in quality.

Figgins family who strongly desire to live a quiet life, make a little wine, and enjoy family and close friends. The only way to gain admittance to the annual release (where Leonetti wine may be purchased) is to be on the winery's mailing list. The mailing list is full and no names are currently being added. In short, there is far too little wine for the current demand, much less for hundreds of additional wine lovers.

### The Wines

In the age of powerful red wines crafted with many layers of flavor—both fruit and oak—Leonetti Cellar wines are among the most popular in the world. Combining intensity of fruit with intensity of oak requires a finesse that few have mastered as well as Gary Figgins. French and American oak barrels of varying ages are used to augment the ripe fruit flavors of Cabernet Sauvignon and Merlot as well as other Bordeaux varietals. Wines available include regular and vineyard designated bottlings of Cabernet, Reserve Cabernet, Merlot and a red table wine Meritage-style blend. Typical Leonetti Merlot offers ripe and plummy fruit with a softer palate than the Cabernet which takes on nuances of coffee, chocolate, mint and eucalyptus. See a well-established wine merchant to beg for these wines.

After the big freeze in Washington State vineyards in 1996, Merlot grapes were in short supply for that vintage. Facing production that was dramatically decreased from the previous year, Gary Figgins turned south to California to purchase quality Merlot fruit to

# Patrick M. Paul Vineyards

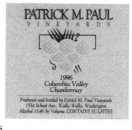

1554 School Ave.
Walla Walla, WA
99362
(509) 526-0676
**Email:** paulte@wwics

**Tasting Room Hours:** Saturday and Sunday, 1 to 4 PM or by appointment.

**Owner:** Mike & Theresa Paul
**Winemaker:** Mike Paul
**First Year:** 1988
**Winery Capacity:** 2,000 Gallons

### Winery History

Research into grape varieties and rootstocks spawned the creation of Patrick M. Paul winery. Vineyard plantings of Cabernet Franc, Pinot Noir, Merlot and Cabernet Sauvignon followed and wine production has been increasing ever since.

### A visit to Patrick M. Paul Winery

Stop by the winery out in the suburbs east of Walla Walla on a weekend.

### The Wines

First releases of Boysenberry and Concord dessert wines found local approval but a bottling of Cabernet Franc from the 1988 vintage was the first step in establishing a reputation with a favorable review in The Wine Spectator. Current releases of Chardonnay and Cabernet Sauvignon have helped pave the way to more recognition.

# Seven Hills Winery

P.O. Box 21
235 E. Broadway
Milton Freewater, OR
97862
(541) 938-7710

**Tasting Room Hours:** May and Sept. open houses or by appointment.

**Owners:** Local Family Shareholders
**Winemaker:** Casey McClellan
**First Year:** 1989
**Winery Capacity:** 5,000 Gallons

## Winery History

The development of Seven Hills Vineyard in the 1980s led to many award-winning wines produced from the vineyard's fruit by local wineries. A son of one of the vineyard owners, Casey McClellan cultivated his interest in winemaking while working at the vineyard in the 1980s. He then studied at U.C. Davis and worked in the California and Portuguese wine industries before beginning Seven Hills Winery in 1988.

## A visit to Seven Hills Cellars

Milton-Freewater is a short drive south from Walla Walla on Highway 11 through scenic hills and farmland. The winery in downtown Milton-Freewater is open during the traditional Walla Walla area May and September weekends. Other visits are by scheduled appointment.

## The Wines

Richly structured Cabernet Sauvignon and Merlot are the focus at Seven Hills Winery. Intensely fruity red wines framed with toasty oak beckon the consumer to drink now but will age gracefully to further develop bottle bouquet. Other varietals are occasionally produced including Sauvignon Blanc, Chardonnay, Gewurztraminer and Riesling.

# Walla Walla Vintners

P.O. Box 1551
Mill Creek Road
Walla Walla, WA 99362
(509) 525-4724
FAX (509) 525-4134

**Tasting Room Hours:** None

**Owners/Winemakers:** Alan Jones, Myles Anderson, Gordon Venneri
**First Year:** 1995
**Winery Capacity:** 4,900 Gallons

Three Walla Walla area wine entrepreneurs produced some pretty good wines from a few recent vintages and have made quite a reputation in a short time. Taking a similar approach to marketing that is serving other Walla Walla wineries, the trio offer their wines through open houses in May and near Labor Day. Red wines of Cabernet Sauvignon, Cabernet Franc and Merlot have won high praise and the group's Washington State Cuvee blend sold quickly during its May release in 1998.

Does this early success portend great things to come? Is this winery destined to be another Leonetti-style success story? Stay tuned for further developments.

### Bruce Hiebert
### Chef/Owner
### Patit Creek Restaurant

*I'm sure that many experienced Northwest wine tourists have heard of Bruce Hiebert's Patit Creek Restaurant. I often wonder how many make the trek all the way from Seattle or Portland to the town ot Dayton to enjoy the experience first hand. You should make the trip.*

*Bruce and Heather Hiebert have made their out-of-the-way restaurant into a destination for all those who crave fine cooking in Eastern Washington. Using the freshest ingredients and classical technique, the chef creates both innovative and traditional offerings. Heather's desserts are a perfect ending to the evening and the couple make sure to have the local wines that everyone asks for on their well-thought-out wine list.*

*The decor is unexpected, the wait staff is down home and friendly, and the drive from Walla Walla isn't all that long when you remember the traffic jams that clogged your last trip into the big city for dinner!*

## ❖ A RECIPE FROM PATIT CREEK RESTAURANT ❖

## Sauteed Breast of Duckling with Port and Black Currant Sauce

Serves 6
Accompanying wine:
Walla Walla Vintners Cabernet Sauvignon

### Ingredients

- 3   whole boneless duck breasts, skin on, cut in half
-     oil

- 3   whole shallot, peeled and minced
- 2/3   cup port wine
- 1   cup dry red wine
- 3   Tbs. black currant preserves
- 2   Tbs. Dijon mustard
- 1   tsp. grated orange peel
- 2   cups beef broth
- 1/2   cup heavy cream
- 1/4   cup butter, cut in pieces

Heat a large saute pan over medium-high heat with a thin film of oil. Score duck skin with a sharp knife and add duck to the pan, skin side down. Cook, turning occasionally, until skin is crisp and desired doneness is reached. (5 to 6 minutes for medium-rare to medium). Remove duck to an ovenproof plate and hold in a warm oven (250° to 275° F.).

Discard rendered fat from pan, turn heat to high, and add the next 7 ingredients. Boil until reduced by half. Add the cream and continue boiling until fairly thick. Remove pan from the heat and whisk in the butter a little at a time. Remove duck from the oven, slice thinly, and serve with the sauce.

# Waterbrook

Rt. 1, Box 46
McDonald Rd.
Lowden, WA
99360
(509) 522-1918, FAX (509) 529-4770
Email: wbrook@bmi.net

**Tasting Room Hours:** Daily, Noon - 5 PM

**Owners:** Eric and Janet Rindal
**Winemaker:** Eric Rindal
**First Year:** 1984
**Winery Capacity:** 30,000 Gallons

## Winery History

Out past the onion farms and wheat fields, a half-mile from Frog Hollow Road, Eric and Janet Rindal converted an asparagus storage building into an attractive little winery they called Waterbrook. Hard work and inspiration got the building cleaned up and ready for business by the 1984 crush when the first Waterbrook wines were made. The wines gained immediate popularity for clean varietal flavors and fruity character. A larger winery building was added during 1987 and 1988 to increase the variety and amount of wine produced. Maturity of the winery's Cottonwood Creek Vineyard near Walla Walla has increased production of Waterbrook's favored varietal, Chardonnay.

Currently, Waterbrook wines have a following across the country and across the seas. This is a very successful winery run by folks who know what they're doing.

## A visit to Waterbrook

Just a short drive south from Highway 12, Waterbrook offers visitors the chance to taste several current releases of both red and white wines. The informative tasting room staff makes this stop worthwhile for serious wine connoisseurs.

## The Wines

Waterbrook's first releases of Chardonnay and Sauvignon Blanc won them a loyal following, and the addition of Merlot and Cabernet cemented a relationship with NW wine lovers. Chardonnays (regular and reserve) are round and rich, buttery and toasty. Ripe and fruity reds also offer ample toasty oak.

# Woodward Canyon Winery

Rt. 1, Box 387
State Highway 12
Lowden, WA 99360
(509) 525-4129
FAX (509) 522-0927

**Tasting Room Hours:**
Daily, 10 AM to 5 PM

**Owners:** Rick & Darcey Fugman-Small
**Winemaker:** Rick Small
**First Year:** 1981
**Winery Capacity:** 13,500 Gallons

## Winery History

The awards came early for Rick Small, an enthusiastic and spirited winemaker who prefers to concentrate his efforts on a few varietals produced in small volume. Northwest recognition for his efforts included gold medals, wine of the year honors, and best of show awards. The local lovers of barrel-fermented Chardonnay and ripe and toasty Cabernet Sauvignon and Merlot catapulted Woodward Canyon to fame in the 1980s. The 1990s have seen the national discovery of Woodward Canyon.

Currently, Rick Small is soul-searching on the subject of terroir. Debating the suitability of certain varietals to certain vineyard plots has become a quandary. On one hand, the grapes growing there do fine and are the basis for extremely successful wines (Chardonnay, mostly), on the other, would Merlot or Cabernet Franc provide even more exciting character? The evolution of the Northwest wine industry continues.

## A visit to Woodward Canyon

Woodward Canyon Winery is located in a collection of small warehouse-style buildings in 'downtown' Lowden, Washington. Across the highway from the grain elevator and back through the parking lot, a small sign welcomes visitors to the tasting room. Your well-informed host might be assistant winemaker Caleb Foster-Erskine, who pours the wine and explains the winery processes with great passion and intellect.

*Like Charlie's Angels (each with her own red-wine Charlie) Nancy Figgins (Leonetti Cellar), Annie Camarda (Andrew Will Winery) and Darcey Small (Woodward Canyon) pose for a picture at the annual Auction of Northwest Wines in Seattle.*

**The Wines**

Woodward Canyon's fame has come from toasty, mouth-filling Chardonnay and ripe Cabernet Sauvignon with a hearty backbone of oak. The Roza Bergé and Columbia Valley Chardonnays offer vanilla and tropical fruit and a long complex finish. Cabernets are intensely ripe and fruity. Merlot is ripe and focused, evolving as more vineyards come on line.

Rick Small released a 1993 Special Selection in 1998 that he put on the market for $75. He didn't apologize in his newsletter, but instead compared it with the finest first growth Bordeaux. Red wine fans, the gods are once again sitting in Rick Small's corner. In our tasting of his current releases, the wines were more complex, better structured, long in the finish . . . and they were damned good before! If you were bored with Woodward Canyon wines recently, the time to come back and try them again is now. Write for Rick Small's witty and insightful winery newsletter to keep posted on developments.

# WALLA WALLA ACCOMMODATIONS

## Green Gables Inn

922 Bonsella, Walla Walla 99362 (509)525-5501
This historic mansion has been converted into a pleasant B & B with each room having its own bath. The quiet, tree-lined streets for which Walla Walla is famous are yours for evening or morning strolling. An efficiency unit is available for families.

## Mill Creek Inn

Rt. 4, Box 251, Mill Creek Road, (509) 522-1234
Greg and Vanessa Finch invite guests to stay at their sensitively restored 1900s homestead on the same property as Glen Fiona Winery. Two cottages and a farm house suite are available and lodging includes an expanded continental breakfast.

## Pony Soldier Motor Inn

325 East Main, (509) 529-4360, (800) 634-PONY
This motel complex is just east of downtown Walla Walla and offers outdoor pool, sauna, cable TV, free continental breakfast. Air-conditioned rooms.

## The Marcus Whitman

107 N. 2nd - (509) 525-2200  The historic Marcus Whitman Hotel has been modernized to become one of the nice places to stay in Walla Walla. Once associated with a Black Angus Motor Inn, the hotel portion is now consolidated under one name. Restaurant, pool, air-conditioned rooms.

# WALLA WALLA AREA DINING

## Patit Creek Restaurant

725 E. Dayton Ave., Dayton - (509) 382-2625
Not in Walla Walla, but the finest gourmet dining in the area. A relaxing 40-minute drive through the farmland leads to Bruce and Heather Hiebert's kitschy dining room, decorated with vintage show-biz memorabilia. Fresh regional ingredients are innovatively prepared with superb sauces and a deft touch with entrees. Excellent NW wine list featuring many hard-to-find bottlings. Reservations required on weekends. Tues. - Sat.

## Merchants Limited

21 E. Main - (509) 525-0900  A bright spot in town with delicious baked goods, a broad selection of fine wines and many deli items for the hungry wine lover. Go to Merchants to grab a latte and a cinnamon roll, then watch the world go by from a cafe table out front or from a seat in the mezzanine. Not to be missed if you're around at breakfast time.

## Jacobi's

416 N. 2nd, (509) 525-2677,  A Walla Walla favorite, located in the former Northern Pacific Depot. Pizza and deli fare are the draws.

## The Addition

16 S. Colville, (509) 529-7336 - Another downtown eatery offering a wide variety of cooking styles. Northwest wines dominate the wine list.

## The Iceburg

W. Birch at 9th, Walla Walla  (509) 529-1793
Terrific hamburgers, shakes and fries.

## Alkali Flats Cafe

Highway 12 in Touchet (say "two-she"), 4 miles west of Lowden - Remember the stories you heard about how hard work in the fields creates a ravenous appetite? Well, this is where the local hard workers come to enjoy a satisfying meal! Straight forward breakfasts and lunches served with a smile. No alcohol, no credit cards, lots of friends and food.

# WALLA WALLA ACTIVITIES

## Hot Air Balloon Stampede & Winery Open House

This popular local festival takes place on the first or second weekend in May. Check with one of the local wineries to find out who's open at what times and when the hot air balloons will be flying.

## Pioneer Park

This oasis just east of downtown has 47 acres of shaded play area with a duck pond, kiddie pool and playground. A small aviary displays exotic waterfowl and pheasants. The quiet location is a great venue for morning walks. Division & Alder.

**Lori McKean-Casad & Tony Casad**

## ❖ A RECIPE FROM LORI MCKEAN-CASAD ❖

# Caramelized Walla Walla Onion and Bacon Tart with Northwest Merlot

Makes 1 - 10-inch tart, or 1 - 9-inch pie (serves 6 to 8)
Accompanying wine: Canoe Ridge Vineyard Merlot

### Pastry

1-1/2 cups unbleached flour
1/2 cup butter, chilled and divided into 1/2-inch pieces
1/2 tsp. salt
2-3 Tbs. cold water, as needed

### Filling

| | | | |
|---|---|---|---|
| 3 | pieces bacon, diced | 1/2 | tsp. salt |
| 2 | tsp. reserved bacon grease | 1/4 | tsp. freshly ground black pepper |
| 2 | large Walla Walla sweet onions, sliced | 1/2 | cup crumbled fresh goat cheese |
| 2 | tsp. sugar | 1/2 | cup grated Swiss cheese |
| 3 | eggs | | sour cream |
| 1/2 | cup sour cream | | sprigs of fresh thyme, |
| 1/4 | tsp. white pepper | | optional garnish |

*Lori McKean-Casad, author of the bestselling* Northwest Best Places Cookbook, Pacific Northwest Flavors *and others, brings us her recipe to pair with Canoe Ridge Merlot:*
"*During a visit to the Canoe Ridge Winery in Walla Walla, Washington, I spoke with winemaker John Abbott about his favorite foods to serve with Merlot. We agreed that the sweet earthy flavors of Walla Walla sweet onions are a wonderful match with a rich, fruity Northwest Merlot. Inspired by our talk, I created my own recipe. If you can't locate Walla Walla onions, use other sweet onions, such as Vidalia or Texas Sweets.*"
*Lori's husband Tony Casad is an accomplished chef who develops and promotes NW specialty food products.*

Place the flour, salt and chilled butter in a food processor. Pulse until butter is reduced to pea-size bits. With processor running, add ice water, 1 tablespoon at a time, until mixture comes together to form a stiff dough. Turn out onto a floured surface, knead lightly and form into a pancake, about 1/2-inch thick. Let rest 10 minutes, then roll out to a circle, approximately 11-inches in diameter. Line a 10-inch fluted tart pan with a removable bottom (or a 9-inch pie plate) with the pastry. Turn edges back under the crust and crimp. Chill pastry while preparing filling.

Saute diced bacon in a large, heavy-bottomed skillet, until crisp. Drain bacon on paper towels, reserving 2 teaspoons of bacon grease in the skillet. Stir in the onion slices and sugar and cook over medium high heat, stirring frequently, until onions are dark brown and caramelized, about 15 minutes. Set mixture aside to cool slightly.

In a mixing bowl, whisk eggs lightly. Whisk in sour cream, white pepper, salt and black pepper. Stir in the cheeses.

Preheat oven to 375° F. Spread onion and bacon mixture evenly over the bottom of the pastry. Pour the sour cream mixture over the onions in the prepared pastry shell, smoothing the top. Bake tart for about 30 minutes, or until a knife inserted in the center comes out clean and pastry is golden brown. Serve warm or at room temperature. If desired, garnish each serving with a dollop of sour cream and a sprig of thyme.

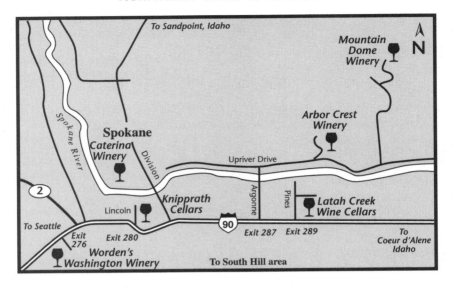

## SPOKANE AREA TOURING

Whether you're traveling to Spokane for the Lilac Festival in May, a golfing vacation on some of the Northwest's finest courses in June, or for some winter skiing at Mount Spokane, you'll find some great wineries to tour.

The wineries vary in age, direction and personality. Dedication to quality winemaking seems to be a common theme, although personal preferences sometimes bend this rule. Utilizing fruit grown in the Columbia Valley, Spokane's wineries don't have local viticultural heritage but they seem content to enjoy the growth of Washington wine and the high quality obtained from Columbia Valley fruit.

Most of the facilities have regular tasting rooms and convenient hours of operation to accommodate visitors. **Arbor Crest Wine Cellars** is located at the historic Cliff House estate a few miles east of downtown. The great view from the mansion and a tour of the grounds should not be missed. You'll find **Caterina Winery** just north of downtown, in the historic Broadview Dairy building. The tasting room and gift shop are great complements to Mike Scott's fine wines. **Latah Creek Wine Cellars** is east of downtown in a Spanish mission style building near the Spokane River.

At **Worden Winery**, the tasting room is located in a log cabin, in a pine forest with nice picnicking on the grounds.

**Knipprath Cellars** is open Friday, Saturday and Sunday in a converted storefront in downtown Spokane. The owners are often on hand to pour their current releases. Open by appointment in the foothills southwest of Mount Spokane is **Mountain Dome Winery** specializing in sparkling wine. If you love French Champagne you should definitely call Michael and Patricia Manz for an appointment to see their remarkable facility.

Outside of town, **China Bend Vineyards** practices organic farming near Kettle Falls and offers their latest releases for sale at their tasting room.

Another local field trip might be Northwest to Sand Point, Idaho where you can visit **Pend Orielle Winery**. Check the Idaho wineries section for information on this new venture.

*Arbor Crest Cliff House above the Spokane River.*

# Arbor Crest Wine Cellars

N. 4705 Fruithill Rd.
Spokane, WA 99207
(509) 927-9463
FAX (509) 927-0574

**Tasting Room Hours:** Daily, Noon - 5 PM
Must be 21 years or older to enter the estate.

**Owners:** David and Harold Mielke
**Winemaker:** Mikhail Brunshteyn
**First Year:** 1982
**Winery Capacity:** 150,000 Gallons

**Winery History**

Owners David and Harold Mielke began Arbor Crest Winery as a brotherly project and a diversification from their family's fruit packing business. Their success has been complete with award-winning varietals being produced annually since the first harvest in 1982. The restoration of Arbor Crest Estate into a visitor facility is complete and the historic site is open daily for visits and wine tasting. The actual winemaking currently takes place at another Spokane location.

**A visit to Arbor Crest**

The Arbor Crest Estate is a remarkable collection of structures built in 1924 by Royal N. Riblet, a wealthy Spokane businessman. His impressive stone mansion above the Spokane River is accompanied by a gazebo and landscaped grounds that make a wonderful afternoon's exploration by interested wine lovers. Marmots climb the rocky cliff and chatter at intruders and the dozens of personal touches left by Royal Riblet are intriguing and, at times, mystifying. Wine tasting is offered in the lower level of the mansion where several of Arbor Crest's releases may be sampled. Visitors must be 21-years or older due to the dangerous cliffs that are, in places, unfenced.

**The Wines**

Producing a wide selection of varietals, Arbor Crest has developed a consistent style of high quality wines. Whites include crisp and aromatic Sauvignon Blanc, Semillon and a blend named Cameo Reserve Grand Cepage that are delightful seafood wines. Toasty Chardonnay and Reserve Chardonnay are joined on the sweeter side by Muscat Canelli, Johannisberg Riesling, Late Harvest Riesling and Jardin des Fleurs blush. Red wine lovers enjoy ripe and fruity Cabernet-Merlot, Merlot and Cabernet Franc, as well as Cameo Reserve Merlot and Cabernet Sauvignon.

# Caterina Winery

905 N. Washington
Spokane, WA 99201
(509) 328-5069, FAX (509) 325-7324
**Email:** mscott@caterina.com

**Tasting Room Hours:** Daily, Noon to 5 PM

**Owner:** The Caterina Trust
**Winemaker:** Michael Scott
**First Year:** 1993
**Winery Capacity:** 22,000 Gallons

**Winery History**

Beginning life as the Steven Thomas Livingstone winery up the street on Division, Caterina Winery is now operated by Livingstone cellarmaster and manager Michael Scott. Purchase of the winery equipment and wine inventory was made possible through local investors with the facility being moved to the Broadview Dairy Building near the

*Continued on next page.*

*Mike Scott at Caterina Winery in Spokane.*

Spokane Riverfront Park. This historic site was shared with a milk processing plant and the Broadview Dairy Museum until 1998. Caterina Winery occupies the lower level of the building with the entrance on the south side facing Cavanaugh's Inn at the Park. The remainder of the building is now vacant with development plans under discussion.

### A visit to Caterina Winery

The decor of the Caterina tasting room in an Italianate style serves the romantic history of the current owners. It is indeed a charming space for enjoying the wine tasting and for browsin the wide assortment of unique gifts. The location of the winery is within walking distance of Riverfront Park (just up Washington Street across the Spokane River) and just across the street from Cavanaugh's Inn at the Park. This well-appointed hotel is a superb headquarters for out-of-town wine tourists to explore Spokane.

### The Wines

Mike Scott continues to excel in his winemaking at Caterina. Chardonnay and Reserve Chardonnay each offer qualities of ripe tropical fruit and barrel fermentation with the Reserve taking on more of the buttery, toasty quality. A seafood-friendly Sauvignon Blanc is a runaway bestseller across the country for its crisp and appealing style. Merlot and Cabernet Sauvignon are rich and full-bodied wines that have been rewarded with acclaim from both consumers and wine critics. A delicious Cabernet Rosé was produced in 1997 to rave reviews from Caterina's hometown fans in Spokane. Mike Scott looks forward to ongoing success with fruit from the Wahluke Slope.

# China Bend Vineyard

3596 Northport Flat Creek Rd.
Kettle Falls, WA 99141
(509) 732-6123
**Web:**
www.chinabend.com

**Tasting Room Hours:** Daily 11 AM to 5 PM or by appointment.

**Owner/Winemaker:** Bart Alexander
**First Year:** 1995
**Winery Capacity:** 3,500 Gallons

About 90 miles northwest of Spokane along the northern reaches of the Columbia River, Bart Alexander and his partners operate an organic vineyard and organic vegetable farm. Making organic, unsulfited wines was the next step and these are released under the China Bend Vineyard label. Proprietary wines include Lake Roosevelt Red, Victory Red and Victory White. A varietal Lemberger is also produced.

The location is off the beaten track in a very beautiful, but unvisited, part of Washington State, call for directions.

# Knipprath Cellars

163 S. Lincoln St.
Spokane, WA 99201
(509) 624-9132
**Email:** winemaker@
knipprath-cellars.com
**Web:** www.knipprath-cellars.com

**Tasting Room Hours:** Daily, 11:30 AM to 6 PM Monday through Saturday; Noon to 5 PM on Sunday.

**Owners:** Henning and Patricia Knipprath
**Winemaker:** Henning Knipprath
**First Year:** 1991
**Winery Capacity:** 10,000 Gallons

### Winery History

"Knipprath Cellars was started in 1991 by a small circle of friends and is dedicated to producing the finest hand-crafted wines available." An Air Force pilot based at nearby Fairchild AFB, Henning Knipprath is the winemaker for the group and his name is carried on the winery label. The small winery operation is currently located in the "future downtown arts and entertainment district" of Spokane, near the WWP Steam Plant!

### A visit to Knipprath Cellars

Knipprath (pronounced "nip rath") Cellars offers special tastings and visits to the winery on weekends or by appointment. Henning Knipprath or his friends or partners, are your hosts in the tasting room. Tours of the small production facility are offered if you have an interest.

### The Wines

Current releases from Knipprath include Chardonnay, Fume Blanc, Gewurztraminer, Muscat Blanc, White Riesling in the white category. Red wines include Pinot Noir, Moonstruck Merlot, Roswell Red (Lemberger) and Positron Port. Must be the Air Force humor coming through!

# Latah Creek Wine Cellars

E. 13030 Indiana
Spokane, WA 99216
(509) 926-0164
FAX (509) 926-0710

**Tasting Room Hours:** Daily, 9 AM to 5 PM

**Owner & Winemaker:** Mike Conway
**First Year:** 1982
**Winery Capacity:** 35,000 Gallons

### Winery History

A California wine veteran, Mike Conway left his assistant winemaker's job at Parducci to come north and make wine for Jack Worden at Worden's Washington Winery. Two years later in 1982 he started his own enterprise in partnership with Mike Hogue. Today, according to the original plan, he is now sole proprietor of the winery.

### A visit to Latah Creek Wine Cellars

Styled after 'Spanish Mission' architecture, the winery is just off Interstate 90 east of Spokane on Indiana Road. Latah Creek's tasting room is open year 'round pouring samples of the broad range of wines produced

here. Also on display in the tasting room is a collection of artwork by Yakima wildlife artist, Floyd Broadbent. Each vintage a different painting is featured on the Latah Creek label. The winery's well-stocked gift shop offers all manner of wine-related items for sale.

### The Wines

Latah Creek produces a delicious Chenin Blanc, Riesling and other wines but the Chardonnay produced by Mike Conway is consistently well balanced and enjoyable. Also try the powerful Merlot and Cabernet Sauvignon and unique Maywine.

# Mountain Dome Winery

16315 E. Temple Rd.
Spokane, WA 99207
(509) 928-BRUT
(928-2788)
**Web:** www.
mountaindome.com

**Tasting Room Hours:** By appointment

**Owners:** Michael and Patricia Manz
**Winemaker:** Michael Manz
**First Year:** 1984
**Winery Capacity:** 6,000 Gallons

### Winery History

Up in the foothills of Mount Spokane in a beautiful forest of conifers is the dome-shaped home of Dr. Michael Manz and his family. Nearby, the winery-named-after-the-home is now completed and is equipped with the most modern gear for producing methode champenoise sparkling wine. Dr. Manz knows what he likes and it's not André extra dry from California. His favorite sparklers include top of the line vintage and non-vintage brut Champagnes from France and his goal is to make wines of that quality. The winery building has recently been expanded to increase production.

### A visit to Mountain Dome Winery

The winery is open by appointment to those keen on taking a look at the sparkling wine operation. You may write to be included on the Mountain Dome mailing list.

*Continued on next page.*

**The Wines of Mountain Dome Winery**

Production of sparkling wine at Mountain Dome has been increasing steadily since the first small lots were laid down 'sur lie' in 1984. The grape crush in 1988 was 16 tons - 10 tons more than in 1987. Crush in 1992 was 45 tons.

The first release took place in October of 1992 with Mountain Dome's Washington State Brut from the 1988 vintage. A delightful wine with aromas of toast and pear drops that showed the finesse and complexity of the finest sparkling wines. Later releases have been equally delicious with a Brut and Brut Rosé offered and other older cuvees yet to be released. *Seattle Times* wine columnist Tom Stockley dubbed the Mountain Dome sparklers "the best Northwest sparkling wine" and I could certainly make a case for agreeing with him.

Search these wines out in local area wine shops or call the winery to inquire about availability in your locale.

# Worden's Washington Winery

7217 W. 45th
Spokane, WA 99204
(509) 455-7835

**Owner:** Jack Worden
**Winemaker:** Paul Vandenburg
**First Year:** 1980
**Winery Capacity:** 50,000 Gallons
**Tasting Room Hours:** Daily, Noon to 5 PM

**Winery History**

The first winery to open its doors in Spokane and one of the first to begin serious winemaking in Washington, Worden's has continued to produce quality wines from fruit grown in the Columbia Valley.

**A visit to Worden's Winery**

Worden's Washington Winery is nestled in a forest of pine trees on the western outskirts of Spokane. The A-frame cabin that serves as tasting room seems an appropriate structure in

*Worden Winery tasting room west of Spokane, Washington.*

the quiet, woodsy setting quite remarkably close to Interstate 90. This popular stopping place is great for picnicking and relaxing under the Ponderosa pines.

**The Wines**

An unusual approach to red wine making (until recent years!) was the 50/50 blending of Worden's Cabernet/Merlot. The softening effect of the Merlot makes the wine drinkable at a younger age and provides pleasant drinking for those with less of a 'red wine palate'. Chardonnay, Gewurztraminer, Riesling and Chenin Blanc are also made.

# SPOKANE AREA ACCOMMODATIONS

## Cavanaugh's Inn at the Park

W 303 North River Dr. - 800-THE-INNS, (509) 326-8000   New hotel downtown with all the luxury amenities you can ask for. The five-story atrium lobby offers two restaurants and lounges while three heated pools, and fitness center keep you physically active. Suites with fireplaces, view rooms and rooms with balconies. $69 and up.

## Waverly Place

709 W. Waverly Pl. off Division - (509) 328-1856 Relaxation in a quiet neighborhood is the name of the game at this north-of-downtown bed and breakfast. Adjacent to a charming park, guests may take their morning stroll under shady trees with promise of a delicious breakfast to follow.

## Sheraton Spokane

322 N. Spokane Falls Court, 99220  (509) 455-9600  On the river and visible from much of downtown, this is another of Spokane's fine hotels. The atrium pool and spacious rooms and suites are but two of the quality features. Moderately priced considering the amenities.

# SPOKANE AREA DINING

## Luna

5620 S. Perry, (509) 448-2383  William and Marcia Bond operate this modest restaurant on Spokane's South Hill. A variety of cuisines are represented on the frequently changing menu and the wine list is exceptional. Open for lunch, dinner and, on weekends, breakfast. Highly rated by local winemakers.

## Patsy Clark's

2208 W. Second Ave. - (509) 838-8300  A luxuriously restored mansion with unique dining rooms restored to their original grace and charm. The menu changes seasonally. Extensive wine list with many Northwest selections.

## Cafe 510

510 S. Freya - (509) 533-0064  Michael Waliser has taken over the former Anaconda Grill and features upscale Mediterranean and Italian food. The only catch is that you bring your wine along with you after you stop by the local Washington liquor store for a $10 banquet permit. It's worth the trouble and you can have any wine you want! Closed Sundays.

## Fugazzi

1 North Post St. - (509) 624-1133  A popular downtown spot for selected specialties that vary with the seasons and the whim of the chef. Fresh bread from the once-in-house bakery is also a draw.

## Milford's Fish House and Oyster Bar

719 N. Monroe  (509) 326-7251  A Spokane institution for many years, this is the choice for fine seafood from NW waters. The busy Oyster Bar offers a place to meet new people in a convivial, yet civilized, atmosphere. A classy place for dinner with a bit of Spokane history for the tourists and locals alike.

# Northwest Microbrews

## Birkebiner Brewpub

35 W. Main, Spokane (509) 458-0854. Stop by the local microbrewery for a pint and some pub grub.

## Hale's Ales

5624 E. Commerce St., Spokane (509) 534-7553. This production facility for Hale's is east of town (off Trent Ave.) and offers informal tours and tasting only.

# SPOKANE AREA ACTIVITIES

## Riverfront Park

This decade-old world's fair site has some fancy stuff for kids to do and attractions for Mom and Dad too.

## Manito Park

South of I-90 off Grand, this park includes various gardens and a conservatory, not tremendously interesting for younger children but an enjoyable outing nonetheless.

## Spokane Lilac Festival

With the coming of spring comes the blooming of Spokane's namesake flower. Third week in May. Winery events take place at this time.

## Mirabeau Park and Walk in the Wild Zoo

N. Pines & E. Euclid - (509) 924-7220  A unique park and zoo for appreciation of animals in natural habitats. Near Latah Creek Winery.

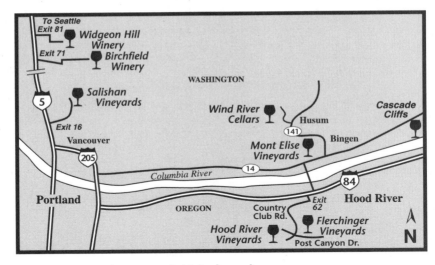

## SW Washington
## & Columbia Gorge Wine Touring

The pastoral farmlands of Southwest Washington and the magnificence of the Columbia River Gorge are the non-enological highlights of touring this area. The icing on the cake is the collection of fine wineries found along the I-5 corridor and in the gorge.

The I-5 traveller can take a break from the rush of the freeway to stop and visit three different wineries between Olympia and Vancouver. Heading south, **Widgeon Hill Winery** is 4 miles east of the freeway near Centralia. Ten miles further on, take exit 71 to visit **Birchfield Winery** in Onalaska. Joan and Lincoln Wolverton are the proprietors at **Salishan Vineyards** just northeast of the town of LaCenter. The winery and the Wolverton's home are at the edge of the vineyard with views of the lush Lewis River Valley. The winery is open Saturdays, 1 - 5 PM, summer and fall.

To make the connection to the Gorge Highway follow the signs to Interstate 205 which bypasses the congestion of the Portland area. Shortly after crossing the Columbia River you'll see signs for Hood River and The Dalles pointing you to I-84.

The Columbia Gorge Highway (I-84) was built in the 1920s and since has provided visitors unequalled panoramas of geologic splendor. The scenic highway bypass is worth the extra driving time for first time visitors to get a peek at the waterfalls and beautiful canyons that line the Oregon side of the Gorge.

Hood River offers two winery stops for traveling wine lovers. Follow Country Club road up and around a few well-marked turns to **Hood River Vineyards**. **Flerchinger Vineyards** is a newer operation located nearby on Post Canyon Drive. Both wineries are open 11 AM to 5 PM daily, except winter months.

Across the Hood River Bridge to Washington you may visit **Mont Elise Vineyards** winery and tasting room in downtown Bingen. A drive up Highway 141 through White Salmon to Husum is the first half of a scenic adventure to the **Wind River Cellars** (formerly Charles Hooper Winery). The second half is the quiet forest drive up the hill to the winery. You'll enjoy the views of Mount Hood from the winery and vineyard.

Travelling east on Highway 14 leads to **Cascade Cliffs** winery near Wishram. Be sure to visit the nearby Maryhill Museum and Stonehenge replica.

## Birchfield Winery

921-B Middle Fork Road
Onalaska, WA 98570
(360) 978-5224
FAX (360) 978-5225

**Tasting Room Hours:**
Daily, 10 AM to 2 PM,
August, September and October

**First Year:** 1995

A small, family-owned winery purchasing grapes from Eastern Washington vineyards and producing Cabernet Sauvignon, Merlot, Lemberger, Pinot Noir, Chardonnay and Semillon. To find the tasting room, take exit 71 from I-5 and travel east 2 miles to the Jackson Highway. Turn left and follow north to Middle Fork Road where you turn right and travel 3.5 miles to the winery on your left.

Wines tasted have been cleanly made and exhibit ripe fruit and toasty oak nuances.

## Cascade Cliffs Winery

8866 Highway 14
P.O. Box 14
Wishram, WA 98673
(509) 767-1100

**Tasting Room Hours:** Weekends, Apr. - Oct., 11 AM to 5 PM, also most summer weekdays

**Owner/Winemaker:** Bob Lorkowski
**First Year:** 1985

**Winery History**

Across the highway, towering basalt cliffs rise 400 feet above Columbia Cliffs Vineyard giving the name to both vineyard and winery. Kenn and Linda Adcock planted the vineyard and built the small winery in 1985. Kenn is semi-retired from the label business and enjoys tending the vineyard and making the wine. His love for the area includes touring the surrounding countryside on his motorcycle. At press time, the winery was sold to Bob Lorkowski an experienced Northwest winemaker who was looking for his own venue.

**A visit to Columbia Cliffs**

Located near the famous Maryhill Museum (home of several Rodin sculptures and other rare original art) and near the replica of Stonehenge, Columbia Cliffs offers a unique micro-region for the study of several academic disciplines. The grandeur of the Columbia Gorge stimulates an interest in geology, as well. Wind surfers come from many nearby river sites to taste wine and procure supplies for their post-surfing relaxation.

**The Wines**

A wide selection of wines including Merlot, Petit Sirah, Pinot Noir, Nebbiolo, Cabernet Sauvignon, Muscat of Alexandria and Sauvignon Blanc are produced. Red wines are aged in several types of oak and are rich and flavorful. With the new ownership the wines may take a new direction.

## Flerchinger Vineyards

4200 Post Canyon Dr.
Hood River, OR 97031
(541) 386-2882
(541) 326-2023

**Tasting Room Hours:**
Daily, 11 AM to 5 PM

**Owners:** Flerchinger Family
**Winemaker:** Joe Flerchinger
**First Year:** 1994
**Winery Capacity:** 5,500 Gallons

**Winery History**

The Flerchinger family operates one of Oregon's newest wine operations in the scenic Hood River Valley. Enjoy your picnic on the winery grounds and taste the winery's Chardonnay, Dry Riesling, White Riesling, Blush, Cabernet Sauvignon and Merlot. The winery has a 6-acre vineyard nearby where they grow Riesling and Chardonnay. Follow Country Club Road 1.4 miles up the valley from exit 62 off I-84. Turn left on Post Canyon Drive.

# Hood River Vineyards

4693 Westwood Drive
Hood River, OR 97031
(541) 386-3772
FAX (541) 386-5880

**Tasting Room Hours:**
Daily, 11 PM to 5 PM,
March to November. Closed Dec. thru Feb.

**Owners:** Bernie and Anne Lurch
**First Year:** 1981
**Winery Capacity:** 10,000 Gallons

### Winery History

Orchardist and Hood River businessman Cliff Blanchette began a second career growing grapes in the hills above the Columbia River in the late 1970s and bonded his winery in 1981. The winery and tasting room provided employment for several family members during the 1980s. The winery was sold in 1993 and the new owners have continued to produce the same selection of wine that established HRV's fine reputation.

### A visit to Hood River Vineyards

Hood River Vineyards winery with the tremendous view atop the hill is open April through the end of November welcoming wine lovers for tasting or tours 7 days a week. Bring your lunch to enjoy a picnic under the pine trees next to the winery. Take exit 62 from I-84, turn right on Country Club Road, follow to Post Canyon Drive. Turn right on Post Canyon and proceed .8 miles to a right turn up the hill past the vineyard to the winery.

### The Wines

Hood River Vineyard wines come from grapes grown in both Oregon and Washington. Red wines have always been successful here with Merlot, Cabernet Sauvignon and Pinot Noir being very popular. A Zinfandel wine crafted from local grapes is a favorite for lovers of hearty reds with the spicy character that works so well with hearty foods. Also, small amounts of Petite Syrah and Nebbiolo are offered. Chardonnay and White Riesling are available for whites.

# Mont Elise Vineyards

315 West Steuben
Bingen, WA 98605
(509) 493-3001

**Tasting Room Hours:**
Daily, 11:30 AM
to 5 PM

**Owners:** The Charles Henderson Family
**Winemaker:** Chuck Henderson, Jr.
**First Year:** 1975
**Winery Capacity:** 18,000 Gallons

### Winery History

Chuck Henderson, Sr. is one of the pioneers of fruit production along the Columbia Gorge. His efforts with Walter Clore in identifying local microclimates for winegrapes led others to plant vitis vinifera on nearby slopes. The original winery was named Bingen Wine Cellars but later changed to honor Chuck's daughter, Elise. His son, Chuck Jr., studied winemaking at U.C. Davis and has handled winemaking duties recently.

### A visit to Mont Elise Vineyards

Dressed up Bavarian style, the town of Bingen on the Washington side of the Columbia Gorge plays up its German-immigrant heritage to attract the business of sightseers traveling through the area. The winery tasting room offers a picture-window view into the winery operation below. Visitors can often see some of the winemaking operations taking place or at least inspect the winery equipment while sampling a selection of Mont Elise wines.

### The Wines

Mont Elise Vineyards has long been hailed as one of the foremost producers of Northwest Gewurztraminer. The crisp, yet fruity style is not hard and tannic like Alsatian Gewurz, but offers more than just a simple sipping wine. Other varietals are well made, including the red wines Gamay Beaujolais and Pinot Noir.

The Hendersons have experimented with sparkling wine production but the wine has so far only been available at the winery.

## Salishan Vineyards

35011 North Fork Ave.
La Center, WA 98629
(360) 263-2713
FAX (360) 263-3675

**Tasting Room Hours:**
May - Dec., Saturdays,
1 PM to 5 PM, tours by
appointment.

*Salishan*
1990
Washington
Pinot Noir
ALCOHOL BY VOLUME 12%

**Owners:** Lincoln and Joan Wolverton
**Winemaker:** Joan Wolverton
**First Year:** 1977
**Winery Capacity:** 8,000 Gallons

*Joan Wolverton, winemaker at Salishan Vineyards.*

**Winery History**

Salishan is one of the original success stories for Northwest "dreams become reality" wineries. The vineyard near the tiny farming community of La Center, was begun in 1971 with the intention of specializing in Pinot Noir and even the earliest efforts at this varietal won great praise. Today, in addition to well-received Pinot Noir, their Chardonnay and Cabernet get raves from consumers and wine judges alike.

**A visit to Salishan Vineyards**

Just five minutes from I-5 (exit 16 to La Center, then north on Aspen St. and N. Fork Rd.) Salishan Vineyards is a convenient stop during the monotonous drive from Seattle to Portland. Summer Saturday afternoons find winemaker Joan Wolverton dispensing not only award-winning wines but also wine information and insights spiced with her sense of humor. A stop not to be missed!

**The Wines**

Salishan's early reputation came from the fine quality Pinot Noir harvested from their vineyard at the winery. The microclimate is a proven one for this varietal with neighboring vineyards providing grapes for Columbia Winery's Pinot and also other smaller producers.

## Widgeon Hill Winery

121 Widgeon Hill Rd.
Chehalis, WA 98532
(360) 758-0407 or
(360) 736-2815
**Email:**
mills@localaccess.com

**Tasting Room Hours:** Saturday and Sunday, Noon to 5 PM

**Owners:** Joel & Dee Mills
**Winemaker:** Joel Mills
**First Year:** 1996
**Winery Capacity:** 1,100

From grapes purchased in the Yakima Valley Joel Mills produces Cabernet Sauvignon, Merlot, Cabernet Franc, Chardonnay and Chenin Blanc. The wines are handcrafted and oak aged. Their label features fanciful wine country art by local artist of renown, Dixie Rogerson.

To visit the tasting room, take exit 81 from I-5 and follow Mellen Street east to Gold St. Turn right and proceed to Summa St. Turn left and follow Summa as it becomes Salzer Valley Road, turn right on Centralia Alpha Road and right again on Widgeon Hill Road. The winery is about 4 miles east of Interstate 5.

# NORTHWEST WINES & WINERIES

## Wind River Cellars

P. O. Box 215
196 Spring Creek Rd.
Husum, WA 98623
(509) 493-2324
(509) 493-2887
**Email:**
windriverwines@gorge.net

**Tasting Room Hours:** Daily
11 AM to 5 PM

**Owners:** Kris & Joel
Goodwillie
**Winemaker:** Joel Goodwillie
**First Year:** 1985
**Winery Capacity:** 5,000 Gallons

**Winery History**

While living in France, England and
Germany for more than 20 years, Charles and
Beverlee Hooper developed an interest in wine
and viticulture. The dream of planting their
own vineyard and founding a winery began to
grow. With the help of their daughters Kim
and Janet, son Chris and many friends, the first
grapes were planted in 1979 overlooking the
Columbia Gorge. With the opening of the
Charles Hooper Family Winery in 1985, the
dream became a reality.

In 1997, the Goodwillies purchased the
winery and changed the name to Wind River
Cellars. Their focus is less Germanic offering
Chardonnay and Cabernet as well as hard
cider. This energetic couple plans lots of
activities to keep the winery hoppin'.

**A visit to Wind River Cellars**

The alpine-like setting of the property is
complemented by panoramic views of the
Gorge and of Mount Hood in the distance. As
you walk through the terraced vineyard, you
can hear the wind in the nearby fir trees and
imagine yourself in the Mosel or Rheingau. A
great site for picnics, you can find the winery
by following Spring Creek Rd. from Husum.

**The Wines**

The wines made at Hooper Family Winery
showed the original owners passion for
Germanic wines. The Goodwillies are
planning to offer additional varieties like
Chardonnay and Cabernet Sauvignon.

## COLUMBIA GORGE ACCOMMODATIONS

### Columbia Gorge Hotel

4000 Westcliff Drive, Hood River, OR 97031
(541) 386-5566, out of state: 1-800-345-1921
This famous hotel hosted famous personalities
from the 1920s upon completion by timber
baron Simon Benson. The hotel today offers
quiet elegance and a magnificent view of the
Gorge. The "World Famous Farm Breakfast" is
included for guests. Expensive

### Vagabond Lodge

4070 Westcliff Dr., Hood River, OR 97031 (541)
386-2992 Right next door to the CGH and half
the price! Some of the view rooms rival the
best of their famous neighbor.

### Lakecliff Estate

3820 Westcliff Dr., Hood River, OR 97031, (541)
386-7000 In this city of many enjoyable B & Bs,
this one stands out for its history, location and
view of the latest action to come down the
Gorge. Friendly hosts, delicious breakfast,
varied accommodations to suit all tastes.

### Orchard Hill Inn

Rt. 2, Box 130 - Oak Ridge Road, White
Salmon, WA 98672 (509) 493-3024 Up in the
hills across the valley from Charles Hooper
Winery, this secluded bed and breakfast is
nestled along the White Salmon River. Three
rooms are available in the main house or a
separate 8-bed bunkhouse.

### Skamania Lodge

Stevenson, Washington (800) 221-7117, or (509)
427-7700 From the folks who brought you
Salishan and The Salish comes the spectacular
Skamania Lodge tucked into the woods above
the Columbia Gorge. Adjacent to the fantastic
Columbia Gorge Interpretive Center, this
complex also features an outstanding golf
course. The restaurant is fabulous — great
wine list!

# COLUMBIA GORGE DINING

## Stone Hedge Inn

3405 Cascade Drive, Hood River (541) 386-3940 The food and service at this elegant restaurant wins raves from locals and visitors alike. Well-prepared seafood and meats are complemented by local fresh produce and a NW/Continental cooking style. Beautiful grounds and a nice collection of wines.

## Mesquitery

1219 12th St., Hood River (541) 386-2002 Check out the mesquite grill for superb steak, seafood and other specialties. Non-smoking dining room, microbrews and wine.

## Ole's Supper Club

2620 W. 2nd St., The Dalles (541) 296-6708 With a name like this you might not stop by unless you knew that was one of the best places in the Northwest to capture a superb bottle of wine and enjoy it with straightforward preparations of prime rib, seafood, game and other seasonal entrees. The secret to the wine selection is the attached wine shop.

# COLUMBIA GORGE AREA MICROBREWS & BREWPUBS

## Full Sail Brewing Company

506 Columbia St., Hood River (541) 386-2281. The windsurfing craze and microbrewing mania swept into Hood River virtually at the same moment. Full Sail Brewing began operation in 1987 and continues to grow each year. The WhiteCap Pub offers the beer lover views of the brewing operation on one side of the room and views of the windsurfing action on the river from the other side. Step out on the view deck to quaff in the warm summer sunshine. Full Sail Amber Ale is one of the Northwest's best selling craft beers, available in bottle or on draught. Beer fans will also want to try Full Sail Pilsner, WasSail Winter Ale, Brown Ale, Red Ale and IPA. Or perhaps a pint of Top Sail Porter, Springbock, Mercator Doppelbok, Oktoberfest or Old Boardhead Barleywine.

## Big Horse Brew Pub

115 State St., Hood River (541) 386-4411 - A jumping brew pub in downtown Hood River featuring everything from Pale Rider IPA to Dark Horse Dunkel Weizen. Open for lunch and dinner on weekends, dinner only Mon. - Thurs. Live music, sports bar, many house-brewed styles. Nine beers on tap and two of the waitstaff do the tap dance.

## Mt. Hood Brewing Company

87304 E. Government Camp Lp. (541) 272-3724. Drive up to Mount Hood on Highway 26 to enjoy a day of skiing in winter, or a day of hiking in the spring and summer. Then follow your nose to the Mt. Hood Brew Pub following the aroma of fresh-baked pizza, chicken and steak. Brews include the strong Ice Axe IPA, a less potent Pinnacle Extra Special Bitter, Hogsback Oatmeal Stout and Cloud Cap Amber.

# COLUMBIA GORGE ACTIVITIES

## Bonneville Dam

Cascade Locks, OR Come and see where electricity is made. Kids marvel at the size of the dam and the turbines in the power house. In the late summer you can watch salmon jumping up the fish ladder to reach their spawning grounds. A small park in Cascade Locks is great for picnicking.

## Maryhill Museum

Maryhill, WA Sam Hill, son-in-law of James J. Hill, built this mansion for his wife, but it's now a fantastic, if lonely, art museum. A large

collection of Rodin sculptures, a museum of local indian artifacts, a large chess set collection, even a replica of Stonehenge (down the road a few miles) hold fascination for children of all ages. Picnicking outside.

## Columbia Gorge Interpretive Center

Stevenson, Washington This new 23,000 square foot, $10.5 million museum opened in 1995 featuring cultural and natural history exhibits which highlight the development of the Columbia River and document the first inhabitants of the Gorge and later residents.

# FAMOUS QUOTATIONS ABOUT WINE

Fill every beaker up, my men,
pour forth the cheering wine,
There's life and strength in every drop,-
thanksgiving to the vine!
*Albert Gorton Greene, Baron's Last Banquet*

When wild with much thought,
'tis to wine I fly, to sober me.
*Herman Melville, Mardi*

Wine is the mirror of the mind.
*John Lyly*

No nation is drunken where wine is cheap;
and none sober where the dearness of wine
substitutes ardent spirits as the common beverage.
*Thomas Jefferson*

Wine is proof that God loves us
and wants us to be happy.
*Benjamin Franklin*

A man will be eloquent if you give him good wine.
*Ralph Waldo Emerson*

I wonder often what vintners buy
Half so precious as the stuff they sell.
*Edward Fitzgerald, The Rubaiyat of Omar Khayyam*

Let us have wine and women, mirth and laughter,
Sermons and soda water the day after.
*Lord Byron, Don Juan*

This wine should be eaten, it is too good to be drunk.
*Jonathan Swift*

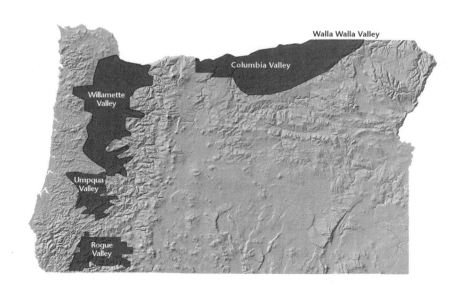

# Oregon
# Wine Touring

# NORTHWEST WINES & WINERIES

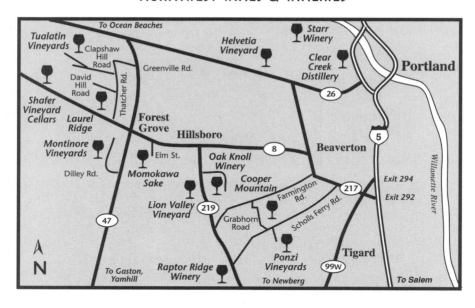

## PORTLAND AREA AND WASHINGTON COUNTY TOURING

Portland, the City of Roses, is a beautiful urban environment where the citizens care very much about livability and style. The surrounding bedroom communities of Beaverton, Hillsboro and Forest Grove offer a mix of residential and farm usage with wineries one of the more recent iterations of the latter.

In Northwest Portland, **Clear Creek Distillery**, regionally famous maker of eau de vie (and now a single malt Scotch!) is open by appointment. A few miles west the former Starr & Brown winery is now Brown-less and has reverted to the name **Starr Winery**. It's not open for visitors. On Broadway not far from Lloyd Center, **Oregon Wines on Broadway** is now a satellite tasting room for St. Innocent

A few minutes south of Washington Square in Beaverton, **Ponzi Vineyards** welcomes visitors on weekends from Noon to 5 PM and weekdays from 10 AM to 5 PM. Their picnic area is a shady summer retreat for snacking and wine sipping. Just northwest of Ponzi, **Cooper Mountain Vineyards** winery is open Friday through Sunday from Noon to 5 PM.

**Oak Knoll Winery** is a few miles further west and is open daily from Noon to 5 PM.

Nearby, the new **Lion Valley Vineyards** is open weekends for tasting and sales.

Four wineries (and one sake producer!) are open to the public near Forest Grove. **Tualatin Vineyards** is open weekends at their location in the picturesque farmland north of town. **Shafer Vineyard Cellars** is also open on weekends just down the road in Gales Creek. Their shady veranda is just the spot for a picnic. The historic site of **Laurel Ridge Winery** on David Hill Road lays claim to being one of Oregon's oldest wine producers. The winery is open daily from Noon to 5 PM. **Montinore Vineyards**, southwest of town on Dilley Road, welcomes wine lovers in their visitor center daily, from Noon to 5 PM.

**Momokawa Sake** is open for tasting and sales of their unique products just off the Tualatin Valley Highway. This is a not-to-be-missed learning experience for wine lovers.

Some Portland-area wineries have no tasting facilities or choose to be open by appointment only. **Antica Terra**, **Helvetia Vineyards**, **Nicholas Rolin**, **Raptor Ridge** and **Andrew Rich** can be contacted by mail or phone to inquire about a visit.

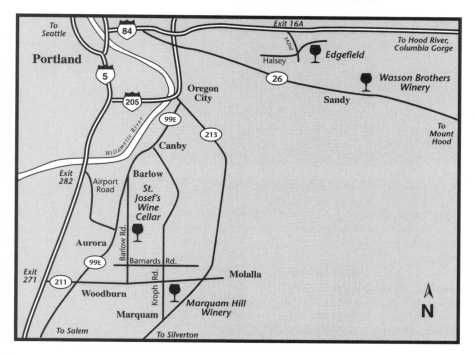

## EAST PORTLAND AND CLACKAMAS COUNTY TOURING

The Clackamas County area, east and southeast of Portland, has a few wineries tucked away for wine lovers to visit on a weekend jaunt from the Rose City. This area of Oregon has many different faces, those of agriculture sometimes take a back seat to developments of condominiums, but take heart, all the wineries here are doing well!

In this age of recycling, the McMenamins (of brewpub fame) reclaimed the local poor farm and created **Edgefield**, a unique collection of restored buildings that include a lodge (like a B & B), theater, pub, restaurant and winery. Almost to Troutdale off the Wood Village exit from Interstate 84.

**Wasson Brothers Winery** in Sandy, near Mount Hood, is on the route of skiers and hikers to and from the mountain. Grape wines as well as fruit and berry wines are the draw. Look for the storefront winery on Highway 26.

Joe and Kirk Fleischmann of **St. Josef's Wine Cellar** in Canby make a very nice Zinfandel from grapes purchased near The Dalles. Chardonnay and Pinot Noir are also available as well as Gewurztraminer and Riesling. The winery offers picnic tables for your enjoyment out by the lake and vineyard.

Not far from St. Josef's, **Marquam Hill Vineyards** offers a similar rural experience with vineyard, lake and expansive picnic area that is available for receptions, reunions and weddings.

# Adams Vineyard Winery

**Winemaker:**
Lynn Penner-Ash
**First Year:** 1981

### Winery History

Portlanders Peter and Carol Adams bonded Adams Vineyard Winery in 1981. This solidified the family's commitment to the making of fine wine in the Pacific Northwest, since they owned a vineyard in the Chehalem Mountains near Newberg. In 1994 the Adams Vineyard brand was acquired by Paul Hart of Rex Hill Winery. The former Adams facility in NW Portland is now closed.

### The Wines

Rex Hill winemaker Lynn Penner-Ash carries on the Adams Vineyard label by producing the wines at Rex Hill. Grapes from the Adams Vineyard are used to produce a Pinot Noir and Chardonnay (blended with wines from other vineyard sources).

# Antica Terra

6120 NE 22nd Ave.
Portland, OR 97211

**Owners/Winemakers:**
Marc Peters, Marty Weber
**First Year:** 1996

### Winery History

Two partners from the east purchased a 28-acre parcel of land in the Amity Hills in the late 1980s, intent on discovering the joys of wine growing in Oregon. In 1990, densely-spaced vineyard planting was begun with a variety of Pinot Noir clones. "The vineyard sits on a gently sloping hillside of well-drained soil underlain by sandstone and siltstone formed from old alluvium - *la antica terra*." Yields on the vineyard are kept low to develop concentrated flavors. There is currently no winery facility, the wine is made at an existing winery.

### The Wines

Although experimental lots of Pinot Noir were made in 1994 and 1995, the first commercial vintage for Antica Terra was 1996.

# Clear Creek Distillery

1430 NW 23rd Ave.
Portland, OR 97210
(503) 248-9470
FAX (503) 248-0490

**Tasting Room Hours:**
By appointment

**Owner and Winemaker/Distiller:**
Stephen R. Mc Carthy
**First Year:** 1985
**Production Capacity:** 100,000 Gallons

### Winery History:

Native Northwesterner Stephen McCarthy graduated from Reed College in Portland and then attended NYU law school. Success in business followed with Steve well-aligned on the fast track. Along came a trip to France in 1982 where Stephen enjoyed his first taste of traditional eau-de-vie, the 'water of life' distilled in many villages in Alsace from local fruits and berries. This was of particular interest to McCarthy because his family owned a large pear orchard in Hood River. Eau-de-vie de poire, pear brandy, seemed like the perfect answer to surplus pears.

Experiments with distillations led to purchases of more and more specialized equipment and to better and better prototype eaux-de-vie. In 1987 a decision was made to finance a commercial distillery. The Oregon liquor board proved to be a friend, not an enemy, and helped secure the necessary permits to allow commercial production and sale of the brandy in state liquor outlets. Today, the Clear Creek product line includes not only eaux-de-vie, but several other digestifs of note.

### A visit to Clear Creek Distillery

If you are fascinated by eaux-de-vie, brandy, grappa and the like, Steve McCarthy will show you around his operation by appointment. The rows of barrels and gleaming copper stills are a delight to the eye. A well-informed host, Steve is a wealth of information on the history and making of

*Continued on page 124.*

## ❖ A RECIPE FROM CLEAR CREEK DISTILLERY ❖

# Clear Creek Fruit Cake

*Serve with Clear Creek Apple or Pear Brandy*

| | |
|---|---|
| 1-1/2 | cups dried pineapple, chopped |
| 1-1/2 | cups dried apricots, chopped |
| 2 | cups dried pears, chopped |
| 2 | cups dried apples, chopped |
| 2 | cups dark raisins or dried cranberries |
| 1 | cup golden raisins |
| 1 | cup Clear Creek Pear Brandy |
| 3 | cups all-purpose flour |
| 2 | tsp. baking powder |
| 2 | tsp. ground cinnamon |
| 1 | tsp. salt |
| 1/2 | tsp. each: ground nutmeg, allspice, ground cloves |
| 2 | cups walnuts |
| 1-1/2 | cups hazelnuts |
| 1-1/2 | cups whole almonds |
| 2 | cups pecans |
| 4 | eggs, beaten frothy |
| 1-3/4 | cups brown sugar, firmly packed |
| 1-1/4 | cup applesauce |
| 3/4 | cup melted butter |
| 1/2 | cup molasses |

*"All regional food and wine is idiomatic. Great regional pairings in the Northwest build on our Asian and European food and wine ancestry, but finds its own unique Northwest style. We are not all the way there yet, but we are getting closer."*

*Steve McCarthy and his wife, artist Lucinda Parker have enjoyed travels that have contributed to their creative processes and have been the motivation for changes in their lives.*

*Perfecting the distillation techniques that create authentic fruit brandies has been Steve's goal for over a decade, and the couple has enjoyed experimenting with food accompaniments like this recipe for "fruitcake that finally beats its bad rap"* as one writer at The Oregonian *observed.*

Preheat oven to 300° F. Grease eight 3-1/2 inch by 6 inch loaf pans, or to make individual servings, substitute two 8-ounce cleaned pineapple cans for each loaf pan.

In a mixing bowl, combine the dried fruits and pour brandy over tossing well to coat the fruit. Let stand for 30 minutes. In another large bowl, sift together the flour, baking powder, cinnamon, salt and spices. Stir in the nuts. Add the brandy/fruit mixture and blend thoroughly.

Combine the beaten eggs, brown sugar, applesauce, melted butter and molasses in a small bowl. Beat until the ingredients are well-blended and smooth. Combine the egg mixture with the flour mixture and stir well to evenly coat all the fruit and nuts with batter. Pour the batter into greased loaf pans and fill 3/4 full. Bake for 1 hour. The cakes are done when the sides begin to pull away from the edge of the pans and a toothpick inserted in the middle comes out clean. They should be a rich, mahogany color.

Cool loaves in pans for about 15 minutes, then turn out on a cake rack. When thoroughly cooled, wrap in cheesecloth that has been soaked in additional pear brandy. Cover with foil and store in an airtight container or refrigerator until ready to serve. The cake is best after being aged at least two or three weeks. Makes 8 small loaves.

eaux-de-vie.

**The Spirits**

The eaux-de-vie produced at Clear Creek include versions made from pear, apple, blue plum, raspberry and cherry. Each of these is effusively fruity to the nose and offers a complex palate and long finish.

Grappa made from Pinot Gris, Pinot Noir and Muscat are delightful "digestifs" and the Gewurztraminer "Marc" (pronounced "mar") is pungent and fiery.

The most recent additions to the Clear Creek line are Oregon Brandy – the traditional grape-based spirit famous around the world – and Oregon single malt scotch whiskey. Having been among the first to taste this smoky, heart-starting elixir from the barrel, I was truly excited that someone had brought quality to this style of beverage distilled in the U.S. If you are at all a fan of Scotch, you should add a bottle of Steve's single malt to your lineup to compare with whiskeys made in Scotland. It's not a better tot, but it is a fine drink to warm a cold winter's night.

# Cooper Mountain Vineyards

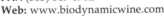

9480 SW Grabhorn Rd.
Beaverton, OR 97007
(503) 649-0027
FAX (503) 649-0702
**Web:** www.biodynamicwine.com

**Tasting Room Hours:** May - Oct., Friday, Saturday, Sunday - Noon to 5 PM; Feb. - April and November, Saturday and Sunday only.

**Owner:** Robert Gross
**Winemakers:** Bob Gross, Rich Cushman
**First Year:** 1987
**Winery Capacity:** 15,000 Gallons

**Winery History**

A career-related move to Portland in the mid-1970s led Bob and Corrine Gross to the purchase of the Cooper Homestead located just south of Beaverton. The 1865 homestead is located on an extinct volcano and proved to have excellent potential as vineyard land. The first acres of Pinot Noir, Chardonnay and Pinot Gris were planted in 1978. Grapes flourished on the site and the Gross family was content to

sell their harvests to other Oregon vintners who made award-winners by the dozens. In 1987 Bob Gross fermented both Pinot Noir and Chardonnay under the tutelage of Rich Cushman and launched Cooper Mountain Vineyards, the winery. A loss to all who enjoyed her good humor and dedication, Corrine Gross died of cancer in 1995.

**A visit to Cooper Mountain Vineyards**

A large winery building and cozy tasting room adjoin the Cooper Mountain Vineyard near Beaverton. Accessible from either Farmington or Scholls Ferry Roads, the site offers a magnificent southwest view and a grassy knoll for picnicking.

**The Wines**

Regular and reserve bottlings of Pinot Noir and Chardonnay have been well received by fans of Cooper Mountain Vineyards. Pinot Gris is the favored varietal and offers a delightful alternative for pairing with seafood and lighter meats.

# Edgefield

2126 S.W. Halsey St.
Troutdale, OR 97060
(503) 669-8610

**Tasting Room Hours:**
Daily, Noon to 8 PM

**Owners:** McMenamins
**First Year:** 1990

**Winery History**

Edgefield Manor, built in 1911, served for several decades as the Multnomah County Poor Farm. The farm, dairy, cannery and meat packing plant employed many in a self-sufficient system. As the Poor Farm was phased out in the late 1940s, the main lodge was used as a nursing home until 1982.

The McMenamin clan purchased Edgefield in 1990 from Multnomah County and began a remarkable restoration project. The complex now contains Bed and Breakfast-style accommodations in the main lodge and Administrator's House. The Edgefield Winery and Brewery were two of the first parts of the restoration to be completed (the McMenamins are, after all, Oregon's pre-eminent brewpub

*The tasting room at Edgefield winery.*

entrepreneurs!).

## A visit to Edgefield

Head east from Portland on I-84 to Troutdale and take the Wood Village exit #16A. Follow 238th Dr. S. to the first light and turn left on Halsey St. for one-half mile. The Edgefield complex has something for everyone including its own theater, pub, restaurant, etc. The winery offers it's own candle-lit cellar for tasting and relaxing.

## The Wines

A wide variety of wines are produced here. Sample Rieslings, Nouveau Pinot Noir, Cabernet Sauvignon, Pinot Gris, Sauvignon-Chardonnay, Port and sparkling wine.

# Helvetia Vineyard

22485 NW Yungen Hill Road
Hillsboro, OR 97124
(503) 647-5169
**Email:** helvwine@aol.com

**Tasting Room Hours:** By appointment or during Memorial Day, Thanksgiving weekends

**Owners:** John Platt, Elizabeth Furse
**Winemakers:** John Platt, Paul Gates
**First Year:** 1996

John Platt and Elizabeth Furse purchased land west of Beaverton in 1980 and planted grapes in 1982. Today, 10 acres of Pinot Noir and Chardonnay provide grapes for Helvetia Winery production. Take Helvetia/Shute Road exit from Highway 26, follow Helvetia Road north for 3.5 miles. After curve, turn right on Bishop Road, then right on Yungen Lane to the winery.

# Laurel Ridge Winery

David Hill Road
P.O. Box 456
Forest Grove, OR 97116
(503) 359-5436

**Tasting Room Hours:** Daily, Noon to 5 PM. Closed January

**Owners:** David & Susan Teppola
**Winemaker:** Pascal Valadier
**First Year:** 1986
**Winery Capacity:** 26,000 Gallons

## Winery History

This property has a long and varied history going back to the 19th century when vineyards were originally planted at the site, and the farmhouse was built. The wine boom of the 1970s saw first the Charles Coury Winery in residence, then an operation named Reuter's Hill Winery gave it a go, hoping that naming the place after the original settler would bring good luck. It didn't. The Reuter's Hill wine inventory was sold off at $1 a bottle during Thanksgiving weekend of 1980. After six years of dormancy the property was purchased and resurrected by a partnership of families already successful in various businesses, most notably grape growing.

## A visit to Laurel Ridge Winery

The current owners have spruced up the farmhouse and grounds and offer visiting wine lovers a nice lawn on which to enjoy their picnic. The acres of vineyards spread out behind the winery make a restful wine country vista. The Laurel Ridge site is just northwest of Forest Grove. Take Thatcher Road then turn left down David Hill Road. A couple of tight curves in the winery's driveway suggest that leaving the Winnebago at home might be in order, otherwise it's easy for cars to make their way.

## The Wines

Two versions of methode champenoise sparkling wine are produced here along with other still varietal wines. Crisp Sauvignon Blanc and Gewurztraminer are available, as is Pinot Noir, Pinot Blanc, Chardonnays and others.

# Lion Valley Vineyard

35040 SW Unger Road
Cornelius, OR 97113
(503) 628-5458

**Tasting Room Hours:** Weekends, 12 to 5 PM.

**Owner/Winemaker:** Dave Levinthal
**First Year:** 1997

Dave Levinthal spent two years in Burgundy and came to Oregon with that winemaking model in mind. His 4,000-plant-per-acre vineyard is among the most densely planted in the state. Follow Highway 219 for 5 miles south of Hillsboro, then 3 miles west on Unger Road.

# Marquam Hill Vineyards

35803 S. Hwy 213,
Mollala, OR 97038
(503) 829-6677
FAX (503) 829-8810
**Email:** marquam@
oregonwine.org

**Tasting Room Hours:** Daily, 11 to 6 PM; Winter, weekends only

**Owners:** Joe & Marylee Dobbes
**Winemaker:**
Joe Dobbes, Sr.
**First Year:** 1989
**Winery Capacity:** 10,000 Gallons

**Winery History**

Joe and Marylee Dobbes discovered an idyllic life in the rural countryside near the foothills of the Cascades. A small family winery, making wine from grapes grown on the property, welcoming visitors for tasting – it all seemed like just the thing to enhance a nearly perfect location.

**A visit to Marquam Hill Vineyards**

A half-hour drive from I-5 through Woodburn and on toward Mollala leads to Hwy. 213 and a left turn to Marquam Hill Vineyards. The Dobbes' 8-acre lake, expansive vineyard plantings and woodsy clearings are a wonderful place for a family outing and a relaxing picnic.

**The Wines**

Joe Dobbes crafts Pinot Noir, Chardonnay, Pinot Gris, Riesling, Gewurztraminer and Muller Thurgau from grapes grown in the 20-acre estate vineyard.

# Momokawa Sake, Ltd.

920 Elm St.
Forest Grove, OR 97116
(503) 357-7056
FAX (503) 357-1014

**Tasting Room Hours:**
Monday - Saturday,
Noon to 5 PM

**Owner:** Momokawa Sake, Ltd., Grif Frost
**Toji:** Ben Ben
**First Year:** 1992

**Winery History**

Momokawa Sake, a famous Japanese producer, joined forces with Oregon entrepreneur Grif Frost to make the centuries old brewed rice "wine" with local ingredients. The completion of the large sake brewery in 1997 also saw the first release of the first Oregon-made sake. Appreciated like wine, a sake tasting is most revealing to many American consumers who know little of this ancient beverage. Imported Japanese sakes are poured currently but production of a locally-brewed product is imminent.

**A visit to Momokawa**

Not far from Forest Grove and Hillsboro, the Momokawa facility is located on the Tualatin Valley Highway. The traditional Japanese decor and a small Japanese garden outside, give the visitor a sense of experiencing something special. The sake making process is fascinating and is thoroughly explained by the well-informed staff.

**The Sake**

Four versions of Momokawa Japanese sake are currently poured. Tastes range from rare and expensive to traditional "everyday" sake, and from sweeter to dry styles. The newly released Sapphire Blue Oregon Sake is light and crisp with a refreshing flavor that complements food very well.

# Montinore Vineyards

P.O. Box 560
3663 SW Dilley Road
Forest Grove, OR 97116
(503) 359-5012
FAX (503) 357-4313

**Tasting Room Hours:** Daily, Noon to 5 PM, April thru December. Other months, weekends only.

**Owners:** Leo and Jane Graham
**Winemaker:** Jacques Tardy
**First Year:** 1987
**Winery Capacity:** 180,000 Gallons

## Winery History

Montinore (a contraction of Montana-in-Oregon) was the name coined in 1905 for the property now planted with 300 acres of vineyard two miles south of Forest Grove. The property's owner at the time was John Forbis, a former corporate attorney for Anaconda Copper and acquisitions agent for the Oregon Pacific Railroad. In 1965 Mr. and Mrs. Leo Graham purchased the 361-acre ranch and added to the holding with purchases of land from adjacent farms. Consultant Jeffrey Lamy was retained in 1982 to study the site for development and his subsequent investigations led to a complex vineyard planting program commencing in 1983. Almost a dozen different varietals are planted on various slopes about the property comprising 45 different vineyard blocks. Each block has been located to optimize soil type and exposure to varietal. According to research and data everything is in its proper place.

Today, the grapevines have matured, a large, modern winery is in place and a lot of wine is being made. Sales and distribution are the current focus.

## A visit to Montinore Vineyards

The property's stately mansion (Leo and Jane Graham's home, once the home of John Forbis) offers a bit of elegance not often seen in this part of Oregon. The winery visitor center includes displays of grape growing and winemaking equipment as well as a large tasting room. A grand assortment of wine-related gifts are available.

## The Wines

Montinore's huge vineyard provides many varietals for the winemakers to work with. Pinot Noir, Chardonnay, Pinot Gris, Riesling, Gewurztraminer and Muller Thurgau are complemented late harvest wines and proprietary blends.

# Nicolas Rolin Winery

2234 NE 50th
Portland, OR 97213
(503) 282-7542

**Owners:** Trent & Robin Bush
**First Year:** 1990
**Production:** 2,000 Gallons

## Winery History

Named after the French Chancellor of State who made the first endowment of land to the Hospices de Beaune in the 16th century, this small winery is headquartered in Portland. Trent Bush became interested in winemaking while a stockbroker and dedicated most of his vacation time and spare moments to learning the craft. His close friendship with Russ Raney at Evesham Wood and other winemakers helped him develop goals for his own winemaking efforts. Now in the winemaking business full time, Trent produces Pinot Noir and Chardonnay which he distributes to retailers and restaurants in Portland and the nearby area.

## A visit to Nicolas Rolin

The production facility for the winery is not located at the Portland address. Trent can be reached at the above-listed phone number and enjoys discussing his wines and winemaking style. As growth continues, there may be a wine country facility open to the public in some future year.

## Oak Knoll Winery

29700 SW
Burkhalter Rd.
Hillsboro, OR
97123
(503) 648-8198
FAX (503) 648-3377
**Email:** oakknoll@ipinc.com
**Web:** www.oakknollwinery.com

**Tasting Room Hours:** Daily, Noon - 5 PM.
Closed major holidays.

**Owner:** Ron Vuylsteke & Marj Vuylsteke
**Winemaker:** Ron Vuylsteke
**First Year:** 1970
**Winery Capacity:** Over 135,000 Gallons

### Winery History

The 1980s were very important to Oak Knoll Winery. After a decade of mostly fruit and berry wine production, the Vuylsteke family began to concentrate their efforts on varietal grape wines (90% of production). The handwriting was on the wall when the 1980 Oak Knoll Vintage Select Pinot Noir won the Governor's Award for the best varietal in the state at the 1983 Oregon State Fair.

Some things change and some things stay the same. Many of the second generation Vuylstekes are involved directly with winery operations. Steve Vuylsteke is now president of Oak Knoll , John and Tom Vuylsteke work the Oak Knoll cellar and warehouse. Ron Vuylsteke, Sr. continues as winemaker in charge and Marj Vuylsteke is tasting room manager and director of hospitality.

Sales and distribution are up under Steve's leadership and Oak Knoll is among Oregon's best selling wineries in state.

### A visit to Oak Knoll Winery

The Oak Knoll Winery is conveniently located just off Highway 219 outside of Hillsboro. This entrance is well marked but you can also sneak in the back way on Rood Bridge Road from Farmington Road or River Road. The tasting room and gift shop at Oak Knoll are cheerful and their picnic area under the spreading oak tree is always inviting. Take Highway 219 south from downtown Hillsboro and watch for a left turn onto Burkhalter Road.

### The Wines

A complete selection of varietals is produced at Oak Knoll including Pinot Noir, Pinot Gris, Chardonnay, White Riesling, Gewurztraminer and Niagara. The Pinot Noir and Vintage Select Pinot Noir are especially good. Their raspberry dessert wine, Frambrosia, is a favorite with chocolate desserts or just for sipping.

## Ponzi Vineyards

14665 SW Winery Ln.
Beaverton, OR 97007
(503) 628-1227
FAX (503) 628-0354

**Web:**
www.ponziwines.com

**Tasting and Sales:**
Weekends, Noon to
5 PM, weekdays, 10 AM to 5 PM.
January, sales only.

**Owners:** Dick and Nancy Ponzi
**Winemakers:** Dick Ponzi, Luisa Ponzi
**First Year:** 1974
**Vineyard Established:** 1970
**Winery Capacity:** 25,000 Gallons

### Winery History

Dick and Nancy Ponzi arrived in Oregon in the late 1960s from California. They had been working toward finding just the right property to establish a vineyard for two years, and the Tualatin Valley held the answers to all their requirements. A rundown farm with excellent grape-growing potential was purchased near Portland and Nancy began planning and planting the vineyard while Dick taught engineering at Portland Community College.

All the family members pitched-in summers, weekends and most every available time. As the vineyard became winery, Dick became winemaker, drawing on his experience at home winemaking augmented with courses at U. C. Davis.

Widespread acclaim for Ponzi's Pinot Noir and Pinot Gris has the family anxiously anticipating each new vintage. The Ponzi

*The Ponzi winery near Beaverton, Oregon.*

children, Michel, Anna-Maria and Luisa, have all taken positions with the winery operation.

### A visit to Ponzi Vineyards

A short drive in from Scholls Ferry Road leads alongside the original vineyard planting at Ponzi winery. The grassy picnic area in front of the winery is inviting, but most wine lovers come to taste the wines for which Ponzi Vineyards has become internationally famous. Admiration for Ponzi Pinot Noir and Pinot Gris has come from all quarters. Directions to the winery are signed from Highway 99W or take Scholls Ferry Road west from Highway 217 and watch for the signs.

### The Wines

Some bottlings of Ponzi Vineyard Pinot Noir and Pinot Gris are in such high demand that it is often difficult to get some without a visit to the winery. The ripe style of Pinot Noir, tempered by aging in French oak, impresses wine judges consistently and is often rated as the best Northwest Pinot. Also look for Chardonnay, Pinot Gris, Vino Gelato (late harvest Riesling) and a bottling of the ancient Italian variety Arneis.

### By the way . . .

Dick and Nancy Ponzi established one of Oregon's first microbreweries in downtown Portland in 1984. Though now out of the microbrewery business (they sold the brewery a few years ago) you can still visit the Bridgeport Brew Pub in downtown Portland.

# Raptor Ridge Winery

29090 SW Wildhaven Rd.
Scholls, OR 97123
(503) 887-5595
FAX (503) 628-6255
**Email:** wineman@raptorridge.com
**Web:** www.raptorridge.com

**Tasting Room Hours:** No tasting room. Private tastings by appointment.

**Owner and Winemaker:** Scott Shull
**First year:** 1995
**Winery Capacity:** 3,000 Gallons

### Winery History

Scott Shull specializes in producing small lots of Pinot Noir, Pinot Gris and Chardonnay at his Raptor Ridge winery high in the Chehalem Mountains, south of Portland. The winery contracts with selected vineyards to acquire high quality grapes and sells most of the wine direct through its mailing list and web site. Several local outlets carry the Raptor Ridge wines as well.

# Andrew Rich

2734 N.E. 65th Ave.
Portland, OR 97213
(503) 284-6622

**Tasting Room Hours:** No tasting room facility

**Owner/Winemaker:** Andrew Rich
**First Year:** 1995
**1997 Production:** 2,000 cases

### Winery History

Andrew Rich left his home is western Massachusetts for a one-year trip to Beaune, France that was the embarkation on what appears to be a lifelong journey through the world of winemaking. His employment at Bonny Doon winery in California from 1988 to 1994 furthered his love for Rhone-style wines and also enhanced his skills and his confidence to strike out on his own. Rich came to Oregon and made his wine at other bonded facilities in the 1995, 1996 and 1997 vintages. His eccentric

*Continued on next page.*

and irreverent style does not fit into any of Oregon's wine stereotypes but his bottlings have met with great success through limited distribution in selected markets in the Northwest.

### The Wines

Rich's popular Tabula Rasa Rosé was originally vinted from Grenache, but with the demise of that vineyard source with Washington's freeze in 1996, he now crafts a dry and complex wine from Pinot Noir. Andrew Rich Les Vigneaux bottlings are produced from individual, small-vineyard sources and include a 1996 Yakima Valley Cabernet Sauvignon, 1996 Pinot Noir from the St. Herman's Vineyard near Dundee, and a spectacular Gewurztraminer Ice Wine from the Willamette Valley.

Andrew Rich labels are both artistic and clever providing a perfect introduction to great wines that will no doubt establish the vintner as both a maverick and a master in Northwest wine circles.

## Saga Vineyards

30815 S. Wall St., Colton, OR 97017
(503) 824-4600

**Tasting Room Hours:** By appointment

**Owners:** Richard & Julianne Pixner
**Winemaker:** Richard Pixner
**Production:** 2,300 Gallons

### Winery History

Relocating from Austria to Oregon in 1984, Richard and Julianne Pixner bought a plot of land in the foothills of the Oregon Cascades in Clackamas County. Richard learned the skills of grape growing and winemaking as an eager amateur and bonded his winery in 1989.

### A visit to Saga Vineyards

By phoning the Pixners you can make an appointment to visit the winery. As part of a tour including St. Josef's and Marquam Hill, a trip to Saga Vineyards makes a fine day out.

### The Wines

Richard Pixner makes Chardonnay, Pinot Noir, Pinot Gris, Pinot Blanc and the unusual (for Oregon) varietal Veltliner.

## St. Josef's Wine Cellar

28836 South Barlow Rd.
Canby, OR 97013
(503) 651-3190

**Tasting Room Hours:** Thursday through Monday, 11 AM to 5 PM Winters: weekends only

**Owners:** Fleischmann Family
**Winemaker:** Joe & Kirk Fleischmann
**First Year:** 1983
**Winery Capacity:** 35,000 Gallons

### Winery History

Joe Fleischmann traded in his baker's apron and the smell of rising bread dough for the rubber boots of a winemaker and the smell of fermenting wine. The success he achieved in baking is a local legend but the family winery has been making its mark since 1983.

Joe and his son Kirk produce their wines from their ten-acre vineyard and from Zinfandel purchased from The Dalles. When the Zinfandel grapes are just right they make a red wine - big and bold like the Egri Bikaver of their Hungarian ancestors. When the Zin is not as ripe, they make a delicious White Zinfandel.

#### A visit to St. Josef's Wine Cellar

A short four mile drive out Barlow Road from Highway 99E leads you into the Clackamas farm country and to the vineyards and winery of St. Josef's. The winery has facilities for receptions and banquets as well as their cozy tasting room and gift shop. A special attraction for visitors is the magnificent picnic area by the Fleischmann's spring-fed lake behind the winery.

### The Wines

Pinot Noir, Cabernet, Zinfandel, Riesling, Gewurztraminer and Chardonnay are produced.

# Shafer Vineyard Cellars

6200 NW Gales Cr. Rd.
Forest Grove, OR 97116
(503) 357-6604

**Tasting Room Hours:** Weekends,
11 AM to 5 PM, Closed January and February

**Owner and Winemaker:** Harvey Shafer
**First year:** 1981
**Winery Capacity:** 20,000 Gallons

**Winery History**

The lush vineyards spreading out behind Shafer winery were planted in 1973 and now offer the complex fruit from which the finest Pinot Noir and Chardonnay can be crafted. Harvey Shafer has been perfecting techniques to achieve the best full-bodied Pinot Noir and toasty, barrel-fermented Chardonnay.

**A visit to Shafer Vineyard Cellars**

The winery is a 4.5 mile drive west from Forest Grove through quiet farmland. Most of the route is shaded by tall deciduous trees that overhang the road on both sides to form a dappled-green tunnel. Picnicking is available on the veranda or in the gazebo.

**The Wines**

Harvey Shafer's years of winemaking has led to a consistent style that has many fans. In addition to the varietals named above the winery produces Riesling, Gewurztraminer, Muller Thurgau and Sauvignon Blanc.

# Starr Winery

10610 NW St. Helens Rd.
Portland, OR 97231
(503) 289-5974

**Tasting Room Hours:** Not open to the public

**Owners:** Rachel Starr, Bob Hanson
**Winemaker:** Rachel Starr
**Production:** 2,500 Gallons

**Winery History**

Rachel Starr has been producing Chardonnay and Pinot Noir since 1991 under the Starr label and plan to continue annual production of just more than 1,500 cases.

**A visit to Starr & Brown**

The winery has closed its tasting room in Northwest Portland.

# Tualatin Vineyards

10850 NW Seavey Road
Forest Grove, OR 97116
(503) 357-5005
FAX (503) 357-1702

**Tasting Room Hours:** Weekends: Noon to 5 PM. Closed January, February and holidays.

**Owners:** Willamette Valley Vineyards
**Winemaker:** Joe Dobbes
**First Year:** 1973
**Winery Capacity:** 60,000 Gallons

**Winery History**

Tualatin Vineyards was founded by two native Californians who staked their fortunes on the success of the Oregon wine industry. Bill Fuller and Bill Malkmus joined forces in 1973 to establish a small pioneer winery and vineyard 30 miles west of Portland, near Forest Grove. Bill Fuller, whose credentials include a Master's Degree in enology and 9 years experience at Louis Martini Winery, was resident overseer and winemaker at Tualatin, while Bill Malkmus maintained his investment banking business and handled national distribution for Tualatin from his office in San Francisco. In 1997 the winery and vineyards were sold to Willamette Valley Vineyards and the former owners departed.

**A visit to Tualatin Vineyards**

Follow Highway 47 or Thatcher Road south from Forest Grove and watch for signs indicating a left turn to Tualatin Vineyards. Turns onto Clapshaw Hill Road and Seavey Road are less well marked. Drive slowly and keep your eyes peeled. At the winery you'll enjoy a view of the valley, the spacious tasting room, umbrella-shaded picnic tables and quiet country surroundings.

**The Wines**

Tualatin's 85-acre vineyard is now in full production so all wines are 'estate bottled'— made only from grapes grown at the winery. This gives the winemaker greater control and allows split-second decision making at harvest time. Wines include Chardonnay, Gewurztraminer, White Riesling and Pinot Noir.

## Wasson Brothers Winery

41901 Highway 26
Sandy, OR 97055
(503) 668-3124

**Owners:** Jim & John Wasson
**Winemaker:** Jim Wasson
**First Year:** 1982
**Winery Capacity:** 10,000 Gallons
**Tasting Room Hours:** 9 AM to 5 PM, Daily

**Winery History**

Jim Wasson and his twin brother John have been part-time farming in Clackamas County since the 1960s including winegrapes since 1978. In the early 1980s they took up amateur winemaking and became so good at it that Jim quit his plumbing job and opened a winery. Their winery building is right on Highway 26 between Portland and the Mt. Hood recreation areas. A perfect stop for tired skiers on their way home from the slopes!

**A visit to Wasson Brother Winery**

At the Wasson Brothers Winery a mile east of Sandy, Oregon wines are available for tasting and wine-related gifts await your perusal. If you'd rather make your own, the Wasson Brothers will be happy to set you up with home winemaking equipment from the supply shop right in the tasting room. You say you'd rather make beer? Well step over to this counter here! A great place to stop!

**The Wines**

Production at the Wasson Brothers winery is split about half and half between fruit and berry wines and varietal grape wines. The local folks prefer the tasty Loganberry, Blackberry and Rhubarb while the skiers and city folks like the Pinot Noir, Riesling and Chardonnay. Jim Wasson's gold medal efforts with Pinot Noir haven't gone unnoticed by wine consumers or by wine judges. He has developed a style that is enjoyed by all and offers classic Pinot Noir nuances.

# PORTLAND AREA ACCOMMODATIONS

### Northwest Bed and Breakfast Association

Portland - (503) 243-7616  A reservations agency for many attractive B & B's in the Portland area and around the Pacific Northwest.

### The Westin Benson

SW Broadway at Oak - (503) 228-2000  The elegance and consistent good service at this Portland landmark have not diminished at all since its acquisition by the Westin Hotel group. The London Bar and Grill maintains one of the city's best wine cellars with choices for every taste.

### The Heathman Hotel

1001 SW Broadway. - (503) 241-4100  Considered by many THE place to stay in Portland with its elegant atmosphere and attentive service. Well-appointed rooms and attractive common rooms offer a bit of class that is heightened by the namesake restaurant on premises. See recipe for the Heathman Restaurant on facing page.

### Hotel Vintage Plaza

422 SW Broadway. - (503) 228-1212  Portland's own hotel dedicated to the Oregon wine industry. Complimentary wine tasting each evening in the lobby, each room is named after an Oregon winery or vineyard, and attentive service to every detail. Pazzo Ristorante offers Northern Italian cuisine and an impressive wine cellar.

### Riverplace Alexis

1510 SW Harbor Way - (503) 228-3233, (800) 227-1333  If you can afford the best, then you will find it at this showplace on the Willamette River. Superb service and unbeatable ambiance. The Esplanade Restaurant features regular winemaker dinners with Oregon's finest.

### Mallory Hotel

729 SW 15th Ave. - (503) 223-6311, (800) 228-8657  Close to downtown location offers convenience to shopping, etc. Inexpensive, quality accommodations.

## Chef Phillipe Boulot
## The Heathman Hotel

*Philippe Boulot joined Portland's historic Heathman Hotel in 1994. A rising culinary star of the 1990s, Boulot's significant strengths add to Portland's growing reputation as an international food destination.*

*His roots in the culinary arts began with typical chores on a farm in his native Normandy, France. He helped his grandmother make butter and cheese and prepared meals with harvest from their gardens. At the age of sixteen, Boulot began his career with apprenticeships under mentors Joel Robuchon and Alain Senderens in Paris. His training continued under their supervision at restaurants Jamin, L'Archestrate and Maxim's. His career has spanned two decades at major restaurants and hotels where he won several important awards.*

*Striving for "freshness, flavor and truthful presentation on every plate," Boulot creates contemporary regional and international dishes using only the finest seasonal ingredients on the market while combining ethnic touches to produce a relationship of tastes and textures.*

*Boulot's wife Susan is pastry chef at The Heathman. A native Oregonian and a graduate of The Culinary Institute of America, Susan met Philippe when they both worked at L'Archestrate in Paris.*

### ❖ A RECIPE FROM THE HEATHMAN ❖

# Gigot of Lamb de Sept Heures with Puree of Oregon Truffles Flageolet

*Serves 10, Wine: WillaKenzie Estate Pinot Meunier*

| | |
|---|---|
| 1 | leg of lamb |
| 1 | lb. large carrots, chopped fine |
| 1 | lb. spanish onions, chopped fine |
| 1/2 | lb. celery, chopped fine |
| 1 | bouquet garni |
| 1 | cup flour |
| 1 | gallon red wine |
| 2 | cups olive oil |
| 1 | lb. garlic cloves, pureed |
| | salt, pepper, thyme |

Rub the leg of lamb with the garlic puree and season with salt, pepper and thyme. Roast the lamb in a 450° F. oven for 5 minutes.

Saute the carrots, onion and celery in olive oil. Add flour and stir to color. Deglaze with red wine and add leg of lamb, rosemary and bay leaf. Braise over medium to low heat for 7 hours. Remove meat from the pan and strain the sauce.

### For the Puree

| | |
|---|---|
| 2 | lbs. dry flageolet (small kidney beans) |
| 1/2 | lb. bacon |
| 1 | cup each, chopped carrot, chopped onion |
| 1/2 | cup, chopped celery |
| 1 | bouquet garni |
| 1 | lb. Oregon truffles |

Soak the flageolets in cold water overnight then cook in water with the vegetables and bacon. When cooked, puree with the truffles.

Spread the flageolet/truffle puree on each plate and place slices of lamb on top. Sprinkle with reserved sauce and with garlic parsey oil.

# PORTLAND AREA DINING

## Atwater's
111 SW 5th Ave., 30th Floor  (503) 275-3600
Enjoy the view and superb preparations by an
expert kitchen staff. A fancy, button-down
place to bring the in-laws or to celebrate a
special event. Select from many Northwest
wines including special reserves.

## Caprial's Bistro & Wine
7015 SE Milwaukee Ave., (503) 236-6457  With
the continued escalation of Caprial's fame, her
restaurant continues to please both locals and
regional devotees who come here for the
experience of being in Caprial's Kitchen! The
name of the game is Northwest innovative
cuisine and, for wine lovers, the prize is the
ability to pull a bottle off the wine shop
shelves for a minimal corkage fee. Lunch and
dinner, Tues. through Saturday. See Northwest Legend recipe on facing page.

## Genoa
2832 SE Belmont St., (503) 238-1464  This price-
fixed Italian dinner should answer all your
questions about Northern Italian cuisine.
Courses are described as served and include
Northwest ingredients in classical and
contemporary preparations. Expensive but
worth every penny for the experience.

## The Heathman (Hotel)
SW Broadway at Salmon St. (503) 241-4100
Great lunches and dinners feature wonderful
NW specialties with a continental flair brought
to the hotel by Philippe Boulot. Szechuan
salmon and Oregon lamb are two favorites.
Extensive NW wine list is sure to please. See
Northwest Legends recipe on page 133.

## Higgins
1239 SW Broadway - (503) 222-9070  When
Greg Higgins opened his own restaurant
many who had been enjoying his fine cuisine
at the Heathman cheered. Like some Northwest winemakers with wine, Greg Higgins has
a magic touch with Northwest cuisine. His
command performances during the early years
of the Pinot Noir Celebration are legendary.
Go for it!

## Il Fornaio
115 NW 22nd Ave. (503) 248-9400  From the
olive oil poured from on high to dip your
rustic breads to the ample portions to the
nicely thought out wine list, you will find
much to enjoy about Il Fornaio. A California
invention that is making its way to Seattle as
well, this restaurant chain has a lot to do with
good eating and drinking in the Italian style
and nothing to do with cookie cutter, copycat
fast food. Check it out at www.ilfornaio.com.

## Jake's Crawfish House
401 SW 12th -(503) 226-1419  Impeccably fresh
seafood served best when unadorned. Locals
and tourists mingle in the bar before dinner.
A deservedly fine reputation for service and
quality.

## Ron Paul Charcuterie
1441 NE Broadway (503) 284-5347  Great new-
American cuisine featuring the finest local
ingredients and an unyielding emphasis on
quality in preparation and service. The
owner's love affair with local wine shows with
the carefully selected offerings on the trim
wine list.

## Wildwood
1221 NW 21st Ave. (503) 248-9663  Cory
Schreiber's superb and creative cuisine
continues to keep this newish Portland eatery
on top. The chef loves local ingredients and
local wines – a sure sign of good things to eat.
Unique salads, pizzas and delightful preparation with local fish and game. Enjoy Cory's
recipe for Dungeness crab on page 171.

## Zefiro
500 NW 21st Ave., (503) 226-3394  The NW
Portland scene continues to impress with fine
meals and innovative international melange.
Zefiro is evolving with creativity and flair—
still cutting edge. Great people watching from
window seats for the outside or any seat for
the activity inside. Excellent wine list.

### Chef Caprial Pence
### Caprial's Bistro

Caprial Pence shares her talent for creating innovative regional dishes on her popular PBS series, Cooking with Caprial. The show is going into its second year, while Caprial's series produced by The Learning Channel – a 1994 nominee for the James Beard Award for best television cooking show – is currently airing internationally.

After graduating in 1984 from the Culinary Institute of America, Caprial returned to her native Pacific Northwest and in 1986 began working at Fullers Restaurant at the Seattle Sheraton Hotel. She was quickly promoted to Chef de Cuisine, a position she held from 1987 to 1991. Under Caprial's direction, Fullers was a leader in Seattle's nouvelle cuisine, and in 1990 the young chef was honored with the James Beard Award for Best Chef in the Northwest.

In order to be closer to their family, in 1992 Caprial and her husband John moved to Portland and opened their own small neighborhood restaurant, now called Caprial's Bistro. Acclaimed for its eclectic Northwest cuisine, the Bisto continues to draw a faithful crowd, while Caprial and John's weekly in-house cooking classes are always a sellout.

Her series of cookbooks includes: Caprial's Seasonal Kitchen, Caprial's Cafe Favorites, and Cooking with Caprial: American Bistro Fare. Her fourth cookbook, Caprial's Bistro Style Cuisine, was published in April, 1998.

## ❖ A RECIPE FROM CAPRIAL'S BISTRO ❖

# Mushroom Appetizer Baked in Parchment with Gorgonzola

*Serves 6, Wine: Vintage Cameron Pinot Noir*

| | |
|---|---|
| 1 | Tbs. olive oil |
| 3 | cups mushrooms, quartered |
| 1 | head of roasted garlic |
| 1 | Tbs. chopped rosemary |
| 1/2 | cup sliced sundried tomatoes |
| 2 | red bell peppers, roasted and chopped |
| 2-3 | oz. pinot noir |
| 2 | oz. balsamic vinegar |
| | salt and pepper to taste |
| | juice of one lemon |
| 2 | oz. extra virgin olive oil |
| 3-4 | oz. Gorgonzola cheese, crumbled |
| 6 | pieces of parchment paper cut into 6-inch circles |

Heat olive oil in large saute pan, add mushrooms and cook until tender. Add garlic, rosemary, tomatoes, and red peppers and cook for 3 minutes. Add pinot and reduce, then add balsamic vinegar. Season with salt and pepper and finish with lemon and extra virgin olive oil. Remove from heat and let cool.

Place one-sixth of the mushroom mixture in each piece of parchment and top with Gorgonzola. Bring the ends of the paper together and twist like a Hershey's Kiss. Bake on a sheet pan in a 400° F. oven for about 10 minutes. Serve immediately.

Portland is beer crazy! There are more breweries, brewpubs, ale houses and just plain good beer here than anywhere else in America. The brewing pioneers have found ways to grow large without sacrificing quality and the styles are expanding to fill the demand for new tastes. Breweries listed first, then brewpubs.

If you still haven't had enough suds, then stop by the Northwest Microbrewery Festival that takes place each July along the Willamette River waterfront.

## BridgePort Brewing Co.

1313 NW Marshall, Portland (503) 241-7179 Bridgeport was founded in 1984 by Dick and Nancy Ponzi but is now under other ownership. The brewery and pub are located in a century-old building in the downtown "brewing district" and offer the beer lover a look at the operation while sipping a cask-conditioned, hand-pumped draught. Pale Ale, Extra Special Bitter, BridgePort Ale (amber style), BridgePort XX Stout, and old Knucklehead Barleywine are offered regularly with special "brewer's select" ales available on a seasonal basis. The pub offers a limited menu but the delicious pizza, focaccia and sandwiches are just the thing to accompany the excellent draught ales.

## Full Sail Brewing Co. at Riverplace

0307 SW Montgomery, Portland (503) 222-5343, Restaurant (503) 220-1865. The original Full Sail Brewery is in Hood River and was founded in 1987. This production facility at the Riverplace Marina was added in 1992 and adjoins McCormick & Schmick's restaurant. This brewery produces many of Full Sail's specialty beers and the full line of beers is offered for tasting at the restaurant's Pilsner Room. Have a draught while you watch the brewers at work through the glass wall looking into the brewhouse. Tours of the brewing operation are offered Monday through Thursday, 6 AM to 5 PM. Inquire at the restaurant about their special brewers dinners highlighting Northwest microbreweries.

## Hair of the Dog Brewing Co.

4509 SE 23rd, Portland (503) 232-6585 Doug Henderson and Alan Sprints have revived a concept in microbrewing that is not widely used today. Their beers are "bottle-conditioned," or refermented in the bottle to provide the fizz. Not unlike methode champenoise winemaking (or home-brewing), the yeast is employed a second time to provide the bubbles. Bottled-product-only includes Adambier, an old world-style ale and Golden Rose, a Belgian-style fruity ale. Tours are offered by appointment at this small brewery in the warehouse district of SE Portland.

## Portland Brewing Co.

2730 NW 31st, Portland (503) 226-7623, Taproom (503) 228-5269. This is the new production facility for one of Portland's original microbrewers. This state-of-the-art plant features all the latest brewing equipment brought in from Germany to craft the seven ales and lagers offered throughout the western U.S. on draught or by the bottle. The Taproom and Grill is open seven days a week for lunch and dinner with beer-steamed clams, home-made soups, salads and sandwiches offered. Tours of the brewery take place at 1 PM on Saturdays or by appointment. Find this landmark brewery in the Northwest Portland Guilds Lake Industrial District. (Follow St. Helens Rd. to 31st, turn right.)

## Saxer Brewing Co.

5875 Lakeview Blvd., Lake Oswego (503) 699-9524 Named after a German immigrant, Henry Saxer, who opened Portland's first brewery in 1852, the operation began in 1993 brewing handcrafted lagers in the Bavarian tradition. The people's choice of Saxer lagers is their Lemon Lager, a light, refreshing beer with a hint of lemon flavor. More traditional "flavors" include Hefedunkel, Amber Lager and Stout. A powerful Doppelbock is brewed and a Pale Bock is brewed seasonally. Saxer beers are available in 16 states in bottle and keg. Visit the tasting room and brewery off Boones Ferry Rd. (exit 290 from I-5), then right on Jean Rd. in Lake Oswego.

# Star Brewing, Inc.

5231 NE Martin Luther King, Jr., Portland (503) 282-6003  Another revival of a brewery from bygone days, Star Brewing offers a selection of ales throughout Oregon and Washington, both draught and bottle.  This production facility in north Portland brews Hop Gold Ale (a rye beer), India Pale Ale, Nut Brown Ale, Altbier, Imperial Stout and a Raspberry Ale using raspberries added to each keg for the flavoring!  Holidale is their winter seasonal ale, slightly spicy.  There are no tourist facilities at this working brewery.  Call for an appointment to visit.

# Widmer Brewing Co.

929 N. Russell, Portland (503) 281-2437  Kurt and Rob Widmer oversee one of the Northwest's largest family-owned and operated breweries.  Now over a decade old, Widmer brewing has expanded into a facility that allows production of sufficient quantities of their popular brews to meet demand.  The first American hefeweizen was brewed by Widmer and continues to be Oregon's bestselling draught microbrew.  Also brewed are Altbier, Dunkelweizen, Festbier, Doppelbock, Bock and Oktoberfest.  The Widmer Gasthaus brewpub and restaurant operates from a corner of the historic building that houses the brewery.  Lunch and dinner are served Monday through Saturday and a Sunday brunch opens the pub at 10 AM.  Tours of the brewery are offered at noon and 1 PM on Saturdays.

These facilities brew their own beer on premise but do not distribute to other outlets. Just a few of the many.

## Lucky Labrador Brewing Co.

915 SE Hawthorne Blvd., Portland  (503) 236-3555.  Whether you sip a Black Lab Stout or quaff a pint of Hawthorne's Best Bitter, you'll feel at home in this funky brewpub in Southeast Portland.  Enjoy a vegi dish or something more carnivorous with your game of steel tip darts.

## McMenamin's Brew Pub Empire

This pair of Oregon brothers have more brewpubs than any other owner.  Famed for taking rundown properties and making them live again!  Try these:

**Bagdad Theater & Pub**, 3702 SE Hawthorne - (503) 232-6676 - Stop in at showtime, pick up a burger and a beer at the bar, find a table in the theater and enjoy your dinner while a first run movie plays.  Not the original concept of dinner theater but not bad!

**The Blue Moon Tavern**, 423 NW 23rd Ave. - (503) 223-3184

**Greenway Pub**, 12272 Scholls Ferry Rd. - (503) 590-1865

**The Ram's Head**, 2282 NW Hoyt - (503) 221-0089

## The Old Market Pub & Brewery

6959 SW Multnomah Blvd. - (503) 244-0450 Located in a huge produce market warehouse out on the way to Ponzi Winery, this new brewpub offers some of the most outrageous ales in town.  Mr. Toad's Wild Red and terrifyingly hoppy Backward Bitter will curl your hair, baldy.

## Tugboat Brewing Co.

711 SW Ankeny - (503) 226-2508  This cozy brewpub is almost hidden away in downtown Portland.  Try the tasty Tex-Mex specialties with a brew from one of the 20 taps.  Noisy blues, rock and and mellow folk liven up the weekends.

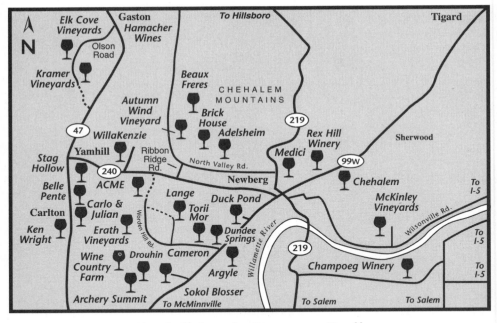

## Yamhill County Touring – North

Yamhill County has virtually filled up with wineries to the point where it takes several days to visit every stop. If you're traveling on one of the holiday weekends when ALL the wineries are open, you really have a lot of touring to do. Drive carefully. **Elk Cove Vineyards** and **Kramer Vineyards**, are just off Highway 47 near Gaston. Don't miss either of these two stops. Both wineries offer estate bottled Pinot Noir, Pinot Gris and Chardonnay. **Hamacher Wines** is not open to the public.

**Autumn Wind Vineyard** is located west of Newberg on North Valley Road and is a great visit. This area, called Ribbon Ridge, has become more developed by in-the-know grape growers. **Beaux Freres**, **Brick House** and **Adelsheim** are in the neighborhood but are not open to the public on a regular basis. The grand **WillaKenzie Estate** is open daily.

Just north of Newberg, **Rex Hill Vineyards** is right on Highway 99W and is open daily. The expansive grounds at Rex Hill make a grand location for an al fresco picnic. Across the highway, **Chehalem** is open by appointment. **McKinley Vineyards** and

**Medici Vineyards** are also open by appointment, while **Champoeg Winery** across the river is open daily.

In and around the town of Dundee, several more wineries are open daily for visits and tasting. **Duck Pond Cellars** is on the highway and **Lange Winery** up the hill is open daily dispensing "dry wine and dry humor." Visit **Torii Mor** winery in the same neighborhood. Two miles west near Crabtree Park is **Erath Vineyards Winery** and south of Dundee just up the hill from the highway you'll find **Sokol Blosser Winery**. Up in the Dundee hills seek out **Wine Country Farm Cellars** and **Archery Summit** (open by appointment). **ACME**, **Cameron** and **Domaine Drouhin** are not open to visitors.

In "downtown" Dundee stands the stately Victorian tasting room for **Argyle** sparkling wines. The new **Ponzi** tasting room is across the road and **Dundee Springs** has sprung up on the west side of the highway as well.

**Ken Wright Cellars, Carlo & Julian, Belle Pente, Stag Hollow** and **Domaine Serene** keep no formal tasting room hours but are often open during holiday weekend events.

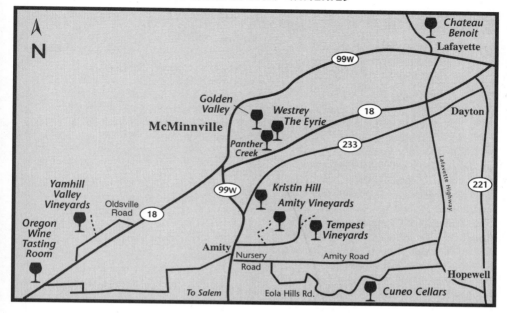

## Yamhill County Touring – South

Heading south from Dundee on Highway 99W you'll discover the wineries of southern Yamhill County. Your first stop might be **Chateau Benoit**, open daily just a couple of miles west of Lafayette. The view from the hilltop winery is grand.

Continuing down 99W to McMinnville you can visit **Panther Creek Cellars, Westrey Winery** and **The Eyrie** by appointment or on the special Yamhill County weekend events on Thanksgiving and Memorial Day. (Eyrie on Thanksgiving only.) Also in McMinnville is the Golden Valley Brewpub and winery for **Golden Valley Vineyards**. Open daily.

South of McMinnville on Highway 18 you'll find **Yamhill Valley Vineyards**. Open daily, YVV offers tasting of their fine wines and an opportunity to enjoy your picnic on a shady deck overlooking their expansive vineyard.

On the eastern side of the county **Amity Vineyards** and **Kristin Hill Winery** are open daily for tastings and informal tours. Amity is one of the area's original wineries while Kristin Hill is one of the newest. Keith Orr's **Tempest Vineyards** is just up Rice Lane (on Karla's Lane) and is open weekends.

Up the serpentine, steep (but worth the drive) Eola Hills Road, Gino Cuneo welcomes visitors to **Cuneo Cellars**. His dedication to red wine should be a beacon to many wine lovers who seek the rich and robust. Saturday noon to 5 PM.

By the way . . . when you're near McMinnville, take the short drive to the **Oregon Wine Tasting Room** at the Lawrence Gallery just north of Sheridan. The resident witty, wine experts serve a little cabaret with the Cabernet and Pinot Noir. How can these talented wine wizards keep track of 15 tasters (or more) while washing glasses, opening bottles and ringing up sales? Catch the act daily and be prepared for a good time.

# ACME Wineworks/ John Thomas Winery

P.O. Box 48
Carlton, OR 97111
(503) 852-6969

**Tasting Room Hours:** No tasting room.

**Owner/Winemaker:** John Thomas
**First Release:** 1993

John Thomas' small vineyard is in the Dundee Hills, near the junction of Worden Hill Road and Highway 240. Small lots of intense, hand-crafted Pinot Noir are released occasionally — when the winemaker/owner deems them ready. Fruit from the Thomas Vineyard is sometimes sold to other wineries in the area.

# Adelsheim Vineyard

16800 NE Calkins Lane
Newberg, OR 97132
(503) 538-3652
FAX (503) 538-2248

**Tasting Room Hours:** No tasting room, but traditionally open Memorial Day Weekend and Thanksgiving Weekend Open Houses

**Owners:** David & Ginny Adelsheim
**Winemaker:** Don Kautzner
**First Year:** 1978
**Winery Capacity:** 35,000 Gallons

**Winery History**
David Adelsheim made a commitment to Oregon winegrowing after a short period of study in Burgundy and after working a couple of harvests with Dave Lett at The Eyrie. The first Adelsheim Vineyard was planted in 1971, following David's acquaintance with several Yamhill County vinifera pioneers. Initial varieties included Pinot Noir, Chardonnay and Riesling. Plantings today also include Pinot Gris and Pinot Blanc. Adelsheim's second

Chehalem Mountain vineyard site, on Calkins Road west of Newberg, is the location of a spacious new winery facility completed in the spring of 1998.

Marketing of the wines has not escaped the scrutiny of the Adelsheim family as David's wife, Ginny, has used her artistic talents to design artisitic labels featuring portraits of family members and close friends. These popular works-of-art-on-the-bottle are some of the Northwest's classic images for label art.

**A visit to Adelsheim Vineyard**
Adelsheim Vineyard is not open for public tours or wine tasting but they are open each Memorial Day Weekend for the Yamhill County celebration "Match Made in Heaven."

**The Wines**
Several excellent Adelsheim Pinot Noirs are produced. In addition to an Oregon appellation, a "Polk County, Seven Springs Vineyard" comes from the Eola Hills. Elizabeth's Reserve, a blend of the best lots of the old estate Pinot Noir, is named for David and Ginny's daughter. Superb Chardonnay and Pinot Gris are readily available, as is a delicious Merlot made from Southern Oregon (Applegate Valley) fruit. Production of Pinot Blanc is increasing as more vineyard plantings come into bearing.

## ❖ A RECIPE FROM CLEAR CREEK DISTILLERY ❖

### Lucinda Parker and Steve McCarthy of Clear Creek Distillery

*"All regional food and wine is idiomatic. Great regional pairings in the Northwest build on our Asian and European food and wine ancestry, but finds its own unique Northwest style. We are not all the way there yet, but we are getting closer."*

*Steve McCarthy and his wife, artist Lucinda Parker have enjoyed travels that have contributed to their creative processes and have been the motivation for changes in their lives.*

*Expanding their culinary horizons has been a pleasant off-shoot of entering the fine spirits business, with both Steve and Lucinda enjoying the additional responsibility of counseling customers on the enjoyment of their brandies and eaux de vie.*

*This recipe for pan-cooked steaks with an apple brandy pan sauce is both simple and delicious.*

# Clear Creek Distillery Steak with Apple Brandy

*Serves 2*
*Serve with: Adelsheim Pinot Noir*

*Recipe by Lucinda Parker*

Ingredients (serves 2 to 4)
| | |
|---|---|
| 2 | top loin steaks, 1-inch thick |
| 1 | tsp. dried thyme |
| | pinch red pepper flakes |
| 2 | cloves garlic, crushed |
| 1 | tbs. vegetable oil |
| 1/4 | cup Clear Creek Apple Brandy |

Trim the steaks of all visible fat. Dry both sides of the meat with a paper towel. Sprinkle both sides lightly with thyme, red pepper and smear with crushed garlic. Heat the oil in a large cast iron skillet over medium heat until almost smoking. Add the steaks and sauté 3 minutes a side for medium doneness. Transfer to a platter and keep warm.

Scraping the bottom of the skillet, boil down the remaining pan juices over high heat for a minute or so until the liquid is reduced and slightly caramelized. Gradually stir in the apple brandy a tablespoon at a time until well blended and the alcohol evaporates, about 2 minutes. Pour the sauce over steaks and serve.

## Amity Vineyards

18150 Amity Vineyards Rd.
Amity, OR 97101
(503) 835-2362
FAX (503) 835-6451

**Tasting Room Hours:**
Daily, Noon to 5 PM,
February 1st through December 23rd.
Several festivals are offered each year. Write or
call the winery to receive mailings.

**Owners:** Myron Redford & Janis Checcia
**President and Winemaker:** Myron Redford
**First Year:** 1976
**Winery Capacity:** 34,000 Gallons

### Winery History

Myron Redford began his career in 1970 as
a cellar worker for the Associated Vintners
winery in Seattle. As he dreamed of having his
own winery, he learned his lessons well and
persevered until the opportunity came his
way. With the help of his mother, Ione, and
close friend Janis Checchia he brought Amity
Vineyards to a place of respect and prominence in the circles of Northwest wine.
Expansion of the winery in 1984 enabled a
production increase from 10,000 to over 20,000
gallons. Meanwhile, continued study of grape
growing and winemaking techniques have
kept Amity Vineyard wines on the plateau of
high quality.

### A visit to Amity Vineyards

As you head up Amity Vineyards Road
you will enjoy vistas through the trees of the
Yamhill County countryside. The rural, low-
tech nature of the experience is echoed in the
tasting bar which is in the corner of the winery.
This location affords a view of the operation in
stasis. A selection of Amity wines are offered
for tasting and a broader selection is available
for sale.

### The Wines

Myron Redford does not prefer over-oaked
Pinot Noir. His Pinots are aged in used French
oak and offer complexity gained from the
additional bottle age he insists upon. The
Winemaker's Reserve is his finest bottling.
The planting of Gamay noir a jus blanc (the
true grape of Beaujolais) at Amity was a
milestone in Oregon viticulture. Myron's

*Myron Redford and Vicky Wettle of Amity
Vineyards.*

research and dedication to this project has
finally yielded results in the fruity,
characterful wine created from these grapes.
Dry Gewurztraminer, Chardonnay, Pinot
Blanc, Riesling, Late Harvest Riesling and a
sulfite-free, organically grown "Ecowine" are
also made.

## Archery Summit

18599 NE Archery
Summit Road
Dayton, OR 97114
(503) 864-4300
FAX (503) 864-4038
**Email:** junew@archerysummit.com

**Owner/Winemaker:** Gary Andrus
**First Year:** 1993
**Production:** 23,000 Gallons

### Winery History

Archery Summit is the project of Gary
Andrus, owner of California's Pine Ridge
Vineyards. His spectacular new winery and
vineyards are on top of the Dundee Hills
bordering properties owned by Domaine
Drouhin and Sokol Blosser. Aging cellars were
bored out of the rock beneath the winery and
are a vision of wine country romance not often
seen in the U.S., much less the Northwest. As
activities have become organized, the winery is
now able to accept serious Pinot-philes for
visits and brief tours. Please call the winery
for an appointment.

**The Wines**

Pinot Noirs from 1993 and 1994 were produced at Pine Ridge from Oregon fruit shipped down in refrigerated trucks. The secret to the success of Archery Summit wines is the ability of the winery to control all aspects of grape production in the estate vineyards. Low crops and meticulous care have yielded stunning results.

The wines are vinted in separate lots based on vineyard source or preferred winemaking styles. The 1996 Brick House Vineyard Pinot Noir was a separate lot and the 100% Whole Cluster Pinot Noir offered the character found in wines produced by this method.

The 1996 Chene D'Oregon Pinot Noir was vinted from the traditional clones of Pommard and Wadenswil and was aged in Oregon oak barrels. The 1996 Jeunesse Pinot Noir was made from the winery's young plantings of Dijon clone Pinot Noir.

# Argyle – The Dundee Wine Company

691 Highway 99W
P.O. Box 280,
Dundee, OR 97115
(503) 538-8520, FAX (503 ) 538-2205

**Tasting Room Hours:** Daily, 11 AM to 5 PM

**Owners:** Brian Croser, Cal Knudsen
**Winemaker:** Rollin Soles
**First Year:** 1987
**Winery Capacity:** 105,000 Gallons

**Winery History**

Argyle was founded in 1987 by Australian vintner Brian Croser. Originally cloaked in secrecy, the operation produced several vintage cuvées for sparkling wine before releasing their first wine and opening their doors to the public. The wait was worth it. Quality methode champenoise sparkling wine from Argyle has become a signature item for anyone wanting to experience the spectrum of Northwest wine. Next to the winery building in downtown Dundee, a delightful Victorian house has been outfitted as a visitor center and tasting room complete with picket fence and flower garden.

**A visit to Argyle**

Just off Highway 99W in Dundee you'll find the quaint tasting room tucked into the parlor of the above-mentioned house. The bright and airy front room is a great place to enjoy samples of Argyle sparkling wine and the still wines made here. A nominal tasting fee is charged for sparkling wine samples, but you are tasting expensive, handmade sparkling wine. Toast your partner with this visit as your first or last stop of the day! A selection of gifts and accessories is offered.

**The Wines**

Methode champenoise sparkling wine is the focus at Argyle and the winery's partnership with grower Cal Knudsen ensures a consistent source of supply of the Pinot Noir and Chardonnay needed. Crisp Brut, Rose Brut and Blanc de Blancs offer forward fruity character that defines Argyle's Northwest style. Pinot Noir, Pinot Gris, Chardonnay and Dry Riesling complete the offerings.

In deference to the former nut processing plant that was converted to the winery, the Argyle reserve Pinot Noir is called Nuthouse Pinot Noir and their late harvest Riesling is similarly dubbed Nuthouse Riesling.

*Wendy and Tom Kreutner of Autumn Wind.*

# Autumn Wind Vineyard

15225 NE North Valley Rd.
Newberg, OR 97132
(503) 538-6931

**Tasting Room Hours:**
Daily, Noon to 5 PM, March - Nov. Weekends only during winter months.

**Owners & Winemakers:**
Tom & Wendy Kreutner
**First Year:** 1987

**Winery History**

Tom and Wendy Kreutner were financial executives who packed their bags and moved to Oregon from Los Angeles in 1977 to satisfy their love for the outdoors. After a short time in the Northwest, the excitement of being involved in the emerging Oregon wine industry proved too appealing to pass by. For two years they studied the Willamette Valley real estate scene until just the right piece of property caught their eye in 1983 - a 52-acre farm near Newberg.

"We worked ourselves silly to plant the first vines in 1984," says owner Wendy Kreutner. "The first plot of land was cleared of cherry trees and prepared for vineyard in just a year." Almost 20 acres are now planted with more vines going in to increase production.

**A visit to Autumn Wind Vineyards**

The small winery in the hills above Newberg offers tasting room facilities in the corner of the winery. Visitors can stroll among the oak barrels and stainless tanks while enjoying samples of Autumn Wind wines.

Outside, picnics at umbrella'd tables are encouraged and sunny-day walks through the vineyard are a relaxing diversion.

**The Wines**

Autumn Wind Vineyard's spicy and toasty Chardonnay and the rich and earthy Pinot Noirs are favorites with wine lovers. Muller Thurgau, Sauvignon Blanc and Pinot Gris are also made. Wendy Kreutner is a superb cook and enjoys offering wine pairing tips to tasting room visitors.

# Beaux Freres

15155 N.E.
North Valley Rd.
Newberg, OR 98132
(503) 537-1137

**Tasting Room Hours:**
No tasting room. Visits by appointment only.

**Owners:** Michael Etzel, Robert Parker, Jr., Robert Roy
**Winemaker:** Michael Etzel
**First Year:** 1991
**Winery Capacity:** 20,000 Gallons

**Winery History**

Just around the NW corner of Ribbon Ridge in the Chehalem Mountains, this operation was begun in 1988 with a 6-acre planting of Pinot Noir. The first harvests were custom-crushed at Ponzi Vineyards in 1991 and 1992, but a winery building on site now handles production. Partial ownership by Wine Advocate publisher Robert M. Parker, Jr. (Michael Etzel's brother-in-law, or *Beaux Freres*) has created excitement for the project greater than would be seen for a new winery operation of its size. The first Pinot Noir wines released in 1993 and 1994 were superb.

Michael Etzel attributes the quality of his wines to the care given to the Pinot Noir vines, now totalling 26 acres. Low crop yield of around two tons per acre and use of predominantly new French oak for aging make for intense, structured wines of character.

The winery is open only by appointment and the one wine produced is sold almost exclusively through a mailing list of regular customers though a little creeps out into restaurants and to select wine merchants.

# Belle Pente Wine Cellars

12470 NE Rowland Rd.
Carlton, OR 97111
(503) 852-6389
**Email:**
bellepente@pnn.com

**Tasting Room Hours:** No tasting room. Visits by appointment only.

**Owners:** Brian and Jill O'Donnell
**Winemaker:** Brian O'Donnell
**First Year:** 1994
**Winery Capacity:** 4,000 Gallons

### Winery History

Home winemakers since 1986, Brian and Jill O'Donnell purchased a 70-acre century farm near Carlton in 1992 and planted two acres of Pinot Noir in 1994. The vineyard has now grown to seven acres with a goal of eventually having 20 to 30 acres producing. A winery building was constructed in 1997 and the winery name, Belle Pente, means "beautiful slope."

### A visit to Belle Pente

The winery is open only by appointment or during special events held in conjunction with the Yamhill County Wineries Association.

### The Wines

Estate Pinot Noir is aged in one third new oak and Pinot Gris is fermented and aged in stainless steel to preserve the fruity quality. Chardonnay is barrel fermented in one half new oak, a mix of French, American and Oregon barrels.

# Brick House Vineyards

18200 Lewis Rogers Ln.
Newberg, OR 97132
(503) 538-5136

**Tasting Room Hours:**
By appointment only.
Open Memorial Day weekend and Thanksgiving Weekend.

**Owners:** Doug & Christine Tunnell
**Winemaker:** Doug Tunnell
**First Year:** 1994
**Production:** 3,000 Gallons

### Winery History

As a foreign correspondent for CBS news, Doug Tunnell traveled the world and had many unique and exciting experiences. The rural life of farming in Yamhill County was both a return to his roots in Western Oregon and a relief from a hectic lifestyle. Today, his Brick House Vineyards focuses on organic farming of vinifera grapes on an eastern slope of Chehalem Mountain. The 26-acre vineyard has been planted to Pinot Noir, Gamay Noir and Dijon clone Chardonnay. While the majority of the vineyard's crop is sold to other wineries, small quantities of Pinot Noir, Gamay Noir and Dijon-clone Chardonnay are now being produced under the Brick House label.

### A visit to Brick House Vineyards

Doug Tunnell's operation was primarily grape growing until Steve Doerner of Cristom Vineyards helped him ferment some Pinot Noir at the Cristom Winery. As Doug gradually made space for his tiny winery he transferred more and more of the winemaking to his converted barn/winery. Though usually open by appointment, Brick House participates in the Memorial Day Weekend and Thanksgiving Weekend wine tasting event in Yamhill County.

# Cameron

P.O. Box 27
8200 Worden Hill Rd.
Dundee, OR 97115
(503) 232-6652

**Owners:** John Paul,
friends and family
**Winemaker:** John Paul
**First Year:** 1984
**Winery Capacity:** 10,000+ Gallons
**Tasting Room Hours:** By appointment only.

### Winery History

Veteran enologist John Paul chose Oregon for his own winery after working in three other famous viticultural regions. John studied winemaking in Burgundy before taking the helm of Napa Valley's Carneros Creek Winery for three years. He then headed to New Zealand for experience in a different climate and setting. He brought to Oregon definite ideas about the wine he wanted to make. In 1987 the winery moved into a new structure built in the hills above Dundee. A partnership with grape grower Bill Wayne led John to look for quarters closer to the viticultural origin of his wines. The winery's large, subterranean barrel cellar allows room to expand production when the need arises.

### A visit to Cameron Winery

Cameron Winery produces only small quantities of wine and the distribution is mostly local. The winery has no regular tasting room hours, but visitors are welcome by appointment or at the Wine Country Thanksgiving event in November.

### The Wines

Cameron Pinot Noir and Chardonnay are unique bottlings made in the personal style of winemaker John Paul. Toasty, buttery Chardonnay with complex aroma and flavor is made in both a regular and reserve version. Similarly, two or more bottlings of Pinot Noir from designated vineyard sources provide a choice for consumers. The Pinot Blanc has been renamed Pinot Bianco Cameroni di Collini Rossi (Pinot Blanc from Cameron of the Red Hills) and the "Clos Electrique" Pinot Noir is a mystery left to the wine lover to discover.

# Carlo & Julian

1000 E. Main St.
Carlton, OR 97111
(503) 852-7432

**Tasting Room Hours:** By appointment and at Yamhill County Winery events.

**Owners:** Annette & Felix Madrid
**Winemaker:** Felix Madrid
**First Year:** 1996

### Winery History

Named after twin brothers in the owners family, Carlo and Julian winery was bonded in 1996. Owner/winemaker Felix Madrid worked for Erath Winery for two years and for Rex Hill for six years before striking out on his own. The Carlo & Julian winery is located in a small building in downtown Carlton.

The winery participates in the two Yamhill County winery events where interested visitors may stop by and sample the wines.

### The Wines

Barrel-fermented Sauvignon Blanc and Gewurztraminer have won a following with their ripe-yet-bone dry style. A vineyard designated Pinot Noir is produced from Croft Vineyard and a Willamette Valley Pinot is blended from three vineyards, including the Carlo and Julian estate vineyard.

# Champoeg Wine Cellars

10375 Champoeg Rd. NE
Aurora, OR 97002
(503) 678-2144
**Email:**
champoeg@teleport.com

**Tasting Room Hours:** May - October, Daily 11 AM to 6 PM, winter: weekends, 12 to 5 PM

**Owners:** Pitterle, Killian and Myers families
**Winemaker:** Elise Pitterle
**First Year:** 1990

### Winery History

From a vineyard planted in 1974, the partnership of families owning Champoeg Wine Cellars made their first wines in 1990.

Previous harvests were sold to other Willamette Valley wineries from 1978 to 1989. The vineyard is planted on the south-facing slope of "La Butte" above the Willamette River near the historic Champoeg State Park. The first estate bottled wines were made in 1992.

### A visit to Champoeg Wine Cellars

By following signs to Champoeg State Park (pronounced "sham poo ick"), the winery is easily reached from Highway 219 near Newberg or from I-5 (Exit 282). You can view the vineyard and winery from the tasting room and enjoy an alfresco picnic on the property.

### The Wines

Pinot Noir, Chardonnay and White Riesling are current releases along with Muller Thurgau and Pinot Gris..

# Chateau Benoit

6580 N.E Mineral
Springs Road
Carlton, OR 97111
(503) 864-2991
FAX (503) 864-2203
Quality Factory Village
Hwy. 101, Lincoln City

**Tasting Room Hours:** Daily, 10 AM to 5 PM

**Owners:** LeCep II, Inc.
**Winemaker:** Fred Benoit
**First Year:** 1979
**Winery Capacity:** 85,000 Gallons

### Winery History

As part of the early beginnings of the Oregon wine rush, physician Fred Benoit and his wife Mary began a project to create a winery steeped in French tradition including the making of sparkling wine by the methode champenoise.

Today Chateau Benoit stands like a French chateau above vineyard and farmland, an imposing structure dominating the skyline as you approach from the valley floor. Expansion of the original facility now allows for special events as well as use of the winery reception hall for weddings, parties and celebrations of all kinds.

*The Chateau Benoit winery near Lafayette, Oregon.*

### A visit to Chateau Benoit

The spectacular hilltop winery and chateau offer a fabulous view of Yamhill County and a grand opportunity to picnic on sunny days. The welcome is warm and friendly. When you're visiting the Oregon Coast, stop by the Chateau Benoit Wine and Food Center (a nifty cafe/tasting room combination) at Lincoln City's factory outlet mall.

### The Wines

The original claim to fame of Chateau Benoit was methode champenoise sparkling wine but most bottlings are now varietal still wines. A non-vintage Brut is yet part of the lineup. Chardonnay, Riesling, Sauvignon Blanc and Pinot Noir are distributed regionally. Pinot Gris, Dry Gewurztraminer, dessert wines and the sparkling Brut are available at the winery or the Lincoln City tasting room.

Production of Reserve wines from Dijon clone grapes have been very well received including both Chardonnay and Pinot Noir.

## Chehalem

31190 NE Veritas Lane
Newberg, OR 97132
(503) 538-4700
FAX (503) 537-0850
**Email:**
harrypn@chehalemwines.com

**Tasting Room Hours:**
Memorial Day and Thanks-
giving weekends or by
appointment.

**Owners:** Harry Peterson-Nedry and Bill &
Cathy Stoller
**Winemakers:** Harry P-N, Cheryl Francis
**First Year:** 1993
**Winery Capacity:** 25,000 Gallons

### Winery History

Wine writer Judy Peterson-Nedry and her
husband Harry have been carefully tending
their Ridgecrest Vineyard in the Chehalem
hills northwest of Newberg since its planting
in 1980. Providing grapes to other vintners for
eight vintages and seeing the quality of the
resulting wines convinced Harry that the time
was right to bond his own facility. In the fall
of 1995 Chehalem completed negotiations to
purchase nearby Veritas Vineyards winery.

### A visit to Chehalem winery

The winery participates in the Memorial
Day and Thanksgiving weekend open house
events and is also open by appointment.

### The Wines

An intensely berry-and-spice Pinot Noir
heads the line with a light and fresh Pinot Gris.
Small lots of toasty Chardonnay and a Gamay
Noir blend named Cerise are also made. The
fine quality grapes from the 1994 vintage
encouraged Harry to begin his Reserve Pinot
Noir program in partnership with his longtime
friend from Burgundy, Patrice Rion. The two
winemakers shared opinions about matters
enological in creating the blend which will be
released under the Chehalem label "Rion
Reserve."

A special lot of Chardonnay, Ian's Reserve,
was released in 1998 in memory of Ian
Peterson-Nedry, Harry and Judy's son who
died in a tragic accident in the fall of 1996.

*Winemakers Harry Peterson-Nedry and Cheryl Francis of Chehalem.*

## Cuneo Cellars

9360 S.E. Eola Hills Rd.
Amity, OR 97101
(503) 835-2782

**Tasting Room Hours:**
Saturday, Noon to 5 PM

**Owners:** Gino Cuneo,
Martin Barrett
**Winemaker:** Gino Cuneo
**First Year:** 1980
**Winery Capacity:** 15,000 Gallons

### Winery History

Among the first wine ventures in the Eola
Hills, the former Hidden Springs Winery
found new life as Cuneo Cellars. Winemaker
Gino Cuneo has a great fondness for rich red
wines and especially Italian varietals. His
small production of Nebbiolo from Yakima
Valley fruit promises to increase with each
vintage and is complemented by his rich and
complex Cana's Feast Cabernet blend.

### A visit to Cuneo Cellars

Enjoy a pleasant drive to the top of the
Eola Hills, then a tasting with owner Gino
Cuneo. A pleasant picnic patio overlooks
adjacent orchards and vineyards.

### The Wines

Pinot Noir, Cabernet-Merlot and Nebbiolo
are the focus of Cuneo Cellars, along with the
above-mentioned Cana's Feast.

## Canlis' Executive Chef Greg Atkinson

*Greg Atkinson came to Canlis in 1997-98. The author of* In Season, Culinary Adventures of a San Juan Island Chef, *summarizes the Canlis philosophy as: "At the entrance to Canlis stands a Kura Door from a seventeenth century Japanese 'Treasure House.' We are Seattle's Treasure House where people celebrate the special events of their lives with our cuisine that celebrates the seasonal bounty of the Pacific Northwest.*

### ❖ A RECIPE FROM CANLIS ❖

# Pear-Shaped Poussin with Green Peppercorns and Morels

*Serves 4 - Serve with Domaine Drouhin Oregon Pinot Noir*

2   poussins, 18 - 24 ounces each
    salt and pepper
    pinch thyme
    Morel Stuffing, recipe follows
2   tablespoons butter
    Green Peppercorn Sauce, recipe follows
    asparagus tips, sautéed morels
    thyme sprigs for garnish

Bone chicken and keep meat intact by cutting first along breast bone, then disjointing wing, then cutting along backbone and disjointing thigh. The aim is to form two half chickens with only the lower leg bone attached. Sprinkle boned half chicken with salt, pepper, and thyme. Preheat oven to 350° F. In each half-chicken, fill hole left from leg bone with 2 tablespoons stuffing and wrap breast meat over the stuffing. Fold thigh meat over breast meat and arrange half chickens, seam side down with bone pointing straight up in a roasting pan. Brush with melted butter and roast, basting occasionally, 35 minutes, or until chicken is cooked through. Transfer chicken to a warm platter and keep warm while preparing sauce. Put an ounce of sauce on each of four warmed plates then arrange sautéed morels and asparagus tips in a circle around the border of the plates. Plant a half chicken in the center of each plate and garnish each one with a sprig of thyme.

## Morel Stuffing

1   slice white bread, crusts removed
1/3 cup heavy cream
1/2 tsp green peppercorns, crushed
1/3 cup finely ground white meat (chicken, veal or turkey)

6   morels, finely diced
    pinch nutmeg
    salt and pepper to taste

Soak bread in cream. In mixing bowl, combine peppercorns, meat, diced morels, nutmeg, salt and pepper. Stir in soaked bread. Use stuffing to fill boned chickens.

## Green Peppercorn Sauce

    pan juices from roasted chicken
1/4 cup cognac
1   cup stock
1/2 cup heavy cream

1   bay leaf
1   tsp. green peppercorns
    sprigs of thyme to garnish each portion

Pour fat away from pan juices. Put pan on burner and de-glaze with cognac. Burn away alcohol and add stock, bring liquid to a boil and strain into a saucepan. Stir in cream, bay leaf and peppercorns, and boil 5 minutes, or until sauce is thickened.

## Domaine Drouhin Oregon

P.O. Box 700,
Dundee, OR 97115
(503) 864-2700
**Web:** www.drouhin.com

**Owner:** Joseph Drouhin
**Winemaker:** Véronique Jousset-Drouhin
**First Year:** 1988
**Tasting Room Hours:** None.
Wines are available nationally.

### Winery History

When the Drouhin family of Burgundy decided to buy land in the Willamette Valley it created such a stir that Oregon's governor made a special announcement and the whole Oregon wine industry was temporarily stunned by the event. The vindication of belief in Oregon's climate seemed now to be complete. An experienced and successful Burgundian producer had staked his reputation on Oregon as a region where fine Pinot Noir wines could be made.

Robert Drouhin and his daughter Véronique visited the area several times and then made arrangements for their first crush in 1988. In 1989, the crush took place in the new Drouhin winery, built on four levels comprising 8-1/2 stories. The hillside construction takes advantage of natural coolness of the earth and permits processing by gravity. The facility is singularly designed to produce Pinot Noir. Véronique Drouhin spends the harvest months each year in Oregon but her permanent home remains in France. Manager Bill Hatcher oversees the operation of the winery with consultation from the Drouhins as necessary. The 180-acre vineyard at the estate is a superb site for growing Pinot Noir.

### A visit to Domaine Drouhin Oregon

The Drouhin winery does not offer tours or tastings. You can get a nice view of the winery from the crush pad at Sokol Blosser or if you take a drive around the Dundee Hills.

### The Wines

There has been but one varietal released at Domaine Drouhin Oregon, Pinot Noir. The

*The Domaine Drouhin Oregon winery in the Dundee Hills.*

regular vintage bottling includes fruit purchased from other growers throughout the Yamhill County area. The Laurene bottling is made exclusively from grapes grown at the Domaine Drouhin estate. Both wines are superb examples of Oregon Pinot Noir and are excellent accompaniments to fine cuisine.

The winery has experimented with Chardonnay and rumor has it that it is a very nice wine. Prospects for release are closely guarded but it seems inevitable that such a successful operation would not expand production to include a quality white wine.

## Domaine Serene

P.O. Box 280
Carlton, OR 97111
(503) 852-7777

**Owners:** Ken & Grace Evenstad
**Winemaker:** Ken Wright
**First Vintage:** 1990
**Winery Capacity:** 2,400 Gallons

### Winery History

Domaine Serene is the project of Ken and Grace Evenstad who established their vineyard near Dundee and bonded their winery in 1994. Ken Wright has been their consulting winemaker since the first vintage and now shares space in their recently acquired facility in nearby Carlton (on Highway 47). Domaine Serene recently moved into a new building and plans to continue production of their Reserve

*Continued on page 152.*

### Jerry Traunfeld
### Chef, The Herbfarm

*The Herbfarm is tucked between two rivers 30 minutes east of Seattle in the foothills of the Cascade Mountains. The farm began 25 years ago when Lola Zimmerman had some extra chives, which she sold from a wheelbarrow at the roadside. From this beginning, The Herbfarm nursery grew until over 600 different herb varieties and 300 different kinds of heritage fruit trees, berries, and edible vines were offered. The Herbfarm also has an Herb Shop as well as a school that offers over 300 classes each year.*

*In 1986, Lola's son Ron and his wife, Carrie Van Dyck, joined The Herbfarm and opened The Herbfarm Restaurant. The little restaurant served prix fixe 6-course luncheons and 9-course dinners featuring only seasonal and regional foods and wines of the Pacific Northwest. For the next 11 years, the restaurant never had an unbooked table and was featured in every major national culinary publication. Chef Jerry Traunfeld was twice nominated for the James Beard Award.*

*The restaurant was completely destroyed by fire in 1997 and will reopen in 1999 featuring deluxe overnight accommodations as well as award-winning cuisine.*

## ❖ A RECIPE FROM THE HERBFARM ❖

## Grilled Salmon with Fennel Pinot Noir Sauce

*Serves 4 - Serve with Domaine Serene Pinot Noir*

6   12-inch dry fennel stalks (optional)
1   pound king salmon fillet
1   tbs. olive oil
1   tsp. chopped fresh fennel or ground fennel seed
    Salt and pepper

Soak the fennel stalks, if using, in cold water for 30 minutes, drain.  Skin and trim the salmon and remove the pinbones with tweezers or needle nose pliers.  Divide into 4 equal pieces.  Stir the oil and fennel seed together in a mixing bowl, add the salmon and toss to coat the fish.  Season with salt and pepper.

Prepare the grill.  When very hot, place the fennel stalks on the coals to create smoke.  Place the fish fillets on the grill, cover and cook until desired doneness, turning once.  Watch the fish carefully and don't let it blacken. Serve while hot with the pinot noir sauce. Garnish with fennel sprigs or blossoms.  4 servings.

### Fennel Pinot Noir Sauce

1   small shallot, minced, about 2 tbs.
2   tsp. unsalted butter
1   cup full-bodied pinot noir
1   tsp. chopped fresh (or ground) fennel seed
1   tsp. sugar
2   tsp. red wine vinegar
3   additional tbs. unsalted butter, room temperature
1   cup chopped fennel leaves (bronze or green)
    Freshly ground black pepper

Melt the 2 tsp. butter in a saucepan over medium heat. Add the shallot and cook, stirring, for about 1 minute, until softened but not brown. Add the pinot noir, fennel seed, sugar, vinegar and salt. Raise the heat to high, bring to a boil, and continue to boil until the mixture is reduced by 2/3. The sauce can be made ahead up to this point.

Bring the reduction back up to a simmer and whisk the butter, 1 tbs. at a time. Stir in the fennel leaves and add black pepper to taste.  Serve immediately.

Pinot Noir and Evenstad Reserve Pinot Noir.

**A Visit to Domaine Serene**

Maintaining no tasting room at the new facility, the owners ask that you write or call for an appointment.

# Duck Pond Cellars

23145 Hwy. 99W
P.O. Box 429
Dundee, OR 97115
(503) 538-3199
FAX (503) 538-3190
**Email:** duckpond@duckpond.com
**Web:** www.duckpondcellars.com

**Tasting Room Hours:** Daily, 11 AM to 5 PM

**Owners:** The Fries Family
**Winemaker:** Greg Fries
**First Vintage:** 1989
**Winery Open:** 1993

**Winery History**

Duck Pond Cellars was founded by Doug and Jo Ann Fries with the first vineyard planted in 1986 in Dundee. Close plant spacing (one meter by two meter) yielded 2,000 vines per acre which will allow a light crop load per vine. Several members of the Fries family are involved with the operation including daughter Lisa Fries Jenkins (sales and marketing), sons Greg Fries (winemaker) and Matt Fries (vineyard and cellar assistant).

**A visit to Duck Pond Cellars**

The winery on Highway 99W just north of Dundee is a popular tourist stop. Friendly staff pour samples and discuss the wines while you can shop for wine, gifts and snacks.

**The Wines**

Quality Pinot Noir, Pinot Gris, Chardonnay, Cabernet Sauvignon, Merlot and other varietals are available. The wines have been received as very good values and are widely distributed.

# Dundee Springs Winery

600 NW Dogwood Ln.
Dundee, OR 97115
(503) 554-8000
FAX (503) 538-3190

**Tasting Room Hours:**
Daily, 11 AM to 5 PM (corner of Hwy. 99 W and Fox Farm Road)

**Owners:** Mary Lynne Perry, Christopher J. Bower
**Winemakers:** John Haw, Jim Kakacek
**First Year:** 1992

A few years in Europe planted the seed for vines and wines in Mary Lynne Perry, one of the proprietors of Dundee Springs Winery. She and partner Chris Bower began planting their (now) 65-acre vineyard in 1990. Small lots of wine were produced beginning in 1992 and the Dundee Springs tasting room opened in 1998. Winery construction is scheduled for 1999. The emphasis is on estate wines utilizing fruit from their vineyard which is cropped at low tonnage per acre.

# Elk Cove Vineyards

27751 NW Olson Road
Gaston, OR 97119
(503) 985-7760
FAX (503) 985-3525

**Tasting Room Hours:**
Daily, 11 AM to 5 PM,
Tours and tour groups by appointment.

**Owners/Winemakers:**
Pat, Joe and Adam Campbell
**First Year:** 1977
**Winery Capacity:** 40,000 Gallons

**Winery History**

Like many Oregon wineries, Elk Cove Vineyards began as a dream of country life and the pursuit of fine winemaking. Both Joe and Pat Campbell are dedicated to the success of Elk Cove – wines and winery. Their son Adam is now an important part of the team, as well. A vineyard expansion in 1985 led to founding a new label, La Bohème. Special grapes from this site west of the estate vineyard created the opportunity for a special, super-premium brand of Pinot Noir and Chardonnay.

### A visit to Elk Cove Vineyards

Easiest access to Elk Cove Vineyards is by Highway 240 from Newberg or Highways 8 or 26 from Portland to Highway 47. The Elk Cove tasting room offers a mini-panorama of the 'cove' filled with vineyard and the helpful tasting room staff offers a wide selection of Elk Cove wines to traveling wine tasters. The winery sponsors jazz concerts and festivals during the spring and summer months. Call for information.

### The Wines

Stylistically these wines demand food. The white wines offer crisp acidity and full-fruitiness to complement a wide range of seafood as well as appetizers and lighter meats. The Pinot Noir is a classic Burgundian treasure of texture and spice that has been greeted with accolades from consumers and wine competitions alike. White varietals include Chardonnay, Pinot Gris, Gewurztra-miner and Riesling. Reds include Pinot Noir (several different vineyard bottlings) and Cabernet Sauvignon. A selection of dessert-style, late harvest wines is designated by the Ultima label.

# Erath Vineyards

9009 NE Worden Hill Rd.
Dundee, OR 97115
(503) 538-3318,
FAX (503) 538-1074
Email: erath.com
Web: www.erath.com

**Tasting Room Hours:** Daily, 11 AM to 5 PM
Tours and groups by appointment.

**Owners:** Dick and Joan Erath
**Winemakers:** Dick Erath, Rob Stuart
**First Year:** 1972
**Winery Capacity:** 120,000 Gallons

**Winery History**

Originally a partnership between wine-maker Dick Erath and lumberman Cal Knudsen (who provided capital to expand the winery/vineyard operation at the beginning), Dick Erath acquired sole ownership of the winery in 1988. Working with his own vineyard sites and with other growers, Dick strives to produce the finest grapes. He jokes that grape growing in Oregon requires some black magic in addition to dedication and skill. The winery is one of the largest in Oregon due to Erath's commitment and innovation. In 1995 the winery revived the Erath Vineyards label, creating once again an accurate presenta-tion of winery ownership and direction.

### A visit to Knudsen Erath Winery

If you enjoy award-winning Pinot Noir and other varietals, Knudsen Erath is an important tasting room to visit. Friendly staff know the wines and the proprietors have thoughtfully stocked a complete line of gifts and logo-ware. Also a nice picnic patio among the oaks and vineyards is provided, complete with winery dog, Fast Eddie, who enjoys sampling gourmet foods. Drive into the Red Hills of Dundee on Worden Hill Road to find the winery near Crabtree Park. Parents can let the kids run off some energy at the park before heading on to the next stop. The winery owners and staff are always looking for a reason to have a party and their Harvest Festival in late summer is legendary. Call for details.

### The Wines

Knudsen Erath has, from the beginning, had a reputation of being the producer of one of Oregon's finest Pinot Noirs. The Vintage Select designation signifies a reserve-style lot that offers depth and complexity along with age-ability for the long haul. Cuisine-friendly Dry Gewurztraminer and Dry Riesling have proven very popular. Also produced are Chardonnay, Cabernet Sauvignon and late harvest Riesling and Gewurztraminer. Soon to join the line will be a Dolcetto from the estate vineyard.

*Diana and David Lett, owners of The Eyrie Vineyards.*

## The Eyrie Vineyards

P.O. Box 697,
Dundee, OR 97115
935 E. 10th,
McMinnville, OR 97128
(503) 472-6315
FAX (503) 472-5124

**Tasting and Tours:** By appointment only or Memorial Day and Thanksgiving Open Houses

**Owners:** David & Diana Lett
**Winemaker:** David Lett
**First Year:** 1970
**Vineyard Planted:** 1966
**Winery Capacity:** 25,000 Gallons

### Winery History

David Lett is in the wine business to make wine. First and foremost his goal is to produce the best possible bottle of wine from the best grapes he can grow. In the world of storybook, castle wineries with views across the vineyards and flocks of eager tour guides, David Lett prefers his quiet back street in McMinnville where he can make his wine.

Since the mid-1960s he has been the proponent and champion of winegrowing in Western Oregon. A decade of grapegrowing separates him from almost every other Oregon winery and he has tried hard to make the time work to his advantage. He stimulated the flurry of Pinot Gris planting when he grafted over his White Riesling vines to the French variety. At times he seems obsessed with the matching of varietal clones to the challenging cool of the Willamette Valley. His style is intense and focused, yet refined.

### A visit to The Eyrie Vineyards

A drive to McMinnville on Thanksgiving Weekend can reward you with a glimpse of this master out of his element. For these few days he welcomes friends, admirers and strangers without appointment to share his wines and enjoy music and warm conversation. After the holidays it's back to work. David and Diana Lett's dedication is complete, their commitment total. Their satisfaction is in knowing that they've made the best wine they can make.

### The Wines

David Lett has had very few failures when it comes to making Pinot Noir. Recent tastings going back to his first vintages reveal a combination of luck and skill in creating wines that gain complexity and character with age while holding off the negative effects of time. Nuances of cherry, spice and plum in the aroma yield to toasty fruit and spice in the mouth. Eyrie wines are best appreciated with characterful cuisine - especially in their youth. Muscat Ottonel, Pinot Gris, Pinot Meunier and Chardonnay are also made.

## Golden Valley Vineyards

980 East Fourth St.
McMinnville, OR 97128
(503) 472-2739
FAX (503) 434-8523
**Email:** pkircher@onlinemac.com

**Owners:** Peter and Celia Kircher
**Winemaker:** John Eliasson
**Production:** 2,000 Gallons

### Winery History

In 1987 Peter and Celia Kircher were operating their commercial fishing boat off Kodiak Island, Alaska when they happened to sample a bottle of 1983 Adelsheim Pinot Noir. Impressed by the quality and potential for Oregon wines, they decided to visit Yamhill County and begin a search for a vineyard site of their own. A prime piece of property was purchased in the Dundee Hills and Saint Herman's vineyard was planted in 1990. Retiring from Alaska salmon fishing in 1993, the Kirchers opened the Golden Valley Microbrewery and Pub in McMinnville.

*Continued on page 156.*

### Nick and Linda Peirano
### Nick's Italian Cafe

Nick Peirano has been a legend in Yamhill County for almost twenty years, with his restaurant serving as the unofficial gathering place for the winemakers of Yamhill County and beyond.

Nick's Italian Cafe on 3rd Street in downtown McMinnville offers fine food with a tradition of excellence that has remained constant. The delicious minestrone soup is made from a family recipe, the pasta courses are sublime (pasta made fresh at the restaurant), and entrees such as rack of lamb, salmon or veal are expertly prepared and served by a staff that is friendly and efficient.

Nick himself is a quiet man whose casual demeanor and sincerity have endeared him to diners for years. Always a close associate of the Oregon wine industry, he has watched it grow and he has hosted legendary tastings of the area's most famous wines.

He was one of the founders of the International Pinot Noir Celebration and directed the kitchen staff for years. He offered his signature dishes as part of the menu when requested.

Nick's is the Oregon wine country just as the Statue of Liberty is New York City. If you're in the neighborhood, don't miss it.

(Note: the photo above was taken at a western-themed, wine country party. Nick's restaurant is strictly Italian!)

## ❖ A RECIPE FROM NICK'S ITALIAN CAFE ❖

# Rosemary Marinated Rack of Lamb

*Serves 4 - Serve with Oregon Pinot Noir*
*Choose your favorite from Adelsheim, Chehalem, Eyrie, Erath, Ponzi or the many others. They are all friends and devotees of Nick's Italian Cafe.*

4　lamb racks, frenched

### Marinade
1/2　cup olive oil
1/2　cup soy sauce
1/4　cup red wine
　　　black pepper to taste
8　cloves garlic, minced
1/4　cup fresh rosemary leaves

Marinate lamb racks 4 to 5 hours, not more.

Cook racks on grill, basting frequently until thermometer inserted in center of meat reads 140° F. for rare, 155° F. for medium-rare.

Alternately, bake in 375-400° F. oven to medium rare tested with thermometer as above..

Success of the pub was immediate and a credit to the owner's good taste and insight. Grapes from Saint Herman's Vineyard are vinified at Panther Creek and bottled under the Golden Valley label.

**A Visit to Golden Valley Vineyards**
The Golden Valley Pub is also the tasting room for the wines of the same name. Great food, great beer . . . why not great wine? See listing under Dining.

**The Wines**
Currently available from Golden Valley are Pinot Noir and Dijon clone Chardonnay.

## Hamacher Wines

40845 SW
Burgarsky Rd.
Gaston, OR 97119
(503) 985-0120

**Owner/Winemaker:** Eric Hamacher
**First Year:** 1995

**Winery History**
Eric Hamacher has worked in the cellars of a dozen different wineries in California as a beginner, assistant winemaker for four years at Chalone, and winemaker for a year at Etude. He discovered Oregon when he worked the 1988 harvest at Rex Hill and has concentrated ever since on Pinot Noir and Chardonnay.

While developing his own Oregon brand since 1995, he worked as winemaker at Medici Vineyard. In addition to giving him a place to make his Hamacher wines, he learned the vineyards and viticulture of the area. Since there is no Hamacher winery as yet, there is no place to visit. The best way to try the wines is to hunt them out at exclusive Oregon wine shops or to call the winemaker.

**The Wines**
Eric Hamacher has distinct winemaking styles that include native yeast fermentation and native malolactic bacteria. He leases vineyard by the acre to control crop size and he oversees all vineyard management.

His wines are highly sought after and a little bit of each 1,400 case annual production goes to select markets nationwide.

## Kramer Vineyards

26830 NW Olson Rd.
Gaston, OR 97119
(503) 662-4545

**Tasting Room Hours:**
Friday through Sunday,
Noon to 5 PM. Closed January and February.

**Owners:** Trudy and Keith Kramer
**Winemaker:** Trudy Kramer
**First Year:** 1989
**Winery Capacity:** 6,500 Gallons

**Winery History**
Kramer Vineyards is a labor of love for Keith and Trudy Kramer. Gold medals at the State Fair for Trudy's homemade raspberry wine started the Kramers thinking that winemaking wasn't all that hard. Vine tending didn't seem too hard either and now they have a thriving 12-acre vineyard at their home/winery estate. Keith Kramer continues to work as a pharmacist (taking the occasional vacation day to work the vineyard or a week or two during crush). Trudy takes care of family matters and handles the day to day chores around the winery. Just a few years of commercial production have shown these energetic entrepreneurs the path to success.

**A visit to Kramer Vineyards**
Just up Olson Road from Elk Cove, Kramer Vineyards welcomes wine lovers with their own style. The knight of the vineyard guards the parking lot and the tasting room is informal and airy. Whether you're partial to delicious fruit wines or well-structured grape varietals, Trudy Kramer has a wine for you. Special events are plentiful here – try the Weird Foods Festival or the Berry Social. Call the winery for details of upcoming events. Being family oriented themselves, Kramer Vineyards offers activities for children and a free beverage for designated drivers.

**The Wines**
Kramer Vineyards' Gewurztraminer, Pinot Gris and Raspberry wine are among the favorites made here. Other varietals include Pinot Noir, Chardonnay, Riesling and Muller Thurgau. Fruit wines vary with the season.

# Kristin Hill Winery

3330 SE Amity-Dayton Highway
Amity, OR 97101
(503) 835-0850

**Tasting Room Hours:** Daily, May - October, Noon to 5 PM, Nov. - April, weekends only.

**Owners:** Aberg Family
**Winemaker:** Eric Aberg
**First Year:** 1990
**Winery Capacity:** 3,000 Gallons

## Winery History

Linda and Eric Aberg are both retired from the U. S. Army and fell in love with wine while stationed in Europe. With some home winemaking experience, the Abergs began to dream of owning their own winery. A search for vineyard land ended in the Willamette Valley where the first vines were planted in 1985. The winery was bonded in 1990 and small lots of selected varietals are produced annually. The grand opening of their tasting room took place in May of 1993.

## A visit to Kristin Hill Winery

Relaxed atmosphere is the order of the day at Kristin Hill where visitors can play catch with winery dog Pinot Gris and most often meet the owners for some barrel tasting.

## The Wines

Kristin Hill produces Pinot Noir, Chardonnay, Riesling, Gewurztraminer and a tasty methode champenoise sparkling wine named Jennifer Falls Brut.

# Lange Winery

18380 NE Buena Vista
P.O. Box 8
Dundee, OR 97115
(503) 538-6476

**Tasting Room Hours:** Daily, 11 AM to 6 PM December through May, weekends only Noon to 5 PM.

**Owners:** Wendy & Don Lange
**Winemaker:** Don Lange
**First Year:** 1987

## Winery History:

Don and Wendy Lange moved to the Willamette Valley from Santa Barbara and have followed the lead of other area residents by taking a leap into winemaking. Six acres of Pinot Noir are now in place at the estate above Dundee and the large winery building is adjacent to the Lange's home.

## A visit to Lange Winery

Drive up Worden Hill Road from Dundee and watch for your right turn marked by a sign for Lange Winery. A few twists and turns lead to the attractive winery where owner Wendy Lange is often on hand dispensing "dry wine and dry humor." A great visit.

## The Wines

The wines produced here include Pinot Noir, Chardonnay and Pinot Gris. The Pinot Gris is ripe and toasty while the Chardonnay offers complex nuances of citrus, oak and earth. Don Lange's Pinot Noir has aromas of cherries and spice, delivering a fruity palate and long finish.

# Medici Vineyards

28005 NE Bell Road
Newberg, OR 97132
(503) 538-9668

**Owners:**
Hal & Dot Medici
**Winemaker:** Peter Rosbach
**First Year:** 1995

**Winery History**

The Medici Vineyard has been a source for quality Pinot Noir fruit for almost two decades. A winery was established in 1995 and the first wines were released under the Medici label. Hal Medici welcomes visitors by appointment to look around the winery and vineyard with a great view of the valley.

# McKinlay Vineyards

7120 Earlwood Rd.
Newberg, OR 97132
(503) 625-2534

**Tasting Room Hours:** By appointment.

**Owners:** Matt & Holly Kinne
**Winemaker:** Matt Kinne
**First Year:** 1989

**Winery History**

Matt Kinne is doing what he wants to do. The challenge of making high quality wine and establishing a small vineyard is a good complement to his family life. Winery, home and vineyard are located on a thirty-acre plot just above the Willamette River near Newberg. Matt's U.C. Davis training and experience in the California and Oregon wine industries prepared him well for his independent operation. Production is increasing with the estate vineyard bearing since 1994.

**A visit to McKinlay Vineyards**

McKinlay Vineyards is open for the traditional Oregon wine industry holidays and by appointment. Matt Kinne encourages visitors to call and come out for a visit.

**The Wines**

Pinot Noir and barrel-fermented Chardonnay are currently produced as well as Pinot Gris. The winemaker believes in diversity of both site and cooperage to make the most interesting, complex wines.

# Panther Creek Cellars

455 N. Irvine
McMinnville, OR 97128
(503) 472-8080, FAX (503) 472-5667

**Tasting Room Hours:** By appointment.

**Owner:** Ron Kaplan
**Winemaker:** Mark Vlossak
**First Year:** 1985
**Winery Capacity:** 20,000 Gallons

**Winery History**

Founded by winemaker Ken Wright in 1986—and then nurtured to success—Panther Creek Cellars was rescued from a bitter business dispute in 1994 by Iowan Ron Kaplan. A lover of Burgundy wine and French cooking, Kaplan discovered the Oregon wine scene in 1991. His search for a suitable winery property led to the purchase of Panther Creek and his fast friendship with Ken Wright. Although Wright has founded his own winery (see Ken Wright Cellars) he helped Kaplan get organized and begin a new era at Panther Creek. Winemaker Mark Vlossak came on board just after the change of ownership.

**A visit to Panther Creek Cellars**

Located in the original power plant building for the city of McMinnville built in 1924, Panther Creek enthusiastically welcomes visitors by appointment. The winery opens for Memorial Day Weekend and Wine Country Thanksgiving events.

**The Wines**

A rich and complex style of Pinot Noir is being created by Ron Kaplan and Mark Vlossak at Panther Creek. Regular and reserve bottlings are the mainstay, but vineyard designated Pinots from Freedom Hill, Shea and Bednarik vineyards are highly sought after. Chardonnay from Washington's Celilo Vineyard is rich and complex. Melon is made from Oregon's oldest vineyard source for this little-known white French varietal, and is crafted in a light and flavorful style that complements fine cuisine.

## Rex Hill Vineyards

30835 N Highway 99W
Newberg, OR 97132
(503) 538-0666
FAX (503) 538-1409

**Tasting Room Hours:** Daily, 11 AM to 5 PM

**Owners:** Paul Hart and Jan Jacobsen
**President/Winemaker:** Lynn Penner-Ash
**First Year:** 1983
**Winery Capacity:** 75,000 Gallons

### Winery History

Attention to detail and dedication to quality show through in every aspect of Rex Hill Winery. Owners Paul Hart and his wife Jan Jacobsen have produced a splendid facility from a historic nut processing plant just off Highway 99W north of Newberg. Completely refurbished, the building looks from the highway to be a new structure but with the grace and lines of traditional turn of the century architecture. Winemaker Lynn Penner-Ash came on board in 1988 and has definitely influenced Rex Hill's wine styles. Greater responsibility was added to her position when she was named President and C.O.O. in 1993.

### A visit to Rex Hill Vineyards

The tasting room at Rex Hill makes visitors feel at home with elegant decor and a helpful staff. Expansion of the tasting area and the construction of an outside terrace for picnics and musical events add to the enjoyment of a visit to Rex Hill. The Maresh Vineyard Little Red Barn Tasting Room on Worden Hill Road in Dundee is now operated by Rex Hill also. Hours are weekends, Noon to 5 PM.

### The Wines

Rex Hill Pinot Noir has established a very fine reputation for complex aroma and a rich and mouth-filling palate. Vineyard designated Pinots are excellent but limited in production. The Rex Hill Chardonnay and Pinot Gris offer unique styles with barrel-fermentation lending a toasty quality to the wine. The King's Ridge brand offers light and fruity Pinot Noir, Pinot Gris and Chardonnay at a lower price level. The cute Vino d'El Niño label was added to the line in 1998.

*Rex Hill Winery from the hilltop estate vineyard.*

## Sokol Blosser Winery

5000 Sokol Blosser Ln.,
P.O. Box 399
Dundee, OR 97115
(800) 582-6668

**Tasting Room Hours:** Daily, 11 AM to 5 PM
Free tours of winery

**Owners:** Bill and Susan Blosser
**Winemaker:** Russ Rosner
**First Year:** 1977
**Winery Capacity:** 60,000 Gallons

### Winery History

Bill and Susan Sokol Blosser have used their vision of producing world-class wines to build one of Oregon's largest and best known wineries. They both hold prestigious degrees from well-respected universities though neither has a background in chemistry or winemaking. Indeed it was the romance of wine and the challenge of operating a successful winery program that lured them to the vineyard.

### A visit to Sokol Blosser

This winery was among the first in Oregon to bring wine to the consumer with expanded tasting room hours and a friendly, informative manner. The Sokol Blosser tasting room is well-stocked with unusual and unique wine-related gifts and food stuffs. A unique, self-guided vineyard tour is offered, complete with a brochure describing the vines and farming practices. The winery amphitheatre is the site for midsummer pop and jazz concerts that draw crowds from around the region.

*Continued on next page.*

**The Wines**

Two styles of Pinot Noir and Chardonnay are offered at Sokol Blosser. The Yamhill County designation is the "front line" of wines made in a lightier, fruitier style. "Redland" designates the reserve style bottlings of these two varietals. Riesling and Muller Thurgau are also produced.

## Stag Hollow Vineyards

7930 NE Blackburn Road
Yamhill, OR 97148
(503) 662-4022
**Email:**
stagholo@concentric.net

**Tasting Room Hours:** By appointment only.

**Owners:** Mark Huff, Jill Zarnowitz
**Winemaker:** Mark Huff
**First Year:** 1994

Describing their vineyard as "Old World" style, the owners of Stag Hollow emphasize high density planting (3,000 vines per acre) on steep, south-facing slopes. Clonally diverse plantings of Pinot Noir and Chardonnay are augmented by Muscat Ottonel, Early Muscat and experimental blocks of Northern Italian varieties. Grapes are picked as the clusters ripen, wines are made in a concentrated style, and small lots are aged in French oak.

Three different Pinot Noirs were released from the 1996 vintage: Vendange selection (from first grapes picked), Celebré (from second picking) and a new wine made from the grapes with the longest time on the vine.

## Tempest Vineyard

6000 Karlas Lane, Amity, OR 97101
(503) 252-1383

**Owner:** Keith Orr
**First Year:** 1988
**Winery Capacity:** 7,000 Gallons

**Winery History**

As part of the City of Portland maintenance team that repairs traffic signals, Keith Orr needed a creative outlet. Winemaking and grape growing proved just such an escape and Tempest Vineyard was born. After several

*Keith Orr of Tempest Vineyards.*

years production in a leased facility, a new winery was built in 1993 near Amity.

**A visit to Tempest Vineyards**

The winery is open summer weekends or by appointment. Also on the Memorial Day and Thanksgiving weekends.

**The Wines**

Keith Orr crafts Pinot Noir, Chardonnay, Pinot Gris and Gamay Noir from purchased grapes. Plantings at the new winery will include the above varieties and also Pinot Blanc.

## Torii Mor

18325 NE Fairview Dr.
Dundee, OR 97115
Winery: P.O. Box 359
905 E. 10th St.
McMinnville, OR 97128
(503) 839-5004
· FAX (503) 434-5733

**Tasting Room Hours:** May through Nov.: Weekends, Noon to 5 PM

**Owners:** Donald & Trisha Olson
**Winemaker:** Patricia M. Green
**First Year:** 1993
**Winery Capacity:** 4,171 Gallons

**Winery History**

Established in 1992, Torii Mor Winery received high praise for its first full-scale release from the 1993 vintage. Owners Don and Trisha Olson supply grapes from their Dundee Hills vineyard which was planted in

*Continued on page 162.*

## Christine Keff
### Chef/Owner of Flying Fish

*"The best way to understand food and wine pairing is to taste, taste, taste." With this simple statement, Christine Keff defines what great chefs around the world offer as instruction to their staffs.*

*Keff's early training in New York gave her a solid beginning to her culinary career. Studying under Seppi Renggli at the Four Seasons Restaurant was inspiring to Keff and assured her that she had chosen the right career.*

*After opening three restaurants in New York, Keff spent a year travelling the U.S. and the Far East. When she landed in Seattle in 1989 she was excited about combining her culinary travel experiences with Northwest ingredients. As the executive chef at The Hunt Club and Yarrow Bay Grill she won more attention for her innovative cooking style.*

*Keff opened Flying Fish in 1995 to rave reviews from around the country. The restaurant was featured in every major culinary magazine and was touted as Seattle's Best New Restaurant.*

*Check our review of Flying Fish on page 42.*

### ❖ A RECIPE FROM FLYING FISH ❖

# Thai Curry Sea Scallops

*Serves 4 - Wine Recommendation: Torii Mor Pinot Noir*

| | |
|---|---|
| 20 | large sea scallops |
| 2 | Tbs. peanut oil |
| 2/3 | cup chicken stock |
| 1/2 | cup coconut milk |
| | salt |
| 3 | Tbs. curry paste, recipe follows |

Place peanut oil in a large non-stick skillet. Heat to smoking. Remove from flame and quickly add scallops to pan, one by one. Return to flame and sear scallops on one side, then the other. Process should take approximately 4 - 5 minutes; scallops will be medium rare.

Remove scallops to a warm platter and discard excess grease from pan. Add curry paste and sauté briefly. Add chicken stock and reduce by half. Add coconut milk and continue to simmer until sauce is thick enough to coat a spoon. Pour sauce over scallops and serve.

## Curry Paste

| | |
|---|---|
| 1/4 | lb. peeled fresh galangale* |
| 1/4 | lb. peeled ginger |
| 1/4 | lb. peeled fresh tumeric* |
| 1/2 | lb. peeled shallots |
| 1 | head peeled garlic |
| 1 | bunch cilantro |
| | juice of 2 limes |
| 5 | dried Thai chiles, soaked in hot water to soften |
| | peanut oil |

*available at Asian specialty stores

Place all curry paste ingredients in food processor and grind. Add just enough peanut oil to make a paste. Continue to grind until paste is smooth.

1977. This distinctive fruit is ideal for the production of a ripe and fleshy Pinot Noir crafted by Oregon wine veteran Patty Green. Torii Mor, which means "Earth Gate" is a combination of Celtic and Japanese languages.

**A Visit to Torii Mor**

The winery tasting room is just off Worden Hill Road on Fairview Drive. The picturesque setting offers a unique chance to enjoy fine views from the Japanese garden.

**The Wines**

Pinot Noir is presented in a ripe and fleshy style. Pinot Gris, Chardonnay, and Gamay Noir Blanche are also made.

*The tasting room at WillaKenzie Estate.*

# Westrey Wine Co.

1065 East Alpine
McMinnville, OR 97128
(503) 434-6357

**Owners/Winemakers:**
David Autrey, Amy Wesselman
**First Year:** 1993
**Production:** 5,000 Gallons

**Winery History**

David Autrey and Amy Wesselman have accumulated many years experience working for other Oregon wineries as well as stints in Burgundy learning from some of France's finest producers of Pinot Noir. After making their first wines in other wineries on a small-lot basis, Autrey and Wesselman opened their own facility near downtown McMinnville in 1996. The space is efficient for winemaking, but the winery remains open by appointment and during the Yamhill County events on Memorial Day and Thanksgiving weekends.

**The Wines**

A rich and spicy Pinot Noir is Westrey's hallmark style with a barrel-fermented Chardonnay offering something yummy for lovers of white Burgundy. Hard to find but worth a call!

# WillaKenzie Estate

19143 NE Laughlin Rd.
Yamhill, OR 97148
(503) 662-3280
FAX (503) 662-4829

**Tasting Room Hours:**
Daily, 11 AM to 5 PM,
Memorial Day through
Labor Day.

**Owners:** Bernard & Ronni LaCroute
**Winemaker:** Laurent Montalieu
**First Year:** 1995
**Winery Capacity:** 40,000 Gallons
**Tasting Room Hours:** Daily, 11 AM to 5 PM

**Winery History**

Much of Yamhill County offers superb soil and climate for cultivating wine grapes. Much of this soil is named WillaKenzie after the Willamette and McKenzie Rivers that flow together in the center of the Willamette Valley. Finding the right plot of land – and having the resources to develop it – Bernard and Ronni LeCroute named their new estate for these soils. A drip-irrigated, forty-acre vineyard was planted to Pinot Noir, Chardonnay and Pinot Blanc in 1992 and a state-of-the-art 25,000-case winery was completed in time for crush in 1995. Fellow Frenchman Laurent Montalieu, former winemaker for Bridgeview Winery, was placed in charge of the winery.

**A visit to WillaKenzie Estate**

The combination of beautiful rolling hills of vineyards, an attractive tasting room and spectacular wines comes together at WillaKenzie Estate. This property has been built from the ground up with quality and function in mind. The second-floor tasting room and banquet facility look out on vistas of the vineyards and the surrounding valley. Behind the antique tasting bar, a friendly and experienced staff is directed by Elisabeth Schock. Open daily during the summer - don't miss it! Watch for the turn onto Laughlin Rd. off Hwy. 240, 2 miles east of Yamhill.

## The Wines

From practically the first sip, the wine press went ga-ga over Laurent Montalieu's initial releases from WillaKenzie Estate. The Pinot Gris and Pinot Blanc were clean, complex, fruity and refreshing. Subsequent releases of reds have been similarly high in quality as Pinot Meunier, Gamay Noir and several versions of Pinot Noir each demonstrated luscious, mouth-filling flavors framed in oak and offering a lingering finish.

# Wine Country Farm Cellars

6855 Breyman
Orchards Rd.
Dayton, OR 97114
(503) 864-3446, FAX
(503) 864-3446

**Tasting Room Hours:** Daily, 11 AM to 5 PM

**Owner:** Joan Davenport
**First Year:** 1993

## Winery History

Joan Davenport established her popular Bed and Breakfast Inn on a wonderful view site at the top of the Dundee Hills. After rehabilitating a neglected vineyard on the property, she has created her own wine label and tasting room offering current vintages to visitors. At present, Pinot Noir, Chardonnay, Riesling and Muller Thurgau are vinted for the winery at Eola Hills Wine Cellars.

# Ken Wright Cellars

P.O. Box 190,
Carlton, OR 97111
(503) 852-7070
FAX (503) 852-7111

**Tasting Room Hours:** By appointment or during the Memorial Day and Thanksgiving weekend events.

**Owners:** Ken Wright, Dale West
**Winemaker:** Ken Wright
**First Year:** 1994
**Production:** 5,800 Gallons

## Winery History

Following the sale of Panther Creek Cellars, Ken Wright began anew, transforming his solid reputation for intense Pinot Noir and characterful white wines into another viable wine brand. Sticking to his principles of vinifying only superb fruit from the best vineyards Wright is once again a moving force in the Oregon wine scene with his Ken Wright Cellars brand. Minority partner Dale West is handling marketing and sales.

## The Wines

Working out of a facility in Carlton, Wright has released spectacular vineyard-designated Pinot Noirs, as well as superb Pinot Noir blends, Celilo Vineyard Chardonnay and Melon.

# Yamhill Valley Vineyards

16250 SW Oldsville Rd.
McMinnville, OR
97128
(503) 843-3100
FAX (503) 843-2450
**Email:**
info@yamhill.com
**Web:** www.yamhill.com

**Tasting Room Hours:** Daily, 11 AM to 5 PM
(June through Nov.) Weekends only, (March
through May) Closed in winter.

**Owners:** Denis Burger, Elaine McCall,
David & Terry Hinrichs
**Winemaker:** Stephen Cary
**First Year:** 1983
**Winery Capacity:** 24,000 Gallons

### Winery History

A partnership between a pair of Portland
immunologists led to the building of one of
Yamhill County's most attractive wineries.
Combining a 100-acre vineyard planted to
Pinot Noir, Chardonnay, Pinot Gris and White
Riesling with a state-of-the-art winery and
visitor center, Yamhill Valley Vineyards is a
well-planned venture. The Yamhill Valley
Vineyards label features both the Oregon State
bird and the Oregon State flower. The Western
Meadowlark has never before been so honored
with its perch on the Oregon Grape plant.

**A visit to Yamhill Valley Vineyards**

Yamhill Valley Vineyards is tucked away
at the south end of Yamhill County on a 300-
acre estate in the foothills of the Oregon Coast
Range. The well-marked route to Oldsville
Road leads to the long driveway through the
vineyards to the winery. A visit to the facility
includes a tasting of the current release wines
and a brief tour of the winery. The expansive
deck offers a chance to relax and picnic with a
view of the vineyard under shady old oak trees
that grow right up through the structure.

**The Wines**

The initial vintages of Yamhill Valley
Vineyards established a reputation for hearty
Pinot Noir with full body and ripe flavors and
aroma. White Riesling and Chardonnay are
also produced. The mineral-scented, bronze-
colored Pinot Gris is also a favorite.

## YAMHILL COUNTY ACCOMMODATIONS

### Springbrook Farm B & B

30295 N. Highway 99W, Newberg (503) 538-
4606 The McClure family welcomes you to
their hazelnut orchard estate with pool, tennis,
pond and gardens. Carriage house available
for families, small groups.

### Shilo Inn

501 Sitka Ave., Newberg (503) 537-0303 or
(800) 222-2244 Just off the wine route this new
Shilo Inn offers comfort and convenience for
wine travelers. Free continental breakfast and
USA Today newspapers, outdoor pool, indoor
spa. Kitchen units available. Moderate.

### Vineyard Inn Motel

2035 S. Hwy 99W, McMinnville - (503) 472-
4900 Indoor pool, spa, air-conditioned,
convenient to local wineries, continental
breakfast.

### Mattey House

10221 NE Mattey Lane, McMinnville (503) 434-
5058 Owners Jack and Denise Seed traveled the
four corners of the world before becoming
innkeepers at this delightful Victorian-style
bed & breakfast. Located on 10 acres near
Lafayette.

### Steiger Haus

360 Wilson St., McMinnville 97128, (503) 472-
0821 Elegant accommodations in a home south
of downtown. Private baths, landscaped
grounds and a gourmet full breakfast!

### Flying M Ranch

23029 NW Flying M Ranch Rd., Yamhill, 97148
(503) 662-3222 Take a trail ride into the Coast
Range or relax in a romantic cabin by the river.
Also camping and horse corrals.

# YAMHILL COUNTY DINING

## Nick's Italian Cafe

521 E. Third St., McMinnville - (503) 434-4471
Nick's is famous all over Oregon for the fine Northern Italian cuisine and wine country atmosphere. An extensive selection of Oregon wines goes back to the 1970s. The minestrone is to die for. Dinner served Tuesday - Sunday.

## Third Street Grill

729 E. 3rd St., McMinnville - (503) 435-1745
This country- elegant restaurant in a charming house near downtown offers unique preparations featuring local produce and quality cuts of meat. Reservations recommended.

## Tina's

760 Hwy. 99W, Dundee (503) 538-8880 Local game, fresh seafood and other fine ingredients creatively prepared and elegantly served in a tiny outpost of quality cuisine. Extensive list of locally-produced wines. Lunch Tue.-Fri.; dinner, Tue.-Sun. Reservations recommended.

## Augustine's

19706 Hwy. 18, (almost to) Sheridan - (503) 843-3225. Upstairs from the respected Lawrence Art Gallery and the irreverent Oregon Wine Tasting Room, Augustine's has been popular with wine lovers for over a decade. Some of the best preparations feature Northwest seafood, local wines by the glass.

## Golden Valley Brewpub

980 East 4th St., McMinnville (503) 472-2739
Peter and Celia Kircher began this brewpub to support their winery . . . well maybe that's not exactly it, but the success of the brewing venture has been phenomenal! Golden Valley brews include a light Wheat Ale, not-as-light Golden Ale, still-darker Amber Ale, dark Porter – rich but not sweet, and the flagship Red Thistle Irish Ale, hoppy and nice! Peter also brews seasonal ales in styles appropriate to the weather. For eats, try the Tuscan Grilled Chicken or Leg of Lamb, salads, burgers and pizzas are good, too. Kids will love the Golden Valley Root Beer made on premises!

## Red Hills Provincial Dining

276 Hwy. 99W, Dundee - (503) 538-8224
Was that "Provincial" or "Provençal?" Wonderful country specialties remind one of the south of France or other laid back Mediterranean destinations. Innovative appetizers and desserts, plus the requisite fine selection of local wines. Lunch: W-F, dinner W-Sun.

## Kame Japanese Restaurant

228 N. Evans, McMinnville - (503) 434-4326
Owner Mieko Nordin welcomes you to enjoy fine Oregon wines, beer or sake with his creative, family-style Japanese cooking.

# YAMHILL COUNTY ACTIVITIES

## Champoeg State Park

Across the Willamette from Newberg. A full service park with boat access to the river, picnic tables, historic landmarks, fishing, etc. Champoeg winery nearby.

## Crabtree Park

Up Worden Hill Road from Dundee. Adjacent to Knudsen Erath Winery. Nice Picnicking.

## McMinnville City Park

3rd and Adams A well-kept, quiet oasis amid the hustle and bustle of McMinnville. Two play areas, a small creek, picnic tables and clean restrooms. Adjacent to the aquatic center where you can swim laps for a couple of bucks.

## Hot Air Ballooning

See the wine country from the air and enjoy a sparkling wine touchdown when the ride comes to an end! Vista Balloon Adventures, (503) 625-7385.

## Lawrence Gallery

Highway 18 at Sheridan. Browse fine art after sipping some prime vintages at the adjacent Oregon Wine Tasting Room. Augustine's Restaurant features fine Oregon cuisine.

## Oregon Wine Tasting Room

Have some fun getting schooled on local wines by the hip and irreverent staff. Know-it-alls have been known to get huffy when kidded by the (sometimes) wise guy with the corkscrew.

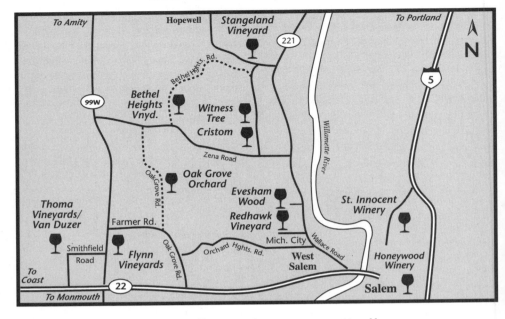

## Salem/Polk County Touring - North

The Eola Hills winegrowing region northwest of Salem is home to some of the Willamette Valley's finest vineyards and many interesting wineries.

In downtown Salem, **Honeywood Winery** on Hines St. offers tasting daily of varietal and fruit wines. **St. Innocent Winery** is open by appointment at their new facility just off the Salem Parkway near Cherry Street..

Leaving downtown Salem for the Eola Hills, follow the signs for Highway 22 (Marion Street Bridge) heading toward the ocean beaches. You'll just cross the Willamette River heading west on the four-lane highway when you exit for West Salem. A right turn on Wallace Road (Highway 221) gets you headed into the action. A few miles ahead, make a left turn on Michigan City Avenue to visit to Tom Robinson's **Redhawk Vineyard**. A friendly welcome in the tasting room and a wide selection of wines (many reds available!) make for a fun stop. Next door, Russ and Mary Raney operate **Evesham Wood** winery open Memorial Day weekend and by appointment.

Continue north on Wallace Road (Hwy. 221) and turn left on Zena Road. Travel west about 1.5 miles to Spring Valley Road (right turn) to visit **Cristom Winery** and **Witness Tree Vineyard**. Both facilities are open daily (except Monday) during the spring and summer. Continue north to find **Stangeland Vineyards** at the junction of Spring Valley Road with Hopewell Road. Open summer weekends, noon to 5.

Back on Zena Road, head west for a mile or two until you see the sign for **Bethel Heights Vineyard**. After visiting the tasting room, enjoy your picnic next to the vineyard. A little navigating on Oak Grove Road leads you to **Oak Grove Orchards Winery**.

**Flynn Vineyards** and the new **Thoma Vineyards-Van Duzer Winery** are located off Highway 99W near the Rickreall junction. Follow Zena Road west to 99W or follow Highway 22.

# EOLA HILLS & POLK COUNTY WINERIES

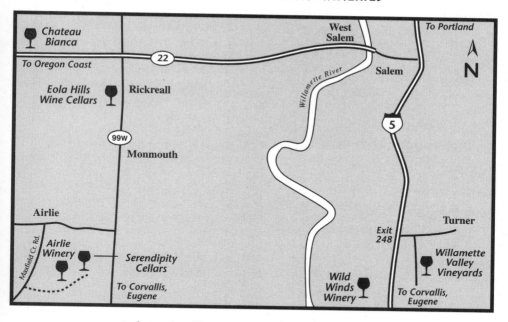

## Salem/Polk County Touring - South

South of Salem the wineries are a little more spread out. Continuing west-bound on Highway 22 as before, you'll find a stoplight on the freeway at Highway 99W. Ten miles west of 99W, and just off Highway 22, is **Chateau Bianca** run by the Wetzel family. A nice stop on your way to the beach!

Retrace your steps to 99W and head south to Rickreall where Eola Hills Wine Cellars is open for informal tours and wine tasting. They offer a special wine tasting brunch on Sundays!

Continue south on 99W through Monmouth then turn right for the town of Airlie (6 miles). Make a left turn in Airlie and travel for another 3 miles to Dunn Forest Road, home of **Airlie Winery** and **Serendipity Cellars**.

Dunn Forest Road is a one-lane, gravel driveway so take it slow for safety and courtesy's sake. At the top of the hill, Glen and Cheryl Longshore welcome you to **Serendipity Cellars**. Glen is the master of the Maréchal Foch grape from which he makes a delightfully fruity and spicy red wine.

Down the hill, Mary Olson and her winemaker Suzy Gagné welcome you to **Airlie Winery**. Mary purchased the winery in 1997 and is excited to have visitors. Stop in and say "Hello."

Back on I-5 you'll find a special reason to pull off for a stop at exit 248. **Willamette Valley Vineyards** is Oregon's original publicly-owned winery and makes a great effort to welcome visitors to their facility. You can picnic with a view of the valley and enjoy the wide selection of wines and gifts in the new visitor center. Climb the observation tower for an even more spectacular view of the surrounding landscape.

Across the highway and up a few twists and turns, **Wild Winds Winery** and vineyard welcomes visitors during special weekend events on Memorial Day and Thanksgiving weekend.

167

*Airlie Winery near Monmouth, Oregon.*

# Airlie Winery

15305 Dunn Forest Rd.
Monmouth, OR 97361
(503) 838-6013
FAX (503) 838-6279
**Email:**
airlie@airliewinery.com
**Web:**
www.airliewinery.com

**Owner:** Mary Olson
**Winemaker:** Suzy Gagné
**First Year:** 1986
**Winery Capacity:** 20,000 Gallons
**Tasting Room Hours:** Weekends, 12 to 5 PM
Closed January and February

## Winery History

Transplanted to Oregon's coast range from the flat Kansas farmlands, Larry and Alice Preedy began growing grapes in their Dunn Forest Vineyard since 1983. Thirty-five total acres are planted to Riesling, Muller Thurgau, Gewurztraminer, Chardonnay, Pinot Noir and Marechal Foch. In 1986 the Preedys built the Airlie Winery and produced 4,000 gallons of wine. Mary Olson, a former executive with U.S. West, purchased the operation in 1997 and with her winemaker Suzy Gagné is making about 9,000 cases per year.

## A visit to Airlie Winery

The owner or winemaker are often your tasting room hosts for weekend visits to Airlie Winery. The winery's covered picnic area includes a delightful pond with a view of the vineyards.

## The Wines

Pinot Noir, Pinot Gris, Chardonnay, Marechal Foch, Gewurztraminer, Riesling and Muller Thurgau are produced.

# Bethel Heights Vineyard

6060 Bethel Heights Road NW,
Salem, OR 97304
(503) 581-2262, FAX (503) 581-0943

**Tasting Room Hours:** Daily, 11 AM to 5 PM during the summer. Other seasons: weekends only. Closed Dec. 24 thru February

**Owners:** Terry & Ted Casteel, Marilyn Webb, Pat Dudley, Barbara Dudley
**Winemaker:** Terry Casteel
**First Year:** 1984
**Winery Capacity:** 15,000 Gallons

## Winery History

A trip to France, a love of wine, and close ties to the Pacific Northwest led the Casteel brothers, Ted and Terry (and their families), to the Willamette Valley in the late 1970s to try their hand at grape growing and winemaking. The families acquired one of the most desirable vineyard sites in the Eola Hills, just northwest of Salem. Fourteen acres of first-year vines came with the property, now 51 acres are planted with Northwest varietals.

As the vines grew and as early harvests were sold to other wineries, the owners discovered what an ideal microclimate they had found. Grapes from the Bethel Heights Vineyard have made some of the Northwest's best Pinot Noir and Chardonnay wines as well as other varietals. In 1983 the time was right to build their own winery and begin production of the first estate wines.

## A visit to Bethel Heights Vineyard

Following signs from Highways 99W or 221, turn onto Zena Road for the 3-plus mile ride to Bethel Heights Road. A picnic at Bethel Heights Vineyard offers a relaxed and quiet setting with views of the rolling hills of vineyard and farmland. Picnic tables are provided for alfresco dining.

Inside, one of the owners or their well-informed staff pours samples of Bethel Heights wine and offers insights into the vine-to-wine transformation that takes place each year at this vineyard-and-winery facility.

*Continued on page 170.*

## Beverly Calder
## BELLA, Baker City, Oregon

*"I've long been a proponent of 'making' your own life happen. That may mean simply observing what is available to you, feeling what you really feel, and pursuing a course that encompasses as many of your needs and desires as possible."*

*Bev Calder has been making her own life happen in several "lifetimes" in Oregon. Studying art at the University of Oregon in the late 1970s she discovered the world of wine. Already an experienced cook and lover of fresh food, she immediately drew this new ingredient into her life and her art education took a back seat to this new passion.*

*Several career moves established her as an Oregon wine authority and an expert on wines of the world. She apprenticed with Phil DeVito as assistant cellarmaster at Salishan Lodge on the Oregon Coast. From there she rose to new heights (literally!) as she established the wine program at Atwater's Restaurant at the top of the U.S. Bank Building in Portland. But her heart was in the wine country.*

*Beverly opened the first "BELLA" in McMinnville in the 1980s and prospered as a purveyor of fine food and wine in an informal setting. Helping out during the beginning years of the International Pinot Noir Celebration in the late 1980s was a thrill, but her most exciting life experience was yet to come.*

*Marrying her soulmate David Gratz in the early 1990s, she moved to faraway Baker City, Oregon and has discovered that life is what you make it. The new BELLA recently moved to Main Street and is thriving. Beverly's warm, friendly smile and infectious laugh have won over the whole town and she is happily selling wine and lattes, catering events and enjoying life to the fullest.*

## A RECIPE FROM
## BEVERLY CALDER AT BELLA

# Roasted Oysters with Rock Shrimp

*Serves 4, Wine: Bethel Heights Pinot Gris*

| | |
|---|---|
| 8 | oysters, in the shell |
| 1 | cup rock shrimp, cut into small pieces |
| 1 | cup freshly grated Parmesan cheese |
| 3/4 | cup fresh bread crumbs |
| 3/4 | cup mushrooms, finely chopped |
| 2 | Tbs. fresh lemon juice |
| 4 | cloves garlic, roasted and diced |
| 1 | Tbs. butter, melted |
| 1/2 | cup cilantro, chopped |

Shuck oysters, leaving in bottom shell. Arrange in baking dish.

Combine remaining ingredients and spoon mixture over each oyster, mounding slightly.

Chill until 15 minutes before serving.

Place oysters in 400° F. oven for 8 to 10 minutes until topping is slightly browned. Serve immediately.

*While BELLA is not located in any wine touring region included in this guide, you may want to visit Beverly when you're in Baker City, Oregon.*

BELLA
1828 Main Street
Baker City, OR 97814
(541) 523-7490

Across the road is the Bethel Heights Farm Bed and Breakfast for those who enjoy a rural setting among forest and vines.

**The Wines**

Crisp acidity in white wines and a nice balance of fruit and toasty oak on the Pinot Noirs are a hallmark of Bethel Heights wines. Recent vintages have seen more variety in special releases including the Reserve Pinot Noir from the "Southeast Block" section of the vineyard. Crisp Chardonnay, Pinot Gris and Pinot Blanc are also made.

## Chateau Bianca

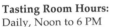

17485 Highway 22
Dallas, Oregon 97338
(503) 623-6181
FAX (503) 623-6230

**Tasting Room Hours:**
Daily, Noon to 6 PM

**Owners:** Wetzel Family
**Winemaker:** Andreas Wetzel
**First Year:** 1991
**Winery Capacity:** 9,600 Gallons

**Winery History**

Helmut Wetzel has been involved in the Oregon wine industry as an investor for over 20 years. The winery venture began in 1991 with all family members participating. Whether working in the vineyard, in the winery, or pouring wine samples in the tasting room, everyone is "hands on" in the business.

**A visit to Chateau Bianca**

Their highway-side location on one of Oregon's busiest tourist routes keeps a stream of visitors coming in. Gifts and specialty foods are offered for sale and visitors may taste wines for a $1 fee, refunded with purchase of wine. Sample Gewurztraminer, Chardonnay, Riesling, Pinot Noir and sparkling wines.

A bed and breakfast will be opening at the winery in the near future.

*Steve Doerner and Paul Gerrie in the barrel cellar at Cristom.*

## Cristom Vineyards

6785 Spring Valley
Road NW
Salem, OR 97304
(503) 375-3068

**Tasting Room Hours:** Tuesday through Sunday, 11 AM to 5 PM
Closed January and February

**Owner:** Paul & Eileen Gerrie
**Winemaker:** Steve Doerner
**First Year:** 1992
**Winery Capacity:** 24,000 Gallons

**Winery History**

The original owners of this property were relatives of the California Mirassous of winery fame. The Oregon venture known as Pellier-Mirassou developed the property and made wine from 1985 until 1991. The winery was purchased by Pennsylvania oil exploration expert Paul Gerrie in 1992. Gerrie is a lover of fine Burgundy and jumped at the opportunity to try his hand at creating some wines in the styles of those he admires from France. Recruiting winemaker Steve Doerner from Calera Winery in California and vineyard manager Mark Feltz from Chalk Hill, Gerrie's team has replanted 40 acres of vineyards and fine tunes blends of Pinot Noir made from purchased and estate grapes. The winery is thriving and the tasting room is welcoming visitors to try the first vintages of Pinot Noir, Chardonnay and Pinot Gris.

### A visit to Cristom Winery

Next door to Witness Tree winery and just around the corner from Bethel Heights Vineyard, Cristom offers correspondingly fine hospitality in their tasting room and gift shop. Enjoy your picnic on the winery deck with a view of the valley!

### The Wines

Steve Doerner is crafting superb Pinot Noir, Chardonnay and Pinot Gris using natural yeasts and minimal handling. Several special bottlings of Pinot Noir and Chardonnay offer the added complexity of vineyard designated sources.

# Eola Hills Wine Cellars

501 S. Pacific
Highway W. (99W)
Rickreall, OR 97371
(503) 623-2405
FAX (503) 623-0350
**Web:** www.eolahillswinery.com

**Tasting Room Hours:** Daily, Noon to 5 PM

**Owner:** Corp. Investor Group,
Tom Huggins, General Manager
**Winemaker:** Kerry Norton
**First Year:** 1986
**Winery Capacity:** 45,000 Gallons

### Winery History

A partnership headed by Tom Huggins is the driving force behind this Polk County winery. Eola Hills owns the nearby 70-acre Oak Grove Vineyard giving the winery access to excellent Pinot Noir, Chardonnay, Cabernet Sauvignon, Sauvignon Blanc and Chenin Blanc. These varietals were made beginning with the 1986 vintage and the winery opened in June of 1988.

### A visit to Eola Hills Wine Cellars

Just south of the junction of highways 99W and 22, Eola Hills offers wine lovers a chance to relax indoors or out, with a picnic area outside and a cafe-style tasting room inside. The proximity of the tasting room to the working winery makes it possible to enjoy a mini-tour without leaving the tasting bar.

Hiring a culinary director for the winery has expanded the gourmet offerings that began with a weekly Sunday brunch years ago. Today, special events like winemaker dinners, themed parties and pre-football game rallies are but a few of the exciting activities taking place at Eola Hills. Check their web site for the current schedule of culinary events.

### The Wines

Rich and hearty reds including Pinot Noir, Cabernet Sauvignon and Merlot offer great appeal for red wine lovers. White wines are varietally true with Pinot Gris, Gewurztraminer and barrel-fermented Chardonnay leading the way. Late harvest style Riesling is crafted when the fruit dictates.

# Evesham Wood Vineyard

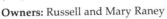

4035 Wallace Rd. NW
Salem, OR 97304
(503) 371-8478

**Owners:** Russell and Mary Raney
**Winemaker:** Russ Raney
**First Year:** 1986
**Winery Capacity:** 7,500 Gallons
**Tasting Room Hours:** By appointment only

## Winery History

Russ and Mary Raney are pursuing a Northwest dream with a small vineyard and a small winery on their property near Salem. The first crush in 1988 included Pinot Noir and Chardonnay. Russ' background includes a degree in viticulture and enology from the German wine institute at Bad Kreuznach. He sold wine retail and wholesale for five years in St. Louis before locating to Oregon and worked as winemaker for Adams Vineyard Winery in Portland in 1984-85. The Evesham Wood name was derived from a fruit growing area of England that Russ and Mary visited on their honeymoon in 1984.

## A visit to Evesham Wood Vineyard

Evesham Wood winery is located at the southern end of the Eola Hills, on an east facing slope above Wallace Road in West Salem . The underground winery building was built as the foundation for the owners home, a remarkable bit of architecture. The winery is open during the Memorial Day and Thanksgiving open houses. Other times by appointment.

## The Wines

Pinot Noir, Chardonnay and Pinot Gris are the varietals produced at Evesham Wood. Small lots of intense and flavorful wines continue to gain popularity nationwide.

# Flynn Vineyards

2200 W. Pacific Hwy.
Rickreall, OR 97371
(503) 623-6505
FAX (503) 623-0908
**Web:**
www.flynnvineyards.com

**Tasting Room Hours:** Weekend only, 11 AM to 5 PM. Weekdays by appointment.

**Owners:** Wayne Flynn,
  Mickey & Jeanne Flynn
**Winemaker:** Bob McRitchie
**First Year:** 1984
**Winery Capacity:** 28,000 Gallons

## Winery History

The first Flynn Vineyard site was purchased and planted in 1982 when Wayne Flynn acquired 50 acres in the southwest Eola Hills. The entire plot was planted to Pinot Noir and another site of 23 acres near Hopewell was added the following spring. Still more land was added to the holding in 1987. The large winery building was constructed in time for the 1990 vintage.

## A visit to Flynn Vineyards

Flynn Vineyards' tasting room is in a corner of the huge open winery, allowing visitors to take a look at the various pieces of equipment and stored wine while they taste. A description of the methode champenoise technique accompanies your tasting.

## The Wines

Winemaker Bob McRitchie is one of Oregon's most experienced vintners. He creates superb quality Pinot Noir, Pinot Gris and Chardonnay, harvested from Flynn's Eola Hills sites, as well as Brut and Blanc de Blanc sparkling wine.

## Wildwood Restaurant
## Cory Schreiber

*"Product, product, product!" is what Cory Schreiber says about the important things that contribute to the success of his restaurant Wildwood in Northwest Portland. Using the freshest ingredients, procured from high quality Northwest purveyors, continues to keep Wildwood on everyone's list of great Portland dining experiences.*

*Cory Schreiber is a 5th generation native of Portland who established a national reputation cooking at San Francisco's exclusive Cypress Club. He came north and opened Wildwood on May 17, 1994.*

*The restaurant honors Portland's Wildwood Trail (a local wilderness landmark) that is depicted in an oil painting above the bar. Portland native and legendary American culinary figure James Beard is paid tribute in a glass and ceramic mural by Oregon artist Liz Mapelli.*

*Check out Wildwood's website at www.wildwoodpdx.com and make plans to stop by for some delicious regional cooking accompanied by superb Northwest wines.*

### ❖ A RECIPE FROM WILDWOOD ❖

# Creamed Crab on Toast with Wild Mushrooms & Thyme

Serves 4 - Accompanying wine:
Evesham Wood Willamette Valley Pinot Noir.

| | |
|---|---|
| 8 | ounces fresh crab meat |
| 3 | shallots, chopped |
| 1/4 | cup white wine |
| 1 | tsp. butter |
| 1/4 | pound wild mushrooms such as morels, black trumpets or chanterelles. Make sure the mushrooms are well cleaned. |
| 2 | tsp. chopped parsley |
| 1 | lemon (zested) |
| 2 | cups heavy cream |
| 1/3 | cup grated aged white cheese such as asiago or parmesan |
| 4 | slices of a heavy crusted bread cut around 1/2-inch thick |
| 1/4 | cup olive oil |
| | Salt and black pepper to taste |

Heat half the olive oil in a pan and brown two of the slices of bread on both sides. Heat the remaining olive oil and brown the other two slices. Set aside.

Warm a large sauté pan over medium heat and melt the butter. Add the shallots and stir in pan for one minute being careful not to brown them. Add the cleaned mushrooms to the pan and continue to cook. When the mushrooms begin to wilt and reduce in size, add the white wine and reduce by half.

Add the heavy cream and turn the heat up to medium high as the cream reduces. Reduce the cream by half in volume and add the crab meat, cheese, lemon zest and juice of half the lemon. Cook for one minute, then add the chopped parsley, season with salt and pepper and remove from the heat. If the mushrooms excreted a lot of moisture, return the cream mixture to the heat to reduce to desired consistency.

Spoon this mixture over each piece of toast and serve. A dressed green salad on top of the creamed crab would make this a complete lunch dish.

# Honeywood Winery

1350 Hines St. S.E.
Salem, OR 97302
(503) 362-4111
FAX (503) 362-4112
(800) 726-4101

**Tasting Room Hours:** M-F, 9 AM - 5 PM, Sat., 10 AM - 5 PM, Sun. 1 - 5 PM.

**Owner:** Paul Gallick
**Winemaker:** Marlene Gallick
**First Year:** 1934
**Winery Capacity:** 60,000 Gallons

## Winery History

The historic Honeywood Winery in downtown Salem began as the Columbia Distilleries just after the repeal of prohibition in 1933. Production at that time was mainly fruit brandies and liqueurs, but soon the owners Ron Honeyman and John Wood decided to make fruit wines instead and the winery was born. Honeywood has operated continuously since that time with the current owner having been at the helm since 1973. Increased production of premium varietal grape wines includes some unique blends with fruit flavors. Honeywood moved to its current location (from the original warehouse) in 1990.

## A visit to Honeywood Winery

Take the Highway 22 exit from I-5 and head west to Hines St. to find the Honeywood Winery just east of downtown Salem. Honeywood offers wine tasting every day along with an extensive selection of wine related gifts in their tasting room.

## The Wines

Honeywood continues to produce quality fruit wines from Willamette Valley harvests including Blackberry, Raspberry, Loganberry, Rhubarb, Plum and others. Varietals from Pinot Noir, Chardonnay, Riesling and Gewurztraminer are also made. A house specialty is white table wine (mostly Riesling) flavored with a small percentage of fruit juice.

# Oak Grove Orchards Winery

6090 Crowley Rd.
Rickreall, OR 97371
(503) 364-7052

**Tasting Room Hours:**
Tuesday thru Sunday, Noon to 6 PM

**Owner & Winemaker:** Carl Stevens
**First Year:** 1987
**Winery Capacity:** 6,000 Gallons

## Winery History

Carl Stevens has been making wine at home for 30 years using fruit that he grows in his orchard and vineyard. A portion of the original family homestead from the 1880s is home to orchards, vineyard and winery.

## A visit to Oak Grove Orchards Winery

A reconstructed building salvaged from an Army facility near Eugene serves as the tasting room for Carl Steven's winery. He moved the building and fixed it up for use both as a tasting room and as an inclement weather picnic site. Outside, picnic tables under the oak trees invite winery visitors to enjoy their repast on sunny days. A note about weekday visits: Carl often has errands to run during the week and winery visitors come mostly on weekends, so if you're coming on a weekday, please call ahead to insure Carl will be there to welcome you.

## The Wines

Carl's chosen varietals are two labrusca (concord) varieties popular in the New York wine growing regions. A Golden Muscat wine is made with 2% residual sugar and a true Concord is available in a dry or off-dry style. The winemaker recommends the dry Concord as a great accompaniment to a spaghetti dinner! Also crafted from estate-grown fruit is a unique Pie Cherry Wine that has a dedicated local following.

## Redhawk Vineyard

2995 Michigan City
Ave. N.W.
Salem, OR 97304
(503) 362-1596, FAX (503) 589-9189

**Tasting Room Hours:** Daily, Noon to 5 PM, May thru Nov.

**Owner/Winemaker:** Tom Robinson
**First Year:** 1989
**Winery Capacity:** 10,000 Gallons

### Winery History

Trained as a schoolteacher and possessing a great sense of humor, Tom Robinson now teaches visitors about wine in his tasting room at Redhawk Vineyard. Learning about wine himself during his days in the hot tub business in Portland, Robinson has chosen to create fanciful labels to help separate his quality table wines from the rest. Grateful Red, Chateau Mootom and Great White (complete with a shark on the label) are but a few of his humorous offerings of less expensive blended wines. The vineyard site was originally developed by Al Alexanderson (one of the founding partners in Hidden Springs Winery) and produces excellent quality wines which Robinson sells as his regular Redhawk bottlings.

### A visit to Redhawk Vineyard

The winery site is just above Highway 221 (Wallace Road) a few miles north of West Salem. The view across the vineyard to the Willamette River and the Cascades is breathtaking on sunny days. Tom Robinson's deadpan sense of humor and mischievous smile intrigues even the most stoic wine lover. A new picnic area in the shady woods behind the winery is a great place to relax.

### The Wines

While fame originally came to Redhawk Vineyard through Grateful Red, the high quality Reserve Pinot Noir and other reds have pushed their way into national reviews and brought well-deserved recognition to the winery. Cabernet Franc, Pinot Blanc, Pinot Gris and Cabernet Sauvignon are also made.

*The tasting room tapestry at Redhawk.*

## Serendipity Cellars

15275 Dunn Forest Rd.
Monmouth, OR 97361
(503) 838-4284
FAX (503) 838-0067
**Email:**
serendip@ncn.com
**Web:** www.ncn.com/~serendip

**Tasting Room Hours:** Daily, Noon to 6 PM, Closed Tuesdays; Winter, weekends only

**Owners:** The Longshore Family
**Winemaker:** Glen A. Longshore
**First Year:** 1981
**Winery Capacity:** 8,000 Gallons

### Winery History

This tiny winery tucked away in a tiny valley near Monmouth is home to a dedicated winemaker and his family, striving each year to maintain an individuality in this era of winery "sameness." Instead of limiting production to the typical varieties grown in Northwestern Oregon, Glen Longshore vinifies a grape called Maréchal Foch into a distinctive, fruity red wine. This grape comes from a family of "French Hybrids," genetic crosses between true vinifera grapes and other varieties bred to provide winter hardiness and resistance to phylloxera insects.

### A visit to Serendipity Cellars

Follow Highway 99W south from Monmouth and turn west on Airlie Road. At the town of Airlie, turn south on Maxfield Creek Road to Dunn Forest Road. Up at the top of the hill on Dunn Forest Road the winery is visible as the lower level of the Longshore home. As the need for more space increases,

*Continued on next page.*

more home becomes winery. The tasting room features a selection of Serendipity Cellars' wines often poured by Glen's wife, Cheryl.

## The Wines

Glen Longshore's hearty reds are touted as lacking the tannic roughness of traditionally made reds. The Marechal Foch, Zinfandel and Cabernet Sauvignon are made in small quantities and are often available only at the winery. Muller Thurgau and Dry Chenin Blanc are Glen's white varieties.

# Stangeland Winery

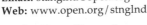

8500 Hopewell Road NW
Salem, OR 97304
(503) 581-0355
FAX (503) 540-3412
**Email:** stanglnd@open.org
**Web:** www.open.org/stnglnd

**Tasting Room Hours:** Summer weekends, Noon to 5 PM

**Owners:** Larry & Kinsey Miller
**Winemaker:** Larry Miller
**First Year:** 1991
**Winery Capacity:** 4,500

## Winery History

Larry and Kinsey Miller planted their vineyard in 1978 as the initial step in producing Stangeland estate wines. Since the winery's opening in 1992, limited production bottlings have been crafted using traditional winemaking methods. Production is expanding each year as more grapes are sourced that meet the winery's quality standards.

## A visit to Stangeland Winery

Located at the corner of Spring Valley Rd. and Hopewell Rd. (just 1/4-mile west of Hwy. 221). The Millers are enthusiastic hosts at the tasting room with a friendly welcome to all. Their slogan is "There are no strangers at Stangeland! The winery offers weekend tasting from Noon until 5 P.M. during the summer as well as Thanksgiving, Memorial Day and Labor Day holiday weekends. Other times by appointment.

## The Wines

Pinot Noir from Stangeland includes a reserve bottling, an estate bottling from 100% Wadenswil clone, Oregon Pinot Noir from Pommard and Wadenswil clones, and Rob Roy Red available only at the winery. Pinot Gris and Chardonnay are each available as estate and reserve bottlings. Gewurztraminer and a blend of Chenin Blanc and Pinot Noir called Stangeland Søndag are also made.

# St. Innocent Winery

1360 Tandem Ave. NE
Salem, OR 97303
(503) 378-1526
FAX (503) 378-1041
Web: www.stinnocentwine.com

**Tasting Room Hours:** Memorial Day and Thanksgiving Weekend events. Other times by appointment.

**Owner:** St. Innocent, Ltd.
**Winemaker:** Mark Vlossak
**First Year:** 1988
**Winery Capacity:** 15,000 Gallons

## Winery History

A comfortable association with wine appreciation and a coincidental career move led to Mark Vlossak's winemaking career and St. Innocent Winery. As physician's assistant to Salem pediatrician Jim Lace, he was shown around the Eola Hills and became interested in the burgeoning wine industry of the early 1980s. Meeting local winemakers and vineyard owners was an important step with home winemaking and U.C. Davis short courses providing hands-on experience. Serving as assistant winemaker at Arterberry Winery in 1987 and 1988 springboarded Vlossak to bonding his own facility in 1988. In 1995 a larger facility was built north of Salem, just off the Salem Parkway.

## A visit to St. Innocent

Currently the winery offers visits only by appointment and on the Thanksgiving and Memorial Day weekend events. From the Salem Parkway, turn east on Cherry St. then turn immediately into the business park area on the north side of the road.

*Mark Vlossak of St. Innocent Winery.*

## The Wines

Mark Vlossak has a well-earned reputation for high quality Pinot Noir, Chardonnay and sparkling wine. A believer in the importance of quality fruit in creating quality wine, he carefully selects the vineyard sources for his bottlings and tracks each vineyard before harvest. Chardonnay from Seven Springs Vineyard and Pinot Noir from O'Connor Vineyard produced the original award-winning results. Recent vintages have seen vineyard designated Pinot Noirs and Chardonnays from O'Conner, Seven Springs and Freedom Hill vineyards.

Mark's first love, sparkling wine, is carefully crafted with labor-intensive methods and great forethought put into each cuvée. A Brut and Blanc de Noir are produced and left several years *en tiriage* before release.

## Thoma Vineyards/ Van Duzer

11975 Smithfield Road, Dallas, OR 97338-9339
(503) 623-6420, FAX (503) 623-4310
**Email:** jkakacek@parducci.com

**Tasting Room Hours:** Weekends, 11 AM to 5 PM. Weekdays by appointment. Winter hours by appointment.

**Owner:** Carl Thoma
**Winemaker:** Jim Kakacek
**First Year:** 1998
**Winery Capacity:** 20,000 Gallons

## Winery History

In the early 1990s William Hill Winery of Napa Valley purchased some land in the Eola Hills to begin an Oregon venture making Pinot Noir, Chardonnay and other wines. Grapes were purchased from existing vineyards and wine was custom made at facilities in both California and Oregon. Wine was released under the Van Duzer label, named for the Van Duzer Corridor, a gap in the Oregon Coast Range that allows the flow of cool marine air into the hot Willamette Valley to moderate the summer climate. Several changes in winery ownership have taken place since then, and the Van Duzer brand will now be produced at the former Schwarzenberg Winery near Rickreall off Highway 99W.

The new owner of this winery is Carl Thoma, CEO of Parducci Wine Estates, a California holding company for several winery properties, including the Van Duzer brand. As personal winery owner, Thoma has created the name Thoma Vineyards and hired winemaker Jim Kakacek to come north and make wine at his new property. Having been the winemaker for Van Duzer wines for two years, Kakacek is looking forward to making the Eola Hills area his home as we go to press. The estate vineyards at the winery include 35 acres of Pinot Noir (some Dijon clone) and 30 acres of Chardonnay.

Look for expanded tasting room hours and exciting wine releases as things get settled in. Another chapter in Oregon winegrowing is about to be written with this property, so be sure to stop by and be counted as one of the first to enjoy it. Turn west on Smithfield Road from Highway 99W to the winery (just north of the junction of Hwys. 99W and 22.

By the way, the nearby Basket Slough Wildlife Refuge is a great place to visit with abundant bird migration taking place during the fall and spring.

*Jerry Sass, owner of Wild Winds Winery.*

# Wild Winds Winery

9092 Jackson Hill Rd. SE
Salem, OR 97306
(503) 391-9991

**Owner/Winemaker:**
Jerry Sass
**First Year:** 1995
**Winery Capacity:** 3,500 Gallons

**Winery History**

Newspaper writer Jerry Sass planted the first two acres of his vineyard in South Salem in 1989 and followed with subsequent plantings in 1991 and 1997. Today a total of eight acres of Pinot Noir (Pommard, Wadenswil, Dijon 115) and Pinot Gris (Colmar clone) are in the ground and the first plantings are producing fruit for estate bottled wines. Careful vineyard management and small yields has produced intense wines of character.

**A visit to Wild Winds**

The winery building at Wild Winds was completed in 1995 and production is slowly increasing with each vintage. Visits to the winery are welcomed by appointment or during the Thanksgiving or Memorial Day weekend events. The winery is across I-5 from Willamette Valley Vineyards and up the hill to the southwest. Call for directions.

**The Wines**

Ripe and spicy Pinot Noir is aged in French oak and is rich and complex. Pinot Gris is fermented in stainless steel, which Sass prefers to show the delicate flavors.

# Willamette Valley Vineyards

8800 Enchanted Way SE
Turner, OR 97392
(503) 588-9463
FAX (503) 588-8894
**Web:** www.wvv.com

**Tasting Room Hours:**
Daily, 11 AM to 6 PM

**Winery Owner:** Publicly Owned,
    James Bernau, President
**Winemaker:** Joseph Dobbes
**First Year:** 1989
**Winery Capacity:** 210,000 Gallons

**Winery History**

"We knew many shared the dream of building and owning a world class winery in Oregon. As 2,620 wine enthusiasts, we pooled our resources to build Oregon's landmark winery and to produce the highest quality, premium wines." Indeed, these shareholders were the beginning of Willamette Valley Vineyards in 1989 and the success has come. Quality winemaking by first winemaker Bob McRitchie (now handled by Joe Dobbes), quality management and a first-class facility have combined to create an example of what good planning can accomplish.

**A visit to Willamette Valley Vineyards**

Just off I-5 south of Salem (take exit 248), this beautiful facility stands out at the top of a hill covered in vineyards. A huge arch welcomes you from the frontage road and the winding driveway leads up to the stylish winery building and visitor center. A well-stocked tasting room invites your enjoyment of wines to sample as well as many gift items and foods to purchase. Terraces for picnicking and the fabulous viewing tower add to the fun.

The winery sponsors jazz concerts and other events, call for information.

**The Wines**

A wide range of varietals are made including Pinot Noir, Pinot Gris, Riesling, Muller Thurgau, Chardonnay and sparkling wines. Intense, oaky reserve red wines are the latest additions to the line offering tannin and wood for long term aging.

# Witness Tree Vineyard

7111 Spring Valley
Road NW
Salem, OR 97304
(503) 585-7874
FAX (503) 362-9765

*Witness Tree Vineyard near Salem.*

**Tasting Room Hours:** Weekends only, 11 AM to 5 PM

**Owners:** Dennis & Carolyn Devine, Derek & Monica Mortimer-Lamb
**Winemaker:** Bryce Bagnall
**First Year:** 1987
**Winery Capacity:** 15,000 Gallons

## Winery History

The Witness Tree Vineyard was planted in 1980 with 46 acres of Pinot Noir and Chardonnay. The name of the winery and vineyard refers to a historic oak "witness tree" that stands above the vineyard. This tree was used as a reference point by early surveyors platting this part of the Willamette Valley. A handsome tasting room was added to the winery building in 1992.

**A visit to Witness Tree Vineyard**

Just above Spring Valley Road, Witness Tree Vineyards welcomes visitors to their visitor center adjacent to the vineyard.

**The Wines**

Strong believers in the future of the Eola Hills as a prime growing area for Pinot Noir and Chardonnay, the owners are taking the necessary steps to ensure that the finest quality wine will be made at their winery. Pinot Noir, Chardonnay and a "Vintage Select" version of each varietal are offered, and a second label Chardonnay under the winery's Aurora label is produced.

# SALEM/EOLA HILLS ACCOMMODATIONS

## Executive Inn

200 Commerical St. SE - (503) 363-4123 (800) 452-7879 Right in the heart of downtown Salem within walking distance of the capitol, Willamette University and shopping. Free health club/racquetball, pool, sauna, jacuzzi. Continental breakfast. Tower suites with hot tubs. Black Angus Restaurant nearby. Moderate.

## State House B & B

2146 State St. - (503) 588-1340 Just a dozen blocks east of Willamette University Mike Winsett and Judy Uselman are constantly improving their handsome four bedroom bed & breakfast. A beautiful back garden borders on Mill Creek complete with hot tub and gazebo. Two regular rooms share a bath, two suites each have a private bath and one has a kitchenette. A bountiful breakfast and cozy terry robes are added amenities. Rates are low, quality is high.

## Marquee House B & B

333 Wyatt Ct. NE, Salem, (503) 391-0837 Not far from the State Capitol and adjacent to Mill Creek, this unique lodging is themed around the movie industry with each guest room having its own personality. Delicious breakfasts feature fresh fruits, egg dishes and baked goods.

## Bethel Heights Farm Bed & Breakfast

6055 Bethel Heights Rd. NW, 97304 (503) 364-7688 Leo and Ervina Anderson have opened their modern view home to lucky overnight guests wishing to be away from the hustle and bustle of the city. Just across the road from Bethel Heights winery and close to many other wine visits, BH Farm offers guest rooms with private baths and patio or deck. Fabulous view and delicious homemade breakfast. The area has been waiting for this one! Moderate.

# SALEM/EOLA HILLS DINING

## Alessandro's Park Plaza

325 High Street SE, Salem (503) 370-9951 Downtown Salem's most elegant restaurant serving Italian cuisine to the downtown and legislative contingent. Traditional dishes are well executed and the wine list features some local bottlings.

## DaVinci's

180 High Street, (503) 399-1413 A garlicky, bistro-style eatery in the downtown Salem business district. Delicious house-made bread, delectable pizzas, tasty entrees and a reason-ably-priced wine list make everyone feel at home. Dine in the balcony if you can.

## Mortons Bistro

1128 Edgewater, West Salem (503) 585-1113 This remarkable find is tucked away under a storefront on West Salem's frontage road. The roar of the freeway just a stone's throw above doesn't reach the dining room and the food is eclectic, regional and delicious. Enjoy an extra bottle of local wine without breaking your bankroll. Elvis has been sighted here.

## Thompson Brewery & Public House

3575 Liberty Rd. S., Salem (503) 363-7286 Part of the McMenamins empire, this south Salem brewpub is in a converted old house and takes advantage of every nook and cranny. Slurp some suds in the "bar" while you watch the ballgame. Dine in the parlor on sandwiches, salads, pizzas and burgers. Be seen on the verandah or grab a picnic table in the side yard to pound down a pint of Terminator stout.

# CORVALLIS & EUGENE AREA WINERIES
## Corvallis & Eugene Area Touring

The southern Willamette Valley is rich in soil, history and academics. The home of Oregon's two state universities is also home to many unique wineries — most of them open weekends in the summer months. From north to south they are:

Just north of Albany, Mike McLain operates **Springhill Cellars** and is open weekends most of the year with a view tasting room and picnic area.

Southwest of Corvallis, follow Llewllyn Road from Highway 99W to find **Bellfountain Cellars** at the home of Rob and Jeanne Mommsen. Carved out of the foothills of the Coast Range, the winery shares a little corner of nature with surrounding forest and field.

Heading south from Corvallis on Highway 99W, your first stop is **Tyee Wine Cellars** on Greenberry Road. The Buchanan family along with Barney Watson and Nola Mosier have created a "quality not quanity" operation on the Buchanan's 100-year-old farm. Picnic out on the grass or under cover.

Further down 99W, a right turn at the town of Monroe leads to **Alpine Vineyards** winery at the home of Dr. Dan Jepsen and family. Dan's medical responsibilities lie at the University of Oregon student health center but his creative outlet and exercise are the vineyard and winery. The winery is currently open by appointment only.

**Broadley Vineyards** has achieved growing fame for their fine Pinot Noirs and is located right on Highway 99W at Monroe. Open by appointment.

Just south on Territorial Road is the vineyard and winery operation owned by Napa winemakers Steve Girard and Carl Doumani. **Benton Lane** is named after the two counties which meet near Monroe. The winery facility was completed in 1998 and plans to be open daily for tasting and sales.

Continuing on Territorial Highway south to Cheshire, turn west to visit **High Pass Winery** on Lavell Road and **Rainsong Vineyards** off Goldson Road.

From Elmira, turn west on Warthen Road and follow the signs to **LaVelle Vineyards**. A delightful picnic area and tasting room (with art gallery) await.

Turn west on Highway 126 to visit **Secret House Vineyards**. Ron and Patty Chappel offer wine tasting and a shady picnic area in the pine woods behind the winery.

**Hinman Vineyards** offers the peace and quiet of the countryside at their vineyard and winery on Briggs Hill Road. A scenic drive through forest and bucolic farmland precedes wine sampling and picnic opportunities at the winery.

You'll see **King Estate** winery on your right as you travel south on Territorial Highway. If you would like a tour of this grand facility, call ahead for an appointment.

You'll find **Chateau Lorane** just a few miles ahead off Siuslaw River Road. Linde and Sharon Kester produce a remarkable assortment of varietals. Open daily.

Tasting and tours by appointment are available at **Houston Vineyards** located off I-5 at exit 189. Steve and Jewelee Houston specialize in Chardonnay.

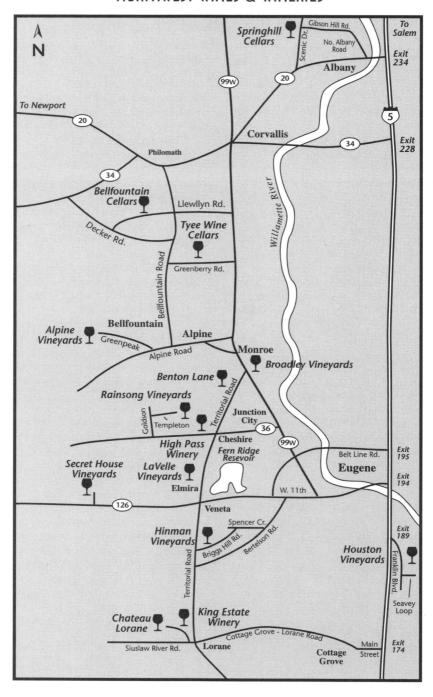

## Alpine Vineyards

25904 Green Peak Rd.
Monroe, OR 97456
(541) 424-5851

**Tasting Room Hours:** By appointment only.

**Owner & Winemaker:** Dan Jepsen
**First Year:** 1980
**Winery Capacity:** 25,000 Gallons

**Winery History**

When Dan and Christine Jepsen returned from two years in Africa working for the Peace Corps, they came to Oregon and planted a vineyard. An amateur winemaker throughout his years at medical school, Dan was attracted to the rural environment, the vigorous outdoor work involved and the prospect that some-where down the line a winery might be in the works. The vineyard was planted in 1976 in a small valley between Corvallis and Eugene where 26 acres of vines now produce grapes for the Alpine Vineyards winery.

**A visit to Alpine Vineyards**

After almost two decades of welcoming visitors to the winery and producing enough wine to handle the demand, Dan Jepsen has slowed down the production and closed the tasting room. Wine lovers may call ahead to see if an appointment to visit is possible.

**The Wines**

Delectable Riesling and Chardonnay complemented the Pinot Noir and Cabernet made during Alpine's biggest years. Call to see what varietals are currently available.

## Bellfountain Cellars

25041 Llewellyn Rd.
Corvallis, OR 97333
(541) 929-3162
**Web:** www.peak.org/
~winemakr/

Bellefountain
Estate
PINOT GRIS
Oregon White Table Wine

**Tasting Room Hours:**
Friday, Saturday and
Sunday, Noon to 6 PM

**Owners/Winemakers:** Rob & Jeanne Mommsen
**First Year:** 1989
**Winery Capacity:** 40,000 Gallons

**Winery History**

In love with the idea of country life, Rob and Jeanne Mommsen traded-in careers in the industrial east to forge a winery and home in the foothills of the Oregon Coast Range near Corvallis. With energy and enthusiasm they have built their home/winery, planted the first 10 acres of vineyard and established a reputation for quality wines.

**A visit to Bellfountain Cellars**

Turn west off Highway 99W on Llewllyn Road to find Bellfountain Cellars just past Fern Rd. The winery and vineyard are in a clearing in the pristine lowland forest with picnic tables and decks arranged to accommodate visitors. The owners encourage picnicking and strolling through the forest or along Bull Run Creek.

**The Wines**

Pinot Noir, Cabernet Sauvignon, Chardonnay, Sauvignon Blanc, Pinot Gris, Riesling and Gewurztraminer are produced.

## Benton Lane Winery

23924 Territorial Hwy.
Monroe, OR 97456
(541) 847-5792

**Owners:** Carl Doumani, Steve Girard
**Winemaker:** Gary Horner
**First Year:** 1991
**Winery Capacity:** 70,000 gallons

**Winery History**

California vintners Carl Doumani and Steve Girard invested in the Oregon wine scene by planting 82 acres of Pinot Noir and Nebbiolo at a site just north of Eugene in 1989. The former Sunny Mountain Ranch totals 2,000 acres in size, so there is room for expansion as the operation grows and additional plantings are planned. The original 80 acres of Pinot are now producing nicely and are the source for the winery's annual vintage Pinot Noir and Reserve Pinot Noir (in most years). The Nebbiolo is curiously unproductive, and rumor has it that it will pay for it's impotence by being grafted over to Pinot Noir.

*Continued on next page.*

In June of 1998, winemaker Gary Horner was hired to oversee the final construction of a new winery and tasting room on the vineyard site just south of Monroe. Horner was an assistant at Bethel Heights Vineyard and most recently worked at Washington Hills Cellars in the Yakima Valley. Previous Benton Lane vintages were custom crushed at another winery but beginning in 1998 their own facility will be home to estate wine production.

**A visit to Benton Lane**

The tasting room is open daily although hours have not been finalized at presstime.

**The Wines**

In addition to Pinot Noir, the winery plans to produce small quantities of Pinot Gris and Viognier for sale at the tasting room only.

# Broadley Vineyards

265 South 5th, Box 160
Monroe, OR 97456
(541) 847-5934
FAX (541) 847-6018

**Tasting Room Hours:** By appointment only.

**Owners:** Craig & Claudia Broadley
**Winemaker:** Craig Broadley
**First Year:** 1986
**Winery Capacity:** 5,000 Gallons

**Winery History**

"City people" turned grape growers and winemakers is how Craig and Claudia Broadley think of themselves after a decade of hard work learning the farming business. Originally involved in publishing and book distribution in San Francisco, the Broadleys found that Oregon was a perfect place to escape to their dream of winery ownership. Their vineyard was planted beginning in 1980 and the winery building acquired in 1986 to accommodate the harvest of 15 acres of Chardonnay and Pinot Noir. Wines were first released in 1988.

**A visit to Broadley Vineyards**

The building now used as a winery for Broadley Vineyards was once a car dealership circa 1930. The winery is open on the Friday, Saturday and Sunday following Thanksgiving. Other visits to the facility are by appointment.

**The Wines**

The Pinot Noirs being produced by Craig Broadley follow his desire to craft Burgundian style wines that accompany food. His Pinot Noir wines are rich and full-bodied and stand with the best of Oregon's finest bottlings. The Claudia's Choice bottling continues to be a top-rated wine around the world.

# Chateau Lorane

27415 Siuslaw
River Rd.
Lorane, OR 97451
(541) 942-8028

**Tasting Room Hours:**
Daily, Noon to 5 PM
(summer months) other months weekends only. Closed January, February

**Owners:** Linde & Sharon Kester
**First Year:** 1992

**Winery History**

Linde and Sharon Kester planted their 30-acre vineyard in 1984 and opened their winery and tasting room to the public in 1992. The beauty of the Coast Range foothills make their site something special with a lake and forest setting.

**A visit to Chateau Lorane**

Travel down Territorial Highway to Lorane or follow the Cottage Grove-Lorane Road from exit 174 off I-5. The winery road is .2 miles west of Lorane on Siuslaw River Rd. The facility may be rented for weddings or other functions accommodating up to 300 people.

**The Wines**

A wide array of varietals are produced from the winery's vineyard and from purchased grapes. Pinot Noir, Chardonnay, Viognier, Sauvignon Blanc, Riesling and Gewurztraminer are joined by Cabernet Franc, Durif, Grignolino, Zinfandel and others.

## High Pass Winery

24757 Lavell Road
Junction City, OR 97448
(541) 998-1447

**Tasting Room Hours:** By appointment.

**Owner/Winemaker:** Dieter Boehm
**First Year:** 1996

**Winery History**

Dieter Boehm is the vineyard manager for High Pass, Priddy and Walnut Ridge Vineyards and makes wines from the grapes he grows at High Pass Winery. Visit the tasting room during Memorial Day or Thanksgiving weekends or by appointment. Follow High Pass Road west to Lavell Road from Junction City or Territorial Highway.

**The Wines**

Dry Riesling, Chardonnay, Sauvignon Blanc, Pinot Gris, Pinot Noir, Cabernet Sauvignon and Merlot are made.

## Hinman Vineyards/ Silvan Ridge

27012 Briggs Hill Road,
Eugene, OR 97405
(541) 345-1945
FAX (541) 345-6174

**Tasting Room Hours:** Daily, Noon to 5 PM

**Owner:** Carolyn Chambers
**Winemaker:** Bryan Wilson
**First Year:** 1979
**Winery Capacity:** 100,000+ Gallons

**Winery History**

As one of a handful of Oregon wineries operating in 1979, Hinman Vineyards was born of enthusiastic partners wishing to make a name in the fledgling wine industry. Growth was rapid and sometimes chaotic, and today a new owner has guided the winery back onto a solid track. Current winemaker Bryan Wilson joined the operation in 1998 and is carrying on the high quality of the Hinman brand and the premium Silvan Ridge reserve wines which win both awards and loyal followers wherever

poured. Wilson has several Oregon vintages under his belt and spent over a decade in the California wine industry.

**A visit to Hinman Vineyards**

A 20-minute drive from Eugene, follow 11th St. (Hwy. 126) to Bailey Hill Rd. Turn left and follow this road for 5 miles, turning right on Spencer Creek Road for 2.5 miles. Turn left on Briggs Hill Road and travel the remaining 3.5 miles to the winery. This large winery complex offers a delightful tasting room/ visitor center where tasting and tours are offered daily.

**The Wines**

From crisp Pinot Gris to complex Pinot Noir to refreshing semi-sparkling Early Muscat, wines made under the Hinman and Silvan Ridge labels offer clean varietal character and good value. Merlot and Cabernet are made from grapes grown in Southern Oregon.

## Houston Vineyards

86187 Hoya Lane
Eugene, OR 97405
(541) 747-4681

**Tasting Room Hours:** By appointment.

**Owners:** Steven & Jewelee Houston
**Production:** 3,000 Gallons

**Winery History**

Steven and Jewelee Houston use only their own grapes in the production of their Chardonnay, but they have chosen to contract with an existing winery to produce wine according to their specifications. As a "custom crush grower" they have wine made from their grapes to their specifications. The Houston Vineyard lies along the Coast Fork of the Willamette River, next to the 2,300 acre Buford County Park off I-5 and just 2 miles east of Eugene. Wine tastings, sales and vineyard tours are available by appointment.

# King Estate Winery

80854 Territorial Road
Eugene, OR 97405
(541) 942-9874, FAX (541) 942-9867
**Email:** king@kingestate.com
**Web:** www.kingestate.com

**Tours and Tastings:** By appointment.

**Owner:** King family, Ed King, President
**Winemaker:** Will Bucklin
**First Year:** 1992
**Winery Capacity:** 400,000 Gallons

## Winery History

Longtime Eugene resident Ed King III is the head of this family-owned enterprise that has entered the Oregon wine industry in a big way. Grapes are harvested from 220 acres of vineyards southwest of Eugene and the huge

*King Estate's barrel aging cellar.*

winery building and aging cellar (constructed during 1992-93) is approaching full production. The vineyard operation includes the King Estate-owned, state-of-the-art, vine propagation and nursery facility called Lorane Grapevines. Grafted cuttings are prepared for planting at the King Estate vineyard and are also sold to other wineries. The 110,000 square foot winery and aging cellar is remarkable for both function and style. You can admire the facility on the cover of this book.

*The dining room at King Estate winery.*

## A visit to King Estate Winery

Tourist facilities for this large operation are limited to showing small groups through the operation by appointment. Highlighting the work being done in the culinary arts is also part of the tour. The first cookbook on Oregon Pinot Gris was published by King Estate in 1994—a beautiful and useful guide to pairing food with this Northwest-favored varietal. This was followed by their similarly successful Pinot Noir cookbook in 1996.

Expanded visitor facilities are in the plans as King Estate grows and more resources are made available to welcome guests.

## The Wines

King Estate crushed only purchased grapes in the early years and released Pinot Gris, Chardonnay and Pinot Noir with favorable reviews. Estate grapes are used in greater proportion as the estate vineyards come into full production.

Pinot Gris and Pinot Noir are the majority of the production with reserve versions of each wine also offered. Crisp, clean Pinot Gris is varietally true with complexity gained through vinification of grapes from different clones and vineyard sites. King Estate's Pinot Noir has also been very successful with French oak aging adding complexity. Chardonnay is produced in a barrel-fermented style, and in 1992 King Estate released its first Cabernet Sauvignon.

**Julia Potter**
**Culinary Director**
**King Estate Winery**

*During her undergraduate days at the University of Oregon in Eugene, Julia Potter delved into the culinary arena by joining Stephanie Pearl Kimmel as sous chef in her catering business. Later managing daily operations for Kimmel's Excelsior Cafe, Potter flourished in the restaurant and hospitality industry.*

*Joining King Estate as Assistant Culinary Director in 1993, Potter has since bcome the winery's Director of Hospitality/Culinary. Julia plans and executes all menus, including the development of food and wine pairings. She focuses on using fresh, seasonal ingredients from King Estate's 1.5 acre organic garden whenever possible.*

*In addition to her culinary passion, Potter coordinates all hospitality events at King Estate, provides direction for the organic garden, manages the production of King Estate's food specialty line (preserves, berry infused vinegars, etc.) and oversees the landscaping for the entire Estate.*

## ❖ A RECIPE FROM KING ESTATE ❖

# Roast Salmon with Wild Blackberry Basil Vinegar Sauce

Serves 4
Accompanying wine: King Estate Pinot Gris or Pinot Noir

| | |
|---|---|
| 1 | cup white wine (Pinot Gris) |
| 1 | cup blackberry vinegar * |
| 1/2 | cup shallots chopped fine |
| 3 | teaspoons green peppercorns (whole) |
| 1/2 | cup heavy cream |
| 12 | oz cold unsalted butter, cut into 1-in cubes |
| | Salt and freshly ground white pepper to taste |
| 4 | 6-oz salmon fillets |

Place shallots, green peppercorns, wine, and vinegar in a heavy medium saucepan and boil over medium high heat until the wine and vinegar has reduced by about 2/3 of original volume. Add cream and continue to cook over low heat until all that is left are the shallots and a very small amount of the reduction of wine and cream.

Still over low heat, whisk in 4 cubes of butter at a time, adding more as the butter blends into the sauce. When all the butter is blended in, remove the saucepan from the flame and keep in a warm place until needed.

Roast salmon filets at 500° F for 10 minutes.

Pour sauce over fish and serve immediately with grilled summer vegetables and roasted potatoes. Garnish with Chiffonade of basil and a few fresh blackberries.

## Blackberry Basil Vinegar

Using 1 gallon of champagne vinegar, add 1/2 dozen pints of blackberries and 2 cups of fresh basil leaves. Infuse for 2-3 weeks, strain, and bottle. The extra amount of blackberry basil vinegar is fabulous as a vinaigrette for salads and marinades. Vinegar will keep for approximately two years.

# LaVelle Vineyards

89697 Sheffler Road
Elmira, OR 97437
(541) 935-9406
FAX (541) 935-7202

**Tasting Room
Hours:** Daily, Noon to 6 PM, Memorial Day
through October. November through May,
Noon to 5 PM weekends only.

**Owners:** Doug & Susan LaVelle
**Winemaker:** Gary Carpenter
**First Year:** 1995

## Winery History

A more romantic winery story you'll
rarely hear than the tale of the discovery and
purchase of LaVelle Vineyards. Doug and
Susan LaVelle had always wanted to take a
hot air balloon ride over the vineyards.
Soaring over the Napa Valley, they discovered
the romance of the wine country and began
dreaming of owning a winery. They knew the
Napa Valley was too expensive so a search in
Oregon was begun. Lo and behold the
former Forgeron Vineyard winery property
was for sale and the LaVelle's became part of
the Oregon wine scene!

## A visit to LaVelle Vineyards

The Forgeron Winery was always a
popular stop with wine lovers who enjoyed
the gardens, picnic area and art gallery in the
mezzanine above the tasting room. It has all
been restored and made even better by the
new owners and they invite visitors to stop by
and enjoy their wines and their hospitality as
fellow lovers of the Oregon wine country.

## The Wines

Pinot Noir, Chardonnay, Pinot Gris,
Riesling, Chenin Blanc, Muller Thurgau and a
sparkling wine from Pinot Noir cuvee are
made under the LaVelle label.

# Rainsong Vineyards Winery

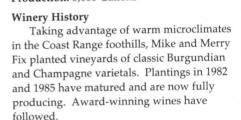

92989 Templeton Rd.
Cheshire, OR 97419
(541) 998-1786

**Tasting Room Hours:**
By appointment

**Owner/Winemaker:** Michael Fix
**First Year:** 1988
**Production:** 5,000 Gallons

## Winery History

Taking advantage of warm microclimates
in the Coast Range foothills, Mike and Merry
Fix planted vineyards of classic Burgundian
and Champagne varietals. Plantings in 1982
and 1985 have matured and are now fully
producing. Award-winning wines have
followed.

## A visit to Rainsong Vineyards

Follow Highway 36 from Eugene through
Cheshire. Turn right on Goldson Road and
cross Hall Road to Templeton. The winery and
tasting room are located on the edge of a small
pond where a picnic area is available to
visiting wine lovers. The tasting room is open
for the Memorial Day and Thanksgiving
weekends.

## The Wines

"Burgundian varietals" Pinot Noir and
Chardonnay are the focus of this family run
operation as well as methode champenoise
sparkling wines.

# Secret House Vineyards

88324 Vineyard Lane
Veneta, OR 97487
(541) 935-3774

**Tasting Room Hours:**
11 AM to 5 PM,
Wednesday through
Monday. Closed Xmas through March 1.

**Owners:** Ron and Patty Chappel
**First Year:** 1991
**Winery Capacity:** 5,000 Gallons

## Winery History

Full-time entrepreneurs, Ron and Patty Chappel have a large vineyard to maintain, a tasting room to handle and a beautiful picnic area under Ponderosa pine trees to offer visitors. With the owners previously involved in importing fine arts from the Far East, the tasting room has intriguing touches of the orient as well as a beautiful gardenia bush in the corner that blooms as testament to Patty's green thumb.

## A visit to Secret House Winery

Just two and a half miles west of Territorial Highway on Route 126, the winery is a convenient stop for those heading to the Oregon coast. Samples of several wines are offered and picnicking is encouraged on the winery grounds. A winery Blues Festival is presented the second weekend in August and the Long Tom Music Festival takes place the first Saturday after Labor Day.

## The Wines

Pinot Noir, Chardonnay, Riesling, Late Harvest Riesling and sparkling wine are produced here.

# Springhill Cellars

2920 NW Scenic Dr.
Albany, OR 97321
(541) 928-1009

**Tasting Room Hours:**
June through November,
1 PM to 5 PM, weekends.
Closed January through March.

**Owners:** Mike & Karen McLain,
Merv Anthony
**Winemaker:** Mike McLain
**First Year:** 1988
**Winery Capacity:** 6,000 Gallons

## Winery History

Shortly after Mike McLain planted his first acres of vineyard, he also expanded his real estate business to include vineyard land. The land values around Corvallis and Albany are much more reasonable than in the Dundee Hills and the suitability for vineyard is excellent. Gary Budd joined the enterprise in the late 1980s to help out as winemaker and Springhill's 1988 Pinot Noir won a gold medal and the Governor's award at the Oregon State Fair. Gary Budd is no longer involved but Mike McLain continues to produce award-winning Pinot Noir.

## A visit to Springhill Cellars

A short jaunt off I-5 (take exit 234 and head west through downtown Albany on Hwy. 20 towards Corvallis, then turn north at the signs on Scenic Dr. 2.1 miles), the winery offers visitors an expansive view of vineyards and the Coast Range for picnics and an enjoyable wine tasting experience.

## The Wines

Mike McLain is striving to make the very finest quality Pinot Noir, Chardonnay, Riesling and Muller Thurgau from the grapes harvested at the winery's Albany vineyard.

# Tyee Wine Cellars

26335 Greenberry Road
Corvallis, OR 97333
(541) 753-8754

**Tasting Room Hours:**
Saturday and Sunday,
Noon to 5 PM (April
through Dec.). Friday through Monday in July
and August.

**Owners:** Dave & Margy Buchanan,
  Barney Watson, Nola Mosier
**Winemaker:** Barney Watson
**First Year:** 1985
**Winery Capacity:** 8,000 Gallons

## Winery History

How many wineries can boast a one
hundred year history of horse racing, sheep
ranching and dairy farming? Grapes now
grow where horses once thundered past the
finish line and sheep pastures have been
turned and planted with vineyards.

Dave and Margy Buchanan are the owners
of the century-old farm that Dave's grandfather began back in the 1880s. Dave's home
winemaking and grape growing led him back
to his alma mater, Oregon State University, to
look up Barney Watson, a U. C. Davis graduate
hired by the school to do research for the
Oregon wine industry. Barney liked the
Buchanan's plans for a vineyard and winery
and a partnership was born.

A good portion of the grapes for Tyee Wine
Cellars current production come from some of
the area's best known vineyards. Estate-grown
wines include Pinot Noir, Pinot Gris, Chardonnay and Gewurztraminer.

## A visit to Tyee Wine Cellars

Rustic farm structures on the Buchanan
farm have been remodeled to serve as winery
and tasting room. New awnings have added a
flair to the presentation, and inside, Margy
Buchanan offers samples of current releases for
visitors. A very friendly welcome makes you
feel right at home. Tyee offers several special
events each year coinciding with the Memorial
Day weekend and Thanksgiving weekend as
well as their own July music event.

An additional building was constructed in
1997 to accommodate winery expansion.

## The Wines

Barney Watson's admitted fondness for
Gewurztraminer has led the winery to great
success with that varietal - a spunky style that
accompanies Asian cooking and other spicy
foods. Tyee's Pinot Gris and Pinot Blanc have
also been popular with wine judges and
consumers at local enological events and are
great with seafood. Chardonnay and Pinot
Noir are also popular with wine lovers.

# CORVALLIS/EUGENE ACCOMMODATIONS

## Towne House Motor Inn

350 SW 4th, Corvallis - (503) 753-4496 A pleasant and modern motor hotel with restaurant, air conditioned rooms and convenient location to downtown and the OSU campus.

## Madison Inn B & B

660 SW Madison, Corvallis - (503) 757-1274 Adjacent to the delightful Central Park, Kathryn Brandis now welcomes guests to her childhood home to enjoy the spacious comfort of a 7 bedroom B & B. Sumptuous breakfasts and shady strolls in the park are also nice.

## Valley River Inn

1000 Valley River Way, Eugene 97401 - (503) 687-0123 This attractive getaway along the Willamette River offers rooms with river views, courtyards, secluded pool area and on-premises dining.

## Eugene Hilton

66 East 6th Ave., Eugene (503) 342-2000 One of the largest buildings in downtown Eugene, the Hilton borders on the Hult Center for the Performing Arts and offers great views from many of its 271 rooms. Indoor pool, spa.

# CORVALLIS/EUGENE DINING

## The Gables

1121 NW 9th St., Corvallis (503) 752-3364 Local and regional ingredients are prepared to highlight freshness and true flavors. The menu leans toward the traditional American preparations that are popular in the country.

## Cafe Central

384 W. 13th, Eugene - (503) 343-9510 A very popular restaurant serving innovative and enjoyable fare for lunch and dinner. Extensive selection of wines, many from NW producers. Lunch, Mon. - Fri., dinner, Mon. - Sat.

## The Excelsior Cafe

754 East 13th Ave. (503) 342-6963 Choice local ingredients are prepared with style and creativity. A wide selection of menu offerings keeps the place crowded but excellent service helps keep pace. Local wines are well represented. Lunch and dinner daily.

## Zenon Cafe

898 Pearl St. (503) 343-3005 International offerings in an upscale environment catering to Eugene's academic crowd. Select your favorite Pinot Noir or Pinot Gris by the glass to accompany Mediterranean, Far Eastern or Middle Eastern specialties.

# CORVALLIS/EUGENE ACTIVITIES

## Jogging and Bicycling

Eugene is acclaimed by runners and bikers as having the most runner/cyclist-friendly attitude of any Northwest city. Bike lanes stripe the roads and bike and jogging paths abound in parks.

## Fern Ridge Reservoir

West of town on Highway 126, offers boating, fishing, water skiing, and more.

## Skinner Butte Park, Spencer Butte Park

These two high points of the area offer great territorial views and profusions of flowers in the summer.

## Van Duyn Candy Factory

Near I-5 off Belt Line. What heartless parent would deny their child a visit to a candy factory?

# CORVALLIS/EUGENE MICROBREWERIES & BREWPUBS

## Oregon Trader Brewing Company

140 Hill St. NE, Albany (503) 928-1931. Jerry and Nancy Mathern operate their small family brewery just a block from the Willamette River in downtown Albany. Enjoy a game of darts or a sandwich with your selection of brew. Hefeweizen, Black Beauty Porter and Chili (hot pepper) Beer are the headliners while tasty Scottish Ale, Imperial Oatmeal Stout and other brews entice experimentation by ardent beer lovers.

## Oregon Trail Brewery

341 SW 2nd St., Corvallis (503) 758-3527. One of Oregon's older microbreweries, Oregon Trail was begun in 1987 and is now headquartered in Corvallis' Old World Center. The gleaming brew kettle is the centerpiece of the uniquely-decorated pub and brewery. Namesake Oregon Trail Ale is a German Kolsch style and wheat beer is represented by Oregon Trail White Ale. Several other popular ale styles are also brewed. Tours are offered by appointment weekdays and the deli-brewpub is open daily.

## Eugene City Brewery

844 Olive St., Eugene (503) 345-8489. "Sandwiched" between two funky, downtown Eugene eateries, the Eugene City Brewery uses these neighbors as outlets for their distinctive ales. West Brothers BBQ and Mona Lizza Pizza proudly pour ECB's Honey Orange Wheat, Black Hole Stout, Red Tape Ale, Best Bitter, IPA and Blackberry Porter.

## Steelhead Brewery & Cafe

199 East 5th Ave, Eugene (503) 686-2739. Located in downtown Eugene's market district, this 150-seat brewery and restaurant offers the spirit of an English pub. Spent brewing grain is baked into the pub's fresh bread and pizza crust. Try the light Hefeweizen, Steelhead Amber, Bombay Bomber IPA, Porter, Oatmeal Stout and several rye malt concoctions including one made with Oregon raspberries. Tours by appointment, outdoor seating, open daily.

# UMPQUA VALLEY WINERIES

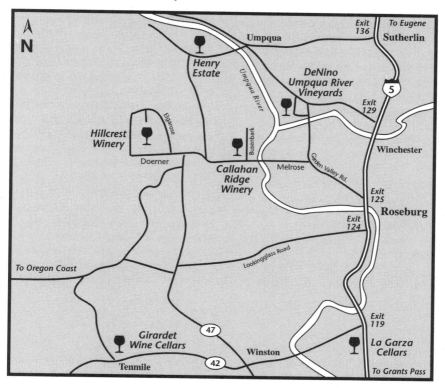

## UMPQUA VALLEY TOURING

The extended valley of the Umpqua River winds through parts of Oregon rich in nature and rich in lore. The rushing streams of the Cascade Foothills offer up quiet corners for the fly fisherman to ply his or her trade. The likes of Ernest Hemingway and Zane Grey came here to fish decades before any winery was conceived. Today, the sport remains, but several good wineries compete for the attention of visiting tourists.

The north part of this region finds **Henry Estate Winery** and **DeNino Umpqua River Estate** perched along the river. Henry Estate is open daily and offers a broad range of varietals poured by family members in the tasting room. Dino and Debra DeNino open their tasting room daily during the summer months. Look for their "Dino's Deli and Wine Shop" in downtown Roseburg.

In the middle part of the valley—the area known as Garden Valley—you'll find **Callahan Ridge Winery**, home to some of Oregon's most appealing red wines. Pioneering **HillCrest Vineyard** keeps regular hours daily with owner Richard Sommer on hand.

South of Roseburg, at freeway exit 119, **La Garza Cellars** is making superb wines and accumulating many awards. Enjoy lunch at the winery restaurant on site!

**Girardet Cellars** is operated by former astrophysicist Philippe Girardet and his wife Bonnie. Their dedication to Umpqua-area winemaking and grape growing reached the decade milestone in 1993.

# Callahan Ridge Winery

340 Busenbark Lane,
Roseburg, OR 97470
(541) 673-7901
**Email:**
winenet@rosenet.net

**Tasting Room Hours:** April through October,
Daily, 11:30 AM to 5:30 PM

**Owners:** Mary Sykes
**Winemaker:** Steve Anderson
**First Year:** 1987
**Winery Capacity:** 45,000 Gallons

**Winery History**

Callahan Ridge winery was founded by
Frank and Mary Sykes-Guido along with
Oregon native and German-trained winemaker
Richard Mansfield. After the death of her
husband, Mary Sykes is now the sole owner.
The wide selection of quality varietals
produced at Callahan Ridge helped establish
the Umpqua Valley as one of Oregon's premier
wine growing regions. Grapes are procured
from several sources including the winery's
4.5-acre vineyard (planted to Chardonnay,
Cabernet and Pinot Noir), Elkton Vineyards
(just 15 miles from the Pacific Ocean) and from
Doerner Ranch at the base of the Callahan
Range.

**A visit to Callahan Ridge Winery**

The barn-style building, constructed in
1878 using hand-hewn beams, houses the
tasting room for Callahan Ridge and is open
for tours and tasting daily from April through
October. Picnicking is encouraged in a shady
field beside the winery. Follow Garden Valley
Road 2 miles from I-5, then turn left on
Melrose and travel 1.3 miles to Busenbark Rd.

**The Wines**

Among the many varietals produced at
Callahan Ridge their Pinot Noir is often among
Oregon's best. Also available are: Riesling,
Dry Gewurztraminer, Cabernet Sauvignon,
Merlto, White Zinfandel, Sauvignon Blanc,
Chardonnay and Select Harvest Riesling.

# DeNino Umpqua River Estate

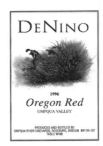

451 Hess Road
Roseburg, OR 97470
(541) 673-1975

**Tasting Room Hours:**
Daily, Noon to 5 PM

**Owner/Winemaker:** Greg
"Dino" DeNino
**First Year:** 1988
**Winery Capacity:** 5,000 Gallons

**Winery History**

The DeNino family has opened up their
winery on the banks of the Umpqua River in
the Garden Valley section of Roseburg. Wines
are made from grapes harvested at the family's
30-acre vineyard at the winery site.

**A visit to Umpqua River Vineyards**

Take exit 129 from I-5 and follow Del Rio
Road to the Old Garden Valley Road then head
south to Hess Lane. Nearby River Forks Park
is a nice stop to run the kids. The winery
tasting room is open daily, April through
September. A picnic area overlooks the private
boat dock on the Umpqua River.

**The Wines**

Greg DeNino crafts hearty Cabernet and
Merlot as well as Sauvignon Blanc, Semillon
and Chenin Blanc. Several blended red wines
that recall the winery slogan: "Enjoy Bordeaux
varietals with Italian winemaking methods!"

# Girardet Wine Cellars

895 Reston Road,
Roseburg, OR 97470
(541) 679-7252
FAX (541) 679-9502

**Tasting Room Hours:** Daily, 11 AM to 5 PM, April to October; Winter: Saturdays only or by appointment.

**Owners:** Philippe and Bonnie Girardet
**Winemaker:** Seth Stefanich
**First Year:** 1983
**Winery Capacity:** 25,000 Gallons

## Winery History

Although the 25-acre vineyard dates from the Girardet's arrival in Oregon in 1972, they were at first content to sell the output of their vineyard to other wineries. The winery began in 1983 and they hired enologist Bill Nelson to guide them through the first crush and to counsel them on proper selection of equipment. Today, Seth Stefanich (trained by enologist Patricia Green) handles the day to day winemaking duties.

## A visit to Girardet Winery

The winery and tasting room are open daily during the summer. The vineyard is just outside the tasting room door and informal tours are available if time permits. Bonnie Girardet is often your hostess.

## The Wines

The blending of wines holds the key to success for Philippe Girardet who takes as much pride in his Oregon Vin Blanc and Oregon Vin Rouge as he does in his Chardonnay or Pinot Noir. Each of the blended wines includes generous portions of grape cultivars frequently referred to as 'French hybrids.' By blending these unusual varieties with Chardonnay and Pinot Noir (and other premium varietal wines) Philippe achieves a complexity and balance that serves as a fine accompaniment to Northwest cuisine. Girardet Cabernet Sauvignon and Vin Rouge are widely lauded and Girardet Baco Noir is both delicious and a rare find.

# Henry Estate Winery

P.O. Box 26,
687 Hubbard Creek Rd.
Umpqua, OR 97486
(541) 459-5120
FAX (541) 459-5146
**Email:** henryest@rosenet.net
**Web:** www.henryestate.com

**Owners:** Scott and Sylvia Henry
**Winemaker:** Scott Henry
**First Year:** 1978
**Winery Capacity:** 35,000 Gallons
**Tasting Room Hours:** Daily, 11 AM to 5 PM

## Winery History

The science of engineering and the science of winemaking have come together many times in the evolution of Oregon's wine industry. Aeronautical engineer Scott Henry began his transition from drafting table and 'T' square to tractor and wine barrel in 1972 when he planted the first of 35 acres of vinifera grapes on the family ranch in the Umpqua Valley. As part of his scientific dedication to viticulture, Scott Henry developed a trellising system that is now used world wide, the Scott Henry Trellis.

Many family members are involved in the operation of the Henry Winery and vineyard. No fewer than four "Scotts" can be found on the payroll including Scott Henry, Jr. and a couple of other "Scotts" related to the clan by marriage or friendship.

## A visit to Henry Estate Winery

Your hosts in the tasting room are often family members who have long histories in the Umpqua Valley. In addition to thorough knowledge of Henry Estate wines, they can provide valuable assistance to visitors to the area. Shaded picnic tables invite the visitor to enjoy an afternoon of food and wine alongside the Umpqua River. Tours of the winery and vineyard are available for those interested.

## The Wines

The wines made at the Henry Winery include many 'estate bottled' selections produced from the Chardonnay, Gewurztraminer, Pinot Noir and Riesling grown at the

*Continued on next page.*

Henry Ranch. The attractive and affordable Pinot Noir and Red Table Wine (also 100% Pinot Noir) have attracted the most attention among Northwest consumers and wine experts. The Estate Pinot Noir receives more skin contact and produces a heartier wine with greater aging potential.

# HillCrest Vineyards

240 Vineyard Lane
Roseburg, OR 97470
(800) 736-3709
FAX (541) 440-9695
Email: finewine@sorcom.com

**Tasting Room Hours:** Daily, 11 AM to 5 PM
Tours available. Tour groups welcome

**Owner/Winemaker:** Richard H. Sommer
**First Year:** 1963
**Winery Capacity:** 41,000 Gallons

## Winery History

Richard Sommer is the original pioneer of the Oregon wine industry. More than three decades have elapsed since he first planted grapes in the Umpqua Valley in 1961 after intensive study of the soils and climate of Western Oregon. The current 35 acres of estate vineyard are in the area that Sommer feels produce the finest Germanic Rieslings in the Northwest.

## A visit to HillCrest Vineyard

To find HillCrest, head west from I-5 (Garden Valley Rd.), bear left on Melrose, right on Doerner, then right again on Elgarose. About 10 miles total. The winery offers picnic tables on an attractive deck for tasters to enjoy a lunch or snack with a sip of wine. Inclement weather has been allowed for with seating inside the tasting room also. Tours of the winery and vineyards are offered.

## The Wines

Hillcrest White Riesling accounts for the majority of the winery's production. Each vintage produces slight nuances but the mature vineyards now have an unmistakable aroma and bouquet that are detectable each year. The Riesling is fermented to retain two to three percent residual sugar to balance the acidity. An enticingly spicy Gewurztraminer is made each year, and the Cabernet Sauvignon and Pinot Noir continue to astound wine lovers with their long life and distinctive varietal character.

# La Garza Cellars

491 Winery Lane
Roseburg, OR 97470
(541) 679-9654
FAX (541) 679-3888

**Tasting Room Hours:**
Daily, 11 AM to 5 PM
(summer); other times:
Wed.-Sun., 12 - 4 PM

**Owner:** Donna Souza-Postles
**Winemaker:** Leonard Postles
**First Year:** 1975
**Winery Capacity:** 2,500 Gallons

## Winery History

In 1969 Jon Marker came north from California with some friends and founded Jonicole Winery just off I-5 near Winston. A vineyard was planted in the early 1970s and a substantial winery was built on the site. A few vintages of quality wine were made, then something went wrong. The winery succumbed to troubles during the early 1980s and laid abandoned until Donna Souza-Postles revived the property with a group of investors in 1992. The winery is up and running again, vineyards are restored and a gourmet restaurant has been opened on the premises! The potential for this scenic corner of the valley has always been great and now things are in superb condition for a visit.

## A visit to La Garza Cellars

Just a half mile west of the freeway at exit 119, La Garza Cellars is a convenient and tranquil stop for traveling wine lovers. Bring your own picnic or enjoy the tasty fare offered by the winery's Gourmet Kitchen restaurant.

## The Wines

While the La Garza Cabernet Sauvignon is a perennial gold medal winner, be sure to try their Chardonnay, Merlot and Riesling as well. Wines from other Northwest wineries are offered for tasting and for sale in the handsome tasting room.

# SOUTHERN OREGON WINERIES

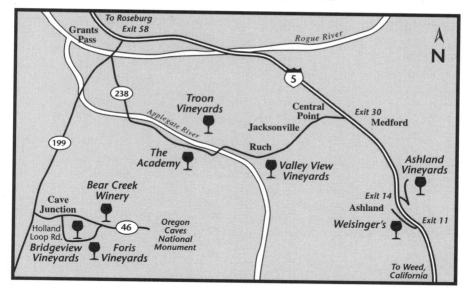

## SOUTHERN OREGON TOURING

This part of Oregon is such a wonderland of recreational possibilities that wine lovers often recreate first and think wine tasting second. However, if you've made it this far down I-5, it would be a shame not to enjoy the hospitality of the fine wineries located here.

A half hour down Highway 199 from Grants Pass, make the turn onto the Oregon Caves Highway to visit **Bridgeview Vineyards** winery with their expansive vineyard, shady picnic area and impressive winery. Not to be outdone, nearby **Foris Vineyards** offers equally relaxing surroundings, fine wine tasting and a sense of the forested Illinois Valley landscape.

Six miles east of Cave Junction on the Oregon Caves Highway you'll find **Bear Creek Winery**. This is the former Siskiyou Vineyards winery, recently purchased and revived by Bridgeview winemaker Rene Eichmann. The Bear Creek tasting room is pouring wines from other area wineries as well as their own.

Backtrack up Highway 199 to pick up Highway 238 for a scenic drive along the Applegate River to **Valley View Vineyards**. The places where the road crosses the river offer some pretty views and some tempting glances at swimming holes in hot weather. Valley View is just south of the town of Ruch.

While you're on this drive you will pass by the locations of **Troon Vineyards** and **The Academy** winery. Neither are open to the public, but you can probably find their wines in local wine shops and restaurants.

After a visit to Valley View, be sure to spend an hour or more in the town of Jacksonville where you'll find a pioneer spirit and many interesting restaurants and shops.

Further south down the I-5 corridor – in the town that the bard made famous – **Ashland Vineyards** is just a short drive from the freeway and provides tasty wines and a delightful picnic area. **Weisinger's Winery** is a short drive on the other side of the interstate and offers lots of specialty foods and gifts in their tasting room.

Several Ashland breweries offer something for the beer lover to write sonnets over.

## Academy Winery

THE ACADEMY

1995 CHARDONNAY
OREGON

18200 Highway 238
Grants Pass, OR  97527
(541) 846-6817

**Owner/Winemaker:**
Barnard Smith
**First Year:** 1996

Retired industrial engineer Barnard Smith moved to southern Oregon to plant a vineyard and make wine during his sunset years. With his wife Betty tending the vines, Smith makes small lots of Cabernet Sauvignon, Pinot Noir and Chardonnay – all from grapes grown at his five-acre vineyard near Applegate. Wines from The Academy are available locally in and around Grants Pass. Call the owner if you would like to come out and look around the tiny operation.

## Ashland Vineyards

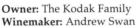

1994 Merlot
Oregon's Rogue Valley

2775 E. Main
Ashland, OR 97520
(541) 488-0088
FAX (541) 488-5857

**Owner:** The Kodak Family
**Winemaker:** Andrew Swan
**First Year:** 1988
**Winery Capacity:** 12,000 Gallons
**Tasting Room Hours:** Daily, 11 AM to 5 PM

**Winery History**

Pilot Bill Knowles combined his love of flying with his love of wine by planting his vineyard and building his winery just a few blocks from the Ashland airport. Tiring of the winery business, Knowles sold the winery to enthusiastic Oregon newcomers Phil and Kathy Kodak in 1995.

**A visit to Ashland Vineyards**

The graceful swans on this winery's label also appear in the pond out behind the winery and tasting room. Take care not to picnic too near the water as these birds sometimes belie their beauty by aggressively pan-handling for your lunch.

**The Wines**

Cabernet Sauvignon and Merlot are the focus and are joined by Chardonnay, Sauvignon Blanc, Riesling and Muller Thurgau.

## Bear Creek Winery

6220 Oregon Caves Hwy.
Cave Junction, OR  97523
(541) 592-3977, FAX (541) 592-2127

**Owner/Winemaker:** Rene Eichmann
**First Year:** 1998

The former Siskiyou Vineyard facility on the Cave Junction Highway has been revived by Rene Eichmann, winemaker for Bridgeview Vineyards under the name Bear Creek Winery.

He is cleaning up and expanding the 20-acre vineyard on the property and readying the tasting room for visitors. Until his own red wines have been bottled, the tasting room is offering tasting and sales of wines from other area wineries.

## Bridgeview Vineyards

Bridgeview
Vineyard and Winery

Blue Moon
OREGON RIESLING

Alcohol 11.6% by Volume

4210 Holland Loop Rd.
Cave Junction, OR 97523
(541) 592-4688
FAX (541) 592-2127
**Email:** e300456.cdsnet.net
**Web:** www.webtrail.
.com/bridgeview/

**Tasting Room Hours:** Daily, 11 AM to 5 PM

**Owners:** Robert & Lelo Kerivan
**Winemaker:** Rene Eichmann
**First Year:** 1986
**Winery Capacity:** 200,000 Gallons

**Winery History**

One of Oregon's largest wineries, Bridgeview Vineyards has earned a reputation for fine wines and consistent quality. The 75-acre vineyard surrounding the winery includes Pinot Noir, Chardonnay, Pinot Gris, Riesling, Gewurztraminer and other varietals.

Rene Eichmann now coordinates winemaking efforts and production of the winery's award-winning bottlings.

**A visit to Bridgeview Vineyards**

Turning east off Highway 199 in Cave Junction, follow the Oregon Caves Highway to Holland Loop Road (right turn) and on to the winery. The Bridgeview winery owners have established a showplace destination on the vineyard grounds, with a large deck and numerous tables overlooking the vineyards and lake. The large oak trees and rustic winery form a pleasant background for an afternoon of picnicking and sipping wine.

**The Wines**

Bridgeview Vineyards offers Pinot Noir, Pinot Gris and Chardonnay along with the winery owner's favorites - Germanic varietals of Riesling and Gewurztraminer. Recent bottlings of rich and flavorful Merlot are made from grapes purchased from other Rogue Valley area vineyards.

The biggest hit by far for Bridgeview has been the popular "Blue Moon" label wines bottled in the stunning cobalt blue bottles that stand out on store shelves. Blue glass has a mysterious appeal to wine buyers and several wine importers have imitated Bridgeview by bringing in their wine in the cool blue bottle.

# Foris Vineyards

654 Kendall Road
Cave Junction, OR 97523
(541) 592-3752

**Tasting Room Hours:**
Daily, 11 AM to 5 PM

**Owners:** Ted & Meri Gerber, Russell & Elizabeth Berard
**Winemaker:** Sarah Powell
**First Year:** 1987
**Winery Capacity:** 78,000 Gallons

**Winery History**

The history of Foris Vineyards is the history of grape growing in the Illinois Valley - the farming area east of Cave Junction. The first five acres of vines were planted back in 1973 - about the same time that the Willamette Valley wineries were just starting up. Ted Gerber brought his family to Oregon to escape the urban lifestyle and fast pace of California - a farm and vineyard seemed the perfect choice. The first Foris varietals were fermented at a nearby winery, but since 1987 the wine has been made at the Foris winery at the vineyard.

**A visit to Foris Vineyards**

Wine tasting is offered in the cozy Foris tasting room adjacent to the winery. Meri

Gerber's craft of weaving grape vines into fanciful wreaths and baskets is on display and many items are for sale. Tours of the winery are available by appointment.

**The Wines**

Foris Vineyards has been growing mighty fast during the 1990s, making five times as much wine in 1997 as in 1990. Sarah Powell has a superb touch with many varietals and has quality grapes from many vineyard sources to work with. Pinot Noir and Chardonnay are the two most important varietals made, but Foris Merlot and Cabernet Sauvignon are frequent award winners in regional competitions. Look for vineyard-designated versions of Merlot and Cabernet, also. Other varietals available under the Foris label include Gewurztraminer, Pinot Gris, Pinot Blanc, Early Muscat and Pinot Noir Port.

# Troon Vineyards

1475 Kubli Road
Grants Pass, OR 97525
(541) 846-6562

**Owners:** Dick Troon
**First Year:** 1993

A longtime vineyard owner (first vines planted in 1972), river guide Dick Troon waited until 1993 to make his first wine. With help from southern Oregon winemaker Donna Divine, he vinified some of the outstanding Chardonnay, Cabernet and Zinfandel from his 10-acre vineyard for his own label. Recently he also released some sparkling Cabernet "Blanc de Noirs."

The winery is not open to the public, but you can seek out Troon Vineyards' wines in the area around Grants Pass.

# Valley View Vineyard

1000 Upper Applegate Road
Jacksonville, OR 97530
(541) 899-8468
(800) 781-9463
**Email:** vvvwine@valleyview
winery.com
**Web:** www.valleyviewwinery.com

**Owners:** The Wisnovsky Family
**Winemaker:** John Guerrero
**First Year:** 1978
**Winery Capacity:** 45,000 Gallons
**Tasting Room Hours:** Daily, 11 AM to 5 PM

**Winery History**

Encouraged by the success of other southern Oregon grape growers, the Wisnovsky family planted Valley View Vineyard in 1972. The vineyard site near the scenic Applegate River offered a micro-climate suitable for production of Cabernet Sauvignon and Merlot in addition to Chardonnay. The vineyard and winery were named after a small winery pioneered by Peter Britt in the 1850s. The 30-acre vineyard matured slowly leading to the winery's bonding in 1978. That first year produced an astounding Cabernet that beat several first growth Bordeaux in a blind tasting.

**A visit to Valley View Vineyards**

The Valley View winery tasting room near the town of Ruch on Highway 238 welcomes visitors to taste the wine and tour the winery facility. Valley View wines are widely available in the town of Jacksonville.

**The Wines**

Valley View's reputation for fine red wines is well-deserved. Chardonnay, Merlot, Cabernet Sauvignon and Zinfandel are made in a ripe, toasty style under the Rogue Valley appellation, and offer plenty of power for current consumption or aging. The "Anna Maria" brand honors the family matriarch with reserve-style bottlings and additional blends and varietals.

# Weisinger's of Ashland

3150 Siskiyou Blvd.
Ashland, OR 97520
(541) 488-5989
**Email:** john@weisingers.com
**Web:** www.weisingers.com

**Tasting Room Hours:** Wednesday through Sunday, 11 AM to 6 PM

**Owners:** John & Sherita Weisinger
**Winemaker:** John & Eric Weisinger
**First Year:** 1988
**Winery Capacity:** 15,000 Gallons

**Winery History**

John and Sherita Weisinger founded their winery on a hill southeast of Ashland with a beautiful view of the Rogue Valley and the Cascade Mountains. A small vineyard is on the property but wine is made mostly from grapes purchased from other Rogue Valley Vineyards.

**A visit to Weisinger's of Ashland**

Not far from I-5, take exit 14 if you're southbound, turn right, then left on Tolman Cr. Rd. to Siskiyou Blvd., turn left. Northbound take exit 11 directly onto Siskiyou. The winery is dressed up in Alpen half-timbered style and continues the theme in the tasting room. Weisinger's offers an "Italian" red blend named Mescolare as a specialty of the house and also a great selection of locally made foods and souvenirs.

Weisinger's has a guest cottage on the property which is available to rent. It was listed as "one of the best places in the Northwest to kiss" in a recent guidebook.

**The Wines**

Cabernet Sauvignon, Merlot, Pinot Noir, Chardonnay, Gewurztraminer, Semillon and a red Bordeaux blend named Petite Pompadour are offered.

# UMPQUA AND SOUTHERN OREGON ACCOMMODATIONS

## Best Western Garden Villa

760 NW Garden Valley Blvd., Roseburg - (541) 672-1601, (800) 547-3446 (OR), (800) 528-1234 (U.S.) West of I-5 near the Garden Valley Shopping Center. Pool, spa, air conditioned. Restaurant nearby.

## Windmill Inn

1450 NW Mulholland Dr., Roseburg - (541) 673-0901, (800) 452-5315 (OR), (800) 547-4747 (U.S.) An attractive chain of motor inns in Southern Oregon. Pool, spa, sauna, air conditioned, CTV, restaurant/lounge.

## Paradise Ranch Inn

7000-D Monument Dr., Grants Pass - (541) 479-4333 A complete resort complex on 300 acres near Grants Pass. Swimming pool, tennis, hiking-biking-jogging trails. Relax in the hot tub, fish in one of the lakes on the property or sharpen your golf game on the putting green.

## Lawnridge House B & B

1304 NW Lawnridge, Grants Pass - (541) 479-5186 Air conditioned cool in summer, cozy fireplace blazing in winter. Two bedrooms plus Bridal Suite. Full breakfast.

## Morical House B & B

668 N. Main St., Ashland -(541) 482-2254 Each room has private bath and air conditioning.

## Winchester Inn B & B

35 South 2nd, Ashland - (541) 488-1113 Seven air conditioned rooms with bath, close to theater. Excellent dining room with good wine list and superb cuisine.

## Steamboat Inn

Hwy. 138, Steamboat, OR 97447, (541) 498-2411, This fly-fishing camp is where the legends came to practice the gentlemanly art of using the Tonkin cane rod. Cabins and cottages are set among the woods and delightful meals are offered by reservation in the lodge.

# UMPQUA / SOUTHERN OREGON DINING

## Tolly's

115 Locust St., Oakland, exit 138 off I-5, (541) 459-3796 Highly recommended by all the local wineries, Tolly's offers the standard steak and seafood dishes preferred in the area but also some specials for visiting city folks. Open for lunch and dinner.

## Jacksonville Inn

175 E. California St., Jacksonville, (541) 899-1900. This fabulous restaurant also offers a place to rest your head in the upstairs guest rooms with private baths. A full breakfast is included with lodging. The restaurant is among the finest in Oregon and the wine list is superb.

*Ashland is so full of unique and enjoyable restaurant experiences that you should dine out for every meal. Two of the best are:*

## Chateaulin

50 E. Main - (541) 482-2264 The best wine list in Ashland accompanies excellent French preparations of veal, seafood and other delights. Near theater.

## Winchester Inn

35 S. 2nd St. - (541) 488-1113 The Winchester offers excellent culinary experiences drawn from many cultures, including Oregon. Outstanding wine list.

# SOUTHERN OREGON ACTIVITIES

## Wildlife Safari

Just south of Roseburg enjoy a drive-through game farm with all manner of beasts. Snack bar and gifts, too!

## Valley of the Rogue State Park

Hwy. 99 East of Grants Pass (I-5 exit 45) Camping and fishing along the Rogue River.

## Oregon Caves National Monument

Kids have to be 6 or older to tour the caves. The nearby Oregon Caves Lodge offers lodging, dining and child care during the summer.

## Fishing

Both the Rogue and Umpqua Rivers are known for excellent fly-fishing. Check with the locals to find out where the fish are biting.

## Umpqua Brewing Company

328 SE Jackson St., Roseburg (541) 672-0452. Umpqua Brewing is located on the east side of the freeway in the older section of historic downtown Roseburg. The brewpub has seven hand made ales on tap at any time featuring Summer Wheat, Umpqua Gold, Rosegarden White, Douglas Draft, Roseburg Red, Downtown Brown and other styles including stout, bock, weizen and berry beers. The barbecued hamburgers, gourmet pizzas and other food treats are popular as is the brewery's sushi night, the first Friday of every month. Brewery tours are available during normal business hours for groups of five or less. The brewpub is closed for sit-down business on Monday's, but a knock on the back door will enable you to get beer to go or take a tour.

## Wild River Brewing

595 NE 'E' St., Grants Pass, (541) 471-7487 This spectacular brewery in Grants Pass sports a three-level restaurant that is open in the morning for espresso and breakfast, serves a great lunch with delicious microbrews, continues for dinner, then rocks on till midnight. Wood-fired pizza ovens make a mean pie for those who have an appetite. Extra Special Bitter, Kolsch, Imperial Stout and Hefeweizen are joined by seasonal brews Weizen Bock, Blackberry Porter, Oktoberfest, and Cave Bear Barleywine. Enjoy these brews on tap at the brewpub or buy the bottled product to enjoy at home.

The Wild River Brewing original plant and brewhouse is down the highway in Cave Junction. This location features back-woodsy decor and down-home cooking. Breads and pizza dough are made from scratch and topped with fresh ingredients. Stop by for some tasty brew and delicious cooking.

## Rogue Brewery and Public House

318 Water St., Ashland (541) 488-5061. Rogue's Ashland location is right on the bank of Ashland Creek making for a beautiful site to spend an afternoon or evening enjoying fine beer and good food — in the pub or on the deck! One of Oregon's original microbreweries, Rogue offers their tasty Golden Ale, Shakespeare Stout, Ashland Amber and Snow White spiced wheat beer. Other seasonal brews are offered with changes in the weather. The pub opens daily at 11:30 AM for lunch, dinner and evening fun. Winter hours offer a 4 PM opening Mon. - Thurs.

## Caldera Brewing Company

540 Clover Lane, Ashland, (541) 482-HOPS. Jim Mills began his operation making tasty ales for the local tavern and restaurant trade, but he promises to open a brewpub sometime in the future. Look for his Vanilla Wheat, Pale Ale, Oatmeal Stout and Hibernator Dopplebock on draft around town.

*While you're at the coast, stop and visit:*

## Rogue Ales Brewery and Tasting Room

2320 OSU Drive, Newport, (503) 867-3660. This is the original Rogue location and the source for the bottled product that is now sold in 29 states. Across Newport Bay at 765 Bay Blvd. enjoy great foods with your beer at Rogues 180-seat Public House. The brewery tasting room is open daily featuring: Mocha Porter, Mexicali Rogue, St. Rogue Red, Rogue-n-Berry, Oregon Golden, American Amber, Old Crustacean Barleywine, Shakespeare Stout, Smoke Ale, Maierbock Ale, Mo Ale, Mogul Ale and Rogue Ale.

## McMenamins Lighthouse Brew Pub

4157 N. Hwy. 101, Lincoln City (503) 994-7238. Another quality McMenamins location in a new building with modern decor and the great beers that have made this chain famous. Also, coast-inspired lunch and dinner fare.

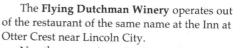

Was it Mark Twain who said, "The mildest winter I ever spent was summer in Tillamook"? Oh, well. The beaches are beautiful, the people are friendly and wine tasting rooms beckon.

In Astoria you simply MUST stop by **Shallon Winery** for a visit with Paul van der Veldt. This charming fellow's unusual wines charm even the snobbiest wine snob.

South of Astoria on Highway 101 you can visit **Nehalem Bay Winery** one mile east of the highway near Mohler.

The **Flying Dutchman Winery** operates out of the restaurant of the same name at the Inn at Otter Crest near Lincoln City.

No other operating wineries are located on the coast but **Chateau Benoit** of Yamhill County has a tasting room at the outlet mall south of Lincoln City.

Almost to the California border near Brookings, you can taste fruit brandies at **Brandy Peak Distillery** off Carpenterville Rd.

# Brandy Peak Distillery

18526 Tetley Road
Brookings, OR 97415
(503) 469-0194

**Tasting Room Hours:**
Tues. - Sat., 1 to 5 PM

**Owners & Distillers:** R.L. and David Nowlin
**First Year:** 1993

A family venture between father and son (R.L. and David Nowlin) this operation produces pear and grape brandies from fruit grown in southern Oregon. Award winning marc, grappa and aged brandies make a fun tasting side trip from the coast.

# Chateau Benoit

Lincoln City Factory Outlet Mall
Highway 101, south end of town

This popular Yamhill County winery keeps their friendly tasting room and cafe open daily.

# Flying Dutchman Winery

301 Otter Crest Loop
Otter Rock, OR 97369
(541) 765-2060
FAX (541) 765-2069

**Tasting Room Hours:**
Daily, 2 PM to 7 PM

**Proprietor:** Richard Cutler
**Winemaker:** Larry Miller
**First Year:** 1998

The popular Inn at Otter Crest condominium resort has added a winery to their Flying Dutchman restaurant overlooking the mighty Pacific Ocean. Larry Miller of Stangeland Winery in the Eola Hills is handling the winemaking duties for the small production (800 gallons in 1997). Chardonnay and Pinot Noir are vinified from fruit grown at the Chehalem Vineyard in Yamhill County.

# Nehalem Bay Winery

34965 Highway 53
Nehalem, OR 97131
(541) 368-5300

**Tasting Room Hours:**
Daily, 9 AM to 6 PM

**Owner & Winemaker:**
Ray Shackelford
**First Year:** 1973

**Winery History**
Tucked into a converted cheese factory, circa 1909, Nehalem Bay Winery has been serving Oregon Coast tourists for over two decades. Originally, only fruit wines were offered – in an age when hardly anyone knew about Oregon Pinot Noir – but now the winery produces mostly grape wines from their own Willamette Valley vineyard source.

**A visit to Nehalem Bay Winery**
The turn from Highway 101 is marked both with a sign to the winery and a state highway sign to the town of Mohler. Drive east one mile then look for the winery in its half-timbered splendor on the right.

**The Wines**
Chardonnay, Gewurztraminer, Pinot Noir, Pinot Noir Blanc, White Riesling, Cranberry and sparkling wine are produced.

# Shallon Winery

1598 Duane St.
Astoria, OR 97103
(503) 325-5978
Email: shallon@aone.com
Web: www.aone.com/
~shallon

RED TABLE WINE

**Tasting Room Hours:**
Daily, "Noonish" to 6 PM

**Owner/Winemaker:** Paul van der Veldt
**First Year:** 1978
**Winery Capacity:** 2,000 Gallons

**Winery History**

A most unusual man is at work in Astoria making some of Oregon's most unusual wines. Paul van der Veldt will serve you a wine reminiscent of berries and cream, and one that takes you back to mom's kitchen and her delicious lemon meringue pie. His latest creation is chocolate orange wine in a thick style you can eat with a spoon! These are the legacies of a retired construction company manager who transformed an Astoria car showroom and meat locker into Shallon Winery.

**A visit to Shallon Winery**

The winery is located right in downtown Astoria about two miles east of the bridge to Washington and a few blocks up the hill from Highway 30 on Duane St. Insist on a tour. The winery part of the building and laboratory are fanciful creations just like the master's wine. Imagination was the driving force behind both. Return to the tasting room to sample the wines about which Paul quips, "It's not that they're so great, they're just unique!"

**The Wines**

Fruit wines are a specialty here including Blackberry, Peach and Apple, but the piece de résistance are the three wines not duplicated in this world – or any other. Enjoy Cran du Lait (made from cranberries, and whey from the local cheese factories), Lemon Meringue Pie wine (with sweet cracker accompaniment to simulate crust), and the latest Pots de Creme, chocolate/orange wine.

# OREGON COAST ACCOMMODATIONS & DINING

### Franklin House B & B

1681 Franklin Ave.,Astoria 97103  (503) 325-5044  Astoria's seafaring heritage goes back over 180 years and this Victorian B & B seems right at home in any decade. Park-like grounds in a quiet location.

### The Stephanie Inn

2740 South Pacific, Cannon Beach 97110 (503) 436-2221  Luxury guest rooms, evening wine tasting, super dining, right on the beach. A great place! See: www.stephanie-inn.com.

### Shilo Inn

Lincoln City (800) 222-2244  This modern accommodation includes indoor pool, kitchens, fireplaces and beachfront!  Great family place.

### Embarcadero Resort Marina

1000 SE Bay Blvd. Newport, 97365  (541) 265-8521  An upscale condo resort on Newport Bay. Indoor pool, spa, kitchens, fireplaces.

### The Ship Inn

#1 Second St., Astoria - on the waterfront (503) 325-0033  Your English hosts have brought their talents for tasty fish & chips and Cornish pasties.  Enjoy the view of river activity with your pint of English ale.

### The Bistro

263 N. Hemlock, Cannon Beach (503) 436-2661 Creative preparation of local seafood is the strong point of The Bistro although all the dishes have pizzaz and the owners and their staff strive for your enjoyment.

### Salishan Lodge Dining Room

Highway 101, Gleneden Beach (541) 764-2371 The chefs at this landmark culinary establishment turn out the finest in continental-Northwest cuisine and their sommelier presides over a wine list numbering to 1,000 selections with over 30,000 bottles in storage. The wine cellar may be toured by appointment.

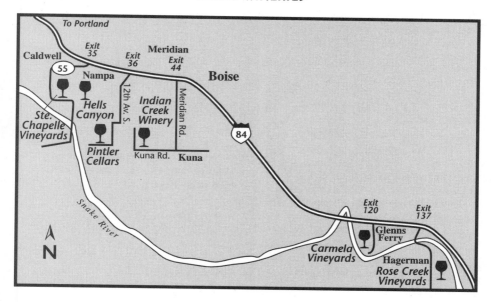

## Idaho Wine Touring

Most of the Idaho wine industry is located in the southwest part of the state where the climatic influence of the Snake River provides excellent growing conditions for grapes. Water from the river for irrigation has long made this part of Idaho an agricultural oasis.

Wine tourists from Seattle or Portland might do well to look into flying to Boise and renting a car. Our last research trip netted a $78 roundtrip from SeaTac (on a nice, quiet Horizon Airlines Fokker twinjet). If you'd rather drive 8 hours, be sure to stop in Baker City and visit our friend Bev Calder at Bella Wine Shop on Main Street.

Whether you arrive by air or by car, your center for touring southern Idaho's wine country will be Boise. Just a dozen miles west of Idaho's capitol city is the winegrowing area around Nampa and Caldwell.

**Ste. Chapelle Winery** is one of the largest in the Northwest with a huge capacity and multiple buildings housing tanks, equipment and a first-class tourist facility. The French cathedral-inspired visitor center offers views of the surrounding vineyards from the tasting room and gift shop.

From Ste. Chapelle, you may want to wander east on Chicken Dinner Road to Symms Road (turn left) to visit **Hells Canyon Winery** and owner Steve Robertson. Tasty wines and a fun conversation await.

**Pintler Cellars** is in the major agricultural area due south of Nampa. This family winery offers a nice picnic area, quality wines and an unbeatable view of the Snake River Valley.

Eight miles east, almost to Kuna, Bill Stowe offers tours and tastings at his **Indian Creek Winery**. His site has the right climate to grow Pinot Noir and he makes both a red wine and a blanc de noir from the grape.

Other Nampa/Caldwell wineries - **Bitner, Koeing, Vickers, Weston** and **Wood River** - have no tourist facilities and a call ahead for an appointment would be wise. **Petros Winery** of Boise also does not have a tourist facility.

A drive of almost two hours through the sagebrush east of Boise is rewarded by a visit to **Carmela Winery** at Glenn's Ferry and **Rose Creek Vineyards** winery in Hagerman. **South Hills Winery** in Twin Falls is by appointment.

North of the Snake River area, visit **Cana Vineyards** in McCall, **Camas and Lifeforce Wineries** in Moscow, and **Pend d'Orielle Winery** in Sandpoint.

## Bitner Vineyard

16645 Plum Road
Caldwell, ID 83605
(208) 454-0086

**Owner:** Ron Bitner
**First Year:** 1993 (winery)

### Winery History

Ron Bitner planted his vineyard in 1982 with the first grapes being harvested in 1985. Chardonnay, Cabernet Sauvignon and Riesling from the 12-acre vineyard were sold to other wineries until 1993 when Bitner used estate grapes to make a Chardonnay under the Bitner Vineyard label. Production is small and presently there is no facility to welcome visitors.

## Camas Winery

110 S. Main St.,
Moscow, ID 83843
(208) 882-0214
**Email:**
scottcamas@turbonet.com

**Tasting Room Hours:**
Tuesday through Saturday, Noon to 6 PM

**Owners:** Stuart & Susan Scott
**Winemaker:** Stuart Scott
**First Year:** 1983
**Winery Capacity:** 4,000 Gallons

### Winery History

Camas Winery traces its name back to the original inhabitants of Northern Idaho, the Nez Perce Indians. A staple food among these tribes was the root of the Camas Lily that grew wild as waving fields of blue flowers throughout the Palouse. Today, replaced by wheat and other crops, the Camas Lily is found only in secluded hollows and on the label of Camas Winery.

Another appreciative consumer of the Camas Lily bulb were the pigs that accompanied the first settlers to the area. The Palouse gained a nickname as "Hog Heaven" as the pigs rooted out the bulbs with great relish. Camas Winery offers a dedication to porcine imbibers in their Hog Heaven Red and Hog Heaven White blended wines.

### A visit to Camas Winery

Co-owner Sue Scott is your charming hostess at the winery tasting room in downtown Moscow. The winery and tasting room are located in a century-old brick building near the corner of First and Main. Follow Highway 95 to First, then follow First to Main St.

### The Wines

The wines are all family-made from grapes grown nearby and include Merlot, Lemberger, Chardonnay, Riesling, sparkling wine and proprietary blends.

## Cana Vineyards

28372 Peckham Rd.
Wilder, ID 83676
(208) 482-7372
**Tasting Room:**
310 East Lake Street
McCall, ID 83638
(208) 634-7600

**Tasting Room Hours:** Tuesday through Sunday, Noon to 7 PM, summer only.

**Owners:** Larry & Meg Dawson
**First Year:** 1992

### Winery History

Cana Vineyards has revived winemaking in the facility originally used by Lou Facelli (see Seattle area) for their initial Idaho winemaking efforts. Larry Dawson makes dry Riesling, Chardonnay, Merlot-Cabernet and a sparkling wine from Riesling. Tours and tastings at the production facility are offered by appointment.

### A visit to Cana Vineyards

In 1995 Cana Vineyards established their McCall tasting room on the second floor of the historic Lake Street Station building. Take Highway 55N to McCall, turn left on E. Lake Street.

# Carmela Vineyards

795 West Madison
P.O. Box 790
Glenns Ferry, ID 83623
(208) 366-2313
FAX (208) 366-2458

**Owner:** Nancy & Roger Jones
**First Year:** 1990
**Winery Capacity:** 37,000 Gallons
**Tasting Room Hours:** Daily, 9 AM to 9 PM

### Winery History

Wow! Finally a winery with its own restaurant and 9-hole golf course! Nancy and Roger Jones purchased this operation from the founding Martell family and are taking it to the next level! Vineyards were planted on the site in the 1980s and they now have 17 acres of quality varietals in production. The winery followed, and a deli-restaurant was added to fill up some of the extra space in the winery building. A golf course was built using equipment already on hand for the other ventures. Bring your clubs when you visit Carmela Vineyards!

Roger Jones is developing more of the property by expanding the golf course, adding some cabins and possibly adding more vineyards.

### A visit to Carmela Vineyards

The winery is now located in the basement of the restaurant/club house building made of native stone. Wine tasting in the pro shop is a bit unusual, but it's part of the fun of the experience. The winery is located two miles south of I-84. Exit at one of the two Glenns Ferry exits and follow signs for Three Islands State Park, you'll go right by the winery. Stop in for a visit!

By the way, don't miss a chance to visit the state park with it's interesting visitor center describing the Oregon Trail crossing of the Snake River that took place nearby. A popular festival re-enacts the pioneer crossing each summer. Modern day pioneers have the advantage of calling the dam operators upstream a day ahead of time to slow the water flow for the crossing!

### The Wines

A few changes in winemakers have taken place at Carmela, due in part to differences of opinion between winemaker and owners. Consultant Mimi Mott is retained to keep an eye on things and make sure the wines are sound. A wide range of varietals is produced, including Cabernet Sauvignon, Merlot, Chardonnay, Riesling, Muscat, Semillon and Cabernet Franc.

# Cocolalla Winery

E. 14550 Bunco Road, Athol, ID 83801
Hwy. 95 North, Milepost 463
(208) 683-2473

**Owner:** Donald & Vivian Merkeley
**Winemaker:** Donald Merkeley
**First Year:** 1986
**Winery Capacity:** 2,000 Gallons

### Winery History

Donald Merkeley's experiments with methode champenoise sparkling wine led to bonding Cocolalla Winery. The winery is located just northeast of Spokane off Highway 95 N. and the wines are sold mostly in the Coeur d'Alene area. The sparkling wine en tiriage is aged in the old Silver Star Mine. No vineyard is owned as Chardonnay and Pinot Noir grapes are purchased from Taggares Vineyard in Othello. Winery visits are by appointment.

## Hegy's South Hills Winery

3099 E 3400 N
P.O. Box 727
Twin Falls, ID
83301
(208) 734-6369, FAX (208) 733-7435

**Owners:** Frank & Crystal Hegy
**First Year:** 1994
**Winery Production:** 1,800 Gallons

Located four miles south of Twin Falls, South Hills Winery produces small quantities of Chardonnay, Riesling, Chenin Blanc, Pinot Noir and Lemberger. The winery specializes in gift and custom bottlings for celebrations and events. Visits by appointment only. Take 1-84 east to Twin Falls, winery is located four miles south of Kimberly on Eastland Drive.

*Steve Robertson and friends at the Hells Canyon tasting room near Caldwell, Idaho.*

**The Wines**
Barrel-fermented Chardonnay and hearty, tannic Cabernet are produced as well as lighter proprietary wines celebrating Steve's love of hunting: Bird Dog White and Retriever Red.

## Hells Canyon Winery

18835 Symms Road
Caldwell, ID 83605
(208) 454-3300

**Owners:** Steve and Leslie Robertson
**First Year:** 1988
**Winery Production:** 5,000 Gallons

**Winery History**
Retired from the restaurant business, sportsman, vineyardist and gourmet Steve Robertson planted Cabernet and Chardonnay in his 20-acre vineyard (one of several reputed to be at the highest elevation in the Northwest). The small operation is just down the road from Ste. Chapelle Winery and has been producing small quantities of wine for local consumption and limited distribution.

**A visit to Hells Canyon Winery**
In 1996-97, Steve expanded the winery building and added a spiffy tasting room with a view of the vineyard. His black Labrador retrievers are friendly and interested in all who stop by for a visit and a taste. Call ahead for an appointment to meet Steve and taste his wines.

## Indian Creek Winery

Rt. 1, 1000 N.
McDermott Rd.
Kuna, ID 83634
(208) 922-4791
FAX (208) 922-4387

**Tasting Room Hours:** Saturday and Sunday, Noon to 5 PM. Weekdays by appointment.

**Owner:** Bill Stowe and four partners
**Winemaker:** Bill Stowe
**First Year:** 1987
**Winery Capacity:** 16,000 Gallons

**Winery History**
When Bill Stowe re-enlisted in the Air Force, he made the military promise they would station him in Idaho. He wanted to prepare for his retirement and had considered farming to be a possibility in the area near Mountain Home Air Force Base.

Bill's brother Mike is a schoolteacher in Davis, California. By taking parttime classes across town at U.C. Davis, he was able to learn quite a lot about grape farming and become a valuable ally to his brother. The two men shared knowledge and Bill planted 20 acres of varietals near Kuna in 1983. Winemaking from

*Bill and Mui Stowe of Indian Creek Winery.*

his own grapes and those of neighboring growers was the next step and Indian Creek Winery was born.

**A visit to Indian Creek Winery**

Bill and Mui Stowe are charming hosts at Indian Creek. Bill's enthusiasm is boundless and he enjoys expanding the winery almost as much as he enjoys making the wines. Mui is a superb cook and she sometimes prepares treats for winery events. In 1997, Bill began construction on a large addition to the winery (almost a whole new winery) The tasting room will be relocated when the addition is finished in 1999.

Indian Creek Winery is located a few miles southwest of Boise near the town of Kuna. Take the first exit west of Boise (Meridian Road) and drive south to Kuna, then turn right (west) to the winery. (With good directions you can drive across the plain directly from Ste. Chapelle - lots of open country and farm acreage.)

**The Wines**

A consistent medal winner has been Bill Stowe's rich and fruity Pinot Noir. Also produced are Riesling, Chardonnay and a refreshing White Pinot Noir. Occasionally, Cabernet Sauvignon and Gewurztraminer are produced.

# Koenig Vineyards

14744 Plum Road
Caldwell, ID 83605
(208) 454-5572

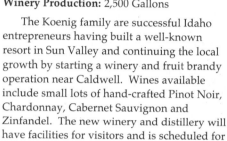

**Owner:** Greg Koenig
**First Year:** 1995
**Winery Production:** 2,500 Gallons

The Koenig family are successful Idaho entrepreneurs having built a well-known resort in Sun Valley and continuing the local growth by starting a winery and fruit brandy operation near Caldwell. Wines available include small lots of hand-crafted Pinot Noir, Chardonnay, Cabernet Sauvignon and Zinfandel. The new winery and distillery will have facilities for visitors and is scheduled for a 1998 opening. Call ahead for directions.

# Life Force Winery

5318 Main St.
Moscow, ID 83843
1193 Saddleridge Rd.
Moscow, ID 83843
(208) 882-9158

**Tasting Room Hours:** Tuesday through Saturday, 10 AM to 5:30 PM; Sunday, Noon to 5 PM.

**First Year:** 1989

Life Force Winery specializes in producing honey wines. Huckleberry and Raspberry honey wines are made as well as two meads: Vandal Gold and Original. The shop offers specialty foods and fine crafts as well as limited wine tasting.

## Pend d'Oreille Winery

1067 Baldy Industrial Park, P.O. Box 1821
Sandpoint, ID 83864
(208) 265-8545
**Email:**
powine@netw.com

**Tasting Room Hours:** Friday and Saturday, Noon to 5 PM, summers. Other times by appointment.

**Owner:** Stephen and Julie Meyer
**First Year:** 1995
**Winery Capacity:** 5,000 Gallons

First off, don't get pegged as a tourist by pronouncing the name anything other than "Pond Oray." NOT "Pend Orry Ell!"

Julie and Stephen Meyer have worked in wineries from Burgundy to California and now have established their own operation in Sandpoint, Idaho. Buying grapes from Idaho and Washington vineyards, they have created a fast following by crafting several award-winning red wines from Pinot Noir, Cabernet Franc and Cabernet Sauvignon. Placing their winery in the recreational and cultural center of northern Idaho has helped develop a local market for the wines in Sandpoint's many fine restaurants.

Find Pend Orielle winery by travelling north out of Sandpoint on Boyer Ave., turn left of Baldy Mountain Road, go 1/2 mile. The winery is on the right.

## Petros Winery

2303 Table Rock Rd.
Boise, ID 83712
(208) 345-6283

**Owners:** Petro and Janet Eliopulos
**First Year:** 1987

### Winery History

The late 1980s saw some wild times in the Idaho wine business. In 1986 Bill Broich left Ste. Chapelle Winery and found new partners to begin The Winery at Spring Creek. His questionable operating practices caused concern with major investors and his interest

was purchased. Petro Eliopulos took the helm and steered the winery to safety under the new name Petros. This brand now offers Chardonnay, Merlot, Cabernet Sauvignon, Late Harvest wines and methode champenoise sparkling wine. No facilities are available for tourists.

## Pintler Cellars

13750 Surrey Lane
Nampa, ID 83651
(208) 467-1200

**Tasting Room Hours:** Friday, Sat., Sunday, Noon to 5 PM

**Owner:** Pintler Family
**Winemaker:** Brad Pintler
**First Year:** 1988
**Winery Capacity:** 15,000 Gallons

### Winery History

Several generations of the Pintler family have farmed the fertile plateau that stretches south to the Snake River from Nampa. In the early 1980s the success of neighboring Ste. Chapelle and other area wineries led the Pintlers to plant a vineyard on their land to accompany the other crops. The vineyard came into bearing in the late 1980s, and a winery with visitor amenities was added.

### A visit to Pintler Cellars

The attractive winery building, picnic area and gazebo are perched atop a hill with a superb view south over the vineyard toward the Snake River and the distant Owyhee Mountains. The tasting room is upstairs to further enhance the view, and tours of the modest winery operation are offered if visitors desire. Take exit 36 from I-84 to head southbound on Franklin Ave. Turn right on 11th Ave. and jog over to 12th Ave. at 3rd St. S. Follow 12th Ave. S. south to a right turn on Missouri Rd., a left on Sky Ranch and finally a right on Surrey Lane to the winery. The route is well signed.

### The Wines

Wine production at Pintler Cellars utilizes the production from their fifteen acres of vines at the winery site. An occasional purchase of

*Winemaker Brad Pintler on the winery deck, with the Snake River and Owyhee Mountains in the distance.*

grapes from nearby vineyards provides additional varietal offerings. A wide range of varietals is produced at Pintler Cellar and all have been well received. Chardonnay, Riesling, Semillon, Cabernet Sauvignon and Pinot Noir are produced.

# Rose Creek Vineyards

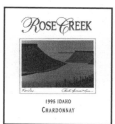

1995 IDAHO
CHARDONNAY

111 West Hagerman
Box 356
Hagerman, ID 83332
(208) 837-4413
FAX (208) 837-6405

**Tasting Room Hours:**
Daily, 11:30 AM to 5:30 PM

**Owners:** Robert Kaplan, Jamie, Susan & Stephanie Martin
**Winemaker:** Jamie Martin
**First Year:** 1984
**Winery Capacity:** 15,000 Gallons

**Winery History**
    While their original location in the lower level of the historic Idaho State Bank was romantic and right on the main highway through Hagerman, there was no room to expand and the winery was growing. At their new location in the retired Idaho Power warehouse complex, several buildings are utilized to make wine, operate the tasting room and store equipment.
    The Martins have dedicated themselves to the success of Rose Creek Vineyards as Stephanie handles the tasting room, describing the wines to frequent visitors from both nearby

and faraway, while Jamie works in the winery or makes deliveries to commercial accounts.

**A visit to Rose Creek Vineyards**
    The long drive from Boise to Hagerman is worthwhile once you turn down into the Hagerman Valley. Located in a rimrock canyon, the town and nearby landmarks share a rocky environment of great beauty. The natural history of the area is a two-day exploration all by itself (Hagerman Fossil Beds, Malad Gorge, Thousand Springs Preserve). At the winery you can enjoy samples of the latest

*Stephanie Martin of Rose Creek Vineyards.*

Rose Creek wines and browse a few crafts and gift items, some of which are locally made.

**The Wines**
    Rose Creek produces their wines from grapes purchased in Idaho and Washington. Chardonnay and Merlot are made from grapes grown in Hagerman, while Riesling is produced from grapes grown in Caldwell. Proprietary wines Basque Red and Basque White celebrate the local population of wine-loving folks of Spanish heritage. Rose Creek Mist and Thousand Springs White Table Wine are good values.

## Ste. Chapelle Winery

14068 Sunnyslope Rd.
Caldwell, ID 83605
(208) 459-7222

**Tasting Room Hours:** Monday thru Saturday, 10 AM to 5 PM; Sunday, Noon to 5 PM

**Owner:** Associated Vintners
**Winemaker:** Kevin Mott
**First Year:** 1976
**Winery Capacity:** 500,000 Gallons+

### Winery History

Ste. Chapelle has come from a small, back-country winery to be one of the five largest wineries in the Pacific Northwest. Each vintage sees a greater production of Idaho wines and continuing success in national and international wine competitions. Originally owned and operated by the Symms family, the winery was sold in 1997 to Associated Vintners, parent of Columbia Winery in Seattle. The challenge of marketing over 120,000 cases of wine each year will be handled through the A.V. organization.

The creation of consumer-oriented wines like the bulk process "champagnes" has allowed Ste. Chapelle to keep low prices on popular varietals like Chardonnay and Riesling. This affordability has made the brand popular with restaurants and also with grocery chains who now offer expanded wine departments in many Northwest markets.

### A visit to Ste. Chapelle Vineyards

The attractive Ste. Chapelle winery is designed in the style of the Paris cathedral for which it is named and provides the visitor a warm welcome complete with a tour of the facility and a tasting of the winery's latest releases. The view from the winery picnic area looks southeast across the Snake River to the Owyhee Mountains.

Jazz concerts are held each Sunday in July to the delight of local music and wine afficionados. Wine and food are available as the music wafts through the vines.

Take exit 35 from Interstate 84 and follow Highway 55 south about 13 miles. The turn to the winery is on your left.

*Winemaker Kevin Mott in front of the Ste. Chapelle Winery visitor center in Caldwell, ID.*

### The Wines

Ste. Chapelle winemaker Kevin Mott produces a broad range of wines to please every palate. From fresh and fruity Riesling, to buttery Chardonnay and crisp Fumé Blanc to hearty Cabernet Sauvignon, Merlot, and even the latest red wine offering, Syrah. Sparkling wines are produced by the bulk method known as Charmat and include a wide range of styles that are sure to please.

## Vickers Vineyards

15646 Sunny Slope Rd
Caldwell, ID 83605

**Owners:** Kirby & Cheryl Vickers
**First Year:** 1992

Kirby Vickers established his vineyard in 1981 and developed an outstanding reputation for high quality Chardonnay fruit. Vineyard designated wines were produced by several Idaho wineries from this fine property. In 1992, Kirby and his wife Cheryl began making small lots of barrel-fermented Chardonnay in the basement of their home adjacent to the vineyard. Fine tuning the fermentation and aging of the wine has become Kirby's passion, and his results have been very favorable.

No visits or tastings are possible, but Vickers Vineyards Chardonnay is available at Boise area restaurants and distribution may be expanded depending on production levels.

# Weston Winery

16316 Orchard St.
Caldwell, ID 83605
(208) 459-2631

**Owner/Winemaker:**
Cheyne Weston
**First Year:** 1982

A veteran of the Nampa/Caldwell winemaking scene, Cheyne Weston was making wine across the road from Ste. Chapelle when the winery was just entering its expansion period in the 1980s. Some wines have been very good and some didn't turn out so well, but longevity has been on the side of this local entrepreneur.

The winery moved from its former location and now offers tastings by appointment. The vineyard is one of several claimed to be at the highest elevation in the area at 2,750 feet.

# Wood River Cellars

2606 San Marco Way
Nampa, ID 83686
(208) 888-9358

**Owner:** Wendy Thompson
**Winemaker:**
Dennis McArthur
**First Year:** 1994

A small vineyard of Merlot, Cabernet Franc and Pinot Gris was established in 1994 to begin the venture that is now Wood River Cellars. Recently Chardonnay and Cabernet Sauvignon have been planted as well and in 1996 the owners had their first crush of estate fruit. There is no visitor facility and production is very small, but Wood River Cellars shows promise and will no doubt grow to a point where this will be another favorite touring stop of Idaho wine lovers.

# Mission Mountain Winery

U. S. Highway 93, Box 100
Dayton, MT 59914
(406) 849-5524

**Owner:** Dr. Thomas J. Campbell
**Winemaker:** Tom Campbell, Jr.
**First Year:** 1984
**Winery Capacity:** 15,000 Gallons

### Winery History

Back in the early 1980s Tom Campbell planted vineyards near Flathead Lake in Northwestern Montana on property owned by he and his father, T. J. Campbell, a Missoula physician. Early efforts were troubled by frost but frost-hardy varieties were selected and overhead sprinklers were installed to combat the problem. Montana grapes are now harvested and vinted into Pinot Noir red wine and methode champenoise sparkling wine. Mission Mountain Winery received Montana's first winery bond. Winemaker Tom Campbell, Jr. owns Horizon's Edge Winery in Zillah in Washington's Yakima Valley.

### A visit to Mission Mountain Winery

The winery tasting room is open daily, May through October, from 10 AM to 5 PM. You'll find it just off Highway 93 near Flathead Lake.

### The Wines

Mission Mountain Pale Ruby Champagne is among the very best in the Northwest. Also produced are Riesling, Blanc de Noir, Pinot Noir, Chardonnay, Merlot, Cabernet Sauvignon, Muscat Canelli and Blush.

Idaho is most famous for its beautiful, unspoiled wilderness and recreational opportunities. Many visitors to Idaho travel by RV and there are many campgrounds to cater to those bringing their "motel room on wheels." Other visitors may prefer staying in the accomodations listed below:

## Cavanaugh's Motor Inn

645 Pullman Rd., Moscow - (208) 882-1611, (800) THE-INNS Large indoor spa, restaurant and lounge, suites with jacuzzi. Adjacent to the University of Idaho. Moderate.

## Red Lion Motor Inn Riverside

2900 Chinden Blvd., Boise - (208) 343-1871 Located on the Boise River, gourmet restaurant, seasonal dining on banks fo the river. Pool, pets O.K. Moderate to expensive.

## University Inn

2360 University, Boise - (208) 345-7170 Restaurant and lounge, kids stay free, air-conditioned rooms, free continental breakfast. Moderate.

## Boisean Motel

1300 S. Capitol Blvd., Boise - (208) 343-3645 Pool, restaurant, kitchens available, parks and museums are closeby.

## Best Western Safari

1070 Grove St., Boise - (208) 344-6556, Toll Free (800) 528-1234 Heated pool, covered parking, free continental breakfast, downtown. Moderate.

## Shilo Inns Nampa Suites

Interstate 84, Exit 36, Nampa - (208) 465-3250, (800) 222-2244 A little worn around the edges, but clean and quiet. Nice indoor pool and spa, restaurant next door, rooms have small refrigerators and microwaves.

## Rock Lodge Motel

Route 30, Hagerman - (208) 837-4822 Air conditioned, kitchens, hot mineral spas, year 'round trout fishing on property, queen beds. Inexpensive.

## Angell's Bar and Grill

999 Main St., Boise - (208) 342-4900 Lunch and dinner in this popular downtown Boise watering hole. Lots of Boise's shakers and movers hang out here on Friday night. Good steaks and seafood, good local wine selection.

## Desert Sage

750 West Idaho St., Boise - (208) 333-8400 Touted by local gourmands as one of the finest eateries in the area, Desert Sage offers creative selections with a fusion flair and a continental twist. The wine list could use a few more local bottlings, rather than the mostly California offerings.

## Ivano's

124 S. 2nd Ave., Sandpoint - (208) 263-0211 Italian food served in a remodelled home just south of downtown Sandpoint. The combination of great food and an outstandingly irreverent wait staff makes this a terrific place for the open minded diner.

## The Plum Tree

604 Third St. S., Nampa - (208) 467-1520 In the heart of downtown Nampa, this restaurant tucked onto the back of the owner's interior design business offers delicious seafood, meats and all the trimmings. Attractive wine list features local bottlings.

## The Sandbar River House Restaurant

Highway 45, Marsing - (208) 896-4124 Right on the Snake River where the highway crosses over, you can spy this cozy jewel from the front door at Ste. Chapelle Winery three miles away. Quality home cooking is the draw and the staff offers personality and humor along with friendly, efficient service. River-view outside dining available in good weather.

## The Snake River Grill

610 State St., Hagerman - (208) 837-6277 A local favorite for fresh-from-the-river trout, catfish and sturgeon.

# BRITISH COLUMBIA WINE TOURING

British Columbia is a superb destination for vacationers. Friendly people, clean air, beautiful scenery, culture, recreation . . . and some truly great wines and wineries! When the first edition of Northwest Wines & Wineries was published in 1986, there was considerable turmoil in the B.C. wine industry. The province's most promising wine region was planted with grape varieties with odd or unpronounceable names, created for cold climates and just plain unpopular with wine drinkers from the United States.

Many changes have taken place in the decade that has passed and we are excited to now include British Columbia for its seemingly unlimited potential to attract wine lovers and keep them happy with quality, recognizable wines, and great opportunities for recreation and enjoyment.

Bringing wine to and from Canada is not nearly as easy as it should be. The authors' experience at both U.S. and Canadian customs suggest that you not take in more than one bottle of wine (duty is quite high for more than this, and it slows down your border crossing).

Coming back to the states with a trunk full of cases of wine seems to surprise the U.S. customs folks, some of whom think that a case of wine should last you a year or more. Duty coming in is just over a dollar (U.S.) per bottle and the inconvenience is not too bad if you're not crossing at a busy time.

Finally, the monetary exchange rate for U.S. citizens is highly favorable. In 1998, a U.S. dollar was worth about $1.40 Canadian, so don't be afraid to buy the better bottlings and leave a generous tip after dinner!

## VANCOUVER ISLAND WINE TOURING

The fun of taking the ferry to Victoria, visiting Butchart Gardens and having tea at the Empress Hotel should now be augmented with at least a day of traveling the wine country from Cobble Hill to Duncan. From Victoria, the trip of about 40 miles takes a little over an hour before you take your first sip of wine.

Travelling up Highway 1 look for a right turn on Fisher Road to find your way to **Cherry Point Vineyards**. The wine shop is open each day and your hosts even have rooms to rent if you want to spend the night!

Heading back to Highway 1 you can visit **Venturi-Shulze Vineyards** by appointment. Don't forget to buy some of their excellent Balsamic vinegar!

Crossing to the west side of Highway 1, you can follow the map to **Blue Grouse Vineyards** for visits on Wednesday, Friday, Saturday and Sunday.

Continuing north on Koksilah Road, you will find **Vigneti Zanatto Vineyards** on Marshall Road – open all afternoons except Mondays.

**Alderlea Vineyards** is just getting started at press time so a call ahead is a good idea. **Chateau Wolff** in Nanaimo is open Saturdays or by appointment.

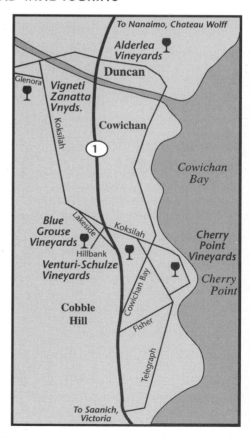

## Alderlea Vineyards

1751 Stamps Road
Duncan, BC V9L 4W4
(250) 743-3834
FAX (250) 746-7122

**Wine Shop Hours:** TBD

**Proprietors/Winemakers:**
Roger & Nancy Dosman
**First Year:** 1998

A new winery opening in the summer of 1998 just north of Duncan. Varieties being produced include Bacchus, Auxerrois, Pinot Gris, Pinot Noir and Marechal Foch.

Traveling north on Highway #1 north of Duncan, turn east on Herd Road, follow to a right turn on Lakes Road then to Stamps Road where a left turn leads to Alderlea Vineyards. The Dosmans also have a bed and breakfast on the farm. Call for more information.

## Blue Grouse Vineyards & Winery

4365 Blue Grouse Road, RR #7
Duncan, BC V9L 4W4
(250) 743-3834
FAX (250) 743-9305

**Proprietor/Winemaker:** Hans Kiltz
**First Year:** 1990

**Wine Shop Hours:** 11 AM to 5 PM, Wednesday, Friday, Saturday and Sunday

Blue Grouse Winery is another that was spawned of the farmgate winery legislation that opened the door to small producers in 1990. Dr. Hans Kiltz, a veterinarian who came to Canada for the peaceful lifestyle suited to raising children, purchased a property with a substantial vineyard already in place and has learned viticulture and winemaking on the fly.

The winery produces a wide range of wines including Pinot Gris, Kerner, Perl of Csaba and a new red "July Muscat."

## Chateau Wolff

2534 Maxey Road
Nanaimo, BC V9S 5V6
(250) 753-9669
FAX (250) 753-0614

**Proprietor/Winemaker:** Harry von Wolff
**First Year:** 1997
**Winery Capacity:** 5,000 gallons

**Wine Shop Hours:** 10 AM to 5 PM, Saturday

Harry and Helga von Wolff opened their winery to the public in the spring of 1998 offering wines from their own vineyard, the northernmost commercial vineyard on Vancouver Island. Capitalizing on a unique microclimate (and extreme protective measures against beavers, rabbits and other pests, Harry released a Pinot Noir and his proprietary blend of Chardonnay and Muller Thurgau called Viva.

After a lifetime crowded with many different careers, Harry von Wolff is excited about the future of winegrowing on Vancouver Island. You can stop by most Saturdays by following Terminal Road in Nanaimo to Bowen Road (turn west) then to E. Wellington Road (turn left) follow to Maxey Road (turn right) and follow to winery entrance.

## Cherry Point Vineyards

840 Cherry Point Road, RR#3
Cobble Hill, BC V0R 1L0
(250) 743-1272
FAX (250) 743-1059
**Web:** www.cherrypoint
vineyards.com

**Proprietors/Winemakers:**
Wayne & Helena Ulrich
**First Year:** 1992

**Wine Shop Hours:** 11:30 AM to 6 PM daily

Wayne and Helena Ulrich came to the wine business after the initial farmgate winery legislation was passed in 1990. Having found a suitable property on Vancouver Island near Cobble Hill, they moved in, planted vineyards and, soon after, began making wine.

Varieties producing in their vineyard include Pinot Blanc, Auxerrois, Ortega, Gewurztraminer, Pinot Noir and Agria. The owners are friends with Gerard and JoAnn Bentryn of Bainbridge Island Winery who have provided helpful information for their grape-growing efforts.

To find the property, drive north on Highway #1, turn right on Fisher Road (south of Duncan), follow to Cherry Point Road (turn right), and look for the wine-cask-guarded entrance to Cherry Point Vineyards.

## Venturi-Schulze Vineyards

4235 Trans Canada
Highway, RR #1
Cobble Hill, BC
V0R 1L0
(250) 743-5630, FAX (250) 743-5630

Visits by appointment only

**Proprietors:** Giordano Venturi and Marilyn Schulze Venturi
**Winemakers:** Giordano & Marilyn Venturi and Michelle Schulze
**First Year:** 1993
**Winery Capacity:** 2,500 gallons

Finding the peaceful lifestyle of Vancouver Island preferable to that of Vancouver, Giordano and Marilyn Schulze moved to the quiet farm country near Cobble Hill on the Trans Canada Highway. They are committed to "making wines that reflect not just our region but the special nature of our own site." Varietals produced include Pinot Gris, Pinot Noir, Madeleine Sylvaner, Kerner, Siegerrebe and Schönburger. A testament to the fine quality of the bottlings is their inclusion on the wine lists of the Empress Room, Sooke Harbour House and The Wickaninnish Inn.

Call for an appointment to visit the winery to buy the wines or the Balsamic style vinegar also made on the farm. A semi-annual newsletter announces special food and wine events.

## Vigneti Zanatta

5039 Marshall
Road, RR #3
Duncan, BC
V9L 2X1
(250) 748-2338
FAX (250) 746-5684

**Proprietor:** Zanatta Family
**Winemaker:** Loretta Zanatta
**First Year:** 1992

**Wine Shop Hours:** May through October, 11 AM to 5 PM, Tuesday and Wednesday; 11 AM to 7 PM, Thursday through Sunday

Located in the Cowichan Valley near Duncan, Vigneti Zanatta is a family effort that has grown slowly over the past decade-and-a-half to finally have their first commercial release in 1992. A vineyard that is heavily protected from deer and birds during harvest is one of the hallmarks of Cowichan Valley winegrowing and Zanatta's is no exception. Varieties Ortega, Cayuga, Leon Millot and others are just as attractive to the wildlife as to wine lovers.

Call the winery before heading out since they often sell out of their small production before the next vintage is released.

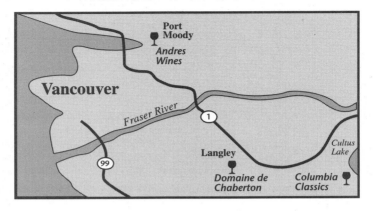

## Andrés Wines - Peller Estates

2120 Vintner Street
Port Moody, BC
V3H 1W8
(604) 937-3411
FAX (604) 937-5487

**Proprietor:** The Peller Family
**Winemaker:** Tony Vlcek
**First Year:** 1961
**Winery Capacity:** 2.75 million gallons

**Wine Shop Hours:** 9 AM to 5 PM, Monday to Friday. Tours, tastings by appointment only.

One of B.C.'s large commercial wineries, Andrés was started by Andrew Peller in 1961. At first making wine from California grape concentrate, the winery grew as grapes were planted in the Okanagan region. In fact, Andrew Peller was instrumental in the creation of Inkameep Vineyard near Oliver, an operation that is an agricultural success story in Anglo-Native Canadian relations.

Andrés scored a major hit in Canada in 1971 with its Baby Duck sparkling wine designed after the Cold Duck wines made popular by California wineries. Expansion led to Andrés building five other wineries across Canada to produce regional wines.

**The Wines**
Today the winery produces premium VQA varietals under the Peller Estates label and most recently has added the Bighorn brand of barrel fermented Chardonnay and crisp "Alsatian-style" Pinot Blanc.

## Columbia Valley Classics Fruit Winery

1385 Frost Road
Lindell Beach, BC
V2R 4X8
(604) 858-5233
Email: drivard@direct.ca

**Proprietor:** John Stuyt and Dominic Rivard
**Winemaker:** Dominic Rivard
**First Year:** 1997
**Winery Capacity:** 10,000 gallons

**Wine Shop Hours:** 10 AM to 6 PM, daily

Begun in 1997, the Columbia Valley Classics fruit winery also processes other agricultural food products. From their 40-acre Bertrand Creek Farm near Cultus Lake, the winery produces an assortment of berry wines (with more to come, say the owners).

You can visit the winery any day by following TransCanada Highway #1 to Chilliwack and take Exit 119 and follow around Cultus Lake to Lindell Beach. In addition to being a fine day trip from Vancouver, this stop is on the way for travelers heading to the Okanagan Valley from the west side via the Canadian route.

## Domaine de Chaberton Estates, Ltd.

1064 - 216th Street
Langley, B.C.
V2Z 1R3
(604) 530-1736
Fax (604) 533-9687

**Proprietors:** Claude and Ingeborg Violet
**Winemakers:** Claude Violet, Elias Phiniotis
**First Year:** 1991
**Winery Capacity:** 75,000 gallons

**Wine Shop Hours:** April 18 to August 30, Tours at 2 PM and 4 PM

Claude and Ingeborg Violet immigrated to Canada in 1981 with their two daughters after having found an acceptable site to start a winery near South Langley in the Fraser Valley. Consulting with local viticulturists, the vineyard was planted to varieties that would mature the grapes in the long, but only moderately warm, western B.C. summer.

The Violet family has a history in the wine business going back to the 17th century in France, and Domaine de Chaberton was indeed named after a former Violet farm in the south of France.

You can find Domaine Chaberton by following Highway 1 east from Vancouver and taking the 200th St. exit, turn right (south), head to 16th Avenue, turn left and continue to 216th St. where a right turn takes you to the winery.

**The Wines**

With advice from consultant winemaker Elias Phiniotis, Claude Violet makes a full line of white and red wines, most from grapes grown in his own vineyard. Chardonnay, Bacchus, Madeleine Angevine, Madeleine Sylvaner and others complement the reds (mostly made from Okanagan Valley grapes) including Pinot Noir, Merlot and Cabernet Sauvignon/Merlot.

# Wine Tasting, VQA and a few other things . . .

The British Columbia Wine Institute administers the Vintners Quality Alliance program for the province with the stated intent of establishing quality standards covering several areas of wine production.

Essentially, the BC Wine Institute has created rules for wineries to follow if they want to label their wine Product of British Columbia. Among other rules, some of the major ones are: varietal wines must be 85% of the named varietal; to use a viticultural area name (i.e. Okanagan Valley) 95% of the grapes must have come from that area; vintage-dated wines must be 95% from the stated vintage; and Estate Bottled wine must be 100% from grapes grown on land owned or controlled by the bottling winery.

These rules are not foreign to most American wine consumers, since they closely parallel rules laid down for U.S. wineries by the BATF regulatory agency.

To wear the VQA label, however, wines must further be evaluated by a tasting panel of industry experts and be judged to be of sound quality and closely resemble a standard of the stated varietal in smell and taste. Further, the tasting panel also makes judgements about specialty wines (late harvest, nouveau, sparkling, etc.) as to the quality and appropriateness of the wine to known standards. Subjectivity has been reduced over the years and nearly everyone seems to be happy with the system.

To the wine drinker, this system has resulted in higher quality BC wines and has encouraged BC vintners to offer better products, competing on an international scale of quality.

A convention used in BC tasting rooms (called wine shops) related to apparent sweetness of wines. The scale in practice seems to work like this:

0 - extremely dry, requires food
1 - not too dry, but still pretty dry
2 - off dry, feel free to sip without food
3-10 - late harvest sweetness
10+ - icewine sweetness (syrup to honey)

# NORTHWEST WINES & WINERIES

What great scenery! What great wines! What friendly people! What a long drive!

If only the Okanagan and Similkameen Valleys were just an hour from Seattle, we would be there every other weekend. Even with the six to seven hour drive, the area is certainly worth visiting at least once each year.

The centerpiece of the valley is 70-mile long Lake Okanagan, a body of water that is not only beautiful but serves to cool the climate in summer and warm the winter's chill. In an area that has long been known for apples, peaches and other crops, the wine grape is just now gaining ground to launch the region's wineries to new heights.

At the south end of the region, from Osoyoos to Okanagan Falls, a half-dozen-plus wineries are growing fast. The "Golden Mile" near Oliver is a bench of warm climate hillside where grapes thrive and some of the area's finest wineries are located. Most are open daily for tours and tasting. Allow at least a day to tour this exciting area.

Penticton is home to the B.C. Wine Information Center which is a great spot to begin your tour of the Naramata area on the east side of Lake Okanagan. Seven wineries are in this area and each offers a breathtaking view of the lake from their property. Another great day of wine touring and picnicking!

Travelling up the west side again, you'll have to visit Sumac Ridge and Scherzinger Wineries near Summerland. After stopping for lunch at The Cellar Door at Sumac Ridge, continue north to Peachland and Westbank to visit five more vintners. If you missed lunch, Hainle Vineyards offers gourmet meals on their veranda. Visits to the three wineries at Westbank makes a sensible end to day three.

Kelowna is home to Ogopogo, a mythical monster said to inhabit Lake Okanagan. Wine lovers often sight the beast on windy evenings after a hard day of wine touring. Also near Kelowna are some spectacular wineries to visit that each have their own special place in the region's wine history and culture. North of town the wineries become further apart, though just as appealing.

A week in the Okanagan is just barely enough to stop by each winery and sample the stunning wines they are making as the new

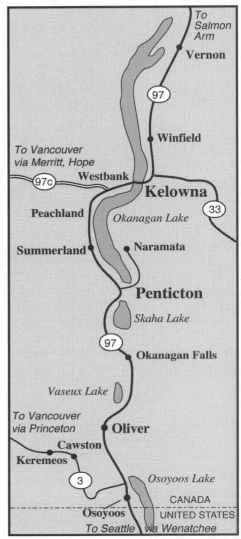

millenium arrives. But do save a few hours for some other recreational pastimes, eh?

Linksters should bring their clubs to enjoy a round of golf at one of the area's 20-plus courses. Quality courses with very reasonable greens fees. Yachtsmen or water skiers are at home on the lake where you can rent a sailboat, houseboat or something faster.

Don't miss the Okanagan wine festivals. The Spring Festival is the last week of April and the Fall Festival takes place during the first part of October.

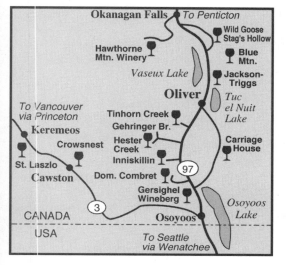

## Southern Okanagan and Similkameen

Just crossing the border from the U.S. a visitor to the Okanagan is presented with a cornucopia of winery stops. A side trip out to the Similkameen Valley offers two winery visits and some delightful scenery. Continuing up Hwy. 97, you discover the "Golden Mile" where grapes are grown along the warm foothills south of Oliver. Winery faciities are first rate and wines to taste are varied and delicious. For American tourists this may be your introduction to varieties such as Ehrenfelser, Auxerrois and others not grown in Washington or Oregon. Winery listings are alphabetical.

## Blue Mountain Vineyards

RR #1, S-3, C-4
(Allendale Road)
Okanagan Falls, BC
V0H 1R0
(250) 497-8244
FAX (250) 497-6160

**Owners:** Ian and Jane Mavety
**Winemaker:** Ian Mavety
**First Year:** 1992

**Wine Shop Hours:** By appointment only

Trained in agriculture at the University of British Columbia, Ian Mavety began farming in the Southern Okanagan in 1971. Planting the hybrid grape varieties recommended at the time, he was one of the first to begin replanting to vitis vinifera (European wine grapes) for the sake of better quality wines.

After the 1988 NAFTA agreement resulted in many growers accepting government subsidies to tear out their hybrid vineyards, Mavety and his wife Jane decided that the clearest path to success was to produce their own wine from the grapes they grew at Blue Mountain Vineyard.

Some enlightening consultation aided the Mavetys in crafting their first successful wines of Pinot Noir, Chardonnay, Pinot Blanc and

Pinot Gris in the early 1990s. The demand for Blue Mountain wines has grown and now virtually all varietal bottlings and the winery's superb sparkling wine are on allocation.

Wine lovers wishing to visit Blue Mountain need to call ahead for an appointment. The winery is located southeast of Okanagan Falls on Allendale Road above the valley.

## Burrowing Owl Estate Winery

Black Sage Road
Oliver, BC

Scheduled for opening spring of 1999, this remarkable facility is a joint venture between the successful Burrowing Owl Vineyards and Cascadia Brands. An underground cave will house the winery and aging cellar to temper the excessive heat of the desert climate of the southeast valley.

## Carriage House Wines

Black Sage Road
RR #1, S-46, C-19
Oliver, BC V0H 1T0
(250) 498-8818

**Proprietors:** Dave & Karen Wagner
**Winemaker:** Dave Wagner
**First Year:** 1998 (vineyard plantings begun in 1993)

**Wine Shop Hours:** 10 AM to 6 PM, summer only, other times by appointment

Currently the only winery facility open on fast-developing Black Sage Road, Carriage House Wines has released Pinot Blanc and Kerner, with Pinot Noir and Chardonnay scheduled to follow shortly. The spectacular view from the desert ridge of Black Sage Road is worth the drive, but keep to marked footpaths to avoid the occasional rattlesnake.

To reach Carriage House, take Road #22 east from Osoyoos and follow it up onto the ridge where it becomes Black Sage Road. Alternately, take Road #9 east from Oliver and turn left on Orchard Grove Lane to head up the hill onto Black Sage Road.

## Crowsnest Vineyards

Surprise Drive
off Lowe Avenue
m.a. RR #1, S-18, C-18
Cawston, BC V0X 1C0
(250) 499-5129

**Proprietors:** Hugh and Andrea McDonald
**Winemaker:** Andrea McDonald
**First Year:** 1995

**Wine Shop Hours:** 10 AM to 6 PM, daily

The union of the son of a British Columbia fruit growing family and the daughter of a Swiss immigrant keen on learning the technology of food and wine processing begat the fledgling Crowsnest Vineyards winery in the Similkameen Valley.

Gradually taking over the McDonald family orchards and replacing them with vineyards began in 1990, and today a full

complement of varieties produce Chardonnay, Riesling, Auxerrois, Merlot and Pinot Noir.

You can find Crowsnest Vineyards by traveling one mile south of Cawston on Highway #3, turn left on Lowe Drive, follow uphill to Surprise Drive, turn left and continue to the winery.

*Olivier Combret at Domaine Combret Winery*

## Domaine Combret Estate Winery

Road 13, Off Hwy. 97
P.O. Box 1170
Oliver, BC V0H 1T0
(250) 498-8878

**Proprietors:** Combret Family
**Winemaker:** Olivier Combret
**First Year:** 1992

**Wine Shop Hours:** By appointment or by chance via winery door intercom. See below.

Robert Combret took advantage of an offer in 1991 to sell his winery in Provence at an attractive price and relocate to British Columbia to begin another family estate with his son Olivier as winemaster. Struggles with bureaucracy over the importation of grapevines from France slowed the project a bit, but today the winery – custom designed for gravity feed by Olivier – is a showplace with vineyards in production to fill the tanks.

The Combret family is excited about the unique terroir on the Oliver bench, a gravelly soil that reminds them of many of the best vineyard sites in France. Their plantings of

Chardonnay, Riesling, Gamay and Cabernet Franc are flourishing.

Visitors to the winery are requested to call ahead but there is a convenient telephone intercom at the winery door to summon your host if your arrival is not previously arranged. From Hwy. 97, take road 13 to the top of the hill and turn right to the winery.

**The Wines**

Domaine Combret offers a crisp Riesling, delicious Chardonnay (partially barrel fermented), a fruity Gamay Noir made using the carbonic maceration technique, a hearty Cabernet Franc and a delicious Riesling Ice Wine that Olivier describes as being like "apple-Calvados" with hints of clove, cinnamon and rose petal. A $5 tasting fee includes a logo glass to take with you.

# Gehringer Brothers Estate Winery

Road #8 at Highway 97
RR #1, S-23, C-4
Oliver, BC V0H 1T0
(250) 498-3537
FAX (250) 498-3510

**Proprietors:** Gehringer Family
**Winemaker:** Walter Gehringer
**First Year:** 1985

**Wine Shop Hours:** July through September: 10 AM to 5 PM, daily,
October through June: Monday - Friday, 10 AM to 5 PM, Saturday, 10 AM to 1 PM

The Gehringer brothers, Walter and Gordon, are the Canadian-born, German-educated winemakers at their family winery on the Oliver bench. Their father Helmut and his brother Karl did the research required to select the proper vineyard site and the winery crushed its first vintage in 1985.

Following Road #8 up from Hwy. 97, the top of the hill offers a choice of right to Gehringer Bros. or left to Hester Creek. Be sure to visit both wineries. The Gehringer tasting room is spacious and a wide selection of varietals is available for sampling.

*Gehringer Brothers wine shop south of Oliver.*

**The Wines**

German training shows great influence on the winemaking style at Gehringer Bros. Sweet reserve is added back to several varieties to provide body and additional fresh fruit flavor. Pinot Gris, Pinot Blanc and Riesling are familiar and delicious, but don't miss the Ehrenfelser and Pinot Auxerrois. Red varieties Pinot Noir, Verdelet and Chancellor lead to a taste of outstanding Riesling Ice Wine. (Note: most wineries have an additional tasting fee for sampling ice wine, usually $2 to $3 per sample)

# Gersighel Wineberg

29690 Highway 97
RR #1, S-40, C-20
Oliver, BC V0H 1T0
(250) 495-3319
FAX (250) 495-3319

**Proprietors:** Dirk De Gussem Family
**Winemakers:** Gerd and Helgi De Gussem
**First Year:** 1995

**Wine Shop Hours:** 9:30 AM to 8 PM, daily

The Belgium-born De Gussem family operates this rustic vineyard and winery just north of Osoyoos. Sons Gerd and Helgi are on hand to pour samples at the tasting room just a stone's throw from Hwy. 97. VQA wines Pinot Blanc, Gewurztraminer, Riesling, Pinot Noir and Merlot are produced along with a blend called Sunset Red.

## Hawthorne Mountain Vineyards

Green Lake Road
P.O. Box 480
Okanagan Falls, BC
V0H 1R0
(250) 497-8267
FAX (250) 497-8073
**Email:** hawthorn@vip.net
**Web:** www.hmvineyard.com

**Proprietors:** Harry McWatters, Bob Wareham
**Winemaker:** Bruce Ewert
**First Year:** 1995

**Wine Shop Hours:** 9 AM to 5 PM, daily

This property has been farmed since the turn of the century when the two Hawthorne brothers homesteaded the land. World War I veteran Major Hugh Fraser bought the isolated farm and worked the land with his loyal Collie dogs until he sold out in 1962.

Albert LeCompte bought the property in 1983 and developed the original producing vineyards and winery on the site. The property was sold in 1995 to Harry McWatters and Bob Wareham and they changed the name from LeCompte Winery to Hawthorne Mountain Vineyards. A huge investment in additional estate vineyard plantings and a thoroughly modern winery promises that HMV will continue to win awards like their recent harvest of medals at the All Canada Wine Championship.

Follow Green Lake Road up the mountain from the north end of Okanagan Falls. A moderately hair-raising, three mile drive is rewarded with superb views of the valley both north and south. Enjoy your picnic on the winery's vine-shaded veranda.

### The Wines

Delicious barrel-fermented Chardonnay, off-dry Riesling, Gewurztraminer and Muscat-Ottonel are produced along with reds, Pinot Meunier, Pinot Noir, Merlot, Cabernet Franc, Lemberger and a Meritage blend. Dessert wines include a late harvest Optima and ice wines from Pinot Blanc and Gewurztraminer. HMV Brut is the winery's sparkling offering.

## Hester Creek Estate Winery

#8 Road off Highway 97
13163 - 326th Street
Oliver, BC V0H 1T0
(250) 498-4435
FAX (250) 498-0651

**Proprietor:** Hans-Jorg Lochbichler
**Winemaker:** Frank Supernak
**First Year:** 1995

**Wine Shop Hours:** June through November, 10 AM to 5 PM, daily; December through May, Monday through Friday only.

The former Busnardo farm and Divino Winery received a new lease on life in 1995 from restaurateur and entrepreneur Hans-Jorg Lochbichler and his innovative winemaker Frank Supernak. The farm, one of the earliest and largest plantings of vinifera in the area, was the project of Italian immigrant Joe Busnardo. His casual ways with tending the vines and making the wines were obstacles to his success, but the new team in charge has moved swiftly to bring things up to muster.

Take Road #8 up the hill and take the left fork to Hester Creek (be sure to leave time to visit Gehringer Brothers next door). The large, vine-covered patio is a great place for a picnic lunch with a bottle of Hester Creek wine.

### The Wines

Three different bottlings of delicious Pinot Blanc illustrate the differences brought to a wine by barrel fermentation and malolactic fermentation. Chardonnay, Cabernet Franc and Merlot are also favorites, along with late harvest Trebbiano and Pinot Blanc Ice Wine.

## Inniskillin Okanagan

Road #11 West
RR #1, S-24, C-5
Oliver, BC V0H 1T0
(250) 498-6663
FAX (250) 498-4566
Toll Free (800) 498-6211
**Web:** www.inniskillin.com

**Proprietors:** Inniskillin Wines
**Winemaker:** Christine Leroux
**First Year:** 1984
**Winery Capacity:** 30,000 gallons

**Wine Shop Hours:** Summer, 10 AM to 5 PM, daily: Winter, Monday through Friday only

A branch of Inniskillin Wines of Ontario, the Okanagan Inniskillin has grown and prospered making VQA wines from the Native Canadian-owned Inkameep Vineyard and from their own Dark Horse Vineyard on Oliver's Golden Mile.

Visitors will find the wine shop just up the hill from Hwy. 97 on Road #11.

**The Wines**

The Dark Horse Vineyard has been producing superb red wines including the winery's award-winning Merlot/Cabernet Franc and Meritage Blend. Also available are Pinot Blanc and Gewurztraminer. From Inkameep, Inniskillin makes Chardonnay, Pinot Noir and several dessert wines including Chenin Blanc Ice Wine and Vidal Ice Wine.

## Jackson-Triggs

Box 1650, Highway 97
Oliver, BC V0H 1T0
(250) 498-4981
FAX (250) 498-6505

**Proprietors:** Allan Jackson, Donald Triggs
**Winemakers:** Sandor Mayer, Bruce Nicholson
**First Year:** 1993

**Wine Shop Hours:** 9 AM to 4:30 PM, Monday through Friday.

Another of the Okanagan's shifts of ownership from a large company (Bright's Wines of Eastern Canada) to consolidated ownership to purchasing of production facilities by former employees.

Nonetheless, wine tourists may still stop by the plant on Hwy. 97 near Oliver for a taste of wine and a tour (10 AM and 2 PM). Current releases of Jackson-Triggs Merlot and Chardonnay have been very popular and the red wine program is reputed to be readying some truly outstanding examples from more recent vintages.

**The Wines**

Okanagan varietals include Chardonnay, Pinot Blanc, Dry Riesling, Gewurztraminer, Blanc de Noir, Merlot, Late Harvest Ehrenfelser and Gewurz., and Riesling Icewine.

## St. Laszlo Estate Winery

Highway 3
Keremeos, BC

Winery owner and grape grower Joe Ritlop is the proprietor of this small operation just southeast of Keremeos. Reports of "rustic wines" dating back as far as the 1979 vintage suggest a very unique tasting awaits each visitor. Not personally tasted.

## Stag's Hollow Winery

Sunvalley Way, RR#1, S-3, C-36
Okanagan Falls, BC
V0H 1R0
(250) 497-6162

**Proprietor/Winemaker:** Larry Gerelus
**First Year:** 1995

**Wine Shop Hours:** 10 AM to 5 PM, daily, May through Thanksgiving. Other times please call ahead

Stag's Hollow Winery southeast of Okanagan Falls enjoys an attractive setting next to their vineyard. Current releases of Chardonnay, Vidal/Ehrenfelser, Pinot Noir and Vidal Reserve will be joined by 1996 oak aged Merlot.

Visitors should look for the attractive stag-themed weather vane atop the winery building next to Wild Goose Vineyards.

## Tinhorn Creek Vineyards, Ltd.

RR #1, S-58, C-10
Oliver, BC V0H 1T0
(250) 498-3743
FAX (250) 498-3228
Toll-free: (888) 484-6467
Email: winery@tinhorn.com
Web: www.tinhorn.com

**Proprietors:** Bob & Barb Shaunessy
**General Manager:** Kenn Oldfield
**Winemaker:** Sandra Oldfield
**First Year:** 1993
**Winery Capacity:** 100,000 gallons

**Wine Shop Hours:** 10 AM to 5 PM, daily

This ambitious and well thought out winery and vineyard program has completed their vineyard planting goal and has vinted a solid offering of wines that will expand in distribution as vineyards mature and supply more fruit. The owner's confidence in the wine industry is evident in the rapid expansion of vineyard plantings (including land acquisition for same) and in creating a first-class winery and visitor center.

Two vineyard sites supply the winery with grapes. The estate vineyard next to the winery on Oliver's Golden Mile is planted to Gewurztraminer, Pinot Gris, Chardonnay, Pinot Noir and Merlot. Across the valley on Black Sage Road the newer Rushmere and Diamondback Vineyards are in a warmer site and are planted to Pinot Gris, Chardonnay, Pinot Noir, Cabernet Franc and Merlot.

The Tinhorn Creek Winery is constructed in such a way that tourists can view the wine production operations from overhead galleries adjacent to the tasting room. A spacious wine shop and well-stocked gift emporium are favorites with visitors. Below the view terrace is a demonstration vineyard where guests may inspect vines and/or fruit depending on the season of their visit.

Follow signs west from Hwy. 97 up the hill to the winery.

### The Wines

U.C. Davis-trained winemaker Sandra Oldfield has come to truly appreciate the winegrowing advantages of the Okanagan Valley with its ability to preserve acidity in vinifera wines. Having two vineyard sites (one cooler, one warmer) to balance and blend as necessary is another advantage.

White wines include Gewurztraminer, Pinot Gris and Chardonnay, each true to varietal and refreshingly crisp. The Pinot Gris has received a kiss of oak and the Chardonnay the added embrace of partial ML fermentation.

Reds tasted included Pinot Meunier, Pinot Noir and Merlot. Spicy notes and toasty oak components are common attributes and each wine offers its hallmark varietal fruit aroma and flavor. Icewine made from the locally grown varietal Kerner is delicious.

## Wild Goose Vineyards & Winery

Sun Valley Way, RR #1,
S-3, C-11
Okanagan Falls, BC
V0H 1R0
(250) 497-8919, FAX (250) 497-6853
Email: wildgoose@img.net

**Proprietors:** Adolf, Roland, Hagan Kruger
**Winemakers:** Adolf and Hagan Kruger
**First Year:** 1990
**Winery Capacity:** 10,000 gallons

**Wine Shop Hours:** 10 AM to 5 PM, daily, April through October

The Kruger family planted 10 acres of vineyard on the southeast side of Okanagan Falls in 1984 after living in Vancouver but being drawn to life in the Okanagan wine country. Adolf Kruger and his sons Hagen and Roland cleared the land for the vineyard and discovered ideal soil to grow winegrapes.

Visitors to the small winery will find one of the family members pouring the wines and answering questions. The winemaking of each wine is explained and the philosophies behind the practices are discussed.

**The Wines**

Using grapes from their own vineyard, the Black Widow Vineyard across the road and from other sites, Wild Goose Winery produces Riesling in off-dry and dry reserve styles, Gewurztraminer (dry and spicy), a refreshing and citrusy Pinot Blanc, and toasty, oak-aged Chardonnay. An off-dry blend named Autumn Gold and a 100% Riesling dessert wine, Autumn Blue are also available.

Reds include Marechal Foch, Pinot Noir, Merlot and Cabernet Sauvignon. Late harvest Riesling and port-style "Pipe" are also made.

*Hagen Kruger at the Wild Goose Winery.*

# British Columbia
# Wine Information Centre

888 Westminster Ave.
West Penticton , BC
(250) 490-2006
**Web:** www.bcwineinfo.com

This facility is located right in the heart of Penticton (next to the Convention Centre and across from "colourful Front Street") and offers a wine range of information on wine touring, general travel and accommodations, and even wine tastings. If you plan to bring back a bottle or two from your vacation, check the wine shop here since they have many wines from all over the province. Out behind the centre is a demonstration vineyard where you can inspect the progress of the current vintage!

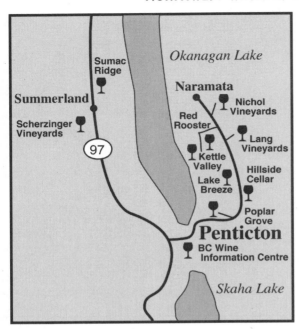

## Penticton, Naramata & Summerland

There is no prettier view on a sunny day than that of vineyards and Okanagan Lake with a ballet of sailboats below and white puffy clouds above. Many winemakers have fallen in love with the view and the climate to establish their lives and their wineries nearby. While the BC Wine Information Centre in Penticton may be the place to find the most wines in one spot, you can strike out on the Naramata Road for an afternoon of sipping and soaking up the sunny ambiance. After that experience, the beautiful drive up the lake to Scherzinger Winery and Sumac Ridge can only be topped by a delicious dinner at The Cellar Door, a gourmet's treasure at your final winery destination.

## Hillside Cellars

1350 Naramata Road
Penticton, BC
V2A 8T6
(250) 493-4424,
FAX (250) 493-6294
**Email:**
info@hillsideestate.com
**Web:** www.hillsideestate.com

**Proprietor:** John Hromyk
**Winemaker:** Eric von Krosigk
**First Year:** 1989

**Wine Shop Hours:** 10 AM to 6 PM, daily

Founded by Czech immigrants Vera and Bohumir Klokocka in 1989, Hillside Cellars was one of the first farmgate wineries licensed in B.C. Replacing orchards with vineyards beginning in 1984, the Klokockas proved that winegrowing along the Naramata bench was possible if one worked hard.

Hillside Cellars has changed ownership and has begun a grander life than the Klokockas could have envisioned on their shoestring budget. A showplace winery has been built and extensive new vineyard plantings are going in to increase production.

Dinners are offered at the winery Saturday nights and the facility is popular for special events and celebrations.

Find Hillside Cellars by heading out Naramata Road from Penticton approximately 4.5 miles. The winery is right by the road.

**The Wines**

Winemaker Eric von Krosigk has crafted a wide variety of wines at Hillside including their flagship Muscat Ottonel and a delicious Gewurztraminer. Other whites include a lightly oaked Pinot Blanc, toasty Chardonnay, Auxerrois, Ehrenfelser and Kerner.

Reds include a nouveau style Gamay, a rich Cabernet Sauvignon, and French oak-aged Merlot and Pinot Noir.

## Kettle Valley Winery, Ltd.

2988 Hayman Road
RR #1, S-2, C-39
Naramata, BC
V0H 1N0
(250) 496-5898, FAX (250) 496-5298
Email: KettleValleyWinery@bc.sympatico.ca

**Proprietors/Winemakers:**
Bob Ferguson and Tim Watts
**First Year:** 1992
**Winery Capacity:** 4,500 gallons

**Wine Shop Hours:** Noon to 5 PM, daily, during summer months

Brothers-in-law and partners in Kettle Valley Winery, Bob Ferguson and Tim Watts have planted their vineyard to Bordeaux red varieties, Pinot Noir and Chardonnay. They have found a niche making hearty red wines and barrel-fermented Chardonnay – not the usual treatment of the variety in the Okanagan.

Visitors can find the winery by turning west at the Naramata Fire Hall and following Debeck Road down toward the lake. Turn left on Hayman Road.

## Lake Breeze Vineyards

Sammet Road off Naramata Road, P.O. Box 9
Naramata, BC V0H 1N0
(250) 496-5659
FAX (250) 496-5894

**Proprietors:** Paul & Verena Moser
**Winemaker:** Garron Elmes
**First Year:** 1996

**Wine Shop Hours:** 10 AM to 6 PM, daily, May through October, Tuesday through Sunday in April. Closed Oct. through April.

The owners of Lake Breeze Vineyards came to British Columbia from South Africa, though both are Swiss born. They farm 13 acres of vineyards producing nine red and white varieties. The superb lake view location offers a patio with food service for those arriving with an appetite and a few moments to linger over a light meal. The striking winery and

*Lake Breeze Vineyards wine shop.*

meticulous landscaping are truly spectacular. Follow signs west from Naramata Road.

**The Wines**
A full range of varietals includes Pinot Blanc, Ehrenfelser, Gewurztraminer, Chardonnay and Semillon. A refreshing Blanc de Noir leads to red wines of Pinot Noir, ripe Cabernet Franc and Merlot. A late harvest blend of Morio Muscat and Pinot Blanc is fruity and the Ehrenfelser Icewine is intense.

## Lang Vineyards, Ltd.

2493 Gammon Road
RR #1, S-11, C-55
Naramata, BC V0H 1N0
(250) 496-5987, FAX (250) 496-5706

**Proprietors:**
Gunther & Kristina Lang
**Winemaker:** Petra Koeller
**First Year:** 1990

**Wine Shop Hours:** 10 AM to 5 PM, daily, May 1st to October 15th. Other times, weekends only.

Gunther and Kristina Lang were the first in their family to emigrate from Germany to British Columbia, but now their parents and Gunther's brother Hans are also living in the province. Buying the vineyard in 1981, the Langs replanted hybrid varieties with vinifera that now produce a delicious selection of Okanagan wines. Find the winery by turning east on Arawana Road to Gammon Road.

**The Wines**
Visitors enjoy several styles of Riesling – from dry to icewine – as well as Auxerrois, Gewurztraminer, Merlot, Pinot Noir, Pinot Meunier and Marchel Foch.

# Nichol Vineyard

1285 Smethurst Road
RR #1, S-14, C-13
Naramata, BC V0H 1N0
(250) 496-5962
FAX (250) 496-4275

**Proprietors/Winemakers:**
Kathleen & Alex Nichol
**First Year:** 1993
**Winery Capacity:** 2,500 gallons

**Wine Shop Hours:** 11 AM to 5 PM, Tuesday through Sunday, May 24 through mid-October. Other times by appointment

Trained in professions more cultural than scientific, Alex and Kathleen Nichol studied wine as a hobby before taking the plunge to buy property for a vineyard and winery in 1988. Up the hill above Naramata Village, their property hugs the slope beneath the granite cliffs that once supported the Kettle Valley Railway. This warmer-than-normal site allows the Nichols to successfully grow Syrah and Cabernet Franc, along with Pinot Noir and St. Laurent (a red variety now grown primarily in Austria). Pinot Gris is the white variety produced from the Nichol Vineyard.

Follow Naramata Road north and take the next right turn after crossing Naramata Creek. Follow Smethurst Road to the right.

# Poplar Grove Winery

1060 Poplar Grove Road
(West off Naramata Road)
Penticton, BC V2A 8T6
(250) 492-2352
FAX (250) 492-9162
**Email:** poplargrove@img.net

**Proprietors:** Ian & Gitta Sutherland
**Winemaker:** Ian Sutherland
**First Year:** 1997

**Wine Shop Hours:** 12 to 5 PM, daily (during summer months)

Ian and Gitta Sutherland purchased a piece of property near Penticton in 1992 that was eight acres of mostly apple orchard. An interest in wine and some home-winemaking experience convinced Ian that he should replace some of the orchard with vineyards like his neighbors at Hillside Winery had done.

Today the orchard is vineyard and Ian buys additional grapes from Inkameep Vineyards. Visit the winery by turning west down Poplar Grove Road just outside of Penticton.

**The Wines**
Partial to Bordeaux-style red wines, Ian makes Cabernet Franc and Merlot along with white wines Chardonnay and Ehrenfelser.

# Red Rooster Winery

910 Debeck Road, RR #1
Naramata, BC V0H 1N0
(250) 496-4041
FAX (250) 496-5674
**Email:**
redrooster@img.net

**Wine Shop Hours:** Daily, 10 AM to 6 PM (summers)

**Proprietors:** Beat and Prudence Mahrer
**Winemaker Consultant:** Eric von Krosigk
**First Year:** 1998

Counted among those who had an appreciation for fine wine but had never made it, Beat and Prudence Mahrer emigrated from Switzerland in 1989 and now have opened a winery! With help from their consultant Eric von Krosigk, they have several wines for sale with others to be released over time. Their property overlooks beautiful Okanagan Lake and is a great place to stop for a taste and perhaps to enjoy a tailgate picnic.

**The Wines**
Red Rooster's first releases are Riesling, Gewurztraminer and a blush made from Merlot, Chardonnay and Riesling. Also available is their methode champenoise sparkling wine. Coming soon are six varieties of icewine, as well as Chardonnay and Merlot table wines. They may have the only Viognier icewine ever made, but only 10 bottles!

## Scherzinger Vineyards

7311 Fiske Road
RR #2, S-68, C-13
Summerland, BC V0H 1Z0
(250) 494-8815

**Proprietors:** Scherzinger Family
**Winemaker:** Edgar Scherzinger
**First Year:** 1994

**Wine Shop Hours:** 10 AM to 6 PM, daily, May through October. Other times please call.

*Crystal Lee, Harry and Kathy McWatters join for a family toast at the winery.*

The hills above Summerland were a favored vacation spot for the Scherzinger family who emigrated from Germany to Vancouver in 1961. Longing for the mountains of his native Black Forest, Edgar bought a farm in Summerland and over the years replaced a struggling cherry orchard with grapevines. His skills as a wood carver are shared with wine lovers as he offers his carvings for sale at the winery. Follow Victoria Road south up the hill to Lewes then right to Fiske St.

**The Wines:**
Gewurztraminer, Chardonnay and Pinot Noir are made at Scherzinger Vineyards.

## Sumac Ridge Estate Winery

Highway 97
P.O. Box 307
Summerland, BC V0H 1Z0
(250) 494-0451
FAX (250) 494-3456
**Email:** info@sumacridge.com
**Web:** www.sumacridge.com

**Proprietors:** Harry McWatters, Bob Wareham
**Winemaker:** Mark Wendenburg
**First Year:** 1970

**Wine Shop Hours:** 9 AM to 5 PM, daily

Firmly committed to the potential of quality varietal wines made in the Okanagan, Harry McWatters has spent the better part of his life working with the government, the wine industry, the vineyardists and others to improve the wines and wine business in British Columbia. Together with his partner Bob Wareham, Harry has expanded their vineyard holdings onto Black Sage Road near Oliver and has begun an ambitious vineyard expansion at their second winery, Hawthorne Mountain Vineyards at Okanagan Falls. The new vineyard at Black Sage Road is providing superb fruit for Sumac Ridge red wines.

The Sumac Ridge winery is just north of Summerland on the east side of Hwy. 97. The adjacent golf course invites you to bring your clubs and enjoy a short round before or after wine tasting. Also at the winery is The Cellar Door Bistro, an elegant restaurant run by talented chef Mark Taylor. This spot is among the best in the Okanagan for a fine meal at lunch or dinner.

**The Wines**
Winemaker Mark Wendenburg crafts a complete line of varietals at Sumac Ridge. Those seeking ripe, full flavored red wines, mellowed by oak aging, will enjoy the Merlot, Cabernet Franc, Cabernet Sauvignon, Pinot Noir and a Meritage Blend of the three Bordeaux varieties. The fruity Chancellor might be a surprise delight to U.S. wine lovers not familiar with this grape. White varieties include Sauvignon Blanc, Pinot Blanc, Chardonnay and a Meritage blend of Sauvignon Blanc and Semillon. Riesling and Gewurztraminer are also produced.

Harry McWatters is very proud of his sparkling wine program and is eagerly anticipating celebrating the new millenium with a special cuvee now resting *en tirage* at the winery. Sumac Ridge's popular Stellar's Jay Brut and Blanc de Noirs Brut are also produced by the methode champenoise.

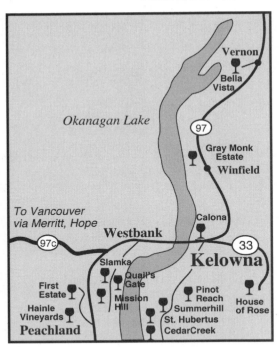

Travelling north, the wine lover discovers Kelowna, the region's center of commerce. Kelowna offers more hotels, restaurants, nightlife and other activities for young and old.

The wine tourist will want to visit the five wineries in Peachland and Westbank before falling into the arms of Kelowna's hustle and bustle. **Hainle Vineyards** and **First Estate Winery** are great stops in Peachland. **Mission Hill Winery**, **Quail's Gate** and tiny **Slamka Cellars** are a trio of attractions in Westbank.

**Calona Winery** in Kelowna is one of the oldest in the Province. The other wineries south of town each offer unique perspectives on BC wine growing. Be sure to visit **Pinot Reach**, **House of Rose**, **Summerhill**, **St. Hubertus** and **CedarCreek** wineries. Heading north, **Gray Monk** near Winfield is not to be missed and **Bella Vista** near Vernon is a unique success story.

## Bella Vista Vineyards

3111 Agnew Road
Vernon, BC V1T 5J8
(250) 558-0770
FAX (250) 542-1221

**Proprietor/Winemaker:** Larry Passmore
**First Year:** 1994

**Wine Shop Hours:** Noon to 5 PM, daily

A skilled home winemaker and a native son of Vernon, Larry Passmore assembled some of his winemaking friends to collectively purchase the local Toriumi farm and vineyard in 1991. Additional grapes were planted and Bella Vista Vineyards had its first vintage in 1993. The winery and hospitality rooms were constructed in 1994. To find the winery, travel west from Hwy. 97 on 30th St. in Vernon to Bella Vista Road. Turn right and head up the hill to the winery at 3111 Agnew Road.

### The Wines

Bella Vista Vineyards offers Marechal Foch, Auxerrois, Chardonnay, Gewurztraminer and other varieties.

## Calona Wines Ltd.

1125 Richter Street
Kelowna, BC V1Y 2K6
(250) 762-3332
FAX (250) 762-2999
Toll free: (800) 663-5086

**Owner:** Corporation
**Winemaker:** Howard Soon
**First Year:** 1935

**Wine Shop Hours:** 9 AM to 6 PM, daily, Victoria Day to Labour Day

Calona is Western Canada's largest winery and has a colorful history that tells a tale of wine marketing and consumer demand through the decades. Taking advantage of the Okanagan's huge production of fruit, the first wines were made from apples. Not a grand success, the owners then switched to grape wines and through the years a remarkable parade of fanciful concoctions were designed to catch the consumer's eye and unsophisticated palate. With the hiring of Elias Phiniotis in 1981, the winery began producing varietally labelled wines in earnest. Early wines were

232

made from vinifera and hybrids including grape created at the Summerland Research Station, Sovereign Opal. With additional vinifera grapes available for winemaking in the 1980s and 1990s Calona has begun working vigorously to gain its share of the varietal wine market. Now, in addition to blended wines with proprietary labels, the winery offers medal-winning Chardonnays, Pinot Blancs, Semillons, Cabernet Sauvignons and other main stream varietals. Current winemaker Howard Soon has been with the winery for almost 20 years and deserves credit for helping bring exciting new bottlings to market.

Visitors will find the winery open for tours and tastings in downtown Kelowna, 12 blocks north of Hwy. 97 on Richter Street.

**The Wines**

Of greatest interest to serious wine lovers, look for Calona's artist series varietals of Chardonnay, Merlot and Cabernet Franc. Upcoming releases will include Pinot Noir, Sauvignon Blanc and Cabernet Sauvignon. Many of these varietals have come from the Burrowing Owl Vineyard near Oliver.

# CedarCreek Estate Winery

5445 Lakeshore Road
Kelowna, BC V1W 4S5
(250) 764-8866
FAX (250) 764-2603
Toll free: (800) 730-9463

**Proprietor:** D. Ross Fitzpatrick
**Winemaker:** Kevin Willenborg
**First Year:** 1986
**Winery Capacity:** 50,000+ gallons

**Wine Shop Hours:** 9:30 AM to 5:30 PM, daily, April through Oct.; 9:30 AM to 5 PM, Monday through Friday, Nov.through March

Successful Canadian businessman and politician Ross Fitzpatrick acquired CedarCreek winery in 1986 and has since developed the brand and the property to prominence in the Okanagan wine community.

The 45 acres of vines at the winery are complemented by the new 45 acre Greata Ranch vineyard near Peachland. New varietals and increased production are making

*Gordon Fitzpatrick, president of CedarCreek.*

CedarCreek an exciting place to watch into the new millenium. Ross Fitzpatrick's son Gordon has taken the reins as winery president and a new winemaker is coming on board for the 1998 vintage. Visitors to the winery can enjoy their picnic at the gazebo adjacent to the vineyard. Find CedarCreek by driving south from downtown Kelowna on Pandosy which turns into Lakeshore Road.

**The Wines**

Dry and off-dry white wines are featured from Chardonnay, Pinot Blanc, Ehrenfelser, Gewurztraminer, Auxerrois, Riesling and Semillon. Reds include Merlot, Pinot Noir, Cabernet-Merlot and Chancellor. Late harvest wines are also made.

# First Estate Cellars

5031 Cousins Road off Trepanier Bench Road
Peachland, BC V0X 1X0
(250) 767-9526, FAX (250) 767-9528
**Email:** olitech@bc.sympatico.ca

**Proprietors:** Gary & Nancy Strachan
**Winemaker:** Gary Strachan
**First Year:** 1989

**Wine Shop Hours:** 10 AM to 4 PM, daily

Longtime Okanagan winemaker and consultant Gary Strachan acquired A & H

*Continued on next page.*

Vineyards winery and opened it as First Estate Cellars in 1998. Two vineyard sites at the property will provide fruit for the winery's planned production. Visitors can find First Estate up the hill from Hainle Vineyards on Cousins Road off Trepanier Bench Road.

**The Wines**

The first releases were Pinot Auxerrois, Dry Gewurztraminer and Marchel Foch.

# Gray Monk Estate Winery

1055 Camp Road
Okanagan Centre, BC
V4V 2H4
(250) 766-3168
FAX (250) 766-3390
Toll free: (800) 663-4205
**Email:** graymonk@okanagan.net
**Web:** www.graymonk.com

**Proprietors:** Heiss Family
**Winemaker:** George Heiss, Jr.
**First Year:** 1982

**Wine Shop Hours:** 10 AM to 5 PM, daily, May through Oct.; 11 AM to 5 PM, Monday through Saturday, Nov. through April.

George and Trudy Heiss came to the Okanagan from Edmonton in 1972 and began planting local hybrid grapes in their vineyard. An encounter with Dr. Helmut Becker, who did research and grape growing trials for the BC wine industry, pointed the way to other varieties which were planted in the Heiss Vineyard. Taking their winery name for the loose Austrian translation of Pinot Gris, Gray Monk winery was opened in 1982. The Heiss family is regarded throughout the region as among the most hospitable, and the friendly welcome extends to visitors at the Gray Monk wine shop. The view Wine Deck offers light lunches and wines by the glass. Drive north from Kelowna on Hwy. 97 and turn left in Winfield on Okanagan Centre Road. Follow the signs to the winery.

**The Wines**

Popular wines from Gray Monk include Gewurztraminer, Pinot Gris, Pinot Noir, Gamay Noir and Merlot. Their white blend named Latitude Fifty is always a favorite.

*Sandra and Tilman Hainle*

# Hainle Vineyards Estate Winery

5355 Trapanier Bench Rd.
P.O. Box 650
Peachland, BC V0H 1X0
(250) 767-2525
FAX (250) 767-2543
Toll free: (800) 767-3109
**Web:** www.hainle.com
**Email:** sandra@hainle.com, tilman @hainle.com

**Proprietors:** Sandra & Tilman Hainle
**Winemaker:** Tilman Hainle
**First Year:** 1988
**Winery Capacity:** 10,000 gallons

**Wine Shop Hours:** 10 AM to 5 PM, Tuesday through Sunday, May through October
1 PM to 5 PM, Thursday through Sunday, November through April

Perched on the hillside above Peachland with a view of the lake through the pines, Hainle Vineyards is the life's work of two thoughtful souls who are clear about what they believe and why. For Tilman Hainle this is reflected in the wines he makes. For Sandra Hainle the muse is food and marketing. Tilman crafts dry wines that are full of flavor and are made from organically grown grapes, while Sandra runs the Amphora Bistro at the winery and produces a delightful newsletter each quarter. The winery's view deck is a grand place to enjoy lunch from the Bistro or relax with a glass of wine. New space at the winery is being readied as a classroom or area for catered events. By the way, the winery (and family) name rhymes with "finely."

**The Wines**

Tilman Hainle's Riesling, Traminer, Pinot Blanc and Ehrenfelser are dry wines that are superb accompaniments to food. They have bracing acidity and a longevity born of Tilman's winemaking style featuring bold aromas and flavors.

Red wines of Pinot Noir and Lemberger are ripe and fruity with notes of smoke (Pinot) or earthy spice (Lemberger).

## House of Rose Vineyards

2270 Garner Road, RR #5
Kelowna, BC V1X 4K4
(250) 765-0802
FAX (250) 765-7762

**Proprietor/Winemaker:**
Vern Rose
**First Year:** 1992
**Winery Capacity:** 10,000 gallons

**Wine Shop Hours:** 10 AM to 5 PM, daily

Retired Alberta schoolteacher Vern Rose and his son Russell operate this charming winery on the eastern outskirts of Kelowna. Self-taught at winemaking and viticulture, the Rose family produces "award-winning wines at affordable prices." Follow Hwy. 33 southeast from Kelowna to Garner Road, turn right and head about 1.5 miles to the House of Rose on your right.

**The Wines**

Chardonnay, Verdelet, Riesling, Perl of Zaba, Auxerrois, Semillon, Marechal Foch and Merlot are produced.

## Larch Hills Winery Ltd.

110 Timms Road
Salmon Arm, BC V1E 2P8
(250) 832-0155
FAX (250) 832-9419
**Email:** LHwinery@shuswap.net
**Web:** www.shuswap.net/mall/Larch Hills Winery

**Proprietors/Winemakers:** Nevrkla Family
**First Year:** 1996

**Wine Shop Hours:** Noon to 5 PM, daily, May through October. Closed Nov. - April

Hans and Hazel Nevrkla operate the Okanagan's northernmost winery at Salmon Arm in the Shuswap Lake area. The drive north from Kelowna is scenic and if you have the time for this trip you can also visit Bella Vista Winery on your way. Ortega and a blend called Northern Lights are current releases.

## Mission Hill Winery

1730 Mission Road
Westbank, BC V4T 2E4
(250) 768-7611
FAX (250) 768-2044
**Email:** brady@markanthony.com

**Owner:** Anthony von Mandl
**Winemaker:** John Simes

**Wine Shop Hours:** 9 AM to 5 PM, daily

Buying a rundown winery in 1981, Anthony von Mandl had a vision for the Okanagan wine country that has proved remarkably accurate. Though he could scarcely have predicted the events that have led to the changes, his predictions about many quality wineries and a burgeoning hospitality industry came true. Hiring New Zealand winemaker John Simes in the early 1990s, von Mandl has seen the wines of Mission Hill improve and go on to win many prestigious awards. A newly completed wine shop and visitor center beckon the wine lover to stop and taste from the wide range of wines. Follow signs from Hwy. 97 onto Boucherie Rd.

**The Wines**

Grand Reserve bottlings include Chardonnay, Pinot Gris, Pinot Noir Riesling, Merlot and Vidal Icewine. The Private Reserve line offers Cab-Merlot, Cabernet Sauvignon, Chardonnay, Chenin Blanc, Merlot, Marechal Foch, Pinot Blanc, Sauvignon Blanc, Chardonnay-Semillon and proprietary blends under the 49 North label. Inexpensive Vintner's Select wines are offered in several varietals and blends.

## Pinot Reach Cellars

1670 Dehart Road
Kelowna, BC V1W 4N6
(250) 764-0078
FAX (250) 764-0771
**Email:** pinot@direct.ca

**Proprietor:** Susan M. Dulik
**Winemaker:** Eric von Krosigk
**First Year:** 1997

**Wine Shop Hours:** Noon to 6 PM, Tuesday through Sunday. Closed Nov. through March

One of the Okanagan's newest wineries, Pinot Reach is the project of owner Susan Dulik and her winemaker Eric von Krosigk. While the winery is new, the vineyard has been supplying grapes to area wineries for many years. Half of the grapes from the winery's 35-acre vineyard were used for Pinot Reach's 1997 production with the other half being sold. Plans are to increase the percentage vinted by the estate. Find the winery by traveling south of downtown Kelowna on Pandosy (to Lakeshore) and turn left on Dehart Road at the Okanagan Mission Community Hall. Follow Dehart to the end, the winery drive leads through the abundant vineyards.

### The Wines

A new sparkling wine is the exciting news at Pinot Reach, but a full line of table wines are also available. Try Bacchus, Riesling, Optima, Pinot Blanc, Pinot Noir, Pinot Blush and Chardonnay.

## Quails' Gate Estate Winery

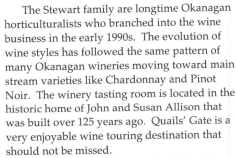

3303 Boucherie Road
Kelowna, BC
V1Z 2H3
(250) 769-4451
FAX (250) 769-3451
**Web:** www.quailsgate.com

**Proprietors:** Stewart Family
**Winemakers:** Jeff Martin
**First Year:** 1990

**Wine Shop Hours:** 10 AM to 5 PM, daily

The Stewart family are longtime Okanagan horticulturalists who branched into the wine business in the early 1990s. The evolution of wine styles has followed the same pattern of many Okanagan wineries moving toward main stream varieties like Chardonnay and Pinot Noir. The winery tasting room is located in the historic home of John and Susan Allison that was built over 125 years ago. Quails' Gate is a very enjoyable wine touring destination that should not be missed.

Visitors to the winery can find it by taking the Boucherie Road exit from Hwy. 97 near Westbank and following south to the winery on your left.

### The Wines

Quails' Gate produces a complete line of varietals and proprietary blends. Proprietor's Selections include Chasselas, Gewurztraminer, and Riesling, as well as a blends called Covey Noir (red) and Harvest White. Limited Release varietals include Cabernet Sauvignon, Chardonnay, Chenin Blanc, Dry Riesling, Merlot, Old Vines Foch and Pinot Noir. Family Reserve Pinot Noir and Chardonnay round out the table wine selection with a late harvest Optima and Riesling Icewine bringing up the sweeter side.

## The Wines

Winemaker Cherie Mirko produces a full line of flavorful varietals and blends for the Gebert's winery. White wines include Riesling, Pinot Blanc, Bacchus, Chardonnay, Chasselas and Okanagan Summer blend. Reds include Marechal Foch, Gamay Noir, Merlot, Pinot Meunier and Northern Summer blend. Icewines of Riesling and Pinot Blanc are also made.

## St. Hubertus Estate Winery

5205 Lakeshore Road
Kelowna, BC V1W 4J1
(250) 764-7888
FAX (250) 274-0499
Toll free: (800) 989-9463
**Email:**
St.Hubertus@awinc.com
**Web:** www.sthubertus.com

**Proprietors:** Leo & Andy Gebert
**Winemaker:** Cherie Mirko
**First Year:** 1992
**Winery Capacity:** 40,000 gallons

**Wine Shop Hours:** 10 AM to 5:30 PM, daily, May through October. Noon to 5 PM, Tuesday through Saturday, November through April.

Swiss emigrants Leo and Andy Gebert are the owners of flourishing vineyards that have been used for grape production as far back as the 1940s. The brothers began their winery in the 1990s making Swiss-style wines from some of the grapes they had been selling to other wineries. Today, the lighter Swiss-style (non-oak aged) wines are produced under the St. Hubertus label while barrel-fermented and barrel-aged wines are sold under the Oak Bay Vineyards brand.

The winery property features a number of buildings including an artist's studio, homes of the proprietors, and the delightful wine shop that is pictured above. The St. Hubertus name comes from the family's home in Switzerland and is also the Swiss patron saint of huntsmen.

## Slamka Cellars

2815 Ourtoland Road,
Lakeview Heights
Kelowna, BC V1Z 2H5
(250) 769-0404
FAX (250) 763-8168

**Proprietor/Winemaker:**
Peter Slamka
**First Year:** 1996

**Wine Shop Hours:** Noon to 5 PM, daily

Peter Slamka's small winery operation is dwarfed by nearby Mission Hill and Quails' Gate wineries but his wines continue to please both consumers and wine judges. Visitors to the wine shop should be sure to check out the proprietor's collection of cork pullers. The winery is reached by following Boucherie Road to Ogden Road then up the hill to Ourtoland Road and right to the winery.

**The Wines**

Slamka Cellars produces the only Auxerrois Icewine in BC but don't rush to the sweet without tasting Peter's dry Auxerrois, Riesling and Pinot Noir. New plantings of Merlot and Lemberger will bear fruit soon.

## Summerhill Estate Winery

4870 Chute Lake Road
Kelowna, BC V1W 4M3
(250) 764-8000
FAX (250) 764-2598
Toll free: (800) 667-3538
**Email:** summerhill@summerhill.bc.ca
**Web:** www.summerhill.bc.ca

**Proprietor:** Stephen R. Cipes
**Winemaker:** Alan C. Marks, Phd.
**First Year:** 1987

**Wine Shop Hours:** 10 AM to 6 PM, daily

Remarkable! Incredible! Unbelievable! These are words one uses to describe the wine country theme park that is Summerhill Winery during the busy tourist season. New York native Stephen Cipes came to the Okanagan to find a parallel career that was less intense than his New York City real estate business. After purchasing a large estate with a spectacular home, he learned to farm the 38 acres of vines on the property. Consultations in the early 1990s with Schramsberg winery owner Jack Davies convinced both men that quality sparkling wine could be made in B.C. Some experimental cuvees were laid down but Davies eventually backed away from the expensive joint venture.

Undaunted, Stephen Cipes worked with local winemaker Eric von Krosigk to develop some of the areas first commercial sparkling wines. Awards for Summerhill's sparkling and still wines are numerous and affirm the founder's insight into the quality of wine grapes grown in the area.

But back to the theme park! Stephen Cipes believes in a strong marketing program and he has created a fantastic complex of attractions that range from culinary to enological to cultural. The winery offers wine tasting of sparkling wines and still wines in a gaily decorated tasting room with the Smokehouse Veranda Restaurant at one end. Champagne tours of the cellars leave the giant sparkling wine sculpture each afternoon on the hour. A reconstructed native village and "working" log cabin and pioneer farm are a short walk from the parking lot. All this and the wines are aged in specially constructed *Pyramids* with the belief that this "pyramid power" will improve the quality of Summerhill's bottlings. What can you say but "O.K. let's taste the wines and see if it really makes a difference!"

*Stephen Cipes and his winemaker Alan Marks.*

### The Wines

Dr. Alan Marks is Stephen Cipes winemaker today and he is doing a remarkable job crafting wines from many varietals. Wines from Ehrenfelser, Pinot Blanc, Chardonnay, Gewurztraminer and Pinot Noir are true to type and very flavorful. The sparkling cuvees are exceptional, and as the flagship for the Summerhill estate they carry the banner well. Medal-winning icewines and late harvest selections are also popular. Personally, our group thinks the pyramid has influence over these bottlings. Almost every Northwest winemaker believes in the power of magic!

## Vancouver

Since there is virtually no wine touring in the immediate Vancouver area, we leave the fine dining and lodging selections to the readers experience and discretion.

## Victoria/Vancouver Island

Some selections on the island for the intrepid wine tourist and those who live a bit higher.

### Cherry Point Vineyards B & B

840 Cherry Point Rd., Cobble Hill - (250) 743-1272, Enjoy a stay not only in the wine country but actually at the winery.

### Dreamweaver B & B

1682 Botwood Lane, Cowichan Bay - (250) 748-7688, A newer Victorian style home overlooking Cowichan Bay.

### Rainbows End B & B

1745 Ordano St., Cowichan Bay - (250) 746-8320, Gray and Sheila Thomson welcome you to their B & B in the center of the region's activities. Take your breakfast by the pool and enjoy birdwatching in the greenbelt.

### North Haven B & B

1747 Herd Road, Duncan - (250) 746-4783, One of the island's most romantic getaways in a restored 1914 manor house. Full breakfast, elegant bedrooms, expansive garden.

### Bluenose Steak & Seafood

1765 Cowichan Bay Road, Cowichan Bay - (250) 748-2841, Informal dining with a water view.

### Sooke Harbour House

Whiffen Spit Road, Sooke - (250) 642-3421, Sinclair Phillip is world famous for the remarkable preparations using local seafood and produce grown on the property. A luxury property and highly rated.

## The Okanagan

This British Columbia vacationland is a favorite for Nordic skiers in the winter and water skiers and golfers in the summer. Dozens of quality lodgings throw open their doors in the spring and restaurants bring out their patio tables. Here are some favorites of the authors in Osoyoos, Oliver, Penticton and Kelowna areas, but there are many more.

## Osoyoos/Oliver

### Jacques Grill

Hwy. 97 in Oliver - (250) 498-4418 Chef Jacques Guerin has been a friend of the wine industry for many years and offers a superb continental menu.

### Mount Kobau Motor Inn

Hwy. 97 at Hwy. 3 in Osoyoos - (800) 977-8711 Clean and comfortable motel with pool, , etc. Located centrally to South Okanagan activities.

## Penticton Area

### The Country Squire

Naramata Village - (250) 496-5416 This regionally famous dinner house serves from 6 PM, Thursday - Sunday. The price fixed menu (select your entree when making reservations) features local specialties with local wines available from the cellar.

### The Cellar Door

at Sumac Ridge Winery, Summerland - (250) 494-3316 - Enjoy superb cuisine at lunch or dinner with a great selection of wines. Mark Taylor's menu offers something for everyone. Great appetizers!

### Theos

687 Main St., Penticton - (250) 492-4019 If you brought your appetite for Greek cooking to the Okanagan, stop at Theos for an evening of all your favorites. Opa!

### Heritage House B & B

11919 Jubilee Road, Summerland - (250) 494-0039, Marsha Clark will make you feel like you've come home again. Cozy rooms, a clawfoot tub, beautiful veranda. Personalized breakfast service by your talented hostess.

*Continued next page.*

## Best Western Inn at Penticton

3180 Skaha Lake Road - (800) 668-6746
Not far from Penticton's beautiful beaches and
parks on Skaha Lake, this newer hotel features
all the amenities you could want.

## Sage Pine B & B

153 Cedar Ave., Kaleden - (250) 497-6383.
Just 15 miles south of Penticton. Spectacular
views of Skaha Lake, outdoor pool.

## Sandy Beach Lodge and Resort

Box 8, Naramata - (250) 496-5765.
This rustic-but-elegant resort features B & B
rooms in the log lodge, two-bedroom cabins for
rent, 400 feet of sandy beach on Lake Okanagan
with rowboats and canoes, pool, tennis . . . and
8 wineries nearby to tour along with some of
the Okanagan's finest dining.

## Peachland on the Lake B & B

3904 Beach Ave., Peachland - (250) 767-3253
A guest suite available in a lakeside location
with kitchen, view and more!

## Okanagan Boat Charters

291 Front St., Penticton - (800) 524-2212
Enjoy part of your wine vacation on the lake!
This operator charters houseboats, sailboats,
and runabouts for fun in the sun on Lake
Okanagan. See www.obc.bc.ca

# Kelowna

## De Montreuil

368 Bernard Ave., Kelowna - (250) 860-5508
Grant de Montreuil cooks fresh regional foods
in his restaurant which is a favorite of many
Okanagan-area vintners. Dinner nightly,
lunch Monday-Friday only.

## Amphora Bistro

Hainle Vineyards, Peachland - (250) 767-2525
Superb cuisine using local ingredients draws
lunch crowds to Sandra Hainle's bistro with
Chef David Forestell adding new dishes to
expand the concept of BC wine country dining.

## Veranda Restaurant

at Summerhill Winery - (250) 764-8000
Enjoy bistro-style food or special appetizers
designed to accompany Stephen Cipes'
sparkling wines. Great view.

## Pandosy Inn

3327 Lakeshore Road Kelowna - (250) 762-5858
Out toward the four lakeside wineries, across
from a beautiful beach park, pool, kitchens,
guest BBQs, etc.

## Hotel Eldorado

500 Cook Rd, Kelowna - (250) 763-7500
This rebuilt mansion along the lake (very near
to area wineries) is the fanciest place in town
and comes complete with a gourmet restaurant
and lakeside boardwalk.

## The Grand Okanagan Lakefront Resort

1310 Water Street, Kelowna - (800) 465-4651
A four-diamond property located on the lake
in downtown Kelowna. Fine dining, elegant
accommodations. Ask about the wine and
cooking gourmet packages.

# APPENDIX

## Wine Touring

## Other Wine Related Information

## Northwest Microbrews

# NORTHWEST REGIONAL WINE EVENTS

The Northwest wine country is well known for hospitality and many wineries and winery groups host elaborate touring events throughout the year. Regional chambers of commerce and wine appreciation societies also stage annual events with wine judgings, walk-around tastings and gourmet meals. Please call the suggested phone numbers to inquire about the exact dates for events listed.

## FEBRUARY
### Newport Oregon Seafood and Wine Festival
This annual event has been popular for over 20 years and includes a wine judging, tasting and seafood for sale to enjoy with the wines. 1-800-COAST44

### Umpqua Greatest of the Grape Festival
A regional wine tasting and competition in Roseburg, Oregon. (541) 672-2648

## MARCH
### McMinnville Food & Wine Classic
A local festival featuring wine tasting and gourmet foods. (503) 472-4033

## APRIL
### Hood River Blossom Festival
Celebrating the bloomin' fruit trees and the bountiful harvest that they bear. Local wineries offer special hospitality at this time.

### Yakima Valley Barrel Tasting Weekend
The last weekend in April, the 20+ wineries in Washington's Yakima Valley invite the public into the cellar to sample upcoming releases from the barrel. A grand time for all and always well attended. (800) 258-7270

## MAY
### Okanagan Spring Wine Festival
First Weekend in May (celebrated around the Canadian holiday for Victoria Day). The wineries of the Okanagan get together and welcome thousands of wine lovers for their springtime extravaganza. Special events, dinners, tastings and much more. Call for a brochure at (250) 861-6654.

### Walla Walla Hot Air Balloon Stampede and Winery Open House
One of the premier hot air balloon events in the nation and a great excuse to visit your friends at Woodward Canyon, Waterbrook, Canoe Ridge Vineyard and other area wineries. (509) 525-0850

### Yamhill County Match Made in Heaven
Memorial Day Weekend. The Yamhill County wineries in Oregon offer wine tasting paired with special foods prepared by local restaurants. A great chance to visit wineries that are not normally open to the public. Be prepared for a nominal tasting fee at many wineries.

### Salem Area Wineries Tastevin Tour
Salem and Eola Hills wineries join up for this Memorial Day Weekend open house featuring wine tasting, food and entertainment at some locations.

## JULY
### International Pinot Noir Celebration
Takes place on the last weekend in July at Linfield College in McMinnville, Oregon. Lots of great Pinot Noirs from around the world and a chance to rub elbows with winemakers from France, California and Oregon! (503) 472-8964.

## NORTHWEST REGIONAL WINE EVENTS

### Enological Society Seattle Chapter Northwest Wine & Food Festival

The last weekend in July sees this 25-year-old event take place at North Seattle Community College. Regional wine judging (the oldest and most prestigious in the area), seminar, walk-around tasting and four-course dinner. www.enosoc.org.

## AUGUST
### Prosser Wine & Food Fair

Summer fun in the heat of Washington's wine country. Always a great opportunity to meet local winemakers and sample Yakima Valley cuisine.

### The Herbfarm Northwest Wine Festival

In Fall City, east of Redmond, Washington, The Herbfarm creates a delightful event for wine tasting and food sampling during the dog days of August. This festival attracts many of the top Northwest wineries that do not attend other events. (800) 866-4372. www.theherbfarm.com.

## SEPTEMBER
### Tri-Cities Catch the Crush Celebration

Washington's Tri-Cities area wineries invite you to come out and see the action during the grape harvest. (509) 588-6716.

## OCTOBER

Okanagan Fall Wine Festival

British Columbia's Okanagan wineries present their almost-20-year-old wine festival with tastings, dinners, wine judging and more. (250) 861-6654.

## NOVEMBER
### Tri-Cities Northwest Wine Festival

Always a sellout, get your tickets early! This annual wine judging, tasting and dinner is very popular. (509) 375-3399.

### Thanksgiving in the Wine Country

In Oregon, almost every wine region rolls out the red carpet for the Thanksgiving weekend (Fri., Sat., Sun.) including special foods, entertainment and new wine releases. Check with your favorite area wineries for details.

In Washington, the Yakima Valley wineries have been offering special Thanksgiving weekend hospitality for several years. (800) 258-7270. The Woodinville area vintners have recently begun a similar seasonal promotion.

### Winery Events

Many Northwest wineries produce monthly events that highlight wine and food, entertainment and education. Some of the most notable ones should be contacted for a schedule of events:

**Chateau Ste. Michelle** - (425) 488-1133
Seattle area - concerts and dinners
**Columbia Winery** - (425) 488-2776
Seattle area - special events, dinner train
**Preston Premium Wines** - (509) 545-1990
Great monthly events in the Tri-Cities
**Silver Lake Cellars** - (425) 486-1900
Monthly special events, live music
**Washington Hills Cellars** - (509) 839-9463
Yakima Valley monthly events
**Worden Winery** - (509) 455-7835
Monthly events in Spokane

**Kramer Vineyards** - (503) 662-4545
Gaston area, Weird Food Fest, many others
**Sokol Blosser Winery** - (800) 582-6668
Yamhill County - Concerts, Events
**Willamette Valley Vnyds.** - (800) 344-9463
Salem area - Concerts, events, dinners

**Ste. Chapelle Vineyards** - (208) 459-7222
(Near Boise - summer concert series)

# NORTHWEST WINE VINTAGES

Residents of the Pacific Northwest enjoy the same weather as wine grapes; Moderate temperatures in the winter, not too hot during the summer. An early spring is always nice, and a summer that lingers into October is appreciated by nearly everyone.

Unfortunately for residents and wine grapes, Mother Nature often deals from the bottom of the deck and gives no warning of weather patterns to come. Frigid winters can freeze vines in Eastern Washington to the ground, and early rains in August and September can delay ripening of Oregon grapes and lead to problems with rot before harvest.

The track record of the most venerable Northwest wineries is 35 years at best, so the learning curve has been steep and slippery for winemakers and grape growers alike. Along with vintage variation one has to consider changes in grape growing technique and changes in winemaking practice. The phrase "hindsight is always 20/20" seems to be appropriate in discussing NW vintages.

## 1997

A fairly normal harvest for both Washington and Oregon with rain falling in some Oregon vineyards and Washington enjoying a nice recovery year from the freeze of 1996. Whites have been delicious from both states and from Idaho as well. Wines tasted in BC indicated that 1997 was a very good year in the Okanagan.

## 1996

Severe freeze damage to Washington grape vines occurred in January and February, reducing the crop by as much as 50%. The fruit that was harvested was excellent - white wines were good and reds

show promise as they are released. Oregon wasn't harmed by freezing and a normal size crop was harvested. Releases of 1996 Pinot Noirs have been judged to be better than the 1995s, not as good as the 1994s.

## 1995

Slow ripening of grapes was the result of a rainy, cool summer. A late hit of warm weather once again saved the bacon of many growers, but the quality of the fruit varied tremendously. As is often the case, certain sites fared well and others did not. Selection of wines for cellaring depends on the producer, not the vintage. A large harvest filled the pipeline with mostly good wine.

## 1994

A warm and ripe vintage that brought Oregon Pinot Noir into the national spotlight once again. Mouthfilling, flavorful wines, packed with fruit and framed with French oak. Washington reds were equally monstrous and the Chards from both states were full bodied and powerful. Many wines sold out by now.

## 1993

A late spring and cool summer made grape growers twitch until a warm, dry fall ripened the grapes. The long hang time helped produce complex, silky reds with finesse and balance. Ageworthy for those with the foresight to lay them away.

## 1992

An early spring and a scorching summer produced a record crop, both in size and early harvest date. Some ungainly reds were made with gnarly tannins, and many whites were simply too ripe for any hope of elegance. Again, a few select sites found balance and made great wines.

# NORTHWEST WINE VINTAGES

## 1991

With a Washington crop half the size of 1992, one might think that some lean, ageable wines were made. A tough harvest season denied winemakers a fair chance and rain in Oregon resulted in mostly average wines. Those who harvested selectively and wisely put some nice white wines into the bottle. Lighter reds have now matured, and the fruit in heavier versions may never outlast the dense tannins.

## 1990

A cool, wet spring reduced the crop size in most Northwest vineyards. A warmer than average summer produced forward red wines that show balance and finesse, if not longevity. Washington whites lost some crisp acidity due to heat during the late summer. If you have 1990s, drink now.

## 1989

A moderate growing season in both Washington and Oregon produced excellent wines, balanced between elegance and power with ripe flavors and moderate tannins. In the mid-1990s these wines were at their prime and some still are. Many Oregon winemakers were in the midst of evaluating different fermentation techniques resulting in a wide variation of Pinot Noir wine styles and quality.

## 1988

A mild winter and average harvest season produced nice wines that were enjoyed until 1994. Further aging seems counterproductive to cellar space utilization.

## 1987

Washington's warm vintage year produced ripe and flavorful Cabernets and Merlots with ample tannins. Some may still have a will to live. Oregon Pinot Noirs initially showed great promise, but the wines seem to have aged prematurely. If they're in your cellar, you waited too long.

### Older Northwest Vintages

Having participated in expansive tastings of well-aged Northwest red wines, it is our opinion that producing Cabernets, Merlots or Pinots that will stand the test of time to 15 or more years is pure luck. When pulling the bags off bottles in some of these "vintage of the decade" expositions, the best wines are most often revealed to be dark horses that no one could have predicted.

Our advice is to keep drinking them within a decade, open the older wines when there is a celebration at hand to raise your spirits anyway, and have a spare bottle of a more recent vintage handy in case you need to reassure your faith in Northwest wine.

## NORTHWEST WINE TRAVEL DISTANCE CHART

Wine touring around the Northwest can involve a fair amount of driving time. While reading flowery and romantic descriptions of wineries, restaurants and bed-and-breakfasts, one often forgets the four or five hours behind the wheel to achieve these far-off delights. Below is a chart of common wine country destinations for all three Northwest states and British Columbia's Okanagan wine center of Penticton. Hopefully this information will help you plan your itinerary with greater accuracy. All distances listed are in U.S. statute miles.

One note of caution, the mileage calculations have been based on the shortest possible route given the best, mid-summer driving conditions. If you are traveling to Yakima, Penticton or other east-of-the-Cascades locations from a western starting point, then keep a weather eye out for pass conditions. Snoqualmie Pass (I-90) is kept open all year except for rare extreme conditions that can close the road for hours at a time. Chains are required infrequently, but studded tires (approved traction devices) are often mandatory during winter travel.

| | Seattle | Portland | Yakima | McMinnville | Tri-Cities | Salem | Spokane | Eugene | Walla Walla | Roseburg | Hood River | Sequim | Boise | Penticton, B.C. |
|---|---|---|---|---|---|---|---|---|---|---|---|---|---|---|
| Seattle | 0 | 175 | 140 | 225 | 222 | 223 | 277 | 289 | 281 | 362 | 239 | 77 | 524 | 301 |
| Portland | 175 | 0 | 228 | 50 | 220 | 48 | 372 | 114 | 239 | 187 | 64 | 228 | 431 | 476 |
| Yakima | 140 | 228 | 0 | 238 | 82 | 234 | 206 | 300 | 141 | 375 | 122 | 217 | 384 | 260 |
| McMinnville | 225 | 50 | 238 | 0 | 270 | 20 | 422 | 86 | 289 | 159 | 114 | 165 | 442 | 526 |
| Tri-Cities | 222 | 220 | 82 | 270 | 0 | 268 | 152 | 334 | 59 | 407 | 156 | 299 | 302 | 347 |
| Salem | 223 | 48 | 234 | 20 | 268 | 0 | 420 | 66 | 287 | 139 | 112 | 276 | 422 | 524 |
| Spokane | 277 | 372 | 206 | 422 | 152 | 420 | 0 | 486 | 160 | 559 | 308 | 354 | 379 | 195 |
| Eugene | 289 | 114 | 300 | 86 | 334 | 66 | 486 | 0 | 353 | 73 | 178 | 342 | 433 | 590 |
| Walla Walla | 281 | 239 | 141 | 289 | 59 | 287 | 160 | 353 | 0 | 426 | 175 | 358 | 252 | 355 |
| Roseburg | 362 | 187 | 375 | 159 | 407 | 139 | 559 | 73 | 426 | 0 | 251 | 415 | 506 | 663 |
| Hood River | 239 | 64 | 122 | 114 | 156 | 112 | 308 | 178 | 175 | 251 | 0 | 292 | 367 | 382 |
| Sequim | 77 | 228 | 217 | 165 | 299 | 276 | 354 | 342 | 358 | 415 | 292 | 0 | 601 | 378 |
| Boise | 524 | 431 | 384 | 442 | 302 | 422 | 379 | 433 | 252 | 406 | 367 | 601 | 0 | 574 |
| Penticton, B.C. | 301 | 476 | 260 | 526 | 347 | 524 | 195 | 590 | 355 | 663 | 382 | 378 | 574 | 0 |

# HOW TO OPEN A BOTTLE OF WINE

Using the traditional waiter's corkscrew is not as difficult as it may seem. A few twists of the wrist and this most comfortable and portable opener is at your command. The key to a successful pull is to get the screw centered in the cork. Missing your aim will result in the screw veering off to the side and coming out the side of the cork.

Use the knife attached to the side of the waiter's corkscrew to score around the capsule (also called a foil, because it is often made of metal foil). Score at the first ridge of the bottle neck, about 1/8" from the top. Remove the capsule top.

Place the corkscrew point-down into the center of the cork. Note that the screw should not be exactly parallel with the neck of the bottle as you begin, but the point should be right in the center of the cork. Now, engage the screw with a twist clockwise while bringing the screw into a vertical position. Continue twisting the screw into the cork until the last turn disappears.

Bring the lever (also called the boot) into position atop the neck of the bottle and apply upward pressure on the opposite end of the handle. The cork should move up and out of the bottle. In the case of an extra-long cork, be careful not to break it by pulling too far. For these cases, pull the cork halfway out then turn the corkscrew in another full turn and pull again.

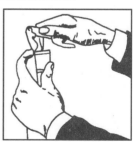

Wipe the neck of the bottle with a napkin (if necessary) and pour the wine. Bits of tartaric acid crystals may be down inside the neck of the bottle and can be removed with the napkin also. Glasses should be filled no more than half full to allow room for swirling and smelling the wine. For a dripless pour, twist the bottle slightly as you raise it after pouring. The drip then runs around the neck of the bottle instead of falling off onto the table.

## A WINE TASTING LEXICON

It is often useful when tasting wines to have a list of descriptors that help identify particular aromas or flavors. The following list describes common aromas in sequence from general (i.e. fruity) to specific (i.e. citrus) to individual (i.e. grapefruit). It is good to practice wine tasting with friends to help build up your aroma-memory of particular wines or wine styles.

### FRUITY

| CITRUS | BERRY | TREE FRUIT | TROPICAL FRUIT | DRIED FRUIT |
|---|---|---|---|---|
| Grapefruit | Blackberry | Apple | Banana | Berry Jam |
| Lemon | Black cherry | Apricot | Melon | Raisin |
| Lime | Black Currant (cassis) | Peach | Pineapple | Prune |
| | Cherry | Pear | | Fig |
| | Raspberry | | | |
| | Strawberry | | | |

### VEGETATIVE

| FRESH | CANNED-COOKED | DRIED |
|---|---|---|
| Bell Pepper | Artichoke | Hay-Straw |
| Cut Green Grass | Asparagus | Tea |
| Eucalyptus | Black Olive | Tobacco |
| Mint | Green Olive | |
| Stemmy | Green Beans | |

### SPICY
Anise, Black Pepper, Cloves, Licorice

### FLORAL
Geranium, Orange Blossomo, Rose, Violet

### NUTTY
Almond, Hazelnut, Walnut

### CARAMELIZED
Butter, Butterscotch, Chocolate, Molasses, Soy Sauce, Toasted Hazelnut

### WOODY
Burnt Toast, Cedar, Charred Wood, Coffee, Oak, Smoky, Vanilla

### EARTHY
Dusty, Forest Floor, Moldy Cork, Mushroom, Musty (Mildew)

### CHEMICAL

| PETROLEUM | SULFUR | PUNGENT | PAPERY | OTHER |
|---|---|---|---|---|
| Diesel | Burnt Match | Acetic Acid (Vinegar) | Wet Cardboard | Fishy |
| Kerosene | Garlic | | | Soapy |
| Plastic | Rubbery | | | |
| Tar | Skunk Cabbage | | | |
| | Wet Dog, Wet Wool | | | |

### MICROBIOLOGICAL
Horsey, Sauerkraut, Sweaty, Yeasty

## WINE PUBLICATIONS AND RATINGS GUIDES

### Northwest Palate Magazine

P.O. Box 10860, Portland, OR 97296-0860, (503) 224-6039, nwpalate@teleport.com

Northwest Palate is a full-color, travel and leisure guide to the Northwest featuring wine ratings for all Northwest states as well as other regions. Good restaurant reviews, food articles, regional happenings.

### Oregon Wine (Newspaper)

644 SE 20th, Portland, OR 97214, (503) 232-7607, orwinepress@aol.com

Features articles on wineries, restaurants, lodgings and Oregon wine country happenings. A handy reference for wine tourists. Free distribution in wineries, by mail: $10 to U.S.A.

### British Columbia Wine Trails

P.O. Box 1319 Summerland, BC V0H1Z0 (250) 494-7733, bcwinetrails@img.net

Full color quarterly tabloid with up-to-date info. on the BC wine country. Tasting notes and good touring information.

### Winepress Northwest

P.O. Box 2608, Tri-Cities, WA 99302-2608 (509) 582-1561, www.winepressnw.com

Some writers at the Tri-Cities Herald and their friends have launched this quarterly wine country magazine with a focus similar to NW Palate but sticking more to the wine side. Currently, their Web site offers a variety of more detailed information.

### The Wine Advocate

P.O. Box 311 , Monkton MD 21111

Robert M. Parker's wine review magazine that wields mighty power in the sales of wines discussed in its pages.

### The Wine Spectator

(800) 752-7799 (subscriptions), (415) 673-2040 (editorial), www.winespectator.com

The glossy, slick wine magazine with hundreds of wine reviews and food/travel features. The Web site is incredibly vast with a search engine for past features, wine reviews and more.

## NORTHWEST REGIONAL WINE INFORMATION ON THE WEB

### Washington Wine Commission

www.washingtonwine.org - A comprehensive site featuring each Washington winery, background and events.

### Oregon Wine Advisory Board

www.mind.net/wine - Listings of Oregon wineries by region, mostly just addresses and phone numbers. Background information and events are also presented.

### Idaho Wines

idahowine.com - A fledgling site with many parts still under construction. Some useful information presented.

### British Columbia Wine Cellar

www.bcwine.com - The most useful site about the wine country of B.C. Informative articles and listings.

### Northwest Gourmet Guides

www.northwest-gourmet.com - Our own site featuring wines, recipes, accommodations and more.

### Mike L's Washington Wine Guide

vintners.net/wawine - The non-profit passion of Mike Lempriere. Comprehensive and non-judgemental, this site is aimed at giving you good information. Labels, photos, history, and much more.

### Wines Northwest

www.winesnw.com - The potential for Susan O'Hara's Northwest wine site is great but the profit motive limits detailed listings to those who sign up for a page.

### Enological Society of the Pacific NW

www.enosoc.org - The Web site of the Seattle Chapter details upcoming events, society news, how to join.

## WINE & FOOD RELATED WEB SITES

### Robin Garr's Wine Lovers Page

**www.wine-lovers-page.com** - Lots of good information and links to other wine sites. Food and wine, wine education, pronounciation guides, more.

### Wine, Beers and Spirits on the Net

**www.ryerson.ca/~dtudor/wine.htm** - Easily the most handy links site on wine and related topics. Wineries around the world (email your request to visit Chateau d'Yquem!), newsgroups, academics. Quit your job, forsake your family and spend several weeks surfing the world of wine.

### UC Davis Official Web Server

**wineserver.ucdavis.edu** - Tune in to the happenings at America's premier school of viticulture and enology. More academia than you could ever digest, plus Ann Noble's wine wheel and other fun stuff.

### Northwest Gourmet Guides

**www.northwest-gourmet.com** - Our own site featuring tasting notes, book reviews and Northwest specialty foods.

### Epicurious

**www.epicurious.com** - From the publishers of Bon Appetit and Gourmet comes this food, wine and travel site with plenty to enjoy. Search the 8,000 recipe Bon Appetit database, plan a trip, and more.

### The Gourmet Market

**www.gourmetmarket.com** - Do you need a new garlic press, but you can't leave your computer? Visit this tempting site.

### HomeArts

**http://homearts.com** - A dandy recipe database plus many other sections about home and hearth.

### The Global Gourmet

**www.foodwine.com** - Articles on wine, food, living. Recipe database by Kate Heyhoe, wine notes by Anthony Dias Blue and Fred McMillin.

### Seattle Caviar

**www.caviar.com** - Learn about Beluga, Sevruga and all their cousins. What wine to serve, prices, history.

## NORTHWEST LODGING WEB SITES

### Bed & Breakfasts of Oregon, Washington and California

**www.moriah.com/inns** - Over 350 B & Bs are listed with descriptions and other essential information.

### British Columbia B & Bs Only

**www.pixsell.bc.ca/bcbb.htm** - A slightly loud but useful site which will guide you to Bed & Breakfast inns throughout B.C.

### Washington Bed & Breakfast Guild

**www.wbbg.com** - Lots of Washington State Bed & Breakfast inns to look at with indexes by city and region.

### On-Line Highways

A great set of sites that provide travel information, points of interest, lodging choices (mostly motels), community information, etc. **www.ohwy.com**
add for each state:
Washington: **/wa.homepage.htm**
Oregon: **/or.homepage.htm**
Idaho: **/id.homepage.htm**
Brit. Columbia: **/bc.homepage.htm**

## FOOD AND WINE PAIRING

| Northwest Favorite Foods | Sparkling Wine | Sauvignon Blanc | Pinot Gris | Pinot Blanc | Semillon | Chardonnay | Riesling | Gewurztraminer | Pinot Noir | Merlot | Cabernet Sauv. | Syrah | Dry Rosé |
|---|---|---|---|---|---|---|---|---|---|---|---|---|---|
| Mild Cheese | ◆ | ◆ | ◆ | ◆ | ◆ |  | ◆ | ◆ |  |  |  |  | ◆ |
| Strong Cheese | ◆ |  |  |  |  | ◆ |  |  | ◆ | ◆ | ◆ | ◆ |  |
| Clams/Mussels |  |  | ◆ | ◆ | ◆ |  |  |  | ◆ |  |  |  | ◆ |
| Oysters | ◆ | ◆ | ◆ | ◆ | ◆ | ◆ |  |  |  |  |  |  |  |
| Dungeness Crab |  |  | ◆ | ◆ |  |  | ◆ |  |  |  |  |  |  |
| Shrimp, Lobster | ◆ | ◆ | ◆ | ◆ | ◆ | ◆ |  |  |  |  |  |  |  |
| Halibut, Cod, Sole |  | ◆ | ◆ | ◆ | ◆ |  |  |  |  |  |  |  |  |
| Salmon |  | ◆ |  |  |  | ◆ | ◆ |  | ◆ | ◆ |  |  | ◆ |
| Poultry | ◆ | ◆ | ◆ | ◆ | ◆ | ◆ |  | ◆ | ◆ |  |  |  | ◆ |
| Pork, Veal |  |  |  |  |  |  |  |  | ◆ | ◆ |  | ◆ | ◆ |
| Lamb |  |  |  |  |  |  |  |  | ◆ | ◆ | ◆ | ◆ |  |
| Ham |  |  | ◆ | ◆ |  |  | ◆ | ◆ | ◆ |  |  |  | ◆ |
| Beef, Venison |  |  |  |  |  |  |  |  |  | ◆ | ◆ | ◆ |  |
| Lite Pasta |  | ◆ |  | ◆ | ◆ |  |  |  | ◆ |  |  |  | ◆ |
| Heavy Pasta |  |  |  |  |  |  |  |  | ◆ | ◆ | ◆ | ◆ |  |
| Pan Asian - Lite | ◆ | ◆ | ◆ | ◆ | ◆ | ◆ | ◆ | ◆ |  |  |  |  |  |
| Pan Asian - Strong |  |  |  |  |  | ◆ |  | ◆ | ◆ |  |  | ◆ | ◆ |

## MATCHING WINES WITH HERBS

| Dominant Herb | White Wine Match | Red Wine Match |
|---|---|---|
| Basil | Sauvignon Blanc, Semillon | Pinot Noir, Merlot |
| Coriander | Sauvignon Blanc, Gewurztraminer | Cabernet Sauvignon |
| Dill | Sauvignon Blanc, Semillon | Cabernet Sauvignon |
| Mint | Chardonnay, Riesling | Cabernet Sauvignon |
| Oregano | Sauvignon Blanc, Semillon | Pinot Noir, Merlot |
| Rosemary | Sauvignon Blanc, Chardonnay | Pinot Noir, Cabernet Sauv. |
| Sage | Riesling | Lemberger, Pinot Noir |
| Tarragon | Chardonnay | Pinot Noir |
| Thyme | Semillon | Lemberger, Merlot |

## NORTHWEST MICROBREW STYLES

Pacific Northwest microbrews (craft beers) are among the finest real ales and lagers. What are real ales and lagers? According to the Reinheits-gebot, a German purity law of the 17th century, beer may be made from only three ingredients: water, malted barley and hops. Northwest craft beers adhere (mostly) to this tradition of making beer from the real thing—no rice adjuncts, corn sugar, artificial flavors.

Beer is made from malted barley (barley grain that has been sprouted then dried) that provides flavor, body and fermentables (to make the alcohol). Hops are added for bittering, flavoring and aromatic qualities.

### Varieties of Microbrew

Beer is divided into two categories—ales and lagers—by the type of yeast used for the fermentation. Ale yeast likes warm temperatures and tends to extract stronger flavors and aromas from the brew. Lager yeast likes cool temperatures and ferments slowly to produce subtle, lighter beers.

### Lager Beers

Most of the imported beers you find from Germany and Holland are lager beers brewed in the style of Pilsners. These rich, malty, hoppy brews are flavorful and mild. Microbrewed lagers from the Northwest (of which there are admittedly quite few) favor this international style.

### Pale Ale

Pale ale is the ale of Britain. **India Pale Ale (IPA)** offers higher hop content and higher alcohol creating a strongly bitter brew that goes well with food. **Bitter** is a lighter style of pale ale with added hops for aroma and bitterness. **Amber Ale** utilizes darker, heavier-roasted malts in the brew giving this beer a rich amber color and a richer, toasty flavor.

### Wheat Beers

**Weizen** are made from a blend of wheat and barley malts, and have a spicy, herbal character that provides flavor interest and food affinity. **Hefe weizen** contains unfiltered yeast sediment that makes the beer cloudy but more flavorful.

### Porter

Still darker malts are added to give the traditional deep brown/mahogany color and the smoky, coffee, chocolate flavors to porters. Porters can be dry or sweet.

### Stout

The style of very dark beer is typified by Guinness Stout—almost black, strongly flavored, very bitter. Stouts are favorites with brewers but many beer lovers find them too bitter.

### Flavored Beers

Many Northwest microbreweries have been tempted into the practice of adding berry, lemon or other flavorings to some of their lighter ales or wheat beers. While this practice is viewed by traditionalists as similar to making wine spritzers by adding 7-Up to your Chardonnay, the brewers continue to do it because the beers are so popular.

I guess the result can be compared to the popularity of the Sloe Gin Fizz in an earlier time . . . and for the same reasons.

If you insist on drinking a berry-flavored beer, let me suggest a natural approach that combines products from both the Northwest beer and wine industries. Try a little shot of Paul Thomas or Hoodsport Raspberry Wine in your regular hefeweizen for a refreshing berry kick. Other berry wineries (Kramer in Oregon, for example) offer multiple berry flavors that can each provide more natural beer flavoring. Cheers!

## BEER LOVERS' WEB SITES

# General Beer Web Sites

### Beer Is My Life

www.beerismylife.com - A fun site with a searchable database of micro-breweries along with tasting notes for brews sampled by the site's authors. Other articles and related topics

### Real Beer

realbeer.com (no www needed) - Send an electronic postcard with a 1950s beer theme or research overseas brewery tours. Lots of sections to this large site.

### All About Beer

www.allaboutbeer.com - Authored by the magazine of the same name is well organized and features searchable databases on many topics. Check out the brew pubs in your area, or the home brew shops. A very good tool when your heading off on a trip and need to know where to have a cold one when you arrive at your destination.

### Beer Info

www.beerinfo.com - A beer site that tends to be aimed at the industry. Sections on running a brewpub or microbrewery are extensive, databases of all types.

### The Beerhunter - Michael Jackson

www.beerhunter.com - Michael Jackson is a beer authority from the U.K. that has helped put the Northwest microbrewing industry on the map with his favorable reviews. His web site is limited but kind of cute with it faux-leather-bound look. Some beer reviews are included.

### Beer Antiques - Breweriana

www.breweriana.com - So you want to start a collection of antique beer coasters (called "beer mats" by the way) or maybe you'd like a statue of the Hamm's Beer Bear for your home rumpus room? This is your place. All kinds of stuff and most of it is for sale at very reasonable prices.

# Food & Beer, Beer Touring

### Northwest Gourmet Guides

www.northwest-gourmet.com - Our own site featuring Northwest beers, beer recipes, brewpub events and more.

# Home Brewing

### The Cellar Homebrew

www.cellar-homebrew.com - A soft spot in my heart sends you to my former employer for their advice on brewing your own ale or lager, from concentrates or all-grain. The shop is located on Greenwood Avenue at N. 145th St. in Seattle. Also good supplies for home winemakers.

### Simental's Homebrewing Page

users.aol.com/simental - A dandy little amateur site with homebrew recipes, helpful hints and an address you can email for personal brewing advice.

# Electronic Beer Postcards

### Cybeer.com

www.cybeer.com - A nice collection of sexist beer promotional postcards (mostly from overseas breweries) that you can send to your female coworkers and . . . no, you better not.

Most national breweries have developed extensive Web sites and many of our local sudsmasters have as well. A few minutes with your favorite search engine should yield URLs that will keep you amused for an evening or a fortnight. Remember to turn the light off and take your empty bottles to the recycling bin.

# NORTHWEST WINES & WINERIES - INDEX OF WINERIES

# NORTHWEST WINES & WINERIES - INDEX OF BREWERIES & BREWPUBS

# NORTHWEST WINES & WINERIES - INDEX OF DINING & LODGING

*Continued on next page.*

# NORTHWEST WINES & WINERIES - INDEX OF DINING & LODGING

# Northwest Guides for Traveling Gourmets from Speed Graphics

If you enjoy touring the Northwest and cooking with Northwest ingredients, you will enjoy these other titles available from Speed Graphics.

## TeaTime in the Northwest
### Sharon & Ken Foster-Lewis
### $16.95

A guide to more than 110 tearoom in Washington, Oregon, British Columbia and Hawaii offering "a sense of place" for each establishment along with address, phone and tearoom hours. This guide is also a cookbook featuring over 90 delicious recipes for sweet and savory teatime treats. Both traditional favorites and unique Northwest tastes make this book a useful addition to any cook's collection. Also included is tea history, tea service and much more.

## The Gourmet's Guide to Northwest Bed & Breakfast Inns
### Anne Nisbet
### $16.95

What is your favorite recipe for breakfast, brunch or tea? Let the foremost Northwest innkeepers add to your recipe chest with this fun tour guide and cookbook. Anne Nisbet has traveled the countryside of Oregon, Washington and Southern British Columbia seeking out delicious recipes that will brighten up the start to any day!

## Food and Wine Northwest Style
### Gilda Barrow-Zimmar & Chuck Hill
### $12.95

Great tastes from the Northwest! Some of the Northwest's finest chefs and gourmet winemakers contributed recipes to this special, useful cookbook. Over 100 recipes for seafood, game, meats, desserts and appetizers. Northwest wine selections are included for each. Informative sidebars on Northwest specialties.

Speed Graphics, 17919 2nd Ave. NW, Seattle, WA 98177
Email: speedgraph@aol.com

# Northwest Gourmet Guides
# Report Form

The growth of the hospitality industry in the Pacific Northwest has created the need for guides to help visitors and active residents find the best and newest places to visit, dine and enjoy an overnight stay. Our guides to the Northwest include TeaTime in the Northwest, The Gourmet's Guide to Northwest Wines & Wineries, and The Gourmet's Guide to Northwest Bed & Breakfast Inns. If you discover a new establishment that you feel would be a good addition to any of these guides, we would be pleased to hear from you. Please fill out the form below and return to the address listed.

Name of Establishment _____

_____

Address _____

_____

Phone _____

Comments _____

_____

_____

Comments about establishments listed in:
__ The Gourmet's Guide to Northwest Wines & Wineries
__ The Gourmet's Guide to Northwest Bed & Breakfast Inns
__ TeaTime in the Northwest

_____

_____

_____

_____

Signed _____
Your Name and Address _____

_____

## *Thank you for your input!*

Return to: Speed Graphics, 17919 2nd Ave. NW, Seattle, WA 98177
Email: speedgraph@aol.com

# Northwest Gourmet Guides
# Report Form

The growth of the hospitality industry in the Pacific Northwest has created the need for guides to help visitors and active residents find the best and newest places to visit, dine and enjoy an overnight stay. Our guides to the Northwest include TeaTime in the Northwest, The Gourmet's Guide to Northwest Wines & Wineries, and The Gourmet's Guide to Northwest Bed & Breakfast Inns. If you discover a new establishment that you feel would be a good addition to any of these guides, we would be pleased to hear from you. Please fill out the form below and return to the address listed.

Name of Establishment _____

_____

Address _____

_____

Phone _____

Comments _____

_____

_____

Comments about establishments listed in:
__ The Gourmet's Guide to Northwest Wines & Wineries
__ The Gourmet's Guide to Northwest Bed & Breakfast Inns
__ TeaTime in the Northwest

_____

_____

_____

_____

Signed_____
Your Name and Address _____

_____

## *Thank you for your input!*

Return to: Speed Graphics, 17919 2nd Ave. NW, Seattle, WA 98177
Email: speedgraph@aol.com

# FAXABLE ORDER FORM (206) 546-4942 (Email: speedgraph@aol.com)

The Gourmet's Guide to
# Northwest Wines & Wineries

*By Chuck Hill with Kurt Krause & Stephen Gaddis*
*Local Authors - Local Experts*

Get this great guide for your customers! All the latest news for Northwest wines and wineries. A great reference for wine touring, wine tasting and cooking the best of Northwest regional cuisine. Retails at just $16.95.

★ ★ Available to your shop at a 50% discount! Minimum order 6 copies.

Mail order with check or prepay with VISA or MasterCard.

Name of Store _____

Proprietor _____

Address _____

City _____ State _____ Zip _____

Phone _____ Email _____

____ Send me your monthly Northwest wines email update

___VISA ___MC   Card No. _____

Exp. Date _____ Signature _____

Speed Graphics • 17919 2nd Ave. NW • Seattle, WA 98177 • (206) 546-8523

★ The Gourmet's Guide to ★
Northwest Wines
& Wineries

★ WINE COUNTRY TOURING ★
FINE DINING  ★ WHERE TO BUY
★ NORTHWEST MICROBREWS ★
NEW! RECIPES FROM NORTHWEST
LEGENDS OF FOOD & WINE

Chuck Hill
with Kurt Krause & Stephen Gaddis